Culture and society

Culture and society

Contemporary debates

•

Edited by

Jeffrey C. Alexander
Steven Seidman

CAMBRIDGE
UNIVERSITY PRESS

Published by the Press Syndicate of the University of Cambridge
The Pitt Building, Trumpington Street, Cambridge CB2 1RP
40 West 20th Street, New York, NY 10011-4211, USA
10 Stamford Road, Oakleigh, Melbourne 3166, Australia

First published 1990
Reprinted 1990, 1991, 1992, 1993, 1994 (twice), 1995

Library of Congress Cataloging-in-Publication Data is available.

A catalogue record for this book is available from the British Library.

ISBN 0-521-35086-7 hardback
ISBN 0-521-35939-2 paperback

Transferred to digital printing 2000

Contents

v

Preface

In the past few years there has emerged a new and powerful interest in the study of culture, an interest that has produced important work throughout the humanities and social sciences. The very richness and diversity of the new cultural studies create certain pedagogical difficulties, however. The new material spans many different disciplines, and it brings into play a fantastic array of theoretical, ideological, and methodological viewpoints. It is not surprising, then, that there exists no single textbook that brings together examples of leading work.

In developing our anthology, we have been attentive not only to this perspectival diversity but to the significant bifurcation of contemporary cultural studies into two distinctive concerns. One is an analytical focus on the interpretation or explanation of culture; the other is a substantive focus on the fate of culture in modern and postmodern society. But whether analytical or substantive, our interest has been in finding selections that illustrate perspectives through empirically arresting work. With the exception of the introductory material, we have not included any purely theoretical statements. That hard choices must be made in a project of this sort goes without saying. In the end, we are surprised and pleased that there has been space for so much.

We would like to express our deep appreciation to Pat Johnson, who managed the labyrinthian task of securing permissions for this project with efficiency and aplomb.

Part I

Analytic debates: Understanding the relative autonomy of culture

Jeffrey C. Alexander

This essay analyzes the principal approaches to culture that are available in the social sciences today and places these debates within the framework of broader theoretical controversies. On the one hand, it is a critical comparison. On the other hand, it has a systematic dimension that casts these arguments in a cumulative form. Far from being aimed at concluding judgments and summary evaluations, the purpose of this essay is to open up doors. In taking up general issues only as they are raised in the readings that follow, this essay will not lose sight of its introductory function.

The initial dichotomy

Two theoretical poles have governed the analysis of action and order since scientific consideration of societies began. The mechanistic conception of action has likened human behavior to a machine that responds automatically, "objectively," and predictably to the stimuli of its environment. The order that is linked to this mechanical action is, correspondingly, seen as a coercive one, affecting action from without by virtue of its powerful force.

In opposition to this view, there has arisen a subjective approach to action and order. According to this approach, action is motivated by something inside the person, by feeling, by perception, by sensibility. The order corresponding to such action is an ideational one. It is composed of nothing other than what exists in people's heads. There is subjective order rather than merely subjective action because subjectivity is here conceived as framework rather than intention, an idea held in common rather than an individual wish, a framework that can be seen as both the cause and the result of a plurality of interpretive interactions rather than a single interpretive act per se. Experience and the meaning of experience become central to this approach.

The concept of culture comes into play to the degree that meaning is

1

conceived of as ordered in this way. Culture is the "order" corresponding to meaningful action. Subjective, antimechanistic order is conceived of as followed for voluntary reasons rather than because of necessity in the mechanistic, objective sense.

The confrontation between Marx and Hegel offers the prototype for the contrast between mechanistic and cultural forms of social science explanations. It also played a crucial historical role in the development of mechanistic and cultural social science explanations themselves. In *The Phenomenology of Spirit* Hegel conceives of historical development as growing out of the frustrations that were experienced because of the limits of each historical period. Each period was described in terms of the framework it provided for meaningful experience. Hegel calls this overarching framework the *Geist*, the spirit of the age, a concept that in the context of German Idealism may be considered equivalent to the contemporary notion of culture.

Because Marx directly confronts Hegel's theory, his work allows the different emphases of a mechanistic approach to be particularly clear. The historical materialist understanding of development that Marx creates in his later writings continues to accept Hegel's notion that later stages were immanent in earlier ones. It describes the source of growth, however, not as subjective frustration but as the objective denial of rational interest. The orders in question are economic and political, which, Marx insists, are not subjective. Indeed, Marx postulates a radical dichotomy between "superstructure" and "base," between consciousness and social being.[1] Cultural phenomena, from legal codes and religious ritual to art and intellectual ideas, are assigned to the superstructure and conceived of as determined by the base. To explain cultural phenomena, one should not investigate their internal structure or meaning but must examine the material elements that they reflect. Because culture is determined by forces outside itself, it does not have autonomy in a causal sense.

In the history of social science subsequent to Marx, methodological, ideological, and presuppositional commitments have led a number of different traditions to continue the mechanistic agenda he laid out. Methodologically, there has been a search for predictability, for visible "real" objects of measurement; ideologically, the liberal and radical sentiment for reform has seemed to imply a need to insist on the "reality" of human

---

1. There are interpretations of Marx's later, or "mature," theory that claim for it a more culturally sensitive, less mechanistic cast. Certainly there are instances of cultural autonomy in Marx's vast corpus, but the central thrust toward mechanism and away from the cultural-autonomy position is unmistakable (see Alexander 1982). It certainly has been as a champion of the anticultural theory that Marx has made his primary imprint on contemporary social science.

suffering in a mechanistic sense; presuppositionally, the immersion of social science in commonsense rationality has made rational actor models easy to understand and, equally important, difficult to refute.

The response to the mechanistic movement has been to reassert that action is meaningful and that culture has ordering power. Yet Marx seems to have succeeded in setting the terms for this debate, even if he was not entirely successful in defining its results. To this day, for example, the opponents of mechanism have defended a subjective approach by maintaining that culture has at least a relative "autonomy" vis-à-vis more materialistic forms.

The case for culture: classical perspectives

Within this overarching response to mechanism, the case for the "autonomy of culture" has been made in fundamentally different ways. Dilthey picked up Hegel's mantle directly, merely substituting naturalistic *Geisten* for Hegel's religious ones. Dilthey stresses the centrality of human experience as the source of meaning, both for the actor and for the analyst. He argues, however, that the need for mutual understanding leads beyond individual experience to shared ideas and, eventually, to the structuring power of cultural systems.

Dilthey emphasizes the internal and subjective location of this structured system. This peculiar location, he argues, demands a special "hermeneutic" method. Hermeneutics is the method of interpretation. To discover the nature of internal and subjective structures is to discover their meaning. Meaning is accessible to analysts only if they interpret cultural structures in and of themselves, rather than trying in the first instance to explain them as the results of other forces, which is the methodological impulse of the mechanistic approach. Interpretation proceeds from understanding, not simply from observation. Dilthey thus contrasts the hermeneutic method of the *Geisteswissenschaften* (the human sciences, literally the "sciences of the spirit") with the observational, explanatory methods of natural science (*Naturwissenschaften*).

Dilthey provides the first and perhaps still the most far-reaching philosophical justification for cultural studies, but he does so in a dualistic way that reflects the one-sided concerns of German Idealism. For him, social phenomena should be studied exclusively from a cultural point of view. He relegates observations about outer mechanistic orders to the mathematical, physical, and biological sciences, and possibly to analytic economics. Dilthey's vision, then, emphasizes the autonomy of culture in a strong, or Idealist, sense. Whether a hermeneutic, interpretive method must be tied to this strong case for culture has been a point of argument ever since.[2]

Dilthey's strong response to mechanism has been challenged from two sides. After discussing these alternatives, both of which develop a "relative autonomy" position, we examine still another general orientation, one that returns to a strong autonomy position but does so in a distinctively anti-hermeneutic way.

In the history of twentieth-century social theory, Parsons has supplied the most sophisticated formal response to mechanism from outside the orthodox hermeneutic tradition. In his "functionalist" approach to society, Parsons has conceptualized the relation between culture and material force not as inner experience versus outer determination but as analytical levels of a unified empirical world. According to Parsons, actors internalize a meaningful order (a cultural system) that is more general than the set of social interactions (the social system) of which they are also a part.

This analytical argument means, on the one hand, that every social act specifies some broader cultural pattern; social action cannot be viewed mechanistically, for it inevitably has some cultural reference. On the other hand, because in analytical terms actions are also part of the social, not only the cultural system, the idealist perspective is also rejected. On the social system level, independent exigencies are conceived of as coming into play, concerns about scarcity and allocation that cannot be deduced from patterns of meaning in and of themselves. Because Parsons also posits the existence of a third analytical system – the personality – he can argue, moreover, that neither cultural coding nor social determinism precludes a role for psychological imperatives. Action is symbolic, social, and motivational at the same time. To carry out a full empirical analysis, then, one would have to understand the concrete interrelationship of all three analytical systems. Although the analytical autonomy of culture is important, in any particular empirical ("concrete") instance it is strongly affected by institutional factors.

Parsons's insistence on the analytical autonomy of cultural, social, and psychological systems promises a way out of the mechanist–subjectivist

2. In the modern period Dilthey's philosophical hermeneutics has been reconceptualized by Gadamer (1975), but its one-sided character has remained. The overly one-sided, or "culturalist," emphasis that I am criticizing in Dilthey's theory must be separated from the problem of whether the method that he and Gadamer worked out for cultural analysis – hermeneutics – is too subjective in the sense of being relativistic. Whether or not Dilthey and Gadamer believe that strong generalizations with claims to objective truth are possible in cultural studies has been a much debated issue (see Alexander 1990). It is not, however, an issue that need concern us directly here, for we are dealing primarily with theoretical rather than metamethodological questions.

dichotomy without giving up on either side. There is space for culture, but it is only a relatively autonomous sphere. There is also the need for analysis of a more mechanistic sort.

The promise of this solution can be neutralized if the separation between these levels is taken in a concrete rather than an analytical way. Functionalist theory can then be taken as recommending that all systems be analyzed independently of one another, insisting only that the relative determining power of the others not be denied. Unfortunately, Parsons's functionalist multilevel model, both because of its inherent difficulty and because of the relatively undeveloped form in which it appears in Parsons's own work, often was taken in precisely this way, allowing functionalist thinking about culture merely to reproduce the mechanistic–subjectivist dichotomy at a higher level. By concretizing the social system as independent of culture, such an approach raises significant problems for an interpretive, culturally sensitive position. Are social system phenomena to be conceived as, in themselves, organized mechanistically, as subject to the laws of necessity rather than to rules of meaning? How can we conceive of the actual interpenetration of cultural and social levels?[3]

It may have been in response to this dilemma that Parsons made a highly consequential recommendation. Functional analysis should be concerned with the "institutionalization" of culture, with how culture becomes part of the real structures of social systems. This focus on institutionalization, Parsons believed, would substantially narrow the cultural interest of sociologists; henceforth, they would focus on "values" rather than on symbol systems as such. Values are symbolic, abstract ways of talking about central institutional problems. They refer to issues like equality versus inequality, spontaneity versus discipline, deference to authority versus critical behavior, and public versus private property. Parsons insists that normative conceptions form around such concrete issues. Actors must make choices between real alternatives; when they do so, normative, or value, standards are evoked. Institutionalization means that one standard or another has become an intrinsic feature of the actor's role. For an individual, group, or collectivity to depart from an institutionalized value brings sanctions; to conform to it brings rewards.

As the readings in this volume under the functional rubric demonstrate, looking at institutions in terms of core values can be extremely revealing. Yet there are fundamental problems with value analysis if it is taken to subsume cultural analysis as such. Because interpretation is limited to

3. Sahlins (1976) raised precisely these objections to Durkheim's earlier functional theory. The acultural quality of Smelser's (1959) important analysis of the industrial revolution – which is usually considered to be the most significant empirical application of the Parsonian schema – has shown that similar questions can, indeed, be raised about Parsons's own.

meanings that can be institutionalized, there is an ironic result: The concepts that value analysis develops for analyzing meaning rely heavily on the vocabulary developed for mechanistic, purely social analysis. One finds little in functionalist analysis about purely symbolic phenomena like ritual, sacralization, pollution, metaphor, myth, narrative, metaphysics, and code.

The social system preoccupation tends, moreover, to narrow the functionalist concern for culture to questions about the impact of culture on stability and instability, processes that depend on the effective distribution of sanctions and rewards. From this perspective, the origins and internal processes of cultural systems are not of primary interest; what is important, rather, is the manner in which a given pattern becomes institutionalized, either through socialization, status elevation, or material rewards. Because of this social focus, functional analysis has often had the effect of separating social science from the interpretive techniques of the humanities. We arrive at the paradoxical situation that the functional approach to meaning has undermined cultural autonomy in significant ways.

Similar problems and similar achievements mark the other fundamental challenge to the strong, idealist case for culture. Ironically, this second challenge has come from within Marxism itself. As the path-breaking work of Gramsci makes clear, however, revolutionary and class-oriented theory can be defined in a manner that steps outside the epistemological straightjacket of Marx's later work. Gramsci identifies Marxism as "praxis theory," a term that comes out of the early, more Hegelian phase of Marx's development; indeed, Gramsci built his critical theory in the course of his dialogue with Croce, the great Italian Hegelian. Because of this formative contact with the hermeneutic tradition, Gramsci took as his starting point the notion that all actors are intellectuals, that the concern with meaning is an inseparable dimension of every human action and every historical form of social order.

Like Parsons, Gramsci distances himself from idealism by insisting that culture be considered as interrelated with, rather than as displacing, mechanistic institutions. He believes that the analysis of social system forces can be separated from the analysis of their meaning. For Gramsci as for Parsons, the social system constitutes culture's major referent; the "real forces" of society oppose or complement culture's meaningful thrust.

Yet Gramsci's cultural Marxism differs from functionalism in fundamental ways. There is a different conception of the social system and, therefore, of culture's place within it. Cultural processes unfold, Gramsci insists, within a sharply divided society, a hierarchy of class domination backed by political power. Culture becomes part of the process of domination. Even the most sophisticated intellectuals take their theoretical reference point from the dominant mode of production; because of their weak institutional position, moreover, they must inevitably come to terms with the powers that be.

The sophisticated intellectual ideas that define the self-understanding of each epoch are carried to the masses by lower quasi-intellectuals, for example, teachers and journalists, actors who are more "organically" linked to the institutions of capitalist society. Gramsci makes an analogy here to the Catholic church. Theologians formulate abstract canons, but it is the parish priests who formulate the doctrine that addresses and explains suffering to the common person.

The ideological domination of masses by intellectuals Gramsci calls "cultural hegemony." Although society is utterly hierarchical, the ruling class does not sustain itself mainly by force. Society is not primarily an economic or political order but a "moral–political bloc." It is held together by what appears to be the voluntary adherence to dominant ideas. We have here the theory of institutionalized culture in a Marxist form.

In Gramsci's view, however, this dominant culture is eventually challenged. His conceptualization of this revolutionary cultural development is just as dependent on a reference to "real circumstances" as his theory of dominant ideas. Because the working class inhabits an objectively exploited and concrete condition, Gramsci believes, their practical consciousness is potentially an imminent one, opposed to the otherworldly or idealized consciousness of the aristocracy and bourgeoisie. Still, Gramsci acknowledges that this latent consciousness cannot become manifest until it is intellectually articulated. Merely practical consciousness is powerless against the intellectual power of dominant ideas. An alternative ideology must first be crystallized, a task performed by Marx and other high socialist intellectuals. With the formation of a revolutionary cadre of organic intellectuals – the leaders and followers of a political party that is more practical and less intellectual – these ideas finally become highly visible and widely available.

Cultural Marxism departs from functional analysis, however, in more than these important explanatory ways. It has an explicitly normative thrust. It is interested not just in explaining or interpreting culture but in evaluating what is "good meaning" versus "bad." This emphasis can be seen in Gramsci's contrast between "rational consciousness" and common sense and religion. His goal is not simply to explain how a counterhegemonic culture can develop, but to show that it can, and will, lead to what he conceives to be a freer and more independent life.

It is undoubtedly true that cultural Marxism improves on functional analysis by emphasizing more strongly the impact of culture on social change. The emphasis on the links between culture and power is, however, a more ambiguous achievement. Speaking of culture primarily as the servant of power undermines the possibility – central to functionalist thought – of conceiving of cultural values as exerting control and regulation over power in turn. In fundamental respects, moreover, Gramsci's approach actually exacerbates the problems of Parsons. Gramsci separates himself from mechanistic Marxism by insisting on culture's relative autonomy from society and action. As with functionalism, however, this insistence on relative autonomy cuts both ways, for it insists on the independence of society and action from culture in turn. Gramsci does not conceive of social system parts – in this case, economic, political, and intellectual groups – as themselves initially constituted by cultural patterns. He describes them, in the end, as reflecting the structures of power and class, mechanistic forces that eventually assume a cultural meaning.

In functionalist theory the differentiation between culture and society led to a narrowing focus on values rather than symbols. In cultural Marxism the concept of "class consciousness" plays much the same role. Although it is defined in terms of cultural meaning, it is located within the social system itself. For this reason, the Marxist analysis of consciousness – like the functionalist analysis of values – often ends up by being much more socially reductive than its endorsement of the relative autonomy of culture might imply. Once again, we see how difficult a truly interdependent relationship between culture and society is to conceive.

The importance to contemporary cultural analysis of semiotics enters at exactly this point. Saussure rejects the notion that social structure or action can ever be understood in culturally unmediated ways. As a linguist, his type case is language. He acknowledges that speech itself is a social action that is psychologically motivated and subject to concrete situational exigencies. He argues, however, that although individual actors can be conceived as responsible for speech acts, they have virtually no control over the language these acts employ. Speaking individuals cannot determine the signs they use. These signs are fixed by the society within very strict limits.

When Saussure speaks about the social determination of language, he is not pointing, as Gramsci might, to the relative power of social institutions. It is the power of language as a symbolic system, an accretion of innumerable social acts, that emerges as an independent force. Language is an abstract code whose structure is determined by laws internal to itself rather than by immediate pressures from the social system. Words are signs that can be decomposed into signifier and signified. Saussure sharply divides the signifier, the sound or material component of the word, from the signified, the concept to which the material sound is attached. He insists that the relation between signifier and signified, between material and ideal component, is "arbitrary." There is no objectively necessary or "real" reason why a particular concept is enunciated by a particular sound; it is so attached only by convention.

Saussure goes one step further still. The word itself cannot be understood by referring to the real social object with which it is coupled by language. That relationship, too, is arbitrarily determined by convention. Meaning is derived from the relationships – the contrasts and similarities – that are established between words, between the signs of the language system. Changes in these relationships are not reflections of changes in the social objects to which they refer. Indeed, in the short run, a sign system is immutable. It develops according to internal laws; the current arrangement of its units can be understood primarily in terms of the earlier traditions from which they have evolved.

If this arbitrary relationship exists between words and things in language, Saussure reasons, why should it not hold in all social institutions and activities? He argues that such must be the case, declaring linguistics to be merely a subcase of semiotics, the more general science of signs. Every social activity is enmeshed in a sign system that works in an analogous way to language. Neither historical development nor social relationship determines this sign system's structure. Its meaning can be understood only by reconstructing the internal codes of the institutional culture itself.

Although semiotics makes a strong case against attempting social analysis without reference to codes, it is an avowedly one-sided analysis. It is concerned with sign systems, not with societies. Even while acknowledging that language systems are social institutions, it suggests that to engage in orthodox semiotics – or "structural analysis," as it has come to be called – means abandoning reference to interactional and situational exigencies as such. Semiotics brings us back, then, to the strong version of autonomy that is proposed by orthodox hermeneutics. Dilthey, too, recommends that we examine social action only from within. Still, there is a crucial difference. For Dilthey, "within" means returning to the patterns of subjective experience. For Saussure, it means seeking out the internal relationships of words. As we will see, semiotics articulates the structure of sign systems in formal terms. Structure consists of intricate patterns of analogies and contrasts that the analyst can locate without reference to the subjective experience of the actors involved. If this injunction were taken seriously, however, it would entail abandoning the search for meaning upon which cultural analysis is based. Whether such an antithesis between cultural structure and meaning is a theoretical necessity has continued to be at issue in the relationship between contemporary semiotics and the other substantive approaches to culture that we examine below.[4]

Approaches to culture: contemporary perspectives

Each of the contemporary approaches to the study of culture can be related to the archetypical variations I have presented.[5] All start with an interest in meaningful rather than intrumental action and with a commitment to the autonomy of symbolic systems from noncultural kinds of determination. They disagree about what this autonomy implies. Just how independent is culture? How should its interrelationship with society be established? They also disagree about the internal composition of culture. What are its key elements, and how are they interrelated? These are the questions that animate debates about culture and society today.

Functionalism

The beauty of functionalist approaches is their ability to intertwine a cultural emphasis with an analysis of real social action. Merton establishes the autonomy of the cultural ethos of science by demonstrating that it is followed not simply because it is efficient but because it is believed in as something good and right. He convincingly demonstrates the norm of "universalism" by showing that when scientists have violated it, for example in times of war, they have felt psychologically compromised and their peers have felt righteously indignant. He shows that "communism" is a scientific norm by pointing out how improbable it would be for scientists to be allowed to keep their research products for themselves. Thus, scientists can compete only for priority of esteem, not for actual intellectual property.

The weakness of functionalist value analysis, I have suggested, is the other side of its strength. Values are often reduced to the very social structures that their supposed analytical autonomy allows them to regulate. Merton has succeeded in identifying an extremely important set of cultural elements, and social scientists influenced by him have documented in great detail the effects of this normative structure on scientific organization and action. The problem is that Merton has not demon-

4. For arguments that the antithesis is unnecessary, see Alexander (1989a, forthcoming).
5. Marxist, semiotic, and functionalist cultural theories all have their viable contemporary versions. Hermeneutics, by contrast, is a general sensibility that affects most contemporary practice.

strated that these values can come from anywhere other than the practice of science itself. When Merton asserts that he is studying the complex of values and norms that "hedge about" science, he treats scientific practice as if it could, in itself, be considered an entirely practical rather than a cultural activity. Thus, because he allows science to exist in the social, not the cultural, system, scientific values come to be conceived as generalizations from actual behavior rather than as derivations from meaningful processes that help to constitute that behavior. It seems plausible to argue, in these terms, that universalism emerges because scientific objectivity must be protected and that communism is a "functional imperative" of science because only in this manner can free access to results be guaranteed. The ethos of science may be learned through precepts and examples, but it is reinforced and stabilized by sanctions. Because it is so institutionalized, Merton alleges, "expediency and morality coincide." But cultural theorists cannot have their cake and eat it too; if they try, the analytical autonomy of culture is lost. If culture is merely expedient, its *raison d'être* as an independent theoretical element disappears.

Lipset's functionalist analysis of culture and politics demonstrates the same strengths and reveals similar weaknesses. Parsons had suggested that social value patterns focus on five central dilemmas, or pattern variables. By showing how these correlate with different kinds of institutional behavior, Lipset makes these normative variables more precise and more credible. The trade-off between universalism and particularism, for example, helps to illuminate why some elites try to incorporate lower groups, whereas others seek to exclude them. Because French employers were particularistic, Lipset suggests, they experienced demands for union representation as morally offensive. In his demonstration of the explosive strains between economic and political values in France and Germany, Lipset also shows that value analysis can illuminate internal complexity and contradiction.

Yet, although Lipset has been careful to locate values at precise points in social structure, he has typically arrived at the value constellations themselves by generalizing from the actual behavior of groups rather than by interpreting the internal dynamics of cultural development. Thus, universalism is seen as having been promoted by the bourgeoisie's revolution of 1789, and its limitation as resulting from the fact that "the forces of the Revolution were not strong enough." In Germany, it was "the pressures stemming from economic change and the rise of new social groupings" that are held to have incited universalism, and the power of older feudal social groupings that are thought to have prevented such values from becoming more widely accepted. Once again, expedience and morality are held to coincide.

Semiotics

In the post–World War II era, structuralism and semiotics posed the principal alternatives to functionalist approaches to meaning.[6] Rather than identifying a small subset of symbols that are institutionalized within the social system, structuralists and semioticians focus on the cultural system per se. Following Saussure's injunction to concentrate on language rather than speech, they insist on the internal integrity of symbolic organization, arguing that this organization must be studied without reference to any other process or level. To do so requires abstraction from any and all concrete exigencies, whether individual contingency or group interest. This abstraction allows the interpreter to construct, or constitute, the symbolic structure of code in an analytically independent way. Only after such a reconstruction has been achieved, semioticians argue, does it become obvious that all concrete temporal processes occur within preexisting patterns of meaning.

The author's own protestations aside, we would be misled if we took Barthes's essay on wrestling as suggesting that semiotics is relevant only to exotica that are outside the boundaries of ordinary social life. Barthes intends this analysis to be paradigmatic for social semiotics as such. This is clear, first of all, in Barthes's insistence that "wrestling is not a sport, it is a spectacle." He argues here for recognizing that action is bound by the structure of a culture rather than viewing wrestling as an ongoing and contingent construction. As language rather than speech, wrestling must be seen as a text. In this sense, it is not really motivated action at all, but something scripted, like a drama, that is performed. It refers not to exigencies in the situation but to meanings that have been long accepted, patterns that wrestlers must learn to "represent." Actors, then, are signs, not personalities. We should study not their interaction but their audience, other actors who are defined as "readers" of the social text's juxtaposed meanings. The actual results of a match do not matter, for wrestling must be thought of not as an event in time but as a performance in a highly structured system of meaning. The results are foretold because wrestlers are actors in a drama that has already been written. Rather than a motivated action in the social system, the match is an emanation of the cultural realm.

6. I am using these two terms synonymously, although in practice they have developed somewhat separate applications. "Semiotics" is the umbrella term, deriving from Saussure's work, and it continues to be the term with which various proponents of formal sign analysis, from literary to sociological studies, identify. "Structuralism" is the name given to the semiotic approach as it has been applied to anthropological concerns, under the impact of the writings of Levi-Strauss, but it has occasionally been applied to extra-anthropological exercises as well.

Sahlins's discussion of food preferences in American society shows what semiotics looks like when it is applied to something that is at the heart of ordinary life. Analytical autonomy is achieved by abstracting from concrete behavior to the cultural realm. When this cultural abstraction is achieved, social elements, like food items, become "correlations in a symbolic system." They can then be seen as elements in an unfolding text, not as figures in a social system. As Sahlins puts it, food "production is a functional moment of a cultural structure." We can also find in this essay a more systematic application of semiotic theory that elaborates some of the basic rules that organize nonlinguistic systems of signs. The patterning of sign systems is organized, like other logical relationships, into analogical and antinomic relationships: Cattle are to pigs as horses are to dogs, as beef is to pork, as human is to nonhuman, as steak is to organ meat, as outer is to inner, as high is to low, and, perhaps, as higher status is to lower status.

The upshot of such a semiotic exercise is not limited to a formally elegant explication of text. By insisting on the complex internal structure of cultural systems, semiotics provides a crucial antidote to the reduction of symbolic codes to values or ideologies, theoretical moves that, we have seen, are typically followed by the reduction of cultural values to generalizations from the mechanistic components of social systems. At the same time, however, the internal and formal emphases of semiotics – its extreme "culturalism" – often turn the error of functional and Marxist analysis on its head. Cultural structures are not only said to inform social patterns but are held to determine them. Thus, Sahlins writes that "the famous logic of maximization" – the profit principle of capitalist societies – "is only the manifest appearance of another Reason," that is, a cultural one. At another point, he suggests that the productive relation between American society and nature, both nationally and internationally, "is organized by specific valuations of edibility and inedibility." But surely the economic logics of social systems must be given their own analytical autonomy as well. Consumption is not only determined culturally, any more than are wrestling matches only symbolic affairs. It is revealing that such one-sided idealism cannot be sustained even by Sahlins himself. When he wants to explain the meaningful relations of different pieces of meat, he relies on a series of relationships that exist outside of semiologics, referring to the sacred value that Americans place on human life and to the economic and racial hierarchies of American society.

Dramaturgy

If functionalism presents an approach to the autonomy of culture that privileges (but does not reduce culture to) the social system, and if semiotics articulates this autonomy through the cultural level, than dramaturgy may be said to articulate cultural autonomy by carving out a special role for the individual. In contemporary sociology, the great theorist of the microworld of individual interaction has been Goffman. In earlier versions of his dramaturgical theory, he often presented norms as the projections of strategic actors. As his work developed, however, he came to acknowledge culture's independent status. Thus, the selection included here begins, "Given a spate of activity that is framed in a particular way. . . ." Yet rather than ending with this acknowledgment of a structured text, Goffman's interest only begins with it. He notes that in the real world of social interaction, individuals are constantly flooded with stimuli in addition to that which is included in the intended cultural frame. Individual actors, then, must have a finely developed capacity for exercising disattention, for simultaneously registering but ignoring, or tuning out, stimuli that threaten to involve them in out-of-frame activity. Audiences, for example, must follow plays while taking account of the entire range of extratheatrical phenomena present to their senses, like the presence of ushers and the creaturely out-of-character qualities of the actors. But the capacity for out-of-frame activity extends beyond disattention, Goffman suggests. Surrounding the central text, there are directional cues that actors must observe if they are to understand who is conducting a piece of framed activity and when. Goffman calls these "connectives" and notes that they extend from punctuation marks in written texts to facial gestures in conversations.

Goffman demarcates a distinctively individualistic contribution to the autonomy of a cultural text that he takes as given. Geertz brings the dramaturgical perspective into the actual process of creating a relatively independent cultural form. At the beginning of his essay on the Balinese cockfight, it appears as if Geertz will embrace the semiotic perspective, for he emphasizes that surrounding the melodrama of the cockfight is a vast body of elaborate rules and texts. It soon becomes clear, however, that Geertz considers such codes hardly sufficient for the cultural task. He describes meaning as something that is imposed, an action that makes reference not only to surrounding rules but to other phenomena as well. In fact, the same genre, cockfight, can be either shallow (trivial, boring) or deep (meaningful, interesting, dramatic). Betting is the device, the means, for making cockfights deep, for increasing the meaningfulness of the event. The reason it does so, Geertz insists, takes us away from the formal analysis of semiotics to more sociological concerns. Heavy bets can be waged only by high-status Balinese, and one heavy bet draws in another. Meaningfulness is intensified because large reputations are put on the line and the results are unpredictable. When the cocks tear into each other in ferocious and bloodthirsty ways, a disturbing message is dramatized about Balinese society at large.

Cockfighting is neither a functional reinforcement of status distinctions – a view Geertz attributes to functionalism – nor an automatic deduction from texts. It is an active, aesthetic achievement, an art form that renders ordinary experience comprehensible by casting it into an exaggerated dramatic form. Geertz insists that it is the actors and the event that create this structure, not the structure that creates the event.

The particular interest of the substantive approaches to culture that we have examined thus far – functionalism, semiotics, and dramaturgy – is not that they represent competing versions of cultural autonomy; these general orientations, after all, were established by the archetypical perspectives discussed earlier. What is more significant, in this context, is that these orientations set out different substantive approaches to cultural autonomy, emphasizing values, formal symbolic relations, and aesthetic, creative performance, respectively. It is here, in their specific and substantive approaches to cultural structures and processes, that the interest of the remaining perspectives also lies. Contemporary cultural analysis in its Weberian, Durkheimian, and Marxian forms differs from classical orthodoxy precisely because work in each of these streams has been affected by the new, postclassical cultural emphases we have examined thus far. Thus, while each of these neoclassical approaches formulates cultural analysis in a manner that distinctively draws upon the founder's work, the manner in which they depart from orthodoxy is as important as the way they elaborate it.

Weberianism

Weber's contribution to thinking about culture and society has traditionally been confined to the "Protestant ethic debate," to arguments about whether Weber was correct in his specific suggestion that Calvinism and Puritanism were a necessary precursor of modern entrepreneurial capitalism. Under the impact of more recent cultural thinking, however, Weber's contribution has been rethought in more general ways. In contrast to notions of institutionally modeled values or formal symbolic relations, Weberians have continued to conceptualize culture as an internally generated symbolic system that responds to compelling metaphysical needs. Religious ideas, theological conceptions of salvation, and the pivotal role of contrasting paths to salvation as defined by ascetic and mystical schemes remain the most distinctive aspects of the Weberian cultural theory. But in current work, the meaning and impact of these ideas are conceived as going beyond issues of self-discipline and rational control;

questions of salvation are understood in terms of more general conceptions of activism, conscience, community, and individuation. Their effect on social institutions is similarly extended beyond the narrow concern with economic activity to issues of political control, democracy, personal comportment, status relations, and intergroup relations.[7]

When Michael Walzer begins his discussion by emphasizing how Calvinism contributed to conscientious, continuous labor, we may think that we are on familiar ground. We soon realize, however, that he is applying this transformative power not to economics but to politics. Puritanism, Walzer suggests, created the critical activism that undergirds our very notion of modern citizenship. In the midst of the social upheavals of early modern Europe, Calvin conceived of human beings as radically estranged from God; yet, at the same time, he believed that certain specially called, or chosen, people could serve as God's instruments for radically reconstructing society. This faith in a transcendent demand for social transformation marked the beginning of ideology in the contemporary sense. Under this transcendental framework, moreover, it is God, not humanity, who becomes the ultimate sanction for earthly conduct. Divine will works through conscience, not through the distribution of earthly wealth or power, and it can manifest itself in any group of human beings, even those in revolt. For the English Puritans, Walzer shows, religious "office" became a secular forum for the denunciation of established economic and political authority, whose self-interested status striving they viewed as sinful and idolatrous. Motivated by their obedience to a new, more abstract and critical discipline, they become revolutionaries capable of engineering massive social transformation. It was thus, Walzer suggests, that the modern commitment to revolution was born, in the subjective reinterpretation and extension of meaning rather than in the mechanistic response to objective necessity.

Pitts, too, begins with the conventional Weberian notion that in order to understand the political and economic structures of modern Western societies, we must return to traditional Christianity. As we enter his text, however, we see that he also generalizes beyond Weber in a series of significant ways. First, he develops the salvation ethic of Catholicism in a much fuller manner than earlier Weberian accounts, suggesting that the more mystical mode of salvation can function as an effective metaphysical outlet in the modern world. Second, Pitts treats the religious symbol

7. In addition to the selections included here in the "Weberian" section, this volume presents another important example of this broader emphasis in the readings of Part II. In "Civil Religion in America," Robert Bellah develops a conception of the relation between secular political religion and modern democratic nation in which the policy can be held to judgment according to a transcendental, otherworldly moral source.

system more formally than Weber, which allows him to conceptualize it as a structure with internal strains. Finally, and most importantly, Pitts translates Weber's salvation theory into a broadly historical account of the cultural specificity of meaningful conduct, personal comportment, and status relations in secular life.

Rather than becoming rational instruments of an abstract and demanding divine will, the status to which Puritans strived, Catholicism has conditioned the French to seek communion with the sacred, embodied not only by the church but by nature and nation as well. Aesthetic, not ascetic, experience becomes the desired condition. By committing acts of "prowess," individuals strive for grace, not through their election via hard and conscientious labor but through spontaneous and elegant performances that reveal the orderliness of an underlying hierarchy of structures and principles. Traditionally, prowess has been associated with the French aristocracy, who exhibited their grace in love, war, dress, housing, conversation, and, above all, in their taste. These aristocratic values were incompatible with some central aspects of industrial capitalism, and Pitts suggests that they slowed down business expansion by attributing more prestige to the consumption of commodities than to their production. More significantly, Pitts argues, the culture of prowess provided a model of bourgeois behavior that pushed French capitalism in a more hierarchical, politically oriented direction.

Semiotics avoids the latent social reduction of value theory by formalizing the internal elements of symbolic systems; in doing so, however, it threatens to empty culture of the socially oriented prescriptions that, according to functionalism, are precisely the elements that make culture so central to the institutional domain. Weberian analysis is more semiotic than work in the dramaturgical or functionalist mode in the sense that it recognizes the internal logic of symbolic systems; at the same time, it is much more historical and social in its approach to culture. If Weberian work relates the internal structures and processes of religion to concerns about salvation, it links competing formulations of salvation to distinctive political, economic, and normative developments. In this way, Weberian theory maintains the autonomy of culture while avoiding formalism.[8]

Durkheimianism

For Durkheimian approaches to culture, religion is also the central component, a focus that similarly allows them to emphasize the internal

8. Among contemporary social science theorists, it is Eisenstadt who has formulated these distinctive qualities of the Weberian approach in the clearest theoretical way. See, for example, Eisenstadt and Curelaru (1976).

complexity and autonomy of symbolic systems while insisting on a social reference that avoids formalism. Apart from such general similarities, however, the parallels between the two approaches end. Unlike Weberian, or functionalist theories for that matter, the Durkheimian approach is not primarily interested in historically specific understandings of cultural processes or comparative approaches to their social and ethical codes. The focus is on the structure and process of meaningful systems, which are taken to be universal regardless of historical time or place. In this respect, the Durkheimian approach is more like the semiotic and structuralist one (see Alexander 1988). Indeed, Saussure was clearly influenced by Durkheim's later work, and Marcel Mauss, whom Levi-Strauss anointed as the founder of anthropological structuralism, was Durkheim's close associate.

Like semiotics, Durkheimian theory views cultural systems as organized into symbolic antinomies. It goes beyond this formalism, however, in several important respects. First, the Durkheimian approach suggests that these antitheses are not just cognitive or logical classifications but separations into the sacred and profane, oppositions that are highly charged both emotionally and morally. These cognitive, emotional, and moral divisions are seen, moreover, as the basis for organized social communities, the members of which experience more or less intense solidarity with one another. Finally, the Durkheimian position stresses that the mediation between symbolic divisions and social solidarities is ritual. Rituals are intensely emotional interactions that focus on sacred symbols. They can arise as responses to symbolic threats or to the diminution of social solidarity with societies or groups.

If contemporary Weberian studies of religion are more broadly cultural and less tied to specific institutional explanations than earlier elaborations of the tradition, this is doubly true of contemporary Durkheimian work. Indeed, until recently, Durkheimian cultural theory was taken to be a prototypically functionalist approach to interpretive understanding, explaining religious and symbolic classifications as reflections of social structure, a mechanistic reduction of cultural autonomy that goes well beyond the ambivalence of Parsonian value theory. One reason for this misunderstanding was the discontinuity in Durkheim's own work. His earlier writing is quite vulnerable to mechanistic interpretations; only in his later writings did a more consistent and well-thought-out approach to cultural autonomy emerge. But if the interpretation of Durkheim's work laid bare this later orientation only in recent years (e.g., Alexander 1982), this is due in large part to the new appreciation of cultural autonomy that has emerged throughout the social sciences and humanities. Only today, within the reinvigorated climate of cultural studies, is it possible to practice Durkheimian sociology in its later, more culturally sensitive form.

Although Mary Douglas's roots in semiotics and functionalism are clear enough, her description of the power of symbolic pollution – which inspires moral, psychological, and existential fear at the same time – is a clear response both to the intellectualist quality of structuralist reasoning and to the reductive elements of functionalism. Douglas believes that the sacred and profane are not only intracultural sources of symbolic classification but sources of strong moral and emotional commitment and, in fact, of social control. "Dirt," she suggests, has nothing to do with hygienic or material conditions; rather, something is dirty, or polluting, because it is inconsistent with the governing symbolic classifications. In contrast to the purity associated with pattern-reinforcing elements, something that is polluted is disorderly, or "matter out of place." To be disorderly, moreover, does not imply randomness but danger; polluted objects are associated with black powers, with the profane. Pollution, then, is a weapon for clarifying and strengthening the dominant symbolic order. By placing blame for disruption on some outside challenger, it clarifies the ambiguity that new elements create, ambiguity that could throw doubt on reigning classifications. In an illustration from simple societies that is certainly just as relevant today, Douglas demonstrates that a leader who abuses the authority of office – who challenges the legitimate symbolic codes of behavior – is conceived as being polluted by the forces of uncontrolled powers and spirits. Pollution can be remedied by rituals of purification, which may include confession, sacrifice, or elaborate relegitimating ceremonies.

Whereas Douglas emphasizes the relation between sacred–profane and social control, giving ritual and social solidarity less play, Victor Turner highlights the Durkheimian emphasis on solidarity and ritual, underemphasizing the independent role of symbolic classifications. Turner begins by arguing for the centrality, in both ancient and modern societies, of rites of passage, which he defines, following Van Gennep, as the movement from a symbolically and institutionally structured position to an antistructural position and back again. In the antistructural or "liminal" phase, participants are seen, by themselves and others, as having ambiguous, indeterminate attributes. Reacting against the status demarcations of more structured social life, in liminal periods actors form tightly knit communities of equals. Because they are forced to cast their old classification system aside, they are viewed as neophytes who can be subjected to new socializing processes. With reaggregation, participants in these rituals assume new status positions, but they do so as actors who have been changed in some fundamental way.

Like Douglas, Turner illustrates his argument with a discussion of kinship, in this case the ancient ritual process involved in the ascension of a king among the Ndembu of Zambia. Before assuming his throne, the king must undergo a liminal period in which he and his wife are physically degraded and verbally humiliated by the common people. After this forced identification with the condition of the lowly, it is believed, the man who assumes the tribe's highest status position will be less likely to abuse his power. But Turner, like Douglas, believes that the ramifications of this perspective go well beyond his specifically ritual theory. As religion becomes merely one segment of a complex and stratified society, he suggests, liminality becomes institutionalized in a way that allows the experience of "communitas" and the notion of the "powers of the weak" to be accessible in more routine ways. Liminality is also recalled by secular conceptions about the mysterious powers of the homeless stranger, who in various genres of popular culture, like the Western, is given the power to bring morality, order, and community back to a society under siege. Turner argues, however, that more than simple reclassification is at stake; liminality can be an incitement to action and social change, as it is in millennial movements, either communist or religious, or in the defiant activities of marginal groups like beatniks, hippies, and punks.

Whereas orthodox Durkheimian theory was considered to have apolitical or even conservative implications, Carroll Smith-Rosenberg's feminist studies demonstrate that the more recent culturalist versions of Durkheimian thought can have a decidedly political and even critical cast. Smith-Rosenberg begins with a historical problem: the unprecedented outpouring of sexually prescriptive literature in the early nineteenth century, "hygienic" literature warning young men about the deadly dangers not only of masturbation but of orgasm itself. Building upon the work of both Douglas and Turner, Smith-Rosenberg warns against viewing this literature in a reductive way, as a reflection of real sexual practices or behavioral problems. Rather, the discussions must be understood as relatively autonomous cultural forms, as distinctively symbolic reformulations of values and social concerns. Once the issues of physiology and hygiene are left aside, it becomes evident that these nearly hysterical discussions were efforts to control threats to the reigning cultural system. The male orgasm was viewed as polluted, as an overpowering, uncontrollable challenge to established relations that could lead to disease and death. Those who practiced "uncontrolled" masturbation or "overheated" sexual relations were assigned a liminal position between masculine and feminine that resembled the stereotypes assigned to male homosexuals.

What had happened, Smith-Rosenberg suggests, was that, via a cultural rather than a rational logic, the male physical body had come to symbolize the social body of early-nineteenth-century America. Threats to disrupt the hierarchy, order, and balance of this society – threats that were, indeed, increasing with the transition from a traditional to a commercial and democratic society – were experienced as threats to health and masculinity. From this symbolic perspective, the suppression of pubescent males made cultural sense, particularly because, in the new world of the market, the apprentice system that had ordered and ritualized their transition to adulthood had disappeared. But if the male orgasm was the carrier of pollution, Smith-Rosenberg asks, what was the source and the cure? Because magical powers could not be invoked in this increasingly secular culture, women emerged in the purity literature as both tempting whore and purifying madonna. The symbolic equivalent of the pure and abstinent male, she suggests, was the frigid woman devoted to hearth and home.

Marxism

Marxism in its orthodox version has formed the great theoretical animus against which the case for a more autonomous approach to culture has most typically been made. In the course of the twentieth century, however, a great internal movement of theoretical revision has sought to rid Marxism of its mechanistic bent. In terms of cultural theory, the most significant reviser was Gramsci, who conceived of bourgeois culture as an independent barrier to the growth of socialism and, hence, the development of a new class culture as the first and most important revolutionary goal. Contemporary Marxist approaches to culture have read Gramsci through the lens of recent cultural theory, and the result has been the emergence of an even less reductionist vision of the relation between culture and economic life.

E. P. Thompson's *The Making of the English Working Class* has been the most influential example of this newly cultural Marxism in the post–World War II period. We hear echoes in it not only of Gramsci but of Weber and Durkheim, and we find references not only to classes but to codes and values. In his effort to explain the growing class consciousness and militance of the English working class, Thompson focuses less on the permutations of economics than on the creation of "community." He traces the origins of the highly organized and self-conscious working class of the industrial period to eighteenth-century local "traditions," which were organized around the "code" of the self-respecting artisan, a code that emphasized decency, regularity, and mutual aid. As the Industrial Revolution spread, this code was extended to ever broader groups of working people, who joined burial and insurance societies and trade unions, not simply for rational economic reasons but to be part of the new cultural milieu.

If the English working class was to become revolutionary, rational knowledge of its conditions and self-interest was not enough. More important, according to Thompson, was the growth of an independent working-class culture. As this culture developed, it joined the artisanal code to the languages of religious brotherhood and socialist idealism. The result was a class culture of collectivist values that emphasized mutual aid, self-discipline, and civil discussion, values that were propagated by political theory and new social organizations like trade unions, but also by mass participation in extensive ceremonies and rituals. Thompson insists that the mass demonstrations through which workers eventually were able to gain recognition were possible only because of this successful cultural transformation, which allowed participants to maintain meaning, solidarity, and self-discipline under difficult political conditions. In Thompson's account, the relative autonomy of culture becomes more than an analytical variable; it becomes a historical and political necessity.

According to orthodox Marxism, capitalist production not only makes manual labor central to life experience but denudes it of meaning, reducing it to a mechanical form. Paul Willis accepts this traditional outlook insofar as he places manual work at center stage and views it as an alienating and exploitive process. He departs radically from orthodoxy, however, by viewing this industrial work as laden with meaning. For Willis, base and superstructure are not even separable, much less hierarchical, domains. "The direct experience of production," he argues, "is worked through and over in the praxis of different cultural discourses."

At the base of workplace culture Willis places the existential confrontation with brutal physical conditions that, because it allows an initial humanization of the workplace, prevents what might otherwise be the total "rout of meaning." Although Willis acknowledges that the physical difficulty of factory labor is decreasing, he maintains that the metaphorical images of strength and bravery remain central to the workplace. They underlie the cultural emphasis on workers' competence and the struggle for informal control over work processes that create symbolic space on the shop labor. They also inform the distinctive language and humor that characterizes shop life. Most significantly, these images of physical prowess and the struggles they inform are worked through symbolic assertions of masculine identity. The self-esteem that workplace culture provides is premised on the belief that weaker people, especially women, are not capable of similar achievements. As a symbol of this differential achievement, the wage packet that the worker takes home guarantees him central status in the family, as well as a certain independence from the demands of wife and children. It is because of this masculine workplace culture, Willis argues, that the hard, brutal nature of factory life comes to be seen as a property of gender rather than as a dehumanizing product of capitalist production itself.

Poststructuralism

The diffuse intellectual movement that has come to be called "poststructuralism" shares Marxism's critical ideology but little of its faith that contemporary conditions will be transformed via the intervention of a self-conscious historical agent like the working class. Although this resignation can be linked to the recent failure of radical social movements, there are also theoretical reasons, for poststructuralism approaches cultural studies not only in the shadow of Marx but under the influence of semiotics and structuralism. Indeed, the approach developed in the late 1960s and 1970s from within both Marxism and structuralism. Against the purely textual references of semiotics and structuralism, writers like Foucault and Bourdieu made a kind of functionalist critique, emphasizing the social links of symbolism to power and social class. Against the structural theory of Marxism, on the other hand, they made a semiotic, antifunctionalist response. They argued that social structures, like classes or political authority, cannot be interpreted as acting "against" culture, for such an understanding implies that the social system is not penetrated by meaning. To use Parsons's terms, if classes or powers have only analytical autonomy from culture, in concrete terms they must be seen as one particular form of embedded cultural codes. This theoretical strategy promises to overcome the mechanistic, "functionalist" implications of even the newly cultural Marxism; the danger is that in doing so, it may replicate the deterministic and antivoluntaristic qualities of the semiotic position it also seeks to critique.[9]

9. If it seems paradoxical to employ Parsons's own analytic–concrete distinction to describe an approach that seeks to overcome the mechanistic possibilities of "functionalism" (and functionalist-like Marxism), the reader should recall my earlier argument that Parsons's more sophisticated understanding of the interpenetration of culture and social system was often converted into a more reductionistic version of three separated systems that confront one another.

The striking theoretical relationship between poststructuralism and Parsonian functionalism – both of which seek some ground between overly social and overly symbolic modes of analysis – can also be used to understand certain problems in the more contemporary theory. Poststructuralism tends to view the social and cultural systems as tightly intertwined – social structures and social actors as mere instantiations of cultural discourses and codes, which, in their turn, are mere reproductions of political and economic constraints. In this sense, poststructuralism fails to acknowledge the systematic conflict between what Parsons called "functional and pattern integration," a conflict between culture and social system that opens up any society to endemic conflicts, strains, and innovation (see the selection from Parsons and Shils in this volume).

For Foucault, the problem with most earlier studies of sexuality is that they are insufficiently cultural. They study the repressiveness or liberality of various discourses about sex but take the "it," sex behavior itself, as if it existed as something apart from these cultural discourses. Foucault argues, to the contrary, that one must account for the way this "it" is spoken about at all, for it is cultural discourse that constitutes the very object that it liberates or oppresses. He insists, moreover, that the way in which "sex" is put into discourse must be considered a form of power; since it deeply affects human behavior, it can be seen as penetrating and controlling everyday pleasure.

Foucault makes this case by reexamining the transition from the overtly more repressive societies of the early modern period – where the expression of sexual deviance, either inside or outside of marriage, was subject to severe punishment – to more modern settings in which therapy and pedagogy have replaced direct punishment. He argues that these more modern developments do not necessarily mean an actual diminution of social control over and discipline of sexual behavior. As they became subjects of therapy and education, sexual acts came to be understood within the framework of increasingly rationalized and abstract discourses, which Foucault suggests should be seen as cultural power disciplining sexuality. Their function has been less the direct interdiction of sex than the creation of new ways of speaking about it. Yet, by defining the categories of contemporary sexuality – such as impotence, perversion, or even "normal heterosexual sexuality" – these discourses created the very objects whose patterns they were to explain. To employ Foucault's evocative language, they implanted principles of classification in the physical bodies of human beings.

But the power of the sex code was not purely a cultural one. Because the discourses demanded constant and curious attention from authorities, they created an entire range of new professional "surveillance" authorities. Again, Foucault insists that these authorities did not emerge in order to combat sexually deviant behavior that was already in existence. To the contrary, he suggests, such behavior was unintentionally evoked by these new agencies of control and by the broader sexual discourses they served. Their professional attention, Foucault claims, reveals less an effort to control the varieties of sexual behavior than an unconscious desire to come into contact with them.

In Pierre Bourdieu's work we find a similar critical inversion of functionalist reasoning with a semiotic slant. According to the common sense of everyday life, Bourdieu writes, the comprehension of material objects is immediate and unforced, and the ability of perception, or perceptiveness, is taken to vary on an individual basis. Following semiotics, Bourdieu suggests that this understanding is illusory. All comprehension is filtered through a priori codes, which, after they are mastered by the observer, become a cultivated ability. Perception, then, is actually a form of cultural deciphering and, following Marx, Bourdieu argues that this ability to decipher is unequally distributed by society. The most important tasks and status positions in society demand complex performances that can be mastered only by those who possess the necessary codes. These codes form the *cultural* wealth of any society, a wealth that can be possessed only by those who have acquired the *symbolic* means to appropriate it. Through the unconscious mastery of the instruments of appropriation, individuals acquire cultural capital.

Families and schools are institutions specializing in the transmission of these cultural codes, which they force upon individuals without their knowledge, determining the perceptual distinctions that individuals will later be able to make. Since families and schools are vastly unequal in their initial access to the most valued cultural codes, their function may be described, in Bourdieu's words, as transmitting "the socially conditioned inequalities of cultural competence." Because class behavior is based on a competence that is transmitted through cultural rather than simply or even primarily through material means, social privilege appears to be a reflection of individual gifts rather than the other way around. Even the members of privileged groups seem to think that their tastes and abilities are natural rather than social. Education transforms socially conditioned inequalities into inequalities of success that are interpreted as inequalities of natural gifts. Culture performs this ideological function as long as this link between culture and education is kept from view.

Conclusion

Recent developments in cultural studies converge in their emphasis on the autonomy of culture from social structure. The meaning of an ideology or belief system cannot be read from social behavior; it must be studied as a pattern in and of itself. Approaches to culture differ from one another in describing precisely what such autonomy implies. Some argue that knowledge of this independently organized cultural system is sufficient for understanding the motives and meaning of social behavior, others that this system must be understood as having been modeled upon processes that already exist in the social system itself. The concrete processes for relating culture, social structure, and action are also decidedly different, ranging from religious ritual, socialization, and education to dramaturgical innovation and the formation of class consciousness. Finally, there is extraordinary disagreement over what is actually inside the cultural system itself. Is culture a set of logically interrelated symbols or is it values that assert desirable social qualities? Is it emotionally charged symbols about the sacred and profane or metaphysical ideas about otherworldly salvation?

One ambition of this introductory essay has been to demonstrate that each of these arguments possesses one element of the truth. We cannot understand culture without reference to subjective meaning, and we cannot understand it without reference to social structural constraints. We cannot interpret social behavior without acknowledging that it follows codes that it does not invent; at the same time, human invention creates a changing environment for every cultural code. Inherited metaphysical ideas form an inextricable web for modern social structures, yet powerful groups often succeed in transforming cultural structures into legitimating means.

Differences between approaches to culture must be respected because culture and society are complex affairs. Culture cannot be studied within the framework of a particular school, or even within the broader limitations of a particular discipline. Anthropology, history, political science, sociology, philosophy, linguistics, literary analysis – each has made distinctively different contributions. If each of the differences we have discussed points to some dimension of reality, however, then the differences taken together point to the need for a more general perspective that can relate each dimension to the others. By discussing these differences in explicitly theoretical terms, and by organizing them around the theme of cultural autonomy, this essay has tried to define the key terms that any more general perspective would involve.

BIBLIOGRAPHY

Alexander, Jeffrey C. (1982). *The Antinomies of Classical Thought: Marx and Durkheim.* Vol. 2 of Alexander, *Theoretical Logic in Sociology* (Berkeley and Los Angeles: University of California Press).
  (1989a). "Action and Its Environments," in Jeffrey C. Alexander, ed. *Action and Its Environments: Towards a New Synthesis* (New York: Columbia University Press), pp. 301–3.
  (1989b). "Durkheimian Sociology and Cultural Studies Today," in Alexander, *Structure and Meaning: Relinking Classical Sociology* (New York: Columbia University Press), pp. 156–73.
  (1990). "General Theory in the Postpositivist Mode: The 'Epistemological Dilemma' and the Case for Present Reason," in Steven Seidman and David Wagner, eds., *Postmodernism and Social Theory* (New York: Basil Blackwell).
  (Forthcoming). "The Promise of a Cultural Sociology: Technological Discourse and the Sacred and Profane, Information Machine," in Neil J. Smelser and Richard Münch, eds., *Theory of Culture* (Berkeley and Los Angeles: University of California Press).

Eisenstadt, S. N., and M. Curelaru. (1976). *The Forms of Sociology: Paradigms and Crises* (New York: Wiley).

Gadamer, Hans-Georg. (1975). *Truth and Method* (New York: Crossroads).

Sahlins, Marshall. (1976). *Culture and Practical Reason* (Chicago: University of Chicago Press).

Smelser, Neil J. (1959). *Social Change in the Industrial Revolution* (Chicago: University of Chicago Press).

   (1988). "Introduction: Durkheimian Sociology and Cultural Studies Today," in Jeffrey C. Alexander, ed., *Durkheimian Sociology: Cultural Studies* (New York: Cambridge University Press), pp. 1–22.

THE CASE FOR CULTURE

- Wilhelm Dilthey, *The human studies*
- Talcott Parsons and Edward Shils, *Values and social systems*
- Antonio Gramsci, *Culture and ideological hegemony*
- Ferdinand Saussure, *Signs and language*

1

The human studies

Wilhelm Dilthey

I shall start from the whole range of facts which forms the firm basis for any reasoning about the human studies. Side by side with the sciences a group of studies, linked by their common subject-matter, has grown naturally from the problems of life itself. These include history, economics, jurisprudence, politics, the study of religion, literature, poetry, architecture, music, and of philosophic world views and systems, and, finally, psychology. All these studies refer to the same great fact: mankind – which they describe, recount, and judge and about which they form concepts and theories.

It cannot be logically correct to distinguish the human studies from sciences on the grounds that they cover different ranges of facts. After all, physiology deals with an aspect of man and is a science. The basis for distinguishing the two classes of disciplines cannot lie in the facts per se. The human studies must be related differently to the mental and the physical aspects of man. And this, indeed, is the case.

In these studies a tendency inherent in the subject-matter itself is at work. The study of language embraces the physiology of the speech-organs as well as the semantics of words and sentences. The chemical effects of gunpowder are as much part of the course of modern war as the moral qualities of the soldiers who stand in its smoke. But, in the nature of the group of disciplines with which we are dealing there is a tendency, which grows stronger and stronger as they develop, to relegate the physical side of events to the role of conditions and means of comprehension. This is the turn towards reflection, the movement of understanding from the external to the internal. This tendency makes use of every expression of life in order to understand the mental content from which it arises. In history we read of economic activities, settlements, wars, and the creating of states. They fill our souls with great images and tell us about the

From "The Construction of the Historical World in the Human Studies" in Wilhelm Dilthey, *Selected Writings,* H. P. Rickman, ed. London: Cambridge University Press, 1976. Excerpted from pp. 170–92. Copyrighted by and reprinted with permission of Cambridge University Press.

historical world which surrounds us: But what moves us, above all, in these accounts is what is inaccessible to the senses and can only be experienced inwardly; this is inherent in the outer events which originate from it and, in its turn, is affected by them. The tendency I am speaking of does not depend on looking at life from the outside but is based on life itself. For all that is valuable in life is contained in what can be experienced and the whole outer clamour of history revolves round it: Goals unknown to nature arise within it. The will strives to achieve development and organization. Only in the world of the mind which creatively, responsibly, and autonomously stirs within us has life its value, its goal, and its meaning.

One can say that in all scholarly work two tendencies assert themselves.

Man finds himself determined by nature, which embraces the sparse, sporadic mental processes. Seen in this way they appear to be interpolations in the great text of the physical world. At the same time our conception of a spatial world is the original basis for our knowledge of uniformities on which we must rely from the outset. We are able to control the physical world by studying its laws. These can only be discovered if the way we experience nature, our involvement in it, and the living feeling with which we enjoy it, recedes behind the abstract apprehension of the world in terms of space, time, mass, and motion. All these factors combine to make man efface himself so that, from his impressions, he can map out this great object, nature, as a structure governed by laws. Thus it becomes the centre of reality for man.

But that same man then turns back to life, to himself. To return to experience, through which alone we have access to nature and to life, the only source of meaning, value, and purpose is the other great tendency which determines scholarly work. From this a second centre comes into being. It gives unity to all that happens to man, what he creates and does, the systems of purposes through which he lives and the outer organization of society in which individuals congregate. Here understanding penetrates the observable facts of human history to reach what is not accessible to the senses and yet affects external facts and expresses itself through them.

The first tendency aims at grasping mental contexts in the language, concepts, and methods of science and so it alienates itself. The other tendency is to seek out, and reflect upon, the unobservable content which manifests itself in the observable outer course of human events. History shows that, through the human studies, man is getting nearer and nearer to his distant goal – self-knowledge.

When we have to deal with states, churches, institutions, customs, books, and works of art we find that, like man himself, they always contain a relationship between what is outside and perceived by the senses and something they cannot reach which is inside.

We must now determine what this inner side is. It is a common error to identify our knowledge of it with psychology. I shall try to eliminate this error by making the following points.

The apparatus of law – books, judges, litigants, defendants at a particular time and place – is, first of all, the expression of a purposive system of laws which makes this apparatus effective. This purposive system is directed towards an unambiguous, external regulation of individual wills: It creates the conditions for the perfect life, as far as they can be realized by compulsion, and delimits the power spheres of individuals in relation to each other, to things, and to the general will. The law must, therefore, take the form of imperatives backed by the power of a community to enforce them. Thus historical understanding of the law in force in a certain community at a given time can be achieved by going back from the outer apparatus to what it manifests, the intellectual system of legal imperatives produced by the collective will and enforced by it. Ihering[1] discusses the spirit of Roman law in this way. His understanding of this spirit is not psychological insight. It is achieved by going back to a mind-created structure with a pattern and law of its own. Jurisprudence, from the interpretation of a passage in the Corpus Juris to the understanding of the whole Roman law and thence to the comparison of legal systems, is based on this. Hence its subject-matter is not identical with the outer facts and occurrences through, and in, which the law takes its course. These facts are the concern of jurisprudence only insofar as they embody the law. The actual capture of the criminal, the illness of witnesses, or the apparatus of execution belong to pathology and technology.

It is the same with aesthetics. The work of a poet lies in front of me. It consists of letters, is put together by compositors and printed by machines. But literary history and criticism are only concerned with what the pattern of words refers to, not – and this is decisive – with the processes in the poet's mind but with a structure created by these processes yet separable from them. The structure of a drama lies in its particular combination of subject, poetic mood, plot, and means of presentation. Each contributes to the structure of the work according to a law intrinsic to poetry. Thus the primary subject-matter of literary history or criticism is wholly distinct from the mental processes of the poet or his reader. A mind-created structure comes into being and enters the world of the senses: We can understand it only by penetrating that world.

These illustrations throw light on the subject-matter of the disciplines under consideration, their nature, and their difference from the sciences. Their subject-matter, too, is not impressions as they are experienced, but

1. R. V. Ihering. German authority on Roman law, 1818–92.

objects created by cognition in order to organize them.[2] In both cases the object is created according to the law imposed by the facts. In this both groups of disciplines agree. But they differ in the way in which their subject-matter is formed, that is, in the procedure which constitutes these disciplines. In the one a mental object emerges in the understanding, in the other a physical object in knowledge.

Now we may pronounce the word *Geisteswissenschaften,* for its meaning is clear. In the eighteenth century, when the need to find a common name for this group of disciplines arose, they were called the moral sciences, *Geisteswissenschaften,* or even the cultural sciences. The change of name alone shows that none of them is quite appropriate for what is to be referred to. So I want to indicate here the sense in which I use the word. It is the sense in which Montesquieu spoke of the spirit of the laws, Hegel of the objective mind, or Ihering of the spirit of the Roman law. To compare the usefulness of this expression with that of others used now will be possible later.

Now we can meet the final requirement for a definition of the human studies. We can distinguish the human studies from the sciences by certain clear characteristics. These are to be found in the attitude of mind, already described, which moulds the subject-matter of the human studies quite differently from that of scientific knowledge. Humanity seen through the senses is just a physical fact which can only be explained scientifically. It only becomes the subject-matter of the human studies when we experience human states, give expressions to them, and understand these expressions. The interrelation of life, expression, and understanding embraces gestures, facial expressions and words, all of which men use to communicate with each other; it also includes permanent mental creations which reveal their author's deeper meaning, and lasting objectifications of the mind in social structures where common human nature is surely, and for ever, manifest. The psycho-physical unit, man, knows even himself through the same mutual relationship of expression and understanding; he becomes aware of himself in the present; he recognizes himself in memory as something that once was; but, when he tries to hold fast and grasp his states of mind by turning his attention upon himself, the narrow limits of such an introspective method of self-knowledge show themselves: Only his actions and creations and the effect they have on others teach man about himself. So he only gains self-knowledge by the circuitous route of understanding. We learn what we once were and how we became what we are by looking at the way we acted in the past, the plans we once made for our lives,

2. Dilthey here assumes the Kantian – as against the empiricist – account of such cases as "seeing a table."

and the professional career we pursued. We have to consult old, forgotten letters and the judgments made about us long ago. In short, we can only know ourselves thoroughly through understanding: But we cannot understand ourselves and others except by projecting what we have actually experienced into every expression of our own and others' lives. So man becomes the subject-matter of the human studies only when we relate experience, expression, and understanding to each other. They are based on this connection, which is their distinguishing characteristic. A discipline only belongs to the human studies when we can approach its subject-matter through the connection between life, expression, and understanding. . . .

The cognition of objects is a temporal process and, therefore, contains memory pictures. As, with the progress of time, experience accumulates and constantly recedes, we come to remember our passage through life. In the same way understanding of other people produces memories of their circumstances and images of different situations. All these memories of external facts, events, and persons are invariably combined with a sense of the context to which they belong. The individual's knowledge of life springs from the generalization of what has thus accumulated. It arises through procedures which are equivalent to induction. The number of cases on which the induction is based constantly increases in the course of a lifetime and the generalizations formed are constantly corrected. The certainty attributable to personal knowledge of life is different from scientific validity, for these generalizations are not methodically made and cannot be formalized.

The individual slant which colours the personal knowledge of life is corrected and enlarged by the common experience. By this I mean the shared beliefs emerging in any coherent circle of people. These are assertions about the passage of life, judgments of value, rules of conduct, definitions of goals and of what is good. It is characteristic of them that they are the products of the *common* life. They apply as much to the life of individuals as to that of communities. As custom, tradition, and public opinion they *influence* individuals and their experience; because the community has the weight of numbers behind it and outlasts the individual, this power usually proves superior to his will. . . .

The lives of individuals are infinitely enriched through their relationships to their environment, to other people, and to things. But every individual is also a point where webs of relationships intersect; these relationships go through individuals, exist within them, but also reach beyond their life and possess an independent existence and development of their own through the content, value, and purpose which they realize. Thus they are subjects of an ideal kind. Some kind of knowledge of reality is inherent in them; standpoints for valuation develop within them; purposes are realized in them; they have a meaning which they sustain in the context of the mind-constructed world.

This is already the case in some of the systems of culture, for instance, art and philosophy, where there is no organization to link their parts. But organized associations also develop. Economic life produces its own associations, science its own research centres, religions develop the strongest of all cultural organizations. The highest development of common goals within a community is found in the family and the state and in the different intermediate forms between them. . . .

This direct relationship between life and the human studies leads, in the latter, to a conflict between the tendencies of life and the goal of science. Because historians, economists, teachers of law, and students of religion are involved in life they want to influence it. They subject historical personages, mass movements, and trends to their judgment, which is conditioned by their individuality, the nation to which they belong, and the age in which they live. Even when they think they are being objective they are determined by their horizon, for every analysis of the concepts of a former generation reveals constituents in them which derive from the presuppositions of that generation. Yet every science implies a claim to validity. If there are to be strictly scientific human studies they must aim more consciously and critically at validity.

Many of the scientific divergences which have recently appeared in the logic of the human studies stem from the conflict between these two tendencies. . . . I find the principle for the settlement of the conflict within these studies in the understanding of the historical world as a system of interactions centered on itself: Each individual system of interactions contained in it has, through the positing of values and their realization, its centre within itself, but all are structurally linked into a whole in which the meaning of the whole web of the social-historical world arises from the significance of the individual parts; thus every value-judgment and every purpose projected into the future must be based exclusively on these structural relationships. We are approaching this ideal principle in the subsequent, general, statements about the connections between the human studies. . . .

Though experience presents us with the reality of life in its many ramifications, we only seem to know one particular thing, namely our own life. It remains knowledge of something unique and no logical aid can overcome this limitation, which is rooted in the way it is experienced. Understanding alone surmounts the limitation of the individual experience and, at the same time, lends to personal experiences the character of knowledge of life. Extending over several people, mental creations, and communities, it widens the horizon of the individual life and, in the human studies, opens up the path which leads from the common to the general.

Mutual understanding assures us of what individuals have in common. They are connected with each other by common, i.e. similar or identical, features. This same relation permeates the whole of the human world. These common bonds are expressed in identity of reason, in sympathy on the emotional plane, and in the mutual commitments of right and duty accompanied by consciousness of obligation.

What persons have in common is the starting-point for all the relations between the particular and the general in the human studies. A basic experience of what men have in common permeates the whole conception of the mind-constructed world; through it consciousness of a unitary self and similarity with others, identity of human nature, and individuality are linked. This is the presupposition for understanding. The degree of methodological certainty achieved by understanding depends on the development of the general truths on which the understanding of this relationship is based.

Thus our example illustrates the double relationship involved in understanding. Understanding presupposes experience and experience only becomes knowledge of life if understanding leads us from the narrowness and subjectivity of experience to the whole and the general. . . .

The totality of understanding reveals – in contrast with the subjectivity of experience – the objectifications of life. A realization of the objectivity of life, i.e. of its externalizations in many kinds of structural systems, becomes an additional basis for the human studies. The individual, the communities, and the works into which life and mind have entered form the outer realm of the mind. These manifestations of life, as they present themselves to understanding in the external world, are, as it were, embedded in the context of nature. The great outer reality of mind always surrounds us. It is a manifestation of the mind in the world of the senses – from a fleeting expression to the century-long rule of a constitution or code of law. Every single expression represents a common feature in the realm of this objective mind. Every word, every sentence, every gesture or polite formula, every work of art, and every political deed is intelligible because the people who expressed themselves through them and those who understood them have something in common; the individual always experiences, thinks, and acts in a common sphere and only there does he understand. Everything that is understood carries, as it were, the hallmark of familiarity derived from such common features. We live in this atmosphere, it surrounds us constantly. We are immersed in it. We are at home everywhere in this historical and understood world; we understand the sense and meaning of it all; we ourselves are woven into this common sphere.

The change of expressions which affect us challenges us constantly to new understanding, but, because every expression and the understanding of it is, at the same time, connected with others, our understanding carries us along naturally from the given particular to the whole. As the relations between what is alike increase, the possibilities of generalizations, already contained in the common features of what is understood, grow.

Understanding highlights a further characteristic of the objectification of life which determines both classification and generalization. The objectification of life contains in itself many differentiated systems. . . .

To summarize. The human studies have as their comprehensive subject-matter the objectification of life. But, insofar as this becomes something we understand, it contains the relation of inner to outer throughout. Accordingly this objectification is always related, in understanding, to experience in which the person becomes aware of his own inner life and capable of interpreting that of others. If the facts of the human studies are contained in this then everything inflexible and everything alien, because it belongs to the images of the physical world, must be removed from the idea of these facts. Every fact is man-made and, therefore, historical; it is understood and, therefore, contains common features; it is known because understood, and it contains a classification of the manifold because every interpretation of an expression by the higher understanding rests on such a classification. The classifying of expressions is already rooted in the facts of the human studies.

Here the concepts of the human studies is completed. Their range is identical with that of understanding, and understanding consistently has the objectification of life as its subject-matter. Thus the range of the human studies is determined by the objectification of life in the external world. Mind can only understand what it has created.

2

Values and social systems

Talcott Parsons and Edward Shils

The theory of action is a conceptual scheme for the analysis of the behavior of living organisms. It conceives of this behavior as oriented to the attainment of ends in situations, by means of the normatively regulated expenditure of energy. . . .

Each action is the action of an actor, and it takes place in a situation consisting of objects. The objects may be other actors or physical or cultural objects. Each actor has a system of relations-to-objects; this is called his "system of orientations." The objects may be goal objects, resources, means, conditions, obstacles, or symbols. They may become cathected (wanted or not wanted), and they may have different significances attached to them (that is, they may mean different things to different people). Objects, by the significances and cathexes attached to them, become organized into the actor's system of orientations. . . .

Actions are not empirically discrete but occur in constellations which we call "systems." We are concerned with three systems, three modes of organization of the elements of action; these elements are organized as social systems, as personalities, and as cultural systems. Though all three modes are conceptually abstracted from concrete social behavior, the empirical referents of the three abstractions are not on the same plane. Social systems and personalities are conceived as modes of organizations of motivated action (social systems are systems of *motivated* action organized about the relations of actors to each other; personalities are systems of motivated action organized about the living organism). Cultural systems, on the other hand, are systems of symbolic patterns (these patterns are created or manifested by individual actors and are transmitted among social systems by diffusion and among personalities by learning). . . .

A *cultural system* is a system which has the following characteristics:

From "Values, Motives, and Systems of Actions," in Parsons and Shils, eds., *Towards a General Theory of Action*. Cambridge, Mass.: Harvard University Press, 1951. Excerpted from pp. 53–60, 105–6, 159–79, © 1951 by The President and Fellows of Harvard College; © 1979 by Helen W. Parsons. Reprinted by permission.

(1) The system is constituted neither by the organization of interactions nor by the organization of the actions of a single actor (as such), but rather by the organization of the values, norms, and symbols which guide the choices made by actors and which limit the types of interaction which may occur among actors. (2) Thus a cultural system is not an empirical system in the same sense as a personality or social system, because it represents a special kind of abstraction of elements from these systems. These elements, however, may exist separately as physical symbols and be transmitted from one empirical action system to another. (3) In a cultural system the patterns of regulatory norms (and the other cultural elements which guide choices of concrete actors) cannot be made up of random or unrelated elements. If, that is, a system of culture is to be manifest in the organization of an empirical action system it must have a certain degree of consistency. (4) Thus a cultural system is a pattern of culture whose different parts are interrelated to form value systems, belief systems, and systems of expressive symbols.

Social systems, personality systems, and cultural systems are critical subject matter for the theory of action. In the first two cases, the systems themselves are conceived to be actors whose action is conceived as oriented to goals and the gratification of need-dispositions, as occurring in situations, using energy, and as being normatively regulated. Analysis of the third kind of system is essential to the theory of action because systems of value standards (criteria of selection) and other patterns of culture, when *institutionalized* in social systems and *internalized* in personality systems, guide the actor with respect to both the orientation to ends and the *normative regulation* of means and of expressive activities, whenever the need-dispositions of the actor allow choices in these matters. . . .

Value-orientation refers to those aspects of the actor's orientation which commit him to the observance of certain norms, standards, criteria of selection, whenever he is in a contingent situation which allows and requires him to make a choice. Whenever an actor is forced to choose among various means objects, whenever he is forced to choose among various goal objects, whenever he is forced to choose which need-disposition he will gratify, or how much he will gratify a need-disposition – whenever he is forced to make any choice whatever – his value-orientations may commit him to certain norms that will guide him in his choices. The value-orientations which commit a man to the observance of certain rules in making selections from available alternatives are not random but tend to form a system of value-orientations which commit the individual to some organized set of rules (so that the rules themselves do not contradict one another). On a cultural level we view the organized set of rules or standards as such, abstracted, so to speak, from the actor who is committed to them by his own value-orientations and in whom they exist as need-dispositions to observe these rules. Thus a culture includes a set of standards. An individual's value-orientation is his commitment to these standards. In either case our analysis of these standards of value-orientation commitment may be the same. . . .

The interaction of ego and alter is the most elementary form of a social system. The features of this interaction are present in more complex form in all social systems.

In interaction ego and alter are each objects of orientation for the other. The basic differences from orientations to nonsocial objects are two. First, since the outcome of ego's action (e.g., success in the attainment of a goal) is contingent on alter's reaction to what ego does, ego becomes oriented not only to alter's probable *overt* behavior but also to what ego interprets to be alter's expectations relative to ego's behavior since ego expects that alter's expectations will influence alter's behavior. Second, in an integrated system this orientation to the expectations of the other is reciprocal or complementary.

Communication through a common system of symbols is the precondition of this reciprocity or complementarity of expectations. The alternatives which are open to alter must have some measure of stability in two respects: first, as realistic possibilities for alter, and second, in their meaning to ego. This stability presupposes generalization from the particularity of the given situations of ego and alter, both of which are continually changing and are never concretely identical over any two moments in time. When such generalization occurs, and actions, gestures, or symbols have more or less the *same* meaning for both ego and alter, we may speak of a common culture existing between them, through which their interaction is mediated.

Furthermore, this common culture, or symbol system, inevitably possesses in certain aspects a normative significance for the actors. Once it is in existence, observance of its conventions is a necessary condition for ego to be "understood" by alter, in the sense of allowing ego to elicit the type of reaction from alter which ego expects. This common set of cultural symbols becomes the medium in which is formed a constellation of the contingent actions of both parties, in such a way that there will simultaneously emerge a definition of a range of *appropriate* reactions on alter's part to each of a range of possible actions ego has taken and vice versa. It will then be a condition of the stabilization of such a system of complementary expectations, not only that ego and alter should *communicate,* but that they should *react appropriately* to each other's action.

A tendency toward consistent appropriateness of reaction is also a tendency toward conformity with a normative pattern. The culture is not only a set of symbols of communication but a *set of norms* for action.

The motivations of ego and alter become integrated with the normative patterns through interaction. . . .

Patterns of value-orientation have been singled out as the most crucial cultural elements in the organization of systems of action [although they are] only part of what has been defined as culture. . . .

[Such] symbol systems in which the evaluative function has primacy may be called "normative ideas" or "regulatory symbols." They are the standards of value-orientation or the value-orientation modes [according to which] the actor has a commitment to orient himself in terms of a *balance* of consequences and implications rather than being free to orient himself to the particular cultural symbol on its immediate and intrinsic merits. Thus his orientation to a particular complex of symbols must conform with the imperatives of the larger system of normative orientation of which it is a part. Otherwise, the normative system becomes disorganized. . . .

A system of evaluative symbol's comprises: (1) a subsystem of standards for solving cognitive problems, (2) a subsystem of standards for solving cathectic or appreciative problems, and (3) a subsystem of "moral" standards for the over-all integration of the various units of the system, the various processes of the system, and the various other standards involved into a single unified system. . . .

The moral value standards, as we can see, are diffuse patterns of value-orientation. They are organizers which define and integrate whole systems of action (and also many subsystems). . . .

Complete consistency of pattern is an ideal type. The moral standards which are actually held and acted upon by a concrete personality or social system cannot possess complete consistency of pattern; it is indeed probable that complete empirical pattern consistency is impossible. The inconsistency of pattern which we frequently observe is engendered by the adjustive problems which arise from the difficulties of articulation of value-orientation systems with personality or social system. It is an empirical problem, growing up from the relation between cultural systems and systems of action and from the coexistence of a plurality of cultural subsystems in the same society or personality.

The evaluation of all the strategically significant categories of the object world is a *functional imperative* of a system of moral standards. It is imposed by the nature of human action. Another principal imperative, which is not necessarily harmonious with the first, is the maximization of the consistency of pattern.[1]

1. Systems of action are functional systems; cultural systems are symbolic systems in which the components have logical or meaningful rather than functional relationships with one another. Hence the imperatives which are charac-

Evaluative orientation confronts situational events which may be both "reinterpreted" and creatively transformed, but only within limits. The recalcitrance of events, particularly the foci of man's organic nature and the scarcity of means or resources, imposes certain functional imperatives on action. There is no necessity, and certainly little likelihood, that all the facts of a situation which in a pragmatic sense must be faced can be dealt with by the actor in accordance with all the canons of a given value system. The various value systems will be differentially selective as to which facts fit and which do not, and how well or how badly, but there will always be some facts[2] that will be *problematical* for every value system. They can be dealt with only on the basis of standards that will be inconsistent with the principal standards of the actor, whatever these may be.

In one sense the *facts* of the system of social objects are more malleable than the other classes. They are, to an important degree, themselves a product of the cultural system prevailing in the action system. Thus both a man and a society are in some measure what they believe. A favourable response from alter never strains ego's own values; the interacting plurality of individuals [who] share common values therefore stands in a sense united in defense against threats to those values. However, there are definite limits to the effectiveness of such common defense if the values in question conflict seriously with functional imperatives of systems of action, which must be dealt with. Some of these functional imperatives make it most improbable that the actual concrete structure of any concrete action system will permit the realization of full consistency of the various parts of *any* value system. There must therefore be some sort of adjustment or accommodation between them. One mode of adjustment is the tendency to "force" the structure of the system of social objects into conformity with the value system, at the cost of increased strain. Another mode of adjustment is to tolerate and in varying degrees to institutionalize into the social system or to internalize in the personality system value patterns which are not [in] harmony with the major emphases of

teristic of the two classes of systems are different. In systems of action the imperatives which impose certain adaptations on the components result from the empirical possibilities or necessities of coexistence which we designate as scarcity, and from the empirical possibilities or necessities of coexistence which we designate as scarcity, and from the properties of the actor as an organism; in cultural systems the internal imperatives are independent of the compatibilities or incompatibilities of coexistence. In cultural systems the systemic feature is coherence; the components of the cultural system are either logically consistent or meaningfully congruous.

2. Problematical facts in the present sense are those which it is functionally imperative to face and which necessitate reactions with value implications incompatible with the actor's paramount value system.

the dominant value system. The inconsistencies of value patterns are intraindividually adjusted through the mechanisms of defense, and interindividually adjusted through such social control mechanisms as isolation and segregation.

It is impossible for a functionally important sector of the social system to be organized and stabilized without some degree of institutionalization, and for a correspondingly important sector of the personality to be organized and stabilized without internalization of values. In those sectors of the system of action which are out of harmony with the dominant value system, "adaptive institutionalization" will tend to occur. There will be a special mode of integration into the action system of that sector of the value-orientation system which is more or less in conflict with the main value-orientation system and its related institutions. There will consequently exist more or less fully institutionalized value-patterns, at variance with the paramount value system; these are "endemic" in the social system, and on occasion may become important foci for structural change. . . .

Inconsistencies within the value system result in strain in the system of action, personal and social. Such inconsistencies often originate through historical circumstances which resulted in exposure to inconsistent value-orientation patterns so that two or more sets may have been internalized or institutionalized in some sector of the system. This source of strain, however, can only add to the original sources of strain inherent in the nature of systems of action. This original source of strain lies in the fact that *no* fully integrated, internally consistent system of value-orientation can be adequate to the functional needs of any concrete system of action. Given the inevitability of strain, there must therefore be adaptive value-integrations in the sectors in which the dominant value-integration is least adequate and which compensate for these inadequacies. Were it not for this basis of malintegration in the nature of action in a system, historical malintegrations would certainly not be either severe or persistent.

Alongside the tendency for inconsistencies in the value system to engender strains in the system of action and vice versa, there is a tendency of systems of action to build up and maintain levels of consistency as high as the exigencies of action will permit. The basis of this tendency rests in the functional need for order which underlies *any* action system, and which entails the need for integration of its cultural components. The need for order is seen in its simplest and most elementary form in the complementarity of role expectations. Without stability and consequently predictability, which is the essence of order, ego and alter could not respond to one another's expectations in a mutually gratifying way. Correspondingly the need-dispositions within a personality system must be organized into a stable pattern as a condition of avoiding frustration and holding down anxiety. The recognition of this need for order in systems of action is the central reason for our introduction of evaluation as one of the few most fundamental categories. The fundamental need for order in a system is the root of the strain which appears when an inconsistent value system is translated into action.

In relatively stable systems of action there are then the two tendencies to build consistent systems of value-orientation and the contrary tendency to generate and to tolerate inconsistent subsystems with the strain which they produce. There will be a delicate dynamic equilibrium between the two maintained by a wide variety of accommodating mechanisms. Empirically the value-orientation is not autonomous except in the sense that it may be treated as an independent variable, interdependent with other variables in a system. Among the basic components of an action system, there is no causal priority of any factor as the initiator of change. Change may come from any source in the system. The outcome will depend on the balance of forces in the system at the time . . . .

The "emanationist" hypothesis which asserts that action is simply a consequence of the prevailing value system cannot be accepted. A further deficiency of this view is its assertion that all sectors of the value system are explicable by logical derivation from the central themes or premises. It is on this account that it is necessary to conceive of both a functional integration of value-orientations and a pattern integration. The latter refers to the extent to which a given pattern or theme of orientation is consistently manifested in the specific evaluative attitudes of the actors throughout the social system. Functional integration refers to the integration of values with systems of action and it therefore involves priorities and allocations of diverse value components among proper occasions and relationships. This is one of the principal aspects of the structure of social systems, and it is by these mechanisms that standards which are not integrated with respect to their patterns are brought into a measure of functional integration sufficient to allow the social system to operate. . . .

The functional inevitability of imperfections of value integration in the social system does not, as we have seen, necessarily destroy the social system, because a set of mechanisms, which are homologous with the mechanisms of defense in the personality, limit the disintegratedness and confine its repercussions. These mechanisms render possible the continued operation of the social system; that is, the interdependent coexistence of the various parts of the system. These mechanisms moreover may even render possible a measure of limited collaboration between the sectors of the society committed in other respects to incompatible values. Just as in the personality certain defense mechanisms keep dangerous impulses below the level of consciousness, thus keeping down the level of anxiety and conflict, so in the social system certain accommodative mechanisms permit contradictory patterns to coexist by allocating them to different situations and groups within the society. The extreme rationalist or the doctrinaire who takes a system of institutionalized values as something to be rigorously and consistently applied in all situations can for this reason be a seriously disturbing influence in a social system.

Social systems and especially large-scale societies are inescapably caught in a very fundamental dilemma. On the one hand, they can only live by a system of institutionalized values, to which the members must be seriously committed and to which they must adhere in their actions. On the other hand, they must be able to accept compromises and accommodations, tolerating many actions which from the point of view of their own dominant values are wrong. Their failure to do so precipitates rebellion and withdrawal and endangers the continuation of the system even at the level of integration which it has hitherto achieved. In this paradox lies a principal source of strain and instability in social systems, and many of the most important seeds of social change.[3]

3. At the same time this situation is, from the theoretical point of view, the main reason for refusing to regard the problems of the integration of systems of cultural value-orientations and of social systems as homologous. It is also the predominant reason why the type of analysis of value-orientation associated particularly with the name of the late Ruth Benedict cannot serve as the sole or even primary basis for an analysis of the dynamic processes of the social system.

3

Culture and ideological hegemony

Antonio Gramsci

It is essential to destroy the widespread prejudice that philosophy is a strange and difficult thing just because it is the specific intellectual activity of a particular category of specialists or of professional and systematic philosophers. It must first be shown that all men are "philosophers," by defining the limits and characteristics of the "spontaneous philosophy" which is proper to everybody. This philosophy is contained in: 1. language itself, which is a totality of determined notions and concepts and not just of words grammatically devoid of content; 2. "common sense" and "good sense"; 3. popular religion and, therefore, also in the entire system of beliefs, superstitions, opinions, ways of seeing things and of acting, which are collectively bundled together under the name of "folklore."

Having first shown that everyone is a philosopher, though in his own way and unconsciously, since even in the slightest manifestation of any intellectual activity whatever, in "language," there is contained a specific conception of the world, one then moves on to the second level, which is that of awareness and criticism. That is to say, one proceeds to the question – is it better to "think," without having a critical awareness, in a disjointed and episodic way? In other words, is it better to take part in a conception of the world mechanically imposed by the external environment, i.e. by one of the many social groups in which everyone is automatically involved from the moment of his entry into the conscious world (and this can be one's village or province; it can have its origins in the parish and the "intellectual activity" of the local priest or aging patriarch whose wisdom is law, or in the little old woman who has inherited the lore of the witches or the minor intellectual soured by his own stupidity and inability to act)? Or, on the other hand, is it better to work out consciously and critically one's own conception of the world and thus, in connection with the labours of one's own brain, choose one's sphere of activity, take an active part in the creation of the history of the world, be

From Gramsci, *Selection from the Prison Notebooks*. New York: International Publishers, 1971. Excerpted from pp. 323–35. Reprinted with permission.

one's own guide, refusing to accept passively and supinely from outside the moulding of one's personality?

Note I. In acquiring one's conception of the world one always belongs to a particular grouping which is that of all the social elements which share the same mode of thinking and acting. We are all conformists of some conformism or other, always man-in-the-mass or collective man. The question is this: Of what historical type is the conformism, the mass humanity to which one belongs? When one's conception of the world is not critical and coherent but disjointed and episodic, one belongs simultaneously to a multiplicity of mass human groups. The personality is strangely composite: It contains Stone Age elements and principles of a more advanced science, prejudices from all past phases of history at the local level, and intuitions of a future philosophy which will be that of a human race united the world over. To criticise one's own conception of the world means therefore to make it a coherent unity and to raise it to the level reached by the most advanced thought in the world. It therefore also means criticism of all previous philosophy, in so far as this has left stratified deposits in a popular philosophy. The starting-point of critical elaboration is the consciousness of what one really is, and is "knowing thyself" as a product of the historical process to date which has deposited in you an infinity of traces, without leaving an inventory.

Note II. Philosophy cannot be separated from the history of philosophy, nor can culture from the history of culture. In the most immediate and relevant sense, one cannot be a philosopher, by which I mean have a critical and coherent conception of the world, without having a consciousness of its historicity, of the phase of development which it represents, and of the fact that it contradicts other conceptions or elements of other conceptions. One's conception of the world is a response to certain specific problems posed by reality, which are quite specific and "original" in their immediate relevance. How is it possible to consider the present, and quite specific present, with a mode of thought elaborated for a past which is often remote and superseded? When someone does this, it means that he is a walking anachronism, a fossil, and not living in the modern world, or at the least that he is strangely composite. And it is in fact the case that social groups which in some ways express the most developed modernity, lag behind in other respects, given their social position, and are therefore incapable of complete historical autonomy.

Note III. If it is true that every language contains the elements of a conception of the world and of a culture, it could also be true that from anyone's language one can access the greater or lesser complexity of his conception of the world. Someone who only speaks dialect, or understands the standard language incompletely, necessarily has an intuition of the world which is more or less limited and provincial, which is fossilised and anachronistic in relation to the major currents of thought which dominate world history. His interests will be limited, more or less corporate or economistic, not universal. While it is not always possible to learn a number of foreign languages in order to put oneself in contact with other cultural lives, it is at the least necessary to learn the national language properly. A great culture can be translated into the language of another great culture and can be a world-wide means of expression. But a dialect cannot do this.

Note IV. Creating a new culture does not only mean one's own individual "original" discoveries. It also, and most particularly, means the diffusion in a critical form of truths already discovered, their "socialisation" as it were, and even making them the basis of vital action, an element of co-ordination and intellectual and moral order. For a mass of people to be led to think coherently and in the same coherent fashion about the real present world, is a "philosophical" event far more important and "original" than the discovery by some philosophical "genius" of a truth which remains the property of small groups of intellectuals.

Connection between "common sense," religion, and philosophy

Philosophy is intellectual order, which neither religion nor common sense can be. It is to be observed that religion and common sense do not coincide either, but that religion is an element of fragmented common sense. Morever common sense is a collective noun, like religion: There is not just one common sense, for that too is a product of history and a part of the historical process. Philosophy is criticism and the superseding of religion and "common sense." In this sense it coincides with "good" as opposed to "common" sense.

Relation between science, religion, and common sense

Religion and common sense cannot constitute an intellectual order, be-cause they cannot be reduced to unity and coherence even within an individual consciousness, let alone collective consciousness. Or rather they cannot be so reduced "freely" – for this may be done by "authoritarian" means, and indeed within limits this has been done in the past.

Note the problem of religion taken not in the confessional sense but in the secular sense of a unity of faith between a conception of the world and a corresponding norm of conduct. But why call this unity of faith "religion" and not "ideology," or even frankly "politics"?

Philosophy in general does not in fact exist. Various philosophies or conceptions of the world exist, and one always makes a choice between them. How is this choice made? Is it merely an intellectual event, or is it something more complex? And is it not frequently the case that there is a contradiction between one's intellectual choice and one's mode of conduct? Which therefore would be the real conception of the world: that logically affirmed as an intellectual choice? or that which emerges from the real activity of each man, which is implicit in his mode of action? And since all action is political, can one not say that the real philosophy of each man is contained in its entirety in his political action?

This contrast between thought and action, i.e. the co-existence of two conceptions of the world, one affirmed in words and the other displayed in effective action, is not simply a product of self-deception. Self-deception can be an adequate explanation for a few individuals taken separately, or even for groups of a certain size, but it is not adequate when the contrast occurs in the life of great masses. In these cases the contrast between thought and action cannot but be the expression of profounder contrasts of a social historical order. It signifies that the social group in question may indeed have its own conception of the world, even if only embryonic; a conception which manifests itself in action, but occasionally and in flashes – when, that is, the group is acting as an organic totality. But this same group has, for reasons of submission and intellectual subordination, adopted a conception which is not its own but is borrowed from another group; and it affirms this conception verbally and believes itself to be following it, because this is the conception which it follows in "normal times" – that is, when its conduct is not independent and autonomous, but submissive and subordinate. Hence the reason why philosophy cannot be divorced from politics. And one can show furthermore that the choice and the criticism of a conception of the world is also a political matter.

What must next be explained is how it happens that in all periods there co-exist many systems and currents of philosophical thought, how these currents are born, how they are diffused, and why in the process of diffusion they fracture along certain lines and in certain directions. The fact of this process goes to show how necessary it is to order in a systematic, coherent, and critical fashion one's own intuitions of life and the world.

What is the popular image of philosophy? It can be reconstructed by looking at expressions in common usage. One of the most usual is "being philosophical about it," which, if you consider it, is not to be entirely rejected as a phrase. It is true that it contains an implicit invitation to resignation and patience, but it seems to me that the most important point is rather the invitation to people to reflect and to realise fully that whatever happens is basically rational and must be confronted as such, and that one should apply one's power of rational concentration and not let oneself be carried away by instinctive and violent impulses. These popular turns of phrases could be compared with similar expressions used by writers of a popular stamp – examples being drawn from a large dictionary – which contain the terms "philosophy" or "philosophically." One can see from these examples that the terms have a quite precise meaning: that of overcoming bestial and elemental passions through a conception of necessity which gives a conscious direction to one's activity. This is the healthy nucleus that exists in "common sense," the part of it which can be called "good sense" and which deserves to be made more unitary and coherent. So it appears that here again it is not possible to separate what is known as "scientific" philosophy from the common and popular philosophy which is only a fragmentary collection of ideas and opinions.

But at this point we reach the fundamental problem facing any conception of the world, any philosophy which has become a cultural movement, a "religion," a "faith," any that has produced a form of practical activity or will in which the philosophy is contained as an implicit theoretical "premiss." One might say "ideology" here, but on condition that the word is used in its highest sense of a conception of the world that is implicitly manifest in art, in law, in economic activity, and in all manifestations of individual and collective life. This problem is that of preserving the ideological unity of the entire social bloc which that ideology serves to cement and to unify. The strength of religions, and of the Catholic church in particular, has lain, and still lies, in the fact that they feel very strongly the need for the doctrinal unity of the whole mass of the faithful and strive to ensure that the higher intellectual stratum does not get separated from the lower. The Roman church has always been the most vigorous in the struggle to prevent the "official" formation of two religions, one for the "intellectuals" and the other for the "simple souls." This struggle has not been without serious disadvantages for the Church itself, but these disadvantages are connected with the historical process which is transforming the whole of civil society and which contains overall a corrosive critique of all religion, and they only serve to emphasize the organisational capacity of the clergy in the cultural sphere and the abstractly rational and just relationship which the Church has been able to establish in its own sphere between the intellectuals and the simple. The Jesuits have undoubtedly been the major architects of this equilibrium, and in order to preserve it they have given the Church a progressive forward movement which has tended to allow the demands of science and philosophy to be a certain extent satisfied. But the rhythm of the movement has been so slow and methodical that the changes have passed unobserved by the mass of the simple, although they appear "revolutionary" and demagogic to the "integralists."

One of the greatest weaknesses of immanentist philosophies in general consists precisely in the fact that they have not been able to create an ideological unity between the bottom and the top, between the "simple" and the "intellectuals." In the history of Western civilisation the fact is exemplified on a European scale, with the rapid collapse of the Renaissance and to a certain extent also the Reformation faced with the Roman church. Their weakness is demonstrated in the educational field, in that the immanentist philosophies have not even attempted to construct a conception which could take the place of religion in the education of children.

One could only have had cultural stability and an organic quality of thought if there had existed the same unity between the intellectuals and the simple as there should be between theory and practice. That is, if the intellectuals had been organically the intellectuals of those masses, and if they had worked out and made coherent the principles and the problems raised by the masses in their practical activity, thus constituting a cultural and social bloc. The question posed here was the one we have already referred to, namely this: Is a philosophical movement properly so called when it is devoted to creating a specialised culture among restricted intellectual groups, or rather when, and only when, in the process of elaborating a form of thought superior to "common sense" and coherent on a scientific plane, it never forgets to remain in contact with the "simple" and indeed finds in this contact the source of the problems it sets out to study and to resolve? Only by this contact does a philosophy become "historical," purify itself of intellectualistic elements of an individual character, and become "life." . . .

The relation between common sense and the upper level of philosophy is assured by "politics," just as it is politics that assures the relationship between the Catholicism of the intellectuals and that of the simple. There are, however, fundamental differences between the two cases. That the Church has to face up to a problem of the "simple" means precisely that there has been a split in the community of the faithful.

This split cannot be healed by raising the simple to the level of the intellectuals (the Church does not even envisage such a task, which is both ideologically and economically beyond its present capacities), but only by imposing an iron discipline on the intellectuals so that they do not exceed certain limits of differentiation and so render the split catastrophic and irreparable. In the past such divisions in the community of the faithful were healed by strong mass movements which led to, or were absorbed in, the creation of new religious orders centered on strong personalities (St. Dominic, St. Francis). . . .

The position of the philosophy of praxis is the antithesis of the Catholic. The philosophy of praxis does not tend to leave the "simple" in their primitive philosophy of common sense, but rather to lead them to a higher conception of life. If it affirms the need for contact between intellectuals and simple [people] it is not in order to restrict scientific activity and preserve unity at the low level of the masses, but precisely in order to construct an intellectual-moral bloc which can make politically possible the intellectual progress of the mass and not only of small intellectual groups.

The active man-in-the-mass has a practical activity, but has no clear theoretical consciousness of his practical activity, which nonetheless involves understanding the world in so far as it transforms it.[1] His theoretical consciousness can indeed be historically in opposition to his activity. One might almost say that he has two theoretical consciousnesses (or one contradictory consciousness): one which is implicit in his activity and which in reality unites him with all his fellow-workers in the practical transformation of the real world; and one, superficially explicit or verbal, which he has inherited from the past and uncritically absorbed. But this verbal conception is not without consequences. It holds together a specific social group, it influences moral conduct and the direction of will, with varying efficacy but often powerfully enough to produce a situation in which the contradictory state of consciousness does not permit of any action, any decision, or any choice, and produces a condition of moral and political passivity. Critical understanding of self takes place therefore through a struggle of political "hegemonies" and of opposing directions, first in the ethical field and then in that of politics proper, in order to arrive at the working out at a higher level of one's own conception of reality. Consciousness of being part of a particular hegemonic force (that is to say, political consciousness) is the first stage towards a further progressive self-consciousness in which theory and practice will finally be

1. A reference to the 11th of Marx's Theses on Feuerbach, which Gramsci interprets as meaning that philosophy (and, in particular, the philosophy of praxis) is a socio-practical activity, in which thought and action are reciprocally determined.

one. Thus the unity of theory and practice is not just a matter of mechanical fact, but a part of the historical process, whose elementary and primitive phase is to be found in the sense of being "different" and "apart," in an instinctive feeling of independence, and which progresses to the level of real possession of a single and coherent conception of the world. This is why it must be stressed that the political development of the concept of hegemony represents a great philosophical advance as well as a politico-practical one.[2] For it necessarily supposes an intellectual unity and an ethic in conformity with a conception of reality that has gone beyond common sense and has become, if only within narrow limits, a critical conception.

However, in the most recent developments of the philosophy of praxis the exploration and refinement of the concept of the unity of theory and practice is still only at an early stage. There still remain residues of mechanism, since people speak about theory as a "complement" or an "accessory" of practice, or as the handmaid of practice. It would seem right for this question too to be considered historically, as an aspect of the political question of the intellectuals. Critical self-consciousness means, historically and politically, the creation of an elite of intellectuals. A human mass does not "distinguish" itself, does not become independent in its own right without, in the widest sense, organising itself; and there is no organisation without intellectuals, that is, without organisers and leaders, in other words, without the theoretical aspect of the theory–practice nexus being distinguished concretely by the existence of a group of people "specialised" in conceptual and philosophical elaboration of ideas. . . .

One should stress the importance and significance which, in the modern world, political parties have in the elaboration and diffusion of conceptions of the world, because essentially what they do is to work out the ethics and the politics corresponding to these conceptions and act as it were as their historical "laboratory." The parties recruit individuals out of the working mass, and the selection is made on practical and theoretical criteria at the same time. The relation between theory and practice becomes even closer the more the conception is vitally and radically innovatory and opposed to old ways of thinking. For this reason one can say that the parties are the elaborators of new integral and totalitarian intelligentsias and the crucibles where the unification of theory and practice, understood as a real historical process, takes place.

2. The reference here is not only to Marx's argument about "ideas becoming a material force," but also to Lenin and the achievement of proletarian hegemony through the Soviet revolution.

4

Signs and language

Ferdinand Saussure

What is language [*langue*]? It is not to be confused with human speech [*langage*], of which it is only a definite part, though certainly an essential one. It is both a social product of the faculty of speech and a collection of necessary conventions that have been adopted by a social body to permit individuals to exercise that faculty. Taken as a whole, speech is many-sided and heterogeneous; straddling several areas simultaneously – physical, physiological, and psychological – it belongs both to the individual and to society; we cannot put it into any category of human facts, for we cannot discover its unity.

Language, on the contrary, is a self-contained whole and a principle of classification. . . . As soon as we give language first place among the facts of speech, we introduce a natural order into a mass that lends itself to no other classification. For language is not complete in any speaker; it exists perfectly only within a collectivity.

In separating language from speaking we are at the same time separating: (1) what is social from what is individual; and (2) what is essential from what is accessory and more or less accidental.

Language is not a function of the speaker; it is a product that is passively assimilated by the individual. It never requires premeditation, and reflection enters in only for the purpose of classification. . . .

Speaking, on the contrary, is an individual act. It is wilful and intellectual. Within the act, we should distinguish between: (1) the combinations by which the speaker uses the language code for expressing his own thought; and (2) the psychophysical mechanism that allows him to exteriorize those combinations. . . .

We have just seen that language is a social institution; but several features set it apart from other political, legal, etc. institutions. We must

From Saussure, *Course in General Linguistics*. New York: McGraw-Hill, 1964 [1916]. Excerpted from pp. 9–17, 65–76. Reprinted with permission of Philosophical Library.

call in a new type of fact in order to illuminate the special nature of language.

Language is a system of signs that express ideas, and is therefore comparable to a system of writing, the alphabet of deaf-mutes, symbolic rites, polite formulas, military signals, etc. But it is the most important of all these systems.

A science that studies the life of signs within society is conceivable; it would be a part of social psychology and consequently of general psychology; I shall call it semiology (from Greek *semeion,* "sign"). Semiology would show what constitutes signs, what laws govern them. Since the science does not yet exist, no one can say what it would be; but it has a right to existence, a place staked out in advance. Linguistics is only a part of the general science of semiology; the laws discovered by semiology will be applicable to linguistics, and the latter will circumscribe a well-defined area within the mass of anthropological facts. . . .

Nature of the linguistic sign

Sign, signified, signifier

Some people regard language, when reduced to its elements, as a naming-process only – a list of words, each corresponding to the thing that it names. For example:

ARBOR

EQUOS

etc.   etc.

This conception is open to criticism at several points. It assumes that ready-made ideas exist before words; it does not tell us whether a name is vocal or psychological in nature (arbor, for instance, can be considered from either viewpoint); finally, it lets us assume that the linking of a name and a thing is a very simple operation – an assumption that is anything but true. But this rather naive approach can bring us near the truth by showing us that the linguistic unit is a double entity, one formed by the associating of two terms. . . .

The linguistic sign unites, not a thing and a name, but a concept and a sound-image. The latter is not the material sound, a purely physical thing, but the psychological imprint of the sound, the impression that it makes on our senses. The sound-image is sensory, and if I happen to call it "material," it is only in that sense, and by way of opposing it to the other term of the association, the concept, which is generally more abstract.

The psychological character of our sound-images becomes apparent when we observe our own speech. Without moving our lips or tongue, we can talk to ourselves or recite mentally a selection of verse. Because we regard the words of our language as sound-images, we must avoid speaking of the "phonemes" that make up the words. This term, which suggests vocal activity, is applicable to the spoken word only, to the realization of the inner image in discourse. We can avoid that misunderstanding by speaking of the sounds and syllables of a word provided we remember that the names refer to the sound-image.

The linguistic sign is then a two-sided psychological entity that can be represented by the drawing:

Concept
_____

Sound-image

The two elements are intimately united, and each recalls the other. Whether we try to find the meaning of the Latin word arbor or the word that Latin uses to designate the concept "tree," it is clear that only the associations sanctioned by that language appear to us to conform to reality, and we disregard whatever others might be imagined.

Our definition of the linguistic sign poses an important question of terminology. I call the combination of a concept and a sound-image a sign, but in current usage the term generally designates only a sound-image, a word, for example (arbor, etc.). One tends to forget that arbor is called a sign only because it carries the concept "tree," with the result that the idea of the sensory part implies the idea of the whole.

"tree"
_____   _____

arbor   arbor

Ambiguity would disappear if the three notions involved here were designated by three names, each suggesting and opposing the others. I propose to retain the word sign [*signe*] to designate the whole and to replace concept and sound-image respectively by signified [*signifié*] and signifier [*signifiant*]; the last two terms have the advantage of indicating the opposition that separates them from each other and from the whole of which they are parts. As regards sign, if I am satisfied with it, this is simply because I do not know of any word to replace it, the ordinary language suggesting no other.

The linguistic sign, as defined, has two primordial characteristics. In enunciating them I am also positing the basic principles of any study of this type.

Principle I: the arbitrary nature of the sign

The bond between the signifier and the signified is arbitrary. Since I mean by sign the whole that results from the associating of the signifier with the signified, I can simply say: The linguistic sign is arbitrary.

The idea of "sister" is not linked by any inner relationship to the succession of sounds *s-o-r* which serves as its signifier in French; that it could be represented equally by just any other sequence is proved by differences among languages and by the very existence of different languages: The signified "ox" has as its signifier *b-o-f* on one side of the border and *o-k-s* (*Ochs*) on the other.

No one disputes the principle of the arbitrary nature of the sign, but it is often easier to discover a truth than to assign to it its proper place. Principle I dominates all the linguistics of language; its consequences are numberless. It is true that not all of them are equally obvious at first glance; only after many detours does one discover them, and with them the primordial importance of the principle.

One remark in passing: When semiology becomes organized as a science, the question will arise whether or not it properly includes modes of expression based on completely natural signs, such as pantomime. Supposing that the new science welcomes them, its main concern will still be the whole group of systems grounded on the arbitrariness of the sign. In fact, every means of expression used in society is based, in principle, on collective behavior or – what amounts to the same thing – in convention. Polite formulas, for instance, though often imbued with a certain natural expressiveness (as in the case of a Chinese who greets his emperor by bowing down to the ground nine times), are nonetheless fixed by rule; it is this rule and not the intrinsic value of the gestures that obliges one to use them. Signs that are wholly arbitrary realize better than the others the ideal of the semiological process; that is why language, the most complex and universal of all systems of expression, is also the most characteristic; in this sense linguistics can become the master-pattern for all branches of semiology although language is only one particular semiological system.

The word symbol has been used to designate the linguistic sign, or more specifically, what is here called the signifier. Principle I in particular weighs against the use of this term. One characteristic of the symbol is that it is never wholly arbitrary; it is not empty, for there is the rudiment of a natural bond between the signifier and the signified. The symbol of justice, a pair of scales, could not be replaced by just any other symbol, such as a chariot.

The word arbitrary also calls for comment. The term should not imply that the choice of the signifier is left entirely to the speaker (we shall see below that the individual does not have the power to change a sign in any way once it has become established in the linguistic community); I mean that it is unmotivated, i.e. arbitrary in that it actually has no natural connection with the signified. . . .

Principle II: the linear nature of the signifier

The signifier, being auditory, is unfolded solely in time from which it gets the following characteristics: (a) it represents a span, and (b) the span is measurable in a single dimension; it is a line.

· While Principle II is obvious, apparently linguists have always neglected to state it, doubtless because they found it too simple; nevertheless, it is fundamental, and its consequences are incalculable. Its importance equals that of Principle I; the whole mechanism of language depends upon it. In contrast to visual signifiers (nautical signals, etc.) which can offer simultaneous groupings in several dimensions, auditory signifiers have at their command only the dimension of time. Their elements are presented in succession; they form a chain. This feature becomes rapidly apparent when they are represented in writing and the spatial line of graphic marks is substituted for succession in time.

Sometimes the linear nature of the signifier is not obvious. When I accept a syllable, for instance, it seems that I am concentrating more than one significant element on the same point. But this is an illusion; the syllable and its accent constitute only one phonational act. There is no duality within the act but only different oppositions to what precedes and what follows.

Immutability and mutability of the sign

Immutability

The signifier, though to all appearances freely chosen with respect to the idea that it represents, is fixed, not free, with respect to the linguistic community that uses it. The masses have no voice in the matter, and the signifier chosen by language could be replaced by no other. This fact, which seems to embody a contradiction, might be called colloquially "the stacked deck." We say to language: "Choose!" but we add: "It must be this sign and no other." No individual, even if he willed it, could modify in any way at all the choice that has been made; and what is more, the community itself cannot control so much as a single word; it is bound to the existing language.

No longer can language be identified with a contract pure and simple, and it is precisely from this viewpoint that the linguistic sign is a particularly interesting object of study; for language furnishes the best proof that a law accepted by a community is a thing that is tolerated and not a rule to which all freely consent.

Let us first see why we cannot control the linguistic sign and then draw together the important consequences that issue from the phenomenon.

No matter what period we choose or how far back we go, language always appears as a heritage of the preceding period. We might conceive of an act by which, at a given moment, names were assigned to things and a contract was formed between concepts and sound-images; but such an act has never been recorded. The notion that things might have happened like that was prompted by our acute awareness of the arbitrary nature of the sign.

No society, in fact, knows or has ever known language other than as a product inherited from preceding generations, and one to be accepted as such. That is why the question of the origin of speech is not so important as it is generally assumed to be. The question is not even worth asking; the only real object of linguistics is the normal, regular life of an existing idiom. A particular language-state is always the product of historical forces, and these forces explain why the sign is unchangeable, i.e. why it resists any arbitrary substitution.

Nothing is explained by saying that language is something inherited and leaving it at that. Cannot existing and inherited laws be modified from one moment to the next?

To meet that objection, we must put language into its social setting and frame the question just as we would for any other social institution. How are other social institutions transmitted? This more general question includes the question of immutability. We must first determine the greater or lesser amounts of freedom that the other institutions enjoy; in each instance it will be seen that a different proportion exists between fixed tradition and the free action of society. The next step is to discover why in a given category, the forces of the first type carry more weight or less weight than those of the second. Finally, coming back to language, we must ask why the historical factor of transmission dominates it entirely and prohibits any sudden widespread change.

There are many possible answers to the question. For example, one might point to the fact that succeeding generations are not superimposed on one another like the drawers of a piece of furniture, but fuse and interpenetrate, each generation embracing individuals of all ages – with the result that modifications of language are not tied to the succession of generations. One might also recall the sum of the efforts required for learning the mother language and conclude that a general change would be impossible. Again, it might be added that reflection does not enter into the active use of an idiom – speakers are largely unconscious of the laws of language; and if they are unaware of them, how could they modify them? Even if they were aware of these laws, we may be sure that their awareness would seldom lead to criticism, for people are generally satisfied with the language they have received.

The foregoing considerations are important but not topical. The following are more basic and direct, and all the others depend on them.

1. The arbitrary nature of the sign. Above, we had to accept the theoretical possibility of change; further reflection suggests that the arbitrary nature of the sign is really what protects language from any attempt to modify it. Even if people were more conscious of language than they are, they would still not know how to discuss it. The reason is simply that any subject in order to be discussed must have a reasonable basis. It is possible, for instance, to discuss whether the monogamous form of marriage is more reasonable and to advance arguments to support either side. One could also argue about a system of symbols, for the symbol has a rational relationship with the thing signified; but language is a system of arbitrary signs and lacks the necessary basis, the solid ground for discussion. There is no reason for preferring *soeur* to sister, *Ochs* to *boeuf*, etc.

2. The multiplicity of signs necessary to form any language. Another important deterrent to linguistic change is the great number of signs that must go into the making of any language. A system of writing comprising twenty to forty letters can in case of need be replaced by another system. The same would be true of language if it contained a limited number of elements; but linguistic signs are numberless.

3. The over-complexity of the system. A language constitutes a system. In this one respect (as we shall see later) language is not completely arbitrary but is ruled to some extent by logic; it is here also, however, that the inability of the masses to transform it becomes apparent. The system is a complex mechanism that can be grasped only through reflection; the very ones who use it daily are ignorant of it. We can conceive of a change only through the intervention of specialists, grammarians, logicians, etc.; but experience shows us that all such meddlings have failed.

4. Collective inertia toward innovation. Language – and this consideration surpasses all the others – is at every moment everybody's concern; spread throughout society and manipulated by it, language is something used daily by all. Here we are unable to set up any comparison between it and other institutions. The prescriptions of codes, religious rites, nautical signals, etc., involve only a certain number of individuals simultaneously and then only during a limited period of time; in language, on the contrary, everyone participates at all times, and that is why it is constantly being influenced by all. This capital fact suffices to show the impossibility

of revolution. Of all social institutions, language is least amenable to initiative. It blends with the life of society, and the latter, inert by nature, is a prime conservative force.

But to say that language is a product of social forces does not suffice to show clearly that it is unfree; remembering that it is always the heritage of the preceding period, we must add that these social forces are linked with time. Language is checked not only by the weight of the collectivity but also by time. These two are inseparable. At every moment solidarity with the past checks freedom of choice. We say *man* and *dog*. This does not prevent the existence in the total phenomenon of a bond between the two antithetical forces – arbitrary convention by virtue of which choice is free and time which causes choice to be fixed. Because the sign is arbitrary, it follows no law other than that of tradition, and because it is based on tradition, it is arbitrary.

Mutability

Time, which insures the continuity of language, wields another influence apparently contradictory to the first: the more or less rapid change of linguistic signs. In a certain sense, therefore, we can speak of both the immutability and the mutability of the sign.

In the last analysis, the two facts are interdependent: The sign is exposed to alteration because it perpetuates itself. What predominates in all change is the persistence of the old substance; disregard for the past is only relative. That is why the principle of change is based on the principle of continuity.

Change in time takes many forms, on any one of which an important chapter in linguistics might be written. Without entering into detail, let us see what things need to be delineated.

First, let there be no mistake about the meaning that we attach to the word *change*. One might think that it deals especially with phonetic changes undergone by the signifier, or perhaps changes in meaning which affect the signified concept. That view would be inadequate. Regardless of what the forces of change are, whether in isolation or in combination, they always result in a shift in the relationship between the signified and the signifier. . . .

Language is radically powerless to defend itself against the forces which from one moment to the next are shifting the relationship between the signified and the signifier. This is one of the consequences of the arbitrary nature of the sign.

Unlike language, other human institutions – customs, laws, etc. – are all based in varying degrees on the natural relations of things; all have of necessity adapted the means employed to the ends pursued. Even fashion in dress is not entirely arbitrary; we can deviate only slightly from the conditions dictated by the human body. Language is limited by nothing in the choice of means, for apparently nothing would prevent the associating of any idea whatsoever with just any sequence of sounds.

To emphasize the fact that language is a genuine institution, Whitney quite justly insisted upon the arbitrary nature of signs; and by so doing, he placed linguistics on its true axis. But he did not follow through and see that the arbitrariness of language radically separates it from all other institutions. This is apparent from the way in which language evolves. Nothing could be more complex. As it is a product of both the social force and time, no one can change anything in it, and on the other hand, the arbitrariness of its signs theoretically entails the freedom of establishing just any relationship between phonetic substance and ideas. The result is that each of the two elements united in the sign maintains its own life to a degree unknown elsewhere, and that language changes, or rather evolves, under the influence of all the forces which can affect either sounds or meaning. The evolution is inevitable; there is no example of a single language that resists it. After a certain period of time, some obvious shifts can always be recorded.

Mutability is so inescapable that it even holds true for artificial languages. Whoever creates a language controls it only so long as it is not in circulation; from the moment when it fulfills its mission and becomes the property of everyone, control is lost. Take Esperanto as an example; if it succeeds, will it escape the inexorable law? Once launched, it is quite likely that Esperanto will enter upon a fully semiological life; it will be transmitted according to laws which have nothing in common with those of its logical creation, and there will be no turning backwards. A man proposing a fixed language that posterity would have to accept for what it is would be like a hen hatching a duck's egg: The language created by him would be borne along, willy-nilly, by the current that engulfs all languages.

Signs are governed by a principle of general semiology: Continuity in time is coupled to change in time.

APPROACHES TO CULTURE: FUNCTIONALIST

- Robert K. Merton, *The normative structure of science*
- Seymour Martin Lipset, *Values and democracy*

5

The normative structure of science

Robert K. Merton

We are here concerned in a preliminary fashion with the cultural structure of science, that is, with one limited aspect of science as an institution. Thus, we shall consider, not the methods of science, but the mores with which they are hedged about. To be sure, methodological canons are often both technical expedients and moral compulsives, but it is solely the latter which is our concern here. This is an essay in the sociology of science, not an excursion in methodology. Similarly, we shall not deal with the substantive findings of sciences (hypotheses, uniformities, laws), except as these are pertinent to standardized social sentiments toward science. This is not an adventure in polymathy.

The ethos of science

The ethos of science is that affectively toned complex of values and norms which is held to be binding on the man of science. The norms are expressed in the form of prescriptions, proscriptions, preferences, and permissions. They are legitimatized in terms of institutional values. These imperatives, transmitted by precept and example and reinforced by sanctions, are in varying degrees internalized by the scientist, thus fashioning his scientific conscience or, if one prefers the latter-day phrase, his superego. Although the ethos of science has not been codified, it can be inferred from the moral consensus of scientists as expressed in use and wont, in countless writings on the scientific spirit, and in moral indignation directed toward contraventions of the ethos.

An examination of the ethos of modern science is only a limited introduction to a larger problem: the comparative study of the institutional structure of science. Although detailed monographs assembling the needed comparative materials are few and scattered, they provide some

From Merton, "Science and Technology in a Democratic Order." *Journal of Legal and Political Sociology* 1 (1942):115–26.

basis for the provisional assumption that "science is afforded opportunity for development in a democratic order which is integrated with the ethos of science." This is not to say that the pursuit of science is confined to democracies. The most diverse social structures have provided some measure of support to science. We have only to remember that the Accademia del Cimento was sponsored by two Medicis; that Charles II claims historical attention for his grant of a charter to the Royal Society of London and his sponsorship of the Greenwich Observatory; that the Academie des Sciences was founded under the auspices of Louis XIV, on the advice of Colbert; that urged into acquiescence by Leibniz, Frederick I endowed the Berlin Academy, and that the St. Petersburg Academy of Sciences was instituted by Peter the Great (to refute the view that Russians are barbarians). But such historical facts do not imply a random association of science and social structure. There is the further question of the ratio of scientific achievement to scientific potentialities. Science develops in various social structures, to be sure, but which provide an institutional context for the fullest measure of development?

The institutional goal of science is the extension of certified knowledge. The technical methods employed toward this end provide the relevant definition of knowledge: empirically confirmed and logically consistent statements of regularities (which are, in effect, predictions). The institutional imperatives (mores) derive from the goal and the methods. The entire structure of technical and moral norms implements the final objective. The technical norm of empirical evidence, adequate and reliable, is a prerequisite for sustained true prediction; the technical norm of logical consistency, a prerequisite for systematic and valid prediction. The mores of science possess a methodologic rationale but they are binding, not only because they are procedurally efficient, but because they are believed right and good. They are moral as well as technical prescriptions.

Four sets of institutional imperatives – universalism, communism, disinterestedness, organized skepticism – are taken to comprise the ethos of modern science.

Universalism

Universalism finds immediate expression in the canon that truth-claims, whatever their source, are to be subjected to preestablished impersonal criteria: consonant with observation and with previously confirmed knowledge. The acceptance or rejection of claims entering the lists of science is not to depend on the personal or social attributes of their protagonist; his race, nationality, religion, class, and personal qualities are as such irrelevant. Objectivity preludes particularism. The circumstance that scientifically verified formulations refer in that specific sense to objective sequences and correlations militates against all efforts to impose particularistic criteria of validity. The Haber process cannot be invalidated by a Nuremberg decree nor can an Anglophobe repeal the law of gravitation. The chauvinist may expunge the names of alien scientists from historical textbooks but their formulations remain indispensable to science and technology. However *echt-deutsch* or hundred-percent American the final increment, some aliens are accessories before the fact of every new scientific advance. The imperative of universalism is rooted deep in the impersonal character of science.

However, the institution of science is part of a larger social structure with which it is not always integrated. When the larger culture opposes universalism, the ethos of science is subjected to serious strain. Ethnocentrism is not compatible with universalism. Particularly in times of international conflict, when the dominant definition of the situation is such as to emphasize national loyalties, the man of science is subjected to the conflicting imperatives of scientific universalism and of ethnocentric particularism. The structure of the situation in which he finds himself determines the social role that is called into play. The man of science may be converted into a man of war – and act accordingly. Thus, in 1914 the manifesto of ninety-three German scientists and scholars – among them, Baeyer, Brentano, Ehrlich, Haber, Eduard Meyer, Ostwald, Planck, Schmoller, and Wassermann – [unleashed] a polemic in which German, French, and English men arrayed their political selves in the garb of scientists. Dispassionate scientists impugned "enemy" contributions, charging nationalistic bias, logrolling, intellectual dishonesty, incompetence, and lack of creative capacity. Yet this very deviation from the norm of universalism actually presupposed the legitimacy of the norm. For nationalistic bias is opprobrious only if judged in terms of the standard of universalism; within another institutional context, it is redefined as a virtue, patriotism. Thus in the process of condemning their violation, the mores are reaffirmed.

Even under counter-pressure, scientists of all nationalities adhered to the universalistic standard in more direct terms. The international, impersonal, virtually anonymous character of science was reaffirmed. (Pasteur: "*Le savant a une patrie, la science n'en a pas.*") Denial of the norm was conceived as a breach of faith.

Universalism finds further expression in the demand that careers be open to talents. The rationale is provided by the institutional goal. To restrict scientific careers on grounds other than lack of competence is to prejudice the furtherance of knowledge. Free access to scientific pursuits is a functional imperative. Expediency and morality coincide. Hence the anomaly of a Charles II invoking the mores of science to reprove the Royal Society for their would-be exclusion of John Graunt, the political arithmetician, and his instructions that "if they found any more such tradesmen, they should be sure to admit them without further ado."

Here again the ethos of science may not be consistent with that of the large society. Scientists may assimilate caste-standards and close their ranks to those of inferior status, irrespective of capacity or achievement. But this provides an unstable situation. Elaborate ideologies are called forth to obscure the incompatibility of caste-mores and the institutional goal of science. Caste-inferiors must be shown to be inherently incapable of scientific work, or, at the very least, their contributions must be systematically devaluated. "It can be adduced from the history of science that the founders of research in physics, and the great discoverers from Galileo and Newton to the physical pioneers of our own time, were almost exclusively Aryans, predominantly of the Nordic race." The modifying phrase, "almost exclusively," is recognized as an insufficient basis for denying outcastes all claims to scientific achievement. Hence the ideology is rounded out by a conception of "good" and "bad" science: The realistic, pragmatic science of the Aryan is opposed to the dogmatic, formal science of the non-Aryan. Or, grounds for exclusion are sought in the extrascientific capacity of men of science as enemies of the state or church. Thus, the exponents of a culture which abjures universalistic standards in general feel constrained to pay lip service to this value in the realm of science. Universalism is deviously affirmed in theory and suppressed in practice.

However inadequately it may be put into practice, the ethos of democracy includes universalism as a dominant guiding principle. Democratization is tantamount to the progressive elimination of restraints upon the exercise and development of socially valued capacities. Impersonal criteria of accomplishment and not fixation of status characterize the open democratic society. Insofar as such restraints do persist, they are viewed as obstacles in the path of full democratization. Thus, insofar as laissez-faire democracy permits the accumulation of differential advantages for certain segments of the population, differentials that are not bound up with demonstrated differences in capacity, the democratic process leads to increasing regulation by political authority. Under changing conditions, new technical forms of organization must be introduced to preserve and extend equality of opportunity. The political apparatus may be required to put democratic values into practice and to maintain universalistic standards.

Communism

"Communism," in the nontechnical and extended sense of common ownership of goods, is a second integral element of the scientific ethos. The substantive findings of science are a product of social collaboration and are assigned to the community. They constitute a common heritage in which the equity of the individual producer is severely limited. An eponymous law or theory does not enter into the exclusive possession of the discoverer and his heirs, nor do the mores bestow upon them special rights of use and disposition. Property rights in science are whittled down to a bare minimum by the rationale of the scientific ethic. The scientist's claim to "his" intellectual "property" is limited to that of recognition and esteem which, if the institution functions with a modicum of efficiency, is roughly commensurate with the significance of the increments brought to the common fund of knowledge. Eponymy – for example, the Copernican system, Boyle's law – is thus at once a mnemonic and a commemorative device.

Given such institutional emphasis upon recognition and esteem as the sole property right of the scientist in his discoveries, the concern with scientific priority becomes a "normal" response. Those controversies over priority which punctuate the history of modern science are generated by the institutional accent on originality. There issues a competitive cooperation. The products of competition are communized, and esteem accrues to the producer. Nations take up claims to priority, and fresh entries into the commonwealth of science are tagged with the names of nationals: Witness the controversy raging over the rival claims of Newton and Leibniz to the differential calculus. But all this does not challenge the status of scientific knowledge as common property.

The institutional conception of science as part of the public domain is linked with the imperative for communication of findings. Secrecy is the antithesis of this norm; full and open communication its enactment. The pressure for diffusion of results is reinforced by the institutional goal of advancing the boundaries of knowledge and by the incentive of recognition which is, of course, contingent upon publication. A scientist who does not communicate his important discoveries to the scientific fraternity – thus, a Henry Cavendish – becomes the target for ambivalent responses. He is esteemed for his talent and, perhaps, for his modesty. But, institutionally considered, his modesty is seriously misplaced, in view of the moral compulsive for sharing the wealth of science. Layman though he is, Aldous Huxley's comment on Cavendish is illuminating in this connection: "Our admiration of his genius is tempered by a certain disapproval; we feel that such a man is selfish and anti-social." The epithets are particularly instructive for they imply the violation of a definite institutional imperative. Even though it serves no ulterior motive, the suppression of scientific discovery is condemned.

The communal character of science is further reflected in the recognition by scientists of their dependence upon a cultural heritage to which they lay no differential claims. Newton's remark – "If I have seen farther it is by standing on the shoulders of giants" – expresses at once a sense of indebtedness to the common heritage and recognition of the essentially cooperative and selectively cumulative quality of scientific achievement. The humility of scientific genius is not simply culturally appropriate but results from the realization that scientific advance involves the collaboration of past and present generations. It was Carlyle, not Maxwell, who indulged in a mythopoeic conception of history.

The communism of the scientific ethos is incompatible with the definition of technology as "private property" in a capitalistic economy. Current writings on the "frustration of science" reflect this conflict. Patents proclaim exclusive rights of use and, often, nonuse. The suppression of invention denies the rationale of scientific production and diffusion, as may be seen from the court's decision in the case of *U.S. v. American Bell Telephone Co.*: "The inventor is one who has discovered something of value. It is his absolute property. He may withhold the knowledge of it from the public." Responses to this conflict-situation have varied. As a defensive measure, some scientists have come to patent their work to ensure its being made available for public use. Einstein, Millikan, Compton, [and] Langmuir have taken out patents. Scientists have been urged to become promoters of new economic enterprises. Others seek to resolve the conflict by advocating socialism. These proposals – both those which demand economic returns for scientific discoveries and those which demand a change in the social system to let science get on with the job – reflect discrepancies in the conception of intellectual property.

Disinterestedness

Science, as is the case with the professions in general, includes disinterestedness as a basic institutional element. Disinterestedness is not to be equated with altruism nor interested action with egoism. Such equivalences confuse institutional and motivational levels of analysis. A passion for knowledge, idle curiosity, altruistic concern with the benefit to humanity, and a host of other special motives have been attributed to the scientist. The quest for distinctive motives appears to have been misdirected. It is rather a distinctive pattern of institutional control of a wide range of motives which characterizes the behavior of scientists. For once the institution enjoins disinterested activity, it is to the interest of scientists to conform on pain of sanctions and, insofar as the norm has been internalized, on pain of psychological conflict.

The virtual absence of fraud in the annals of science, which appears exceptional when compared with the record of other spheres of activity, has at times been attributed to the personal qualities of scientists. By implication, scientists are recruited from the ranks of those who exhibit an unusual degree of moral integrity. There is, in fact, no satisfactory evidence that such is the case; a more plausible explanation may be found in certain distinctive characteristics of science itself. Involving as it does the verifiability of results, scientific research is under the exacting scrutiny of fellow experts. Otherwise put – and doubtless the observation can be interpreted as lese majesty – the activities of scientists are subject to rigorous policing, to a degree perhaps unparalleled in any other field of activity. The demand for disinterestedness has a firm basis in the public and testable character of science, and this circumstance, it may be supposed, has contributed to the integrity of men of science. There is competition in the realm of science, competition that is intensified by the emphasis on priority as a criterion of achievement, and under competitive conditions there may well be generated incentives for eclipsing rivals by illicit means. But, in general, spurious claims appear to be negligible and ineffective. The translation of the norm of disinterestedness into practice is effectively supported by the ultimate accountability of scientists to their compeers. The dictates of socialized sentiment and of expediency largely coincide, a situation conducive to institutional stability.

In this connection, the field of science differs somewhat from that of other professions. The scientist does not stand vis-à-vis a lay clientele in the same fashion as do the physician and lawyer, for example. The possibility of exploiting the credulity, ignorance, and dependence of the layman is thus considerably reduced. Fraud, chicanery, and irresponsible claims (quackery) are even less likely than among the "service" professions. To the extent that the scientist–layman relation does become paramount, there develop incentives for evading the mores of science. The abuse of expert authority and the creation of pseudo-sciences are called into play when the structure of control exercised by qualified compeers is rendered ineffectual.

It is probable that the reputability of science and its lofty ethical status in the estimate of the layman is in no small measure due to technological achievements. Every new technology bears witness to the integrity of the scientist. Science realizes its claims. However, its authority can be and is appropriated for interested purposes, precisely because the laity is often in no position to distinguish spurious from genuine claims to such authority.

The presumably scientific pronouncements of totalitarian spokesmen on race or economy or history are for the uninstructed laity of the same order as newspaper reports of an expanding universe or wave mechanics. In both instances, they cannot be checked by the man-in-the-street and in both instances, they may run counter to common sense. If anything, the myths will seem more plausible and are certainly more comprehensive to the general public than accredited scientific theories, since they are closer to common-sense experience and to cultural bias. Partly as a result of scientific achievements, therefore, the population at large becomes susceptible to new mysticisms expressed in apparently scientific terms. The borrowed authority of science bestows prestige on the unscientific doctrine.

Organized skepticism

Organized skepticism is variously interrelated with the other elements of the scientific ethos. It is both a methodological and an institutional mandate. The temporary suspension of judgment and the detached scrutiny of beliefs in terms of empirical and logical criteria have periodically involved science in conflict with other institutions. Science which asks questions of fact, including potentialities, concerning every aspect of nature and society may come into conflict with other attitudes toward these same data which have been crystallized and often ritualized by other institutions. The scientific investigator does not preserve the cleavage between the sacred and the profane, between that which requires uncritical respect and that which can be objectively analyzed.

As we have noted, this appears to be the source of revolts against the so-called intrusion of science into other spheres. Such resistance on the part of organized religion has become less significant as compared with that of economic and political groups. The opposition may exist quite apart from the introduction of specific scientific discoveries which appear to invalidate particular dogmas of church, economy, or state. It is rather a diffuse, frequently vague, apprehension that skepticism threatens the current distribution of power. Conflict becomes accentuated whenever science extends its research to new areas toward which there are institutionalized attitudes or whenever other institutions extend their control over science. In modern totalitarian society, anti-rationalism and the centralization of institutional control both serve to limit the scope provided for scientific activity.

6

Values and democracy

Seymour Martin Lipset

To compare national value systems, we must be able to classify them and distinguish among them. Talcott Parsons has provided a useful tool for this purpose in his concept of "pattern variables." These were originally developed by Parsons as an extension of the classic distinction by Ferdinand Tonnies between "community" and "society" – between those systems which emphasized *Gemeinschaft* (primary, small, traditional, integrated) values, and those which stressed *Gesellschaft* (impersonal, secondary, large, socially differentiated) values. The pattern variables to be used in the following analysis are achievement–ascription, universalism–particularism, and specificity–diffuseness. According to the achievement–ascription distinction, a society's value system may emphasize individual ability or performance or it may emphasize ascribed or inherited qualities (such as race or high birth) in judging individuals and placing them in various roles. According to the universalism–particularism distinction, it may emphasize that all people shall be treated according to the same standard (e.g., equality before the law), or that individuals shall be treated differently according to their personal qualities or their particular membership in a class or group. Specificity–diffuseness refers to the difference between treating individuals in terms of the specific positions which they happen to occupy, rather than diffusely as individual members of the collectivity.

The pattern variables provide us with a much more sensitive way of classifying values than the older polar concepts of sociology, such as the folk–urban, mechanical–organic, primary–secondary, or *Gemeinschaft–Gesellschaft*, etc. For instance, they make it possible for us to establish differences in value structures between two nations that are at the same end of the *Gemeinschaft–Gesellschaft* continuum, or are at similar levels of economic development or social complexity. They are also useful for describing differences within a society. Thus the family is inherently ascriptive and particularistic while the market is universalistic and achievement oriented – the weaker the kinship ties in a given society, the greater the nation's emphasis on achievement is likely to be. . . .

The values of France and Germany – our politically unstable cases – resemble those of the United States and Britain in many respects. France, through her Great Revolution of 1789, sought to adopt the same syndrome of values which the United States developed: achievement, equalitarianism, universalism, specificity. The Declaration of the Rights of Man, like the Declaration of Independence, proclaims doctrines subsumed by these concepts. Germany has resembled Britain in that the pressures stemming from economic change and the rise of new social groupings in the nineteenth century did not result in a political revolution which proclaimed a new value ethos. Rather, Germany seemingly sought to modify existing institutions and to create diverse value patterns in different hierarchical subsystems in ways very similar to those which developed in Britain. The French failure stems from the fact that, in contrast to America, the forces of the Revolution were not strong enough to sustain value consensus among the key social groupings; in Germany the new combinations of values, though powerful, were basically incompatible with the requirements for a stable non-authoritarian political system.

French society is difficult to classify in terms of basic values. Its internal political tensions flow in large measure from the fact that major social groupings adhere to largely incompatible values. . . .

These internal cleavages result from the fact that the French Revolution succeeded in eliminating neither the old set of ascriptive–particularistic values nor some of their key institutional supports, particularly the Church. A large part of the French bourgeoisie, whose status and economic objectives sustained the Revolution, never completely rejected the traditional value system.[1] . . .

France has maintained particularistic values in commerce and industry more than any other industrial nation. The economic policies of many French small businessmen emphasize the maintenance of the fam-

1. Tocqueville has argued that fear of social revolution led the bourgeoisie to return to Catholicism. As he put it: "The Revolution of 1792, when striking the upper classes, had cured them of their irreligiousness; it had taught them, if not the truth, at least the social usefulness of belief. . . . The Revolution of 1848 had just done on a small scale for our tradesmen what that of 1792 had done for the nobility. . . . The clergy had facilitated this conversion by [giving] . . . to long established interests, the guarantees of its traditions, its customs and its hierarchy." *The Recollections of Alexis de Tocqueville* (London: The Harvill Press, 1948), p. 120.

ily fortune and status. They refuse to take economic risks or to enter into serious competition with one another. The politics of the petty bourgeoisie has stressed the stability of existing business, even though this has limited the economy's potential for expansion. French employers, particularly in small plants, have expected particularistic loyalties from their employees. All through its history, French industry has attempted to deny representation rights to trade unions, and when forced to grant them has undermined these concessions as soon as possible. To permit the unions rights of representation – and thereby to acknowledge universalistic norms – has been seen as morally offensive. The behavior of the French businessman is, of course, more complicated than this brief analysis suggests, since a capitalist system inevitably dictates a considerable degree of universalism. As Francois Bourricaud has pointed out: "Between the 'bourgeois' money criterion and more aristocratic criteria – antiquity of family and connection – the bourgeois hesitates. This ambiguity explains in part, perhaps, why his relations with the workers have been so difficult."[2]

The French working class, on the other hand, has supported in ideology, if not always in action, the revolutionary values of achievement, equalitarianism, universalism. However, it has been faced with a situation in which individual and collective mobility are morally disapproved of by the more privileged orders – although, of course, as in other industrial societies, considerable individual mobility does occur. French workers' efforts to improve their lot through collective action are bitterly resisted by the bourgeoisie, and the emphasis on local particularism inhibits the unions' efforts to form strong nation-wide organizations. There is perhaps no more impressive evidence of the deep moral hostility of many French employers towards unions than the systematic effort to demolish all union rights during the period of the "phony" war, from September 1939 to May 1940. Seemingly both employers and their political representatives in the government put "teaching the workers and unions a lesson" ahead of national unity and, in the last analysis, national survival.

The effort to sustain traditionalist norms within a growing economy has inhibited the creation of a democratic parliamentary system based on achievement and universalism. Every French republic has sought to institutionalize these values, and has given the lower classes equal rights of access to government. In most other countries such rights and norms have led to the tempering of aggressive ideologies in the lower classes; in France it has led to an intensification of these ideologies.

2. Francois Bourricaud, "France," in Arnold M, Rose, ed., *The Institutions of Advanced Societies* (Minneapolis: University of Minnesota Press, 1958), p. 478.

Thus the most disruptive element in French culture has been the cleavage between preindustrial values, supported by the upper classes and the church, which have continued to affect the economic sector, and the legitimacy of the Revolution, which has formally dominated the political structure. The ascriptive, elitist, and particularistic aspects of French values facilitated the emergence of politics along class lines, while the emphasis on equalitarianism, universalism, and achievement has led the less privileged strata to sharply resent their position. Tocqueville pointed to this problem in an exaggerated form when he suggested: "To conceive of men remaining forever unequal upon a single point, yet equal on all others, is impossible; they must come in the end to be equal upon all."[3]

The retention of preindustrial values within French capitalism did not mean, of course, that all of French industry adhered to them. Within large-scale industry as within government, the corollaries of bureaucratization and rationalization emerged: stable definition of rights and duties, systematic universalistic ordering of authority relationships, publicity of decisions, the appearance of personnel experts or specialists in labor relations as a consequence of the division of labor. And though one generally expects workers to be more radical in large-scale industry than in small, in those sections of France where industry was large and bureaucratic – in general the North – the business classes demonstrated a greater willingness to accept trade unions as a legitimate and permanent part of the industrial system; there, syndicalism and Communism were weakest. Before 1914, the Socialists were strongest in the areas of the country with large industry, while the anarcho-syndicalists had their greatest strength in those parts of the nation where the particularistic values of small business were dominant. These differences were paralleled between the two great wars by the variations in support of the socialists and Communists. The Communists, in general, took over the centers of syndicalist strength, though since World War II they have become the party of the French industrial workers almost everywhere.

The picture of a relatively stagnant France with "stalemate" politics, a reluctance to take advantage of economic opportunities, and a low birth rate, which was accurate enough before World War II, has changed drastically since then. The European economic miracle – great and rapid economic growth and a sharp increase in the consumption of mass-produced items – has affected France as much as any country. The net reproduction birth rate, which stood below 100 (the rate at which a population reproduces itself) all during the inter-war years, has hovered around 125 since 1946. A number of observers of the French scene have argued that "the

3. Alexis de Toqueville, *Democracy in America* (New York: Vintage Books, 1956), Voi. 7, p. 55.

combination of 'new men and new attitudes' inherited from the war period has made French society much less different from the societies of other industrial nations."

> In the civil service, in business, in professional organizations, even in the military forces, new groups of "technocrats" appear – men who specialize in the management of a highly industrialized and bureaucratic society, men who earn high incomes without necessarily owning much capital. . . .
>
> Within the business world, a kind of managerial revolution has led to a new conception of profits, in which management and ownership are less tightly fused and in which the firm's power counts more than the owner's fortune.[4]

The emergence of a "modern" France would seem to be negated by the continued strength of the Communists as a party and union movement (CGT) among the industrial workers, and the highly unstable political system. It may be argued, however, that the current instabilities of the political system now reflect the tensions of rapid change super-imposed on a polity whose political leadership has a traditional bent toward uncompromising rhetoric. The Communists have retained most of the working-class electoral following which they secured in the late 1930s and the 1940s. They have not gained new votes, and they have lost a large proportion of their party and trade-union membership. But if the majority of French workers still vote Communist, various opinion surveys suggest a relatively low level of class alienation among the workers. On the "right," the principal version of anti-democratic extremism – the Poujadist movement – secured almost all of its backing from the declining middle-class strata, often in regions that were being economically impoverished. That is, those who found their relative or absolute economic and social position worsening as a result of changes in French society were attracted to a politics that was "against the system." The tensions over the Algerian War similarly involved efforts to resist inherent "modernizing" tendencies. In a real sense, the Gaullist fifth report is engaged in an effort to bring France's polity and values into line with the changing reality of its class and economic structures. But political and organizational loyalties do not disappear quickly, and consequently the political system, in which conflicts over these values are acted out, seems much more resistant to change than are other institutions.

The way in which historic tensions are maintained may be seen most clearly by examining the sources of the perpetuation of value differences

4. Stanley Hoffman, "Paradoxes of the French Political Community," in Hoffman, ed., *In Search of France* (Cambridge: Harvard University Press), p. 61.

between those white-collar workers who are employed in the bureaucracy of industry and those employed by government. In France, it has
not been possible to speak of the "white-collar worker" as such; rather,
there are the sharply differing backgrounds of the *employé* (private em-
ployee) and the *fonctionnaire* (civil servant). As the French sociologist
Michel Crozier has described the situation in his country:

> We meet two opposite types of participation and integration in
> society; one type which [can] be described as paternalistic and
> which is present among traditional white-collar workers (bank
> employees, insurance employees, and those employed in indus-
> try), and an egalitarian type, present in the world of the lower
> civil servants. . . . The same basic psychological situation has
> produced two role types, and with these two roles, two differ-
> ent concepts of society, two sets of religious attitudes, two ap-
> proaches to politics. These differences have tended to decline
> since the second World War, but there are still two different
> worlds which are determined in one case by channels of social
> mobility through the lay and anti-clerical sector of the society,
> and in the other through paternalistic and even confessional
> methods of entrance.[5]

These two non-manual strata are recruited from different sectors of
French society. Private industry tends to secure its employees from the
graduates of the Catholic schools, often on the basis of personal recommendations, and "many private firms examine carefully the family origins . . . of prospective employees." The civil service is recruited almost
exclusively from state schools whose faculties are overwhelmingly on the
political left. Its recruitment procedures and operation emphasize rigorous selection criteria and formal academic achievement. These differences
in the recruitment and membership deeply affect French trade-union political life, since the Catholic trade-union federation (CFTC) and the
liberal Catholic party (the MRP) have their principal base of support in
the white-collar workers employed in private industry, while the socialist-
influenced union federation, *Force Ouvrier* (FO), and the socialist party
(SFIO) have their strongest supporters among the lower echelons of civil
service workers.

> The political consequences of these differences are known; the
> inability of the parties of the Center, of the Third Force, to
> overcome their differences and to form any permanent unity.
> These differences support, and are in turn nourished by, the

5. Michel Crozier, "Classes san consience ou préfiguration de la société sans
classes," *European Journal of Sociology* 1 (1960):244–5.

opposition of the socialist FO and the Catholic CFTC unions, a conflict based in the last analysis on the essential incompatibility between the religious mentality of the old Federation of White-Collar workers, the base of the CFTC, and the lay mentality of the federations of Civil Servants in the FO.[6]

Thus France remains unstable politically. It may currently be in the final process of cultural "modernization," but historic institutional commitments still prevent the emergence of a fully modern domestic politics, one in which the base internal issues revolve around an interest struggle for the division of national income within a welfare state. Rather, issues concerning the basic legitimacy of various institutions, the role of the religious and secular school, and the structure of authority still divide the nation. Historically, the resistance of the French ascriptive and particularistic "right" to accepting changes in power relations within industry, to legitimating (i.e., morally accepting) unions, was in large measure responsible for the fact that the French workers, though possessors of the suffrage before workers elsewhere in Europe, remain alienated from the polity.[7] Conversely, to the extent that the workers have supported extremist tendencies, anarcho-syndicalism, and Communism, the conservative strata have been enabled to feel morally sustained in their refusal to share power. To break through this vicious cycle of extremism and counterextremism is not an easy task, even though the cleavages in basic values may be ending.

The difficulties of the German polity stem from sources which are, in one sense, the obverse of the French. Where France has encouraged political participation by the lower classes but denied them rights in industry, the German system has given the working class rights and protection within industry while limiting their access to the polity. Until 1918 at least, the German aristocratic classes successfully maintained ascriptive and particularistic values in the noneconomic areas of life, while encouraging achievement and universalism, but not equalitarianism, in the economic order. That is, the old upper classes permitted, and sometimes even encouraged, the working class to improve its economic position through social legislation and trade unions. They were not willing, however, to

6. *Loc. cit.*
7. It should also be noted that this alienation cannot be explained primarily by low wages. "In comparison with European wages, they are not low. Higher than in Italy or Holland, certainly not as high as in Sweden or Switzerland, a little lower than in Great Britain, they have been somewhat better in buying power than in Germany and are still at least equal in that respect." Raymond Aron, *France: Steadfast and Changing*, (Cambridge: Harvard University Press, 1962), p. 49.

accede to achievement criteria in the status and political orders. Individuals were still judged and rejected according to their social origins. This meant that, as is usual in an ascriptively oriented status system, political movements emerged based on distinct status or class lines which were buttressed by the class organizations in industry. However, these political groupings could never gain a secure foothold in the political system.

Concretely, the Prussian aristocracy and the Wilhelmine monarchy, while sympathetic to the objectives of the unions in industry, first attempted to suppress the Socialists as a party between 1878 and 1891, and then refused to accept a democratic electoral system in Prussia, the chief state of the Reich, up to the overthrow of the monarchy in 1918. This refusal to allow the workers' political representatives a share in political power forced the Socialist movement to maintain a revolutionary ideological posture which was at complete variance with its social position and aspirations. The workers' movement did not want to destroy the state, but rather to be admitted to it. In southern Germany, where ascriptive status lines were much less rigid than in Prussia, and where the conservative classes admitted the workers' political movements into the body politic, the Socialist parties quickly developed a moderate, reformist, and pragmatic ideology. In these states, the revisionist doctrines of Eduard Bernstein had their earliest and strongest advocates; in some, the Social Democrats supported cooperation with nonsocialist parties, thereby reducing the emphasis on class warfare. In Weimar Germany, the Social Democratic Party developed into a modern organization, and, until the outbreak of the Great Depression and the rise of Nazism, absorbed most of the old Socialist and Communist electoral strength.

Many conservative groups, particularly those which had been involved in the status system of the old empire – for example, the landed aristocracy, the teachers, the professional officers, and much of the civil service – never accepted the Weimar Republic and its universalistic norms.[8] The middle classes wavered between embracing a political system which incorporated the universalistic values that they had long supported and reacting against the challenge to the privileges and the deferential norms they retained as part of the socially privileged. The support which both the old and new middle classes gave to Nazism in the early 1930s has been linked by many observers to the strong German emphasis on ascription and elitism. Faced with a dire economic threat to their status, the middle classes turned to the Nazis, who promised a national socialism which

8. "From 1920 onwards the history of the Weimar Republic was only a rearguard action against the revitalized social forces on which the German state structure had been built under Bismarck: Army, Junkers, big industrialists, and the higher strata of the Civil Service." J. P. Mayer, *Max Weber and German Politics* (London: Faber and Faber, 1956), p. 64.

would restore prosperity and preserve the values of the *Standestaat* (strong respect for hierarchical rankings).

In discussing the pattern variables, I have assumed that the industrial economic order requires a greater application of universalistic, specific, and achievement criteria than do the political and social orders. Employers must deal with workers in terms of these values, and workers, in turn, are constrained to secure a stable, universalistic definition of their rights in industry. The demand for universalistic treatment in the factory is a prime demand of workers in modern society. The demand for universalistic treatment in the political sphere occurs often as part of the struggle in the economic order. On the other hand, the middle and upper classes tend to be more oriented toward maintaining their privileged position in terms of status rather than in economic terms – that is, toward enforcing the norms inherent in elitism. Hence, a working class which has made gains in the economic order will be relatively satisfied, while a middle and upper class which feels threatened in its position of status will react aggressively. It may be contended that in Weimar Germany the majority of the workers were relatively moderate politically because they had secured access to the economic and political orders, while traditional conservative groupings and the middle classes were disposed to accept militant politics in a crisis because their value orientations of elitism and ascription led them to perceive such gains on the part of the workers as a threat to their overall status position and to their sense of "the way things ought to be." . . .

Major changes in [Germany's] value system, which weaken ascriptive values, appear to have been developing since the end of the last [world] war. Two of the major bulwarks of ascriptive and particularistic values in the society no longer exist or have been weakened: the army and the Prussian aristocracy. The major regions of Germany previously dominated by these values (most of old Prussia) are now in Russia, Poland, or Communist East Germany. What is now West Germany is largely composed of areas which even before World War I were willing to admit the working class into the political club. In addition, the upheavals of Nazism and World War II have upset the old German class structure and have reduced the significance of ascriptive elements.

Yet ascriptive, elitist values are far from dead in West Germany. To some extent, the society still emphasizes social origins as a determinant of status, and men are still reacted to in terms of status position – professors, engineers, industrialists, and others are members of an elite. While workers are part of the body politic and not outside it, they have not secured an end to a diffuse emphasis on class. The continued significance of elitist values has been pointed up in a recent study of the German entrepreneurial class. Heinz Hartmann suggests that this stratum has laid claim to diffuse respect: "[M]anagement does not claim elite status with respect to a specific task, area, or group but rather in relation to the total society." In effect, the German *Unternehmer* (entrepreneurs) have laid explicit claim to the deference and authority once received by now decimated classes:

> Management's drive toward ascendancy quite frequently is justified by reference to the death or incapacitation of previous elite groups. When Winschuh, for instance, addressed a conference of Young *Unternehmer* in 1950, he pointed out that "due to the destruction of old elites, the importance of the *Unternehmer* for the formation of a new elite group has increased." He reminded his audience of the "mass annihilation and expatriation of the Elbian feudatory" and called the attention of his listeners to "the decimation of numerous families of officers and civil service officials." . . . All of this led up to the finding that "society needs more authority in leadership, more determination and speed in administration" than it enjoys at the time and that the *Unternehmer* were willing and able to provide all of this.[9]

The West German system is probably moving toward the British or the Swedish model. There is also much more authoritarianism – or perhaps, more accurately, executive power – in Bonn than there was in Weimar. Chancellor Adenauer has played a role much more comparable to that of Bismarck in the Imperial system than to any of the Weimar chancellors, and elections have been fought to a considerable degree as contests for the Chancellorship. Whether Germany will actually maintain itself as a stable democracy, only time will tell. Particularly crucial will be the resolution of the challenge to the values of the privileged classes when the working-class-based Social Democrats actually move toward national office.

9. Hartmann, *Authority and Organization in German Management* (Princeton: Princeton University Press, 1959), p. 242.

APPROACHES TO CULTURE: SEMIOTIC

- Roland Barthes, *The world of wrestling*
- Marshall Sahlins, *Food as symbolic code*

•

7

The world of wrestling

Roland Barthes

The virtue of all-in wrestling is that it is the spectacle of excess. Here we find a grandiloquence which must have been that of ancient theatres. And in fact wrestling is an open-air spectacle, for what makes the circus or the arena what they are is not the sky (a romantic value suited rather to fashionable occasions), it is the drenching and vertical quality of the flood of light. Even hidden in the most squalid Parisian halls, wrestling partakes of the nature of the great solar spectacles, Greek drama and bull-fights: In both, a light without shadow generates an emotion without reserve.

There are people who think that wrestling is an ignoble sport. Wrestling is not a sport, it is a spectacle, and it is no more ignoble to attend a wrestled performance of Suffering than a performance of the sorrows of Arnolphe or Andromaque.[1] Of course, there exists a false wrestling, in which the participants unnecessarily go to great lengths to make a show of a fair fight; this is of no interest. True wrestling, wrongly called amateur wrestling, is performed in second-rate halls, where the public spontaneously attunes itself to the spectacular nature of the contest, like the audience at a suburban cinema. Then these same people wax indignant because wrestling is a stage-managed sport (which ought, by the way, to mitigate its igominy). The public is completely uninterested in knowing whether the contest is rigged or not, and rightly so; it abandons itself to the primary virtue of the spectacle, which is to abolish all motives and all consequences: What matters is not what it thinks but what it sees.

This public knows very well the distinction between wrestling and boxing; it knows that boxing is a Jansenist sport, based on a demonstration of excellence. One can bet on the outcome of a boxing-match: With

1. In Molière's *L'École des Femmes* and Racine's *Andromaque*.

From Barthes, *Mythologies*. New York: Hill and Wang, 1972, excerpted from pp. 115–25. Reprinted with permission of the Estate of Roland Barthes; Annette Lavers, translator; and Jonathan Cape, Ltd. *Mythologies* was first published in French by Editions du Serial in 1957.

wrestling, it would make no sense. A boxing-match is a story which is constructed before the eyes of the spectator; in wrestling, on the contrary, it is each moment which is intelligible, not the passage of time. The spectator is not interested in the rise and fall of fortunes; he expects the transient image of certain passions. Wrestling therefore demands an immediate reading of the juxtaposed meanings, so that there is no need to connect them. The logical conclusion of the contest does not interest the wrestling-fan, while on the contrary a boxing match always implies a science of the future. In other words, wrestling is a sum of spectacles, of which no single one is a function: Each moment imposes the total knowledge of a passion which rises erect and alone, without ever extending to the crowning moment of a result.

Thus the function of the wrestler is not to win; it is to go exactly through the motions which are expected of him. It is said that judo contains a hidden symbolic aspect; even in the midst of efficiency, its gestures are measured, precise but restricted, drawn accurately but by a stroke without volume. Wrestling, on the contrary, offers excessive gestures, exploited to the limit of their meaning. In judo, a man who is down is hardly down at all – he rolls over, he draws back, he eludes defeat, or, if the latter is obvious, he immediately disappears; in wrestling, a man who is down is exaggeratedly so, and completely fills the eyes of the spectators with the intolerable spectacle of his powerlessness.

This function of grandiloquence is indeed the same as that of ancient theatre, whose principle, language, and props (masks and buskins) concurred in the exaggeratedly visible explanation of a Necessity. The gesture of the vanquished wrestler signifying to the world a defeat which, far from disguising, he emphasizes and holds like a pause in music, corresponds to the mask of antiquity meant to signify the tragic mode of the spectacle. In wrestling, as on the stage in antiquity, one is not ashamed of one's suffering, one knows how to cry, one has a liking for tears.

Each sign in wrestling is therefore endowed with an absolute clarity, since one must always understand everything on the spot. As soon as the adversaries are in the ring, the public is overwhelmed with the obviousness of the roles. As in the theatre, each physical type expresses to excess the part which has been assigned to the contestant. Thauvin, a fifty-year-old with an obese and sagging body, whose type of asexual hideousness always inspires feminine nicknames, displays in his flesh the characters of baseness, for his part is to represent what, in the classical concept of the *salaud,* the "bastard" (the key-concept of any wrestling-match), appears as organically repugnant. The nausea voluntarily provoked by Thauvin shows therefore a very extended use of signs: Not only is ugliness used here in order to signify baseness, but in addition ugliness is wholly gathered into a particularly repulsive quality of matter: the pallid collapse of dead flesh (the public calls Thauvin *la barbaque,* "stinking meat"), so that the passionate condemnation of the crowd no longer stems from its judgment, but instead from the very depth of its humours. It will thereafter let itself be frenetically embroiled in an idea of Thauvin which will conform entirely with this physical origin: His actions will perfectly correspond to the essential viscosity of his personage.

It is therefore in the body of the wrestler that we find the first key to the contest. I know from the start that all of Thauvin's actions, his treacheries, cruelties, and acts of cowardice, will not fail to measure up to the first image of ignobility he gave me; I can trust him to carry out intelligently and to the last detail all the gestures of a kind of amorphous baseness, and thus fill to the brim the image of the most repugnant bastard there is: the bastard-octopus. Wrestlers therefore have a physique as peremptory as those of the characters of the *Commedia dell'Arte,* who display in advance, in their costumes and attitudes, the future contents of their parts: Just as Pantaloon can never be anything but a ridiculous cuckold, Harlequin an astute servant, and the Doctor a stupid pedant, in the same way Thauvin will never be anything but an ignoble traitor, Reinières (a tall blond fellow with a limp body and unkempt hair) the moving image of passivity, Mazaud (short and arrogant like a cock) that of grotesque conceit, and Orsano (an effeminate teddy-boy first seen in a blue-and-pink dressing-gown) that, doubly humorous, of a vindictive *salope,* or bitch (for I do not think that the public of the Elysée-Montmartre, like Littré, believes the word *salope* to be a masculine).

The physique of the wrestlers therefore *constitutes a basic sign,* which like a seed contains the whole fight. But this seed proliferates, for it is at every turn during the fight, in each new situation, that the body of the wrestler casts to the public the magical entertainment of a temperament which finds its natural expression in a gesture. The different strata of meaning throw light on each other, and form the most intelligible of spectacles. Wrestling is like a diacritic writing: Above the fundamental meaning of his body, the wrestler arranges comments which are episodic but always opportune, and constantly help the reading of the fight by means of gestures, attitudes, and mimicry which make the intention utterly obvious. Sometimes the wrestler triumphs with a repulsive sneer while kneeling on the good sportsman; sometimes he gives the crowd a conceited smile which forebodes an early revenge; sometimes, pinned to the ground, he hits the floor ostentatiously to make evident to all the intolerable nature of his situation; and sometimes he erects a complicated set of signs meant to make the public understand that he legitimately personifies the ever-entertaining image of the grumbler, endlessly confabulating about his displeasure.

We are therefore dealing with a real Human Comedy, where the most socially-inspired nuances of passion (conceit, rightfulness, refined cruelty, a sense of "paying one's debts") always felicitously find the clearest sign which can receive them, express them, and triumphantly carry them to the confines of the hall. It is obvious that at such a pitch, it no longer matters whether the passion is genuine or not. What the public wants is the image of passion, not passion itself. There is no more a problem of truth in wrestling than in the theatre. In both, what is expected is the intelligible representation of moral situations which are usually private. This emptying out of inferiority to the benefit of its exterior signs, this exhaustion of the content by the form, is the very principle of triumphant classical art. Wrestling is an immediate pantomime, infinitely more efficient than the dramatic pantomime, for the wrestler's gesture needs no anecdote, no decor, in short no transference in order to appear true.

Each moment in wrestling is therefore like an algebra which instantaneously unveils the relationship between a cause and its represented effect. Wrestling fans certainly experience a kind of intellectual pleasure in seeing the moral mechanism function so perfectly. Some wrestlers, who are great comedians, entertain as much as a Molière character, because they succeed in imposing an immediate reading of their inner nature: Armand Mazaud, a wrestler of an arrogant and ridiculous character (as one says that Harpagon[2] is a character), always delights the audience by the mathematical rigour of his transcriptions, carrying the form of his gestures to the furthest reaches of their meaning, and giving to his manner of fighting the kind of vehemence and precision found in a great scholastic disputation, in which what is at stake is at once the triumph of pride and the formal concern with truth.

What is thus displayed for the public is the great spectacle of Suffering, Defeat, and Justice. Wrestling presents man's suffering with all the amplification of tragic masks. The wrestler who suffers in a hold which is reputedly cruel (an arm-lock, a twisted leg) offers an excessive portrayal of Suffering; like a primitive Pieta, he exhibits for all to see his face, exaggeratedly contorted by an intolerable affliction. It is obvious, of course, that in wrestling reserve would be out of place, since it is opposed to the voluntary ostentation of the spectacle, to this Exhibition of Suffering which is the very aim of the fight. This is why all the actions which produce suffering are particularly spectacular, like the gesture of a conjuror who holds out his cards clearly to the public. Suffering which appeared without intelligible cause would not be understood; a concealed action that was actually cruel would transgress the unwritten rules of wrestling and would have no more sociological efficacy than a mad or parasitic gesture. On the contrary, Suffering appears as inflicted with

2. In Molière's *L'Avare*.

emphasis and conviction, for everyone must not only see that the man suffers, but also and above all understand why he suffers. What wrestlers call a hold, that is, any figure which allows one to immobilize the adversary indefinitely and to have him at one's mercy, has precisely the function of preparing in a conventional, therefore intelligible, fashion the spectacle of Suffering, of methodically establishing the conditions of Suffering. The inertia of the vanquished allows the (temporary) victor to settle in his cruelty and to convey to the public this terrifying slowness of the torturer who is certain about the outcome of his actions; to grind the face of one's powerless adversary or to scrape his spine with one's fist with a deep and regular movement, or at least to produce the superficial appearance of such gestures: Wrestling is the only sport which gives such an externalized image of torture. But here again, only the image is involved in the game, and the spectator does not wish for the actual suffering of the contestant; he only enjoys the perfection of an iconography. It is not true that wrestling is a sadistic spectacle: It is only an intelligible spectacle.

There is another figure, more spectacular still than a hold; it is the forearm smash, this loud slap of the forearm, this embryonic punch with which one clouts the chest of one's adversary, and which is accompanied by a dull noise and the exaggerated sagging of a vanquished body. In the forearm smash, catastrophe is brought to the point of maximum obviousness, so much so that ultimately the gesture appears as no more than a symbol; this is going too far, this is transgressing the moral rules of wrestling, where all signs must be excessively clear, but must not let the intention of clarity be seen. The public then shouts "He's laying it on!", not because it regrets the absence of real suffering, but because it condemns artifice: As in the theatre, one fails to put the part across as much by an excess of sincerity as by an excess of formalism.

We have already seen to what extent wrestlers exploit the resources of a given physical style, developed and put to use in order to unfold before the eyes of the public a total image of Defeat. The flaccidity of tall white bodies which collapse with one blow or crash into the ropes with arms flailing, the inertia of massive wrestlers rebounding pitiably off all the elastic surfaces of the ring, nothing can signify more clearly and more passionately the exemplary abasement of the vanquished. Deprived of all resilience, the wrestler's flesh is no longer anything but an unspeakable heap spread out on the floor, where it solicits relentless reviling and jubilation. There is here a paroxysm of meaning in the style of antiquity, which can only recall the heavily underlined intentions in Roman triumphs. At other times, there is another ancient posture which appears in the coupling of the wrestlers, that of the suppliant who, at the mercy of his opponent, on bended knees, his arms raised above his head, is slowly brought down by the vertical pressure of the victor. In wrestling, unlike judo, Defeat is not a conventional sign, abandoned as soon as it is understood; it is not an income, but quite the contrary, it is a duration, a display, it takes up the ancient myths of public Suffering and Humiliation: the cross and the pillory. It is as if the wrestler is crucified in broad daylight and in the sight of all. I have heard it said of a wrestler stretched on the ground: "He is dead, little Jesus, there, on the cross," and these ironic words revealed the hidden roots of a spectacle which enacts the exact gestures of the most ancient purifications.

But what wrestling is above all meant to portray is a purely moral concept: that of Justice. The idea of "paying" is essential to wrestling, and the crowd's "Give it to him" means above all else "Make him pay." This is therefore, needless to say, an immanent justice. The baser the action of the "bastard," the more delighted the public is by the blow which he justly receives in return. If the villain – who is of course a coward – takes refuge behind the ropes, claiming unfairly to have a right to do so by a brazen mimicry, he is inexorably pursued there and caught, and the crowd is jubilant at seeing the rules broken for the sake of a deserved punishment. Wrestlers know very well how to play up to the capacity for indignation of the public by presenting the very limit of the concept of Justice, this outermost zone of confrontation where it is enough to infringe the rules a little more to open the gates of a world without restraints. For a wrestling-fan, nothing is finer than the revengeful fury of a betrayed fighter who throws himself vehemently not on a successful opponent but on the smarting image of foul play. Naturally, it is the pattern of Justice which matters here, much more than its content: Wrestling is above all a quantitative sequence of compensations (an eye for an eye, a tooth for a tooth). This explains why sudden changes of circumstances have in the eyes of wrestling habitués a sort of moral beauty: They enjoy them as they would enjoy an inspired episode in a novel, and the greater the contrast between the success of a move and the reversal of fortune, the nearer the good luck of a contestant to his downfall, the more satisfying the dramatic mime is felt to be. Justice is therefore the embodiment of a possible transgression; it is from the fact that there is a Law that the spectacle of the passions which infringe it derives its value. . . .

Wrestlers, who are very experienced, know perfectly how to direct the spontaneous episodes of the fight so as to make them conform to the image which the public has of the great legendary themes of its mythology. A wrestler can irritate or disgust; he never disappoints, for he always accomplishes completely, by a progressive solidification of signs, what the public expects of him. In wrestling, nothing exists except in the absolute, there is no symbol, no allusion, everything is presented exhaustively.

Leaving nothing in the shade, each action discards all parasitic meanings and ceremonially offers to the public a pure and full signification, rounded like Nature. This grandiloquence is nothing but the popular and age-old image of the perfect intelligibility of reality. What is portrayed by wrestling is therefore an ideal understanding of things; it is the euphoria of men raised for a while above the constitutive ambiguity of everyday situations and placed before the panoramic view of a univocal Nature, in which signs at last correspond to causes, without obstacle, without evasion, without contradiction.

When the hero or the villain of the drama, the man who was seen a few minutes earlier possessed by moral rage, magnified into a sort of metaphysical sign, leaves the wrestling hall, impassive, anonymous, carrying a small suitcase and arm-in-arm with his wife, no one can doubt that wrestling holds that power of transmutation which is common to the spectacle and to religious worship. In the ring, and even in the depths of their voluntary ignominy, wrestlers remain gods because they are, for a few moments, the key which opens Nature, the pure gesture which separates Good from Evil, and unveils the form of a Justice which is at last intelligible.

8

Food as symbolic code

Marshall Sahlins

Historical materialism is truly a self-awareness of bourgeois society – yet an awareness, it would seem, within the terms of that society. In treating production as a natural-pragmatic process of need satisfaction, it risks an alliance with bourgeois economics in the work of raising the alienation of persons and things to a higher cognitive power. The two would join in concealing the meaningful system in the praxis by the practical explanation of the system. If that concealment is allowed, or smuggled in as premise, everything would happen in a Marxist anthropology as it does in the orthodox economics, as if the analyst were duped by the same commodity fetishism that fascinates the participants in the process. Conceiving the creation and movement of goods solely from their pecuniary quantities (exchange-value), one ignores the cultural code of concrete properties governing "utility" and so remains unable to account for what is in fact produced. . . .

In order to frame an answer, to give a cultural account of production, it is critical to note that the social meaning of an object that makes it useful to a certain category of persons is no more apparent from its physical properties than is the value it may be assigned in exchange. Use-value is not less symbolic or less arbitrary than commodity-value. For "utility" is not a quality of the object but a significance of the objective qualities. The reason Americans deem dogs inedible and cattle "food" is no more perceptible to the senses than is the price of meat. Likewise, what stamps trousers as masculine and skirts as feminine has no necessary connection with their physical properties or the relations arising therefrom. It is by their correlations in a symbolic system that pants are produced for men and skirts for women, rather than by the nature of the object per se or its capacity to satisfy a material need – just as it is by the cultural values of men and women that the former normally undertake this production and

From Sahlins, *Culture and Practical Reason*. Chicago: University of Chicago Press, 1976. Excerpted from pp. 166–79. Reprinted with permission of the author and publisher.

the latter do not. No object, no thing, has being or movement in human society except by the significance men can give it.

Production is a functional moment of a cultural structure. This understood, the rationality of the market and of bourgeois society is put in another light. The famous logic of maximization is only the manifest appearance of another Reason, for the most part unnoticed and of an entirely different kind. We too have our forebears. It is not as if we had no culture: no symbolic code of objects – in relation to which the mechanism of supply-demand-price, ostensibly in command, is in reality the servant.

Consider, for example, just what Americans do produce in satisfying basic "needs" for food. . . .

The aim of these remarks on American uses of common domestic animals will be modest: merely to suggest the presence of a cultural reason in our food habits, some of the meaningful connections in the categorical distinctions of edibility among horses, dogs, pigs, and cattle. Yet the point is not only of consuming interest: The productive relation of American society to its own and the world environment is organized by specific valuation of edibility and inedibility, themselves qualitative and in no way justifiable by biological, ecological, or economic advantage. The functional consequences extend from agricultural "adaptation" to international trade and world political relations. The exploitation of the American environment, the mode of relation to the landscape, depends on the model of a meal that includes a central meat element with the peripheral support of carbohydrates and vegetables – while the centrality of the meat, which is also a notion of its "strength," evokes the masculine pole of a sexual code of food which must go back to the Indo-European identification of cattle or increasable wealth with virility.[1] The indispensability of meat as "strength," and of steak as the epitome of virile meats, remains a basic condition of the American diet (note the training table of athletic teams, in football especially). Hence also a corresponding structure of agricultural production of feed grains, and in turn a specific articulation to world markets – all of which would change overnight if we ate dogs. By comparison with this meaningful calculus of food preferences, supply, demand, and price offer the interest of institutional means of a system that does not include production costs in its own principles of hierarchy. The "opportunity costs" of our economic rationality are a secondary formation, an expression of relationships already given by

1. Cf. Benveniste on Indo-European *pasu vīra;* for example: "It is as an element of mobile wealth that one must take the avestic *vīra* or *pasu vīra.* One designates by that term the ensemble of movable private property, men as well as animals." (*Le Vocabulaire des institutions Indoeuropéenes.* Vol. 1. *Économics, parenté, société.* Paris: Edition de Minuit, 1969, p. 49.)

another kind of thought, figured a posteriori within the constraints of a logic of meaningful order. The tabu on horses and dogs thus renders unthinkable the consumption of a set of animals whose production is practically feasible and which are nutritionally not to be despised. Surely it must be practicable to raise some horses and dogs for food in combination with pigs and cattle. There is even an enormous industry for raising horses as food for dogs. But then, America is the land of the sacred dog.

A traditional Plains Indian or a Hawaiian (not to mention a Hindu) might be staggered to see how we permit dogs to flourish under the strictest interdictions on their consumption. They roam the streets of major American cities at will, taking their masters about on leashes and depositing their excrements at pleasure on curbs and sidewalks. A whole system of sanitation procedures had to be employed to get rid of the mess – which in the native thought, and despite the respect owed the dogs themselves, is considered "pollution." (Nevertheless, a pedestrian excursion on the streets of New York makes the hazards of a midwestern cow pasture seem like an idyllic walk in the country.) Within the houses and apartments, dogs climb upon chairs designed for humans, sleep in people's beds, and sit at table after their own fashion awaiting their share of the family meal – all this in the calm assurance that they themselves will never be sacrificed to necessity or deity, nor eaten even in the case of accidental death. As for horses, Americans have some reason to suspect they are edible. It is rumored that Frenchmen eat them. But the mention of it is usually enough to evoke the totemic sentiment that the French are to Americans as "frogs" are to people.

In a crisis, the contradictions of the system reveal themselves. During the meteoric inflation of food prices in the spring of 1973, American capitalism did not fall apart – quite the contrary; but the cleavages in the food system did surface. Responsible government officials suggested that the people might be well-advised to buy the cheaper cuts of meat such as kidneys, heart, or entrails – after all, they are just as nutritious as hamburger. To Americans, this particular suggestion made Marie Antoinette seem like a model of compassion. The reason for the disgust seems to go to the same logic as greeted certain unsavory attempts to substitute horsemeat for beef during the same period. The following item is reprinted in its entirety from the *Honolulu Advertiser* of 15 April 1973:

PROTEST BY HORSE LOVERS

WESTBROOK, Conn. (UPI) – About 25 persons on horseback and on foot paraded outside Carlson's Mart yesterday to protest the store's selling horsemeat as a cheap substitute for beef.

"I think the slaughter of horses for human consumption in

this country is disgraceful," said protest organizer Richard Gallagher. "We are not at a stage yet in the United States where we are forced to kill horses for meat."

"Horses are to be loved and ridden," Gallagher said. "In other words, horses are shown affection, where cattle that are raised for beef . . . they've never had someone pet them or brush them, or anything like that. To buy someone's horse up and slaughter it, that, I just don't see it."

The market began selling horsemeat – as "equine round," "horsemeat porterhouse," and "horseburger" – on Tuesday, and owner Kenneth Carlson said about 20,000 pounds were sold in the first week.

Most butchers who sell horsemeat have purchased "real old, useless horses" which would otherwise be sold "for dogfood and stuff like that," Gallagher said. But "now they're picking up the young horses. We can't buy these horses now, because the killers are outbidding us."

The principal reason postulated in the American meat system is the relation of the species to human society. "Horses are shown affection, where cattle that are raised for beef . . . they've never had someone pet them or brush them, or anything like that."[2] Let us take up in more detail the domesticated series cattle-pigs-horses-dogs. All of these are in some measure integrated in American society, but clearly in different statuses, which correspond to degrees of edibility. The series is divisible, first, into the two classes of edible (cattle-pigs) and inedible (horses-dogs), but then again, within each class, into higher and less preferable categories of food (beef vs. pork) and more and less rigorous categories of tabu (dogs vs. horses). The entire set appears to be differentiated by participation as subject or object in the company of men. Moreover, the same logic attends the differentiations of the edible animal into "meat" and the internal "organs" or "innards." To adopt the conventional incantations of structuralism, "everything happens as if" the food system is inflected throughout by a principle of metonymy, such that taken as a whole it composes a sustained metaphor on cannibalism.

2. "Supposing an individual accustomed to eating dogs should inquire among us for the reason why we do not eat dogs, we could only reply that it is not customary: and he would be justified in saying that dogs are tabooed among us, just as much as we are justified in speaking of taboos among primitive people. If we were hard pressed for reasons, we should probably base our aversion to eating dogs or horses on the seeming impropriety of eating animals that live with us as our friends." (Franz Boas, *The Mind of Primitive Man.* New York: Free Press, 1965 [1938], p. 207.)

Dogs and horses participate in American society in the capacity of subjects. They have proper personal names, and indeed we are in the habit of conversing with them as we do not talk to pigs and cattle.[3] Dogs and horses are thus deemed inedible, for, as the Red Queen said, "It isn't etiquette to cut anybody you've been introduced to." But as domestic cohabitants, dogs are closer to men than are horses, and their consumption is more unthinkable: They are "one of the family." Traditionally horses stand in a more menial, working relationship to people; if dogs are as kinsmen, horses are as servants and nonkin. Hence the consumption of horses is at least conceivable, if not general, whereas the notion of eating dogs understandably evokes some of the revulsion of the incest tabu.[4] On the other hand, the edible animals such as pigs and cattle generally have the status of objects to human subjects, living their own lives apart, neither the direct complement nor the working instrument of human

3. French and American naming practices appear to differ here. Levi-Strauss's observations on the names the French give animals (*The Savage Mind,* Chicago: University of Chicago Press, 1966, pp. 204 ff) apply only fractionally to American custom. A brief ethnographic inquiry is enough to show that the latter is quite complex in this regard. The general rule, however, is that named/unnamed: inedible/edible. The names of both dogs and horses (excluding racehorses) are sometimes "like stage names, forming a series parallel to the names people bear in ordinary life, or, in other words, metaphorical names" (ibid., p. 205) – e.g. Duke, King, Scott, Trigger. More often, however, the names used in English are descriptive terms, likewise metaphorical, but taken from the chain of discourse: Smokey, Paint, Blue, Snoopy, Spot, etc. The French reserve such names for cattle. Our cattle are generally unnamed, except for milk cows, which often have two-syllable human names (Bessie, Ruby, Patty, Rena – these were collected from informants). Work horses – as distinguished from riding horses – also had human names.

4. Edmund Leach develops this point in his important paper on English animal categories as fitting into a systematic set of correspondences between relations to people and relations to animals according to degrees of distance from self ("Anthropological Aspects of Language: Animal Categories and Verbal Abuse. In Eric H. Eneenberg, ed., *New Directions in the Study of Language* [Cambridge, MA: MIT Press, 1964], pp. 23–63). Leach claims the scheme has wide validity, although not universality: Of course, it would require some permutation for peoples who (for example) eat domestic dogs. The Hawaiians treat dogs destined for eating with great compassion, "and not infrequently, condescend to treat them with Poi [pounded taro] from their moughs" (Robert Dampier, *To the Sandwich Islands on H.M.S. Blonde* [Honolulu: University of Hawaii Press, 1971], p. 50). Dogs destined for eating, however, are never allowed to touch meat" (Peter Corney, *Voyages in the Northern Pacific,* [Honolulu: Thos. G. Thrum, 1896 (1821)], p. 117). It is not clear whether they are eaten by the family who raised them, or like Melanesian pigs, similarly coddled in the household, reserved for prestations to others.

activities. Usually, then, they are anonymous, or if they do have names, as some milk cows do, these are mainly terms of reference in the conversations of men. Yet as barnyard animals and scavengers of human food, pigs are contiguous with human society, more so than cattle. Correspondingly, cut for cut, pork is a less prestigious meat than beef. Beef is the viand of higher social standing and greater social occasion. A roast of pork does not have the solemnity of prime rib of beef, nor does any part of the pig match the standing of steak.

Edibility is inversely related to humanity. The same holds in the preferences and common designations applied to edible portions of the animal. Americans frame a categorical distinction between the "inner" and "outer" parts which represents to them the same principle of relation to humanity, metaphorically extended. The organic nature of the flesh (muscle and fat) is at once disguised and its preferability indicated by the general term "meat," and again by particular conventions such as "roast," "steak," "chops," or "chuck"; whereas the internal organs are frankly known as such (or as "innards"), and more specifically as "heart," "tongue," "kidney," and so on – except as they are euphemistically transformed by the process of preparation into such products as "sweetbreads."[5] The internal and external parts, in other words, are respectively assimilated to and distinguished from parts of the human body – on the same model as we conceive our "innermost selves" as our "true selves" – and the two categories are accordingly ranked as more or less fit for human consumption. The distinction between "inner" and "outer" thus duplicates within the animal the differentiation drawn between edible and tabu species, the whole making up a single logic on two planes with the consistent implication of a prohibition on cannibalism.

It is this symbolic logic which organizes demand. The social value of steak or roast, as compared with tripe or tongue, is what underlies the difference in economic value. From the nutritional point of view, such a notion of "better" and "inferior" cuts would be difficult to defend. Moreover, steak remains the most expensive meat even though its absolute supply is much greater than that of tongue; there is much more steak to the cow than there is tongue. But more, the symbolic scheme of edibility joins with that organizing the relations of production to precipitate, through income distribution and demand, an entire totemic order, uniting in a parallel series of differences the status of persons and what they eat. The poorer people buy the cheaper cuts, cheaper because they are socially

5. The meat taxonomy is of course much more complex than these common appellations. Steak, for instance, has a whole vocabulary of its own, in which some organic reference occurs, although usually not the terms applied to the human body (sirloin, T-bone, etc.) Calves' liver is an exception to this entire discussion, the reasons for which I do not know.

inferior meats. But poverty is in the first place ethnically and racially encoded. Blacks and whites enter differentially into the American labor market, their participation ordered by an invidious distinction of relative "civilization." Black is in American society as the savage among us, objective nature in culture itself. Yet then, by virtue of the ensuing distribution of income the "inferiority" of blacks is realized also as a culinary defilement. "Soul food" may be made a virtue. But only as the negation of a general logic in which cultural degradation is confirmed by dietary preferences akin to cannibalism, even as this metaphorical attribute of the food is confirmed by the status of those who prefer it.

I would not invoke "the so-called totemism" merely in casual analogy to the *pensée sauvage*. True that Lévi-Strauss writes as if totemism had retreated in our society to a few marginal resorts or occasional practices. And fair enough – in the sense that the "totemic operator," articulating differences in the cultural series to differences in natural species, is no longer a main architecture of the cultural system. But one must wonder whether it has not been replaced by species and varieties of manufactured objects, which like totemic categories have the power of making even the demarcation of their individual owners a procedure of social classification. (My colleague Milton Singer suggests that what Freud said of national differentiation might well be generalized to capitalism, that it is narcissism in respect of minor differences.) And yet more fundamental[ly], do not the totemic and product-operators share a common basis in the cultural code of natural features, the significance assigned to contrasts in shape, line, color, and other object properties presented by nature? The "development" that is effected by the *pensée bourgeoise* may consist mainly in the capacity to duplicate and combine such variations at will, and within society itself. But in that event, capitalist production stands as an exponential expansion of the same kind of thought, with exchange and consumption as means of its communication. . . .

The modern totemism is not contradicted by a market rationality. On the contrary, it is promoted precisely to the extent that exchange-value and consumption depend on decisions of "utility." For such decisions turn upon the social significance of concrete contrasts among products. It is by their meaningful differences from other goods that objects are rendered exchangeable; they thus become use-values to certain persons, who are correspondingly differentiated from other subjects. At the same time, as a modular construction of concrete elements combined by human invention, manufactured goods uniquely lend themselves to this type of discourse. Fashioning the product, man does not merely alienate his labor, congealed thus in objective form, but by the physical modifications he effects, he sediments a thought. The object stands as a human concept outside itself, as man speaking to man through the medium of things.

And the systematic variation in objective features is capable of serving, even better than the differences between natural species, as the medium of a vast and dynamic scheme of thought: because in manufactured objects many differences can be varied at once, and by a godlike manipulation – and the greater the technical control, the more precise and diversified this manipulation – and because each difference thus developed by human intervention with a view toward "utility" must have a significance and not just those features, existing within nature for their own reasons, which lend themselves to cultural notice. The bourgeois totemism, in other words, is potentially more elaborate than any "wild" variety, not that it has been liberated from a natural-material basis, but precisely because nature has been domesticated. "Animals produce only themselves," as Marx taught, "while men reproduce the whole of nature."

Yet if it is not mere existence which men produce but a "definite *mode of life* on their part," it follows that this reproduction of the whole of nature constitutes an objectification of the whole of culture. By the systematic arrangement of meaningful differences assigned the concrete, the cultural order is realized also as an order of goods. The goods stand as an object code for the signification and valuation of persons and occasions, functions and situations. Operating on a specific logic of correspondence between material and social contrasts, production is thus the reproduction of the culture in a system of objects.

APPROACHES TO CULTURE: DRAMATURGICAL

- Erving Goffman, *Out-of-frame activity*
- Clifford Geertz, *The Balinese cockfight as play*

9

Out-of-frame activity

Erving Goffman

Given a spate of activity that is framed in a particular way and that provides an official main focus of attention for ratified participants, it seems inevitable that other modes and lines of activity (including communication narrowly defined) will simultaneously occur in the same locale, segregated from what officially dominates, and will be treated, when treated at all, as something apart. In other words, participants pursue a line of activity – a story line – across a range of events that are treated as out of frame, subordinated in this particular way to what has come to be defined as the main action.

Of course, individuals can give the appearance of respectful involvement in their declared concern when, in fact, their central attention is elsewhere. And, indeed, the management of these appearances can itself distract from the obligatory focus of attention, producing a specifically interactional tension. But although all of this is of interest, it is not the main one here. My primary concern is to examine what it is that persons are allowed (or obliged) to treat as their official chief concern, not whether or not they actually do so.

Here adopt an imagery. Say that in every circumstance in which an individual finds himself he will be able to sustain a main story line of activity, and that the range of matters so treatable will vary from one setting to another. From the perspective of the participants one might refer here to a capacity, from the perspective of the situation itself, a channel or "track." And using the same metaphor, one could go on to consider some of the channels of subordinated activity – deeds or events managed in what (at least) appears to be a dissociated way.

A significant feature of any strip of activity is the capacity of its participants to "disattend" competing events – both in fact and in appearance – here using "disattend" to refer to the withdrawal of all attention and awareness. This capacity of participants, this channel in the situation, covers a range of potentially distracting events, some a threat to appropriate involvement because they are immediately present, others a threat in spite of having their prime location elsewhere.

Some sense of this arrangement can be obtained by examining extreme cases of disattention. . . . Of course, the classic example here occurs in response to parade-ground military discipline:

> London – A woman visitor to London let out a shriek yesterday as she stood watching the rock-steady guards outside St. James' Palace.
>
> Blood was flowing from the hand of one of the sentries, where he had cut himself on his bayonet. The sentry stood immobile, eyes straight ahead, and upper lip stiff.
>
> The woman who shrieked and another woman ran forward to bandage the guard's hand with a handkerchief.
>
> But he did not move until a police constable had told the orderly officer. A replacement was marched on, and the wounded guard marched off – head high, lip still stiff.[1]

Incidentally, from this anecdote one can deduce that if the individual is to be quite fully assimilated to a uniform element in an overall design – as in choreography in general – then a mechanism will be required for removing failures, and in such a fashion that the removal process itself can be assimilated to the pattern – as though these scenes occurred in submarines and a special lock were required to allow something inside to get outside without flooding everything. Thus, to remove a dancer who has been forced out of frame by cramps, make an unscheduled momentary dropping of the curtain. . . .

Parade-ground decorum raises a general issue about disattention. The regrettable fact (it is believed) is that whenever individuals are incorporated into an activity in roles of some kind, they will, as performers, as human machines, always be faced with their physiology – exhibited in a desire to shift slightly, scratch, yawn, cough, and engage in other side involvements affording "creature release." There are four general means of coming to terms with these little exigencies. One is to suppress them. In middle-class society suppression occurs in almost all social circumstances in regard to flatus. The second is to treat such releases as do occur as though they had not occurred at all. (These are the two solutions employed in parade-ground manners. They may be linked with a formal device by which a performer, in role, can ask permission to step out of ranks to perform his release, becoming, when he does so, alto-

1. *San Francisco Chronicle*, June 17, 1962.

gether out of frame, this being a version of the mechanism already considered in connection with incapacitated uniformed performers who cannot themselves perform a proper exit ceremony.)[2] The third is for the performer to shield his lapse from the perception of others by twists and contortions of various kinds or by restricting his impropriety to a part of his body that is already shielded from view. The fourth is for him to assume liberties, openly attending to his comfort or openly asking permission to do so or sufferance for having done so, the assumption being that the requirements of his role are not so strict as to disallow momentary withdrawal. In these last cases, the actor attends to his creature concerns and the others present disattend his attendance. (In this way, a speaker at the beginning of a talk may momentarily go out of frame in order to greet silently a familiar member of the audience or exchange a nicety with the chairman, and during the talk pause at an appropriate juncture to take a sip of water, clean his glasses, or arrange his notes. Correspondingly, he will be able to sustain certain out-of-frame side involvements, such as toying with his pen or squaring off the objects on the lectern.)

In contrast to parade-ground practices, where very little by way of diversionary side involvement is allowed, there are formal board games such as checkers in which very little by way of discipline is required of performers and diversionary interruptions are easily dissociated from the play in progress. The performer in his capacity as opponent or protagonist is obliged to be mindful of the state of the game and to manage, with more or less physical aplomb, to get his piece to the intended square at the right time; but outside of that, he as a person will be allowed a wide range of side and subordinate activities. Perhaps, as will be argued, because board games are so well designed to generate involvement they do not need formal help in this regard. More to the point, the entities that board games set into play are not persons but pieces, and so perhaps the individuals who direct a set of them can be allowed all manner of lapses – after all, the pieces themselves don't sniffle or scratch or clean their pipes, being indeed as disciplined as tin soldiers.

These two extremes – parade grounds and board games – are themselves to be contrasted with the staging of a drama. The theater even more than the parade ground obliges the performer to refrain from all momentarily motivated creature releases and other side involvements, but it does this in connection with the fact that in the theater these disruptions have a special syntactical value. On the stage a whole "natu-

2. The basic example is the traditional schoolroom signal of a few generations ago, whereby a child indicated by holding up one or two fingers what he wanted to be excused for.

ral" person is projected, a full identity whatever the special role requirements of a particular scene. As such, the performer will have to enact
appropriate creature releases, for obviously the typical discrepancies between performer and role are ones the actor must put into his part if he is
to perform a seemingly genuine, fully rounded person. But, of course,
these little movements and expressions will be judiciously scripted into
the preformulated flow of interaction on the stage and thus will not
constitute genuine side involvements at all. When an actor literally fails to
contain himself during the performance of his part he can, of course,
attempt to assimilate this disruption to the character he is projecting, as
if, in fact, the discrepancy had been part of the script; and fellow performers may attempt to cooperate in this covering, adjusting their own lines
and actions to contain the event "naturally." But if this remedy fails, then
embarrassment will be very deep, deeper, perhaps, than can occur on the
parade ground or any other place of great formality; for what is embarrassed is an identity, not a role, and beyond this the plane of action in
which the other characters have their being, too.[3]

It is clear that on many occasions, not only certain events but also
certain persons will be disattended. Guards, janitors, and technicians all
routinely function as nonpersons, present in a relevant way but treated as
though not present. (At business, governmental, and academic meetings,
a young female will sometimes be present to fetch coffee and paper, relay
messages from outside the room to persons inside, place calls, and so
forth, while expressing by her entire manner – walk, talk, and seating
posture – that she is claiming as little space as possible and that what she
does is to be disattended.) Of course, there are limits. During the Oakland
[California] antiwar demonstrations of 1967, doctors and ministers, labeled as such, expected to be treated as noncombatants, as outside the
fray, but were apparently put upon by the police. They later formally

3. Similarly, when the audience witnesses an actor forgetting his lines and hears
   the prompter providing them, the whole dramatic illusion can be threatened,
   not merely the flubber's contribution to it. Again the issue is the syntactical
   level at which the error occurs. We may speak metaphorically of an actor in
   literal life forgetting his lines and having to be prompted, but it is hard to think
   of an everyday flub that cuts as deeply into unstaged reality as a missed line
   does in a dramatized event. Something like a man forgetting the first name of
   his wife when introducing her would have to be drawn upon. Of course,
   children who put on a play for a school audience can survive all manner of
   breakdown, as can their audience, but that is because no one expects to
   become much encaptured by the play, attention focusing on the effort of the
   little actors, not their efficacy. For the same reason children make, and are
   suffered in making, many gaffes in offstage interaction. That, in part, is what it
   means to be treated as – to "be" – a child.

complained that their rights – rights of being nonplayers in the events – were not respected.

When one examines transformed interaction, such as that presented onstage, one finds, of course, that matters are, as it were, formalized with a rigorous line drawn around the official realm of activity and its characters and relatively great capacity to disattend events not cast as part of this domain. Something of an extreme can be found in non-Western drama. . . .

> European spectators at Chinese plays always find it surprising and offensive that attendants in ordinary dress come and go on the stage; but to the initiated audience the stagehand's untheatrical dress seems to be enough to make his presence as irrelevant as to us the intrusion of an usher who leads people to a seat in our line of vision.[4]

The audience, of course, is not alone in exhibiting a willingness to disattend. The characters projected by the performers systematically disattend the individuals on the other side of the stage, both as playgoers (in that fidgetting, latecoming, and the like can be disattended) and as onlookers (as when riotous cheers and booing are systematically disattended during a boxing match or baseball game).

The scope of disattention varies in pretty [distinctive] ways. It is said that soldiers in the heat of battle can sustain injuries without feeling pain and never sense that anything is wrong with them until they are back at a base camp. I once was present when a fire broke out in a downtown Las Vegas casino. From the second floor smoke and smell began to pour down, fire sirens were heard, firemen rushed in and ran upstairs with equipment, more smoke came down, eventually the firemen left, and all the while on the first floor the dealers continued to deal and the players continued to play. In the same establishment on another night I saw a cocktail waitress get into a fight with a customer, tear the shirt off his back, and have him ejected – all without anyone's much looking up. On the other hand, those who have worked the fields near a road in rural Scotland know that the slightest distraction – a bird, a dog, a tourist walking by – will be reason enough to stop for a moment and examine what is happening. On the theatrical stage, actors projecting play charac-

4. Susanne K. Langer, *Feeling and Form* (New York: Charles Scribner's Sons, 1953), p. 324. Of course, since Langer wrote these words playwrights and directors in search of new gimmicks have employed precisely these stage practices. Nor can one think of a practice no longer employed that might not come to be employed for the novelty to be derived from it. In general, then, there is reason here for speaking of theatrical practices or conventions, not hard and fast rules.

ters may be prepared to treat as not occurring the disturbance caused by latecomers or persons who shake bracelets, cough, sneeze, crinkle candy wrappings, clap prematurely, churn in their seats, and so forth, but will often be unwilling to tolerate being photographed. So, too, sometimes concert artists:

> But the crowning stupidity occurred during Andres Segovia's recital, when a nut in the audience actually stood up and tried to photograph him – at which The Master stopped playing and called out in a touching misuse of the language: "Impossible, please!"[5]

Further, in [the] theater, as suggested there is a marked tendency to focus on one speaker at a time, but still others onstage can engage in some activity meant to be witnessed simultaneously. In radio drama, on the other hand, no such complexity is allowable, for, as suggested, we appear to have less capacity to single out sounds than to single out sights.

Capacities regarding the management of distraction vary quite considerably across time and place. Today the minor adjustment noises that are just tolerated from theater audiences are apparently relatively slight compared to eighteenth-century practice. For in general, playgoer discipline is much stricter now than in most other periods of the Western stage. . . .

One should also consider whether or not some sounds are themselves harder to disattend than others, apart from absolute volume. Apparently in our culture irregularly timed sounds are more distracting than regular ones. More to the point . . . sounds that produce an ambiguity as to what frame they are to be heard in seem to produce distraction.

It has been suggested that during the occurrence of any activity framed in a particular way one is likely to find another flow of other activity that is systematically disattended and treated as out of frame, something not to be given any concern or attention. Drawing loosely on a particular imagery, it was said that the main track carrying the story line was associated with a disattended track, the two tracks playing simultaneously. Now a second stream of out-of-frame activity must be considered, this one even more consequential, perhaps, for the main activity than the first, yet nonetheless – to a degree – kept out of focus.

In doings involving joint participation, there is to be found a stream of signs which is itself excluded from the content of the activity but which serves as a means of regulating it, bounding, articulating, and qualifying its various components and phases. One might speak here of directional signals and, by metaphorical extension, the track that contains them.

The most obvious illustration of directional cues is, of course, literary

5. Reported by Herb Caen, *San Francisco Chronicle*, March 24, 1968.

punctuation, for it comprises one corpus of conventions, one code, that is learned consciously, often all too consciously. In any case, these marks nicely illustrate the special character of the directional stream – the quality of not being attended focally yet closely organizing what is attended.

An interesting part of the directional stream is what might be called "connectives." In all activity, especially spoken activity, it is crucial to be able to locate who is doing what at the moment it is being done. In face-to-face talk, location is usually established for the hearer by judgments of relative intensity of sound as between his two ears, by his identifying the personal style of the speaker, and by seeing the speaker's lip movements. In telephone contact, on those occasions when unfamiliarity prevents voice identification, social categorization (sex, age, class, and so on) usually occurs, names are often given quickly, and it is assumed that only one person at one end will be speaking, all of which, of course, sharply limits the problem. In novels, connectives again occur, namely, tags such as "he said," "he replied," "he answered," coming after a sentence, or somewhat similar ones coming before. (Interestingly, readers demonstrate a nice capacity to wait for a line to be finished before demanding a connective.) And as an alternative to these standard connectives, there is occasional use of mere spatial arrangement, especially when the sense of what is being said makes it very evident who is speaking.

. . . The point here is that although in written dialogue connectives are everywhere and very stereotyped, they are very little seen, and if seen, not seen as something to judge closely for stereotyping – as would be the text itself. . . .

Observe that what is carried in the disattend track can be blotted out, in fact as well as appearance, but not so directional cues, for these must be kept in mind enough so that they can do their work. And because what they do has a framing effect, structuring (or dramatically restructuring) what came before or comes after, the quietest impropriety here can be heard as very noisy. What might ordinarily be handled with ease as something to disattend becomes precarious when it can be read as part of the directional flow. Thus, at an outdoor political rally a dog barking at random can often be disattended more or less effectively; but if the dog happens to chime in so that his bark can be taken as a comment upon something being said, the chime occurring precisely at a response juncture in the saying, it will be hard indeed to manage the difficulty. Laughter or its suppression can become general. A similar disarray occurs . . . when directional statements are unwittingly incorporated into the story line. . . .

I have suggested that in addition to sustaining a story line in any stream of interaction, the individual is also capable of sustaining subordinate channels of activity. This implies that individuals possess a nice capacity to give no outward sign of attention and little, if any, inward concern to something that is, after all, within cognitive reach – and in the case of regulative cues, must be. The issue, I think, is not that the individual at any one moment will be merely simulating interest in the story line but that he establishes himself in the setting and manages himself so that at any juncture, should the need arise, he smoothly carries on his official involvement in the face of something distracting that has begun to occur, including the need to convey furtive signals through the concealment channel. This capacity to cope with a range of disruptions – anticipated and unanticipated – while giving them the minimal apparent attention is, of course, a basic feature of *interaction competency,* one seen to develop with "experience."

10

The Balinese cockfight as play

Clifford Geertz

Cockfights (*tetadjen; sabungan*) are held in a ring about fifty feet square. Usually they begin toward late afternoon and run three or four hours until sunset. About nine or ten separate matches (*sehet*) comprise a program. Each match is precisely like the others in general pattern: There is no main match, no connection between individual matches, no variation in their format, and each is arranged on a completely ad hoc basis. After a fight has ended and the emotional debris is cleaned away – the bets have been paid, the curses cursed, the carcasses possessed – seven, eight, perhaps even a dozen men slip negligently into the ring with a cock and seek to find there a logical opponent for it. This process, which rarely takes less than ten minutes, and often a good deal longer, is conducted in a very subdued, oblique, even dissembling manner. Those not immediately involved give it at best but disguised, sidelong attention; those who, embarrassedly, are, attempt to pretend somehow that the whole thing is not really happening.

A match made, the other hopefuls retire with the same deliberate indifference, and the selected cocks have their spurs (*tadji*) affixed – razor sharp, pointed steel swords, four or five inches long. This is a delicate job which only a small proportion of men, a half-dozen or so in most villages, know how to do properly. The man who attaches the spurs also provides them, and if the rooster he assists wins, its owner awards him the spur-leg of the victim. The spurs are affixed by winding a long length of string around the foot of the spur and the leg of the cock. For reasons I shall come to presently, it is done somewhat differently from case to case, and is an obsessively deliberate affair. The lore about spurs is extensive – they are sharpened only at eclipses and the dark of the moon, should be kept out of the sight of women, and so forth. And they are handled, both in

From: "Deep Play: Notes on the Balinese Cockfight," in Geertz, *The Interpretation of Cultures*. New York: Basic Books, 19. Excerpted from pp. 417–26, 431–6, 443–8. Reprinted by permission of *Daedalus*, Journal of the American Academy of Arts and Sciences, "Myth, Symbol, and Culture," vol. 101, no. 1, Winter 1972, Boston, MA.

use and out, with the same curious combination of fussiness and sensuality the Balinese direct toward ritual objects generally.

The spurs affixed, the two cocks are placed by their handlers (who may or may not be their owners) facing one another in the center of the ring. A coconut pierced with a small hole is placed in a pail of water, in which it takes about twenty-one seconds to sink, a period known as a *tejeng,* and marked at beginning and end by the beating of a slit gong. During these twenty-one seconds the handlers (*pengangkeb*) are not permitted to touch their roosters. If, as sometimes happens, the animals have not fought during this time, they are picked up, fluffed, pulled, prodded, and otherwise insulted, and put back in the center of the ring, and the process begins again. Sometimes they refuse to fight at all, or one keeps running away, in which case they are imprisoned together under a wicker cage, which usually gets them engaged.

Most of the time, in any case, the cocks fly almost immediately at one another in a wing-beating, head-thrusting, leg-kicking explosion of animal fury so pure, so absolute, and in its own way so beautiful as to be almost abstract, a Platonic concept of hate. Within moments one or the other drives home a solid blow with his spur. The handler whose cock had delivered the blow immediately picks it up so that it will not get a return blow, for if he does not the match is likely to end in a mutually mortal tie as the two birds wildly hack each other to pieces. This is particularly true if, as often happens, the spur sticks in its victim's body, for then the aggressor is at the mercy of his wounded foe.

With the birds again in the hands of their handlers, the coconut is now sunk three times, after which the cock which has landed the blow must be set down to show that he is firm, a fact he demonstrates by wandering idly around the ring for a coconut sink. The coconut is then sunk twice more and the fight must recommence.

During this interval, slightly over two minutes, the handler of the wounded cock has been working frantically over it, like a trainer patching a mauled boxer between rounds, to get it in shape for a last, desperate try for victory. He blows in its mouth, putting the whole chicken head in his own mouth and sucking and blowing, fluffs it, stuffs its wounds with various sorts of medicine, and generally tries anything he can think of to arouse the last ounce of spirit which may be hidden somewhere within it. By the time he is forced to put it back down he is usually drenched in chicken blood, but, as in prize fighting, a good handler is worth his weight in gold. Some of them can virtually make the dead walk, at least long enough for the second and final round.

In the climatic battle (if there is one; sometimes the wounded cock simply expires in the handler's hands or immediately as it is placed down again), the cock who landed the first blow usually proceeds to finish off his weakened opponent. But this is far from an inevitable outcome, for if a cock can walk, he can fight, and if he can fight, he can kill, and what counts is which cock expires first. If the wounded one can get a stab in and stagger on until the other drops, he is the official winner, even if he himself topples over an instant later.

Surrounding all this melodrama – which the crowd packed tight around the ring follows in near silence, moving their bodies in kinesthetic sympathy with the movement of the animals, cheering their champions on with wordless hand motions, shiftings of the shoulders, turnings of the head, falling back en masse as the cock with the murderous spurs careers toward one side of the ring (it is said that spectators sometimes lose eyes and fingers from being too attentive), surging forward again as they glance off toward another – is a vast body of extraordinarily elaborate and precisely detailed rules.

These rules, together with the developed lore of cocks and cockfighting which accompanies them, are written down in palm-leaf manuscripts (*lontar; rontal*) passed on from generation to generation as part of the general legal and cultural tradition of the villages. At a fight, the umpire (*saja komong; djuru kembar*) – the man who manages the coconut – is in charge of their application and his authority is absolute. I have never seen an umpire's judgment questioned on any subject, even by the more despondent losers, nor have I ever heard, even in private, a charge of unfairness directed against one, or, for that matter, complaints about umpires in general. Only exceptionally well trusted, solid, and, given the complexity of the code, knowledgeable citizens perform this job, and in fact men will bring their cocks only to fights presided over by such men. It is also the umpire to whom accusations of cheating, which, though rare in extreme, occasionally, arise, are referred; and it is he who, in the not infrequent cases where the cocks expire virtually together, decides which (if either, for, though the Balinese do not care for such an outcome, there can be ties) went first. Likened to a judge, a king, a priest, and a policeman, he is all of these, and under his assured direction the animal passion of the fight proceeds within the civic certainty of the law. In the dozens of cockfights I saw in Bali, I never once saw an altercation about rules. Indeed, I never saw an open altercation, other than those between cocks, at all. . . .

The Balinese never do anything in a simple way that they can contrive to do in a complicated one, and to this generalization cockfight wagering is no exception.

In the first place, there are two sorts of bets, or *toh*. There is the single axial bet in the center between the principals (*toh ketengah*), and there is the cloud of peripheral ones around the ring between members of the audience (*toh kesasi*). The first is typically large; the second typically small. The first is collective, involving coalition of bettors clustering around the owner; the second is individual, man to man. The first is a matter of deliberate, very quiet, almost furtive arrangement by the coalition members and the umpire huddled like conspirators in the center of the ring; the second is a matter of impulsive shouting, public offers, and public acceptances by the excited throng around its edges. And most curiously, and as we shall see most revealingly, *where the first is always, without exception, even money, the second, equally without exception, is never such.* What is a fair coin in the center is a biased one on the side.

The center bet is the official one, hedged in again with a webwork of rules, and is made between the two cock owners, with the umpire as overseer and public witness. This bet, which, as I say, is always relatively and sometimes very large, is never raised simply by the owner in whose name it is made, but by him together with four or five, sometimes seven or eight, allies – kin, village mates, neighbors, close friends. He may, if he is not especially well-to-do, not even be the major contributor; though, if only to show that he is not involved in any chicanery, he must be a significant one. . . .

The Balinese attempt to create an interesting, if you will, "deep," match by making the center bet as large as possible so that the cocks matched will be as equal and as fine as possible, and the outcome, thus, as unpredictable as possible. They do not always succeed. Nearly half the matches are relatively trivial, relatively uninteresting – in my borrowed terminology, "shallow" – affairs. But that fact no more argues against my interpretation than the fact that most painters, poets, and playwrights are mediocre argues against the view that artistic effort is directed toward profundity and, with a certain frequency, approximates it. The image of artistic technique is indeed exact: The center bet is a means, a device, for creating "interesting," "deep" matches, not the reason, or at least not the main reason, why they are interesting, the source of their fascination, the substance of their depth. The question of why such matches are interesting – indeed, for the Balinese, exquisitely absorbing – takes us out of the realm of formal concerns into more broadly sociological and social-psychological ones, and to a less purely economic idea of what "depth" in gaming amounts to.

In deep ones, where the amounts of money are great, much more is at stake than material gain: namely, esteem, honor, dignity, respect – in a word, though in Bali a profoundly freighted word, status. It is at stake symbolically, for (a few cases of ruined addict gamblers aside) no one's status is actually altered by the outcome of a cockfight; it is only, and that momentarily, affirmed or insulted. But for the Balinese, for whom nothing is more pleasurable than an affront obliquely delivered or more painful than one obliquely received – particularly when mutual acquaintances, undeceived by surfaces, are watching – such appraisive drama is deep indeed.

This, I must stress immediately, is not to say that the money does not matter, or that the Balinese is no more concerned about losing five hundred ringgits than fifteen. Such a conclusion would be absurd. It is because money does, in this hardly unmaterialistic society, matter and matter very much that the more of it one risks, the more of a lot of other things, such as one's pride, one's poise, one's dispassion, one's masculinity, one also risks, again only momentarily but again very publicly as well. In deep cockfights an owner and his collaborators, and, as we shall see, to a lesser but still quite real extent also their backers on the outside, put their money where their status is.

It is in large part *because* the marginal disutility of loss is so great at the higher levels of betting that to engage in such betting is to lay one's public self, allusively and metaphorically, through the medium of one's cock, on the line. And though to a Benthamite this might seem merely to increase the irrationality of the enterprise that much further, to the Balinese what it mainly increases is the meaningfulness of it all. And as (to follow Weber rather than Bentham) the imposition of meaning on life is the major end and primary condition of human existence, that access of significance more than compensates for the economic costs involved. . . .

This graduated correlation of "status gambling" with deeper fights and, inversely, "money gambling" with shallower ones is in fact quite general. Bettors themselves form a sociomoral hierarchy in these terms. As noted earlier, at most cockfights there are, around the very edges of the cockfight area, a large number of mindless, sheer-chance-type gambling games (roulette, dice throw, coin-spin, pea-under-the-shell) operated by concessionaires. Only women, children, adolescents, and various other sorts of people who do not (or not yet) fight cocks – the extremely poor, the socially despised, the personally idiosyncratic – play at these games, at, of course, penny ante levels. Cockfighting men would be ashamed to go anywhere near them. Slightly above these people in standing are those who, though they do not themselves fight cocks, bet on the smaller matches around the edges. Next, there are those who fight cocks in small, or occasionally medium matches, but have not the status to join in the large ones, though they may bet from time to time on the side in those. And finally, there are those, the really substantial members of the community, the solid citizenry around whom local life revolves, who fight in the larger fights and bet on them around the side. The focusing element in these focused gatherings,[1] these men generally dominate and define the

---

1. See Erving Goffman, *Encounters: Two Studies in the Sociology of Interaction.* Indianapolis: Bobbs-Merrill, pp. 9–10.

sport as they dominate and define the society. When a Balinese male talks, in that almost venerative way, about "the true cockfighter," the *bebatoh* ("bettor") or *djuru kurung* ("cage keeper"), it is this sort of person, not those who bring the mentality of the pea-and-shell game into the quite different, inappropriate context of the cockfight, the driven gambler reprobate, and the wistful hanger-on, that they mean. For such a man, what is really going on in a match is something rather closer to *potet,* a word which has the secondary meaning of thief or an *affaire d'honneur* (though, with the Balinese talent for practical fantasy, the blood that is spilled is only figuratively human), than to the stupid, mechanical crank of a slot machine.

What makes Balinese cockfighting deep is thus not money in itself, but what, the more of it that is involved the more so, money causes to happen: the migration of the Balinese status hierarchy into the body of the cockfight. Psychologically an Aesopian representation of the ideal/demonic, rather narcissistic, male self, sociologically it is an equally Aesopian representation of the complex fields of tension set up by the controlled, muted, ceremonial, but for all that deeply felt, interaction of those selves in the context of everyday life. The cocks may be surrogates for their owners' personalities, animal mirrors of psychic form, but the cockfight is – or more exactly, deliberately is made to be – a stimulation of the social matrix, the involved system of cross-cutting, overlapping, highly corporate groups – villages, kingroups, irrigation societies, temple congregations, "castes" – in which its devotees live. And as prestige, the necessity to affirm it, defend it, celebrate it, justify it, and just plain bask in it (but not, given the strongly ascriptive character of Balinese stratification, to seek it), is perhaps the central driving force in the society, so also – ambulant penises, blood sacrifices, and monetary exchanges aside – is it of the cockfight. This apparent amusement and seeming sport is, to take another phrase from Erving Goffman, "a status bloodbath".[2] . . .

"Poetry makes nothing happen," Auden says in his elegy of Yeats; "it survives in the valley of its saying . . . a way of happening, a mouth." The cockfight too, in this colloquial sense, makes nothing happen. Men go on allegorically humiliating one another and being allegorically humiliated by one another, day after day, glorying quietly in the experience if they have triumphed, crushed only slightly more openly by it if they have not. *But no one's status really changes.* You cannot ascend the status ladder by winning cockfights; you cannot, as an individual, really ascend it at all. Nor can you descend it that way. All you can do is enjoy and savor, or suffer and withstand, the concocted sensation of drastic and momentary movement

2. Goffman, *Encounters,* p. 78.

along an aesthetic semblance of that ladder, a kind of behind-the-mirror status jump which has the look of mobility without its actuality.

Like any art form – for that, finally, is that we are dealing with – the cockfight renders ordinary, everyday experience comprehensible by presenting it in terms of acts and objects which have had their practical consequences removed and been reduced (or, if you prefer, raised) to the level of sheer appearances, where their meaning can be more powerfully articulated and more exactly perceived. The cockfight is "really real" only to the cocks – it does not kill anyone, castrate anyone, reduce anyone to animal status, alter the hierarchical relations among people, or refashion the hierarchy; it does not ever redistribute income in any significant way. What it does is what, for other peoples with other temperaments and other conventions, *Lear* and *Crime and Punishment* do; it catches up these themes – death, masculinity, rage, pride, loss, beneficence, change – and, ordering them into an encompassing structure, presents them in such a way as to throw into relief a particular view of their essential nature. It puts a construction on them, makes them, to those historically positioned to appreciate the construction, meaningful -- visible, tangible, graspable – "real," in an ideational sense. An image, fiction, a model, a metaphor, the cockfight is a means of expression; its function is neither to assuage social passions nor to heighten them (though, in its playing-with-fire way it does a bit of both), but, in a medium of feathers, blood, crowds, and money, to display them.

The question of how it is that we perceive qualities in things – paintings, books, melodies, plays – that we do not feel we can assert literally to be there has come, in recent years, into the very center of aesthetic theory. Neither the sentiments of the artist, which remain his, nor those of the audience, which remain theirs, can account for the agitation of one painting or the serenity of another. We attribute grandeur, wit, despair, exuberance to strings of sounds; lightness, energy, violence, fluidity to blocks of stone. Novels are said to have strength, buildings eloquence, plays momentum, ballets repose. In this realm of eccentric predicates, to say that the cockfight, in its perfected cases at least, is "disquietful" does not seem at all unnatural, merely, as I have just denied it practical consequence, somewhat puzzling.

The disquietfulness arises, "somehow," out of a conjunction of three attributes of the fight: its immediate dramatic shape, its metaphoric content, and its social context. A cultural figure against a social ground, the fight is at once a convulsive surge of animal hatred, a mock war of symbolical selves, and a formal simulation of status tensions, and its aesthetic power derives from its capacity to force together these diverse realities. The reason it is disquietful is not that it has material effects (it has some, but they are minor); the reason that it is disquietful is that, joining pride to selfhood, selfhood to cocks, and cocks to destruction, it brings to imaginative realization a dimension of Balinese experience normally well obscured from view. The transfer of a sense of gravity into what is itself a rather blank and unvarious spectacle, a commotion of beating wings and throbbing legs, is effected by interpreting it as expressive of something unsettling in the way its authors and audience live, or, even more ominously, what they are.

As a dramatic shape, the fight displays a characteristic that does not seem so remarkable until one realizes that it does not have to be there: a radically atomistical structure. Each match is a world unto itself, a particulate burst of form. There is the matchmaking, there is the betting, there is the fight, there is the result – utter triumph and utter defeat – and there is the hurried, embarrassed passing of money. The loser is not consoled. People drift away from him, look around him, leave him to assimilate his momentary descent into nonbeing, reset his face, and return, scarless and intact, to the fray. Nor are winners congratulated or events rehashed; once a match is ended the crowd's attention turns totally to the next, with no looking back. A shadow of the experience no doubt remains with the principals, perhaps even with some of the witnesses of a deep fight, as it remains with us when we leave the theater after seeing a powerful play well performed; but it quite soon fades to become at most a schematic memory – a diffuse glow or an abstract shudder – and usually not even that. Any expressive form lives only in its own present – the one it itself creates. But, here, that present is served into a string of flashes, some more bright than others, but all of them disconnected, aesthetic quanta. Whatever the cockfight says, it says in spurts. . . .

If one dimension of the cockfight's structure, its lack of temporal directionality, makes it seem a typical segment of the general social life, however, the other, its flat-out, head-to-head (or spur-to-spur) aggressiveness, makes it seem a contradiction, a reversal, even a subversion of it. In the normal course of things, the Balinese are shy to the point of obsessiveness of open conflict. Oblique, cautious, subdued, controlled, masters of indirection and dissimulation – what they call *alus,* "polished," "smooth" – they rarely face what they can turn away from, rarely resist what they can evade. But here they portray themselves as wild and murderous, with manic explosions of instinctual cruelty. A powerful rendering of life as the Balinese most deeply do not want it (to adapt a phrase Frye has used of Gloucester's blinding) is set in the context of a sample of it as they do in fact have it. And, because the context suggests that the rendering, if less than a straightforward description, is nonetheless more than an idle fancy, it is here that the disquietfulness – the disquietfulness of the fight, not (or, anyway, not necessarily) its patrons, who seem in fact rather thoroughly to enjoy it – emerges. The slaughter in the cock ring is not a depiction of how things literally are among men, but, what is almost worse, of how, from a particular angle, they imaginatively are.

The angle, of course, is stratificatory. What, as we have already seen, the cockfight talks most forcibly about is status relationships, and what it says about them is that they are matters of life and death. That prestige is a profoundly serious business is apparent everywhere one looks in Bali – in the village, the family, the economy, the state. A peculiar fusion of Polynesian title ranks and Hindu castes, the hierarchy of pride is the moral backbone of the society. But only in the cockfight are the sentiments upon which that hierarchy rests revealed in their natural colors. Enveloped elsewhere in a haze of etiquette, a thick cloud of euphemism and ceremony, gesture and allusion, they are here expressed in only the thinnest disguise of an animal mask, a mask which in fact demonstrates them far more effectively than it conceals them. Jealousy is as much a part of Bali as poise, envy as grace, brutality as charm; but without the cockfight the Balinese would have a much less certain understanding of them, which is, presumably, why they value it so highly.

Any expressive form works (when it works) by disarranging semantic contexts in such a way that properties conventionally ascribed to certain things are unconventionally ascribed to others, which are then seen actually to possess them. To call the wind a cripple, as Stevens does, to fix tone and manipulate timbre, as Schoenberg does, or, closer to our case, to picture an art critic as a dissolute bear, as Hogarth does, is to cross conceptual wires; the established conjunctions between objects and their qualities are altered, and phenomena – fall weather, melodic shape, or cultural journalism – are clothed in signifiers which normally point to other referents. Similarly, to connect – and connect, and connect – the collision of roosters with the divisiveness of status is to invite a transfer of perceptions from the former to the latter, a transfer which is at once a description and a judgment. (Logically, the transfer could, of course, as well go the other way; but, like most of the rest of us, the Balinese are a great deal more interested in understanding men than they are in understanding cocks.)

What sets the cockfight apart from the ordinary course of life, lifts it from the realm of everyday practical affairs, and surrounds it with an aura of enlarged importance is not, as functionalist sociology would have it, that it reinforces status discriminations (such reinforcement is hardly necessary in a society where every act proclaims them), but that it provides a metasocial commentary upon the whole matter of assorting human beings into fixed hierarchical ranks and then organizing the major part of collective existence around that assortment. Its function, if you want to call it that, is interpretive: It is a Balinese reading of Balinese experience, a story they tell themselves about themselves. . . .

APPROACHES TO CULTURE: WEBERIAN

- Michael Walzer, *Puritanism and revolutionary ideology*
- Jesse R. Pitts, *French Catholicism and secular grace*

11

Puritanism and revolutionary ideology

Michael Walzer

A politics of conflict and competition for power, of faction, intrigue, and open war is probably universal in human history. Not so a politics of party organization and methodical activity, opposition and reform, radical ideology and revolution. The history of reform and revolution is relatively short compared, for example, with that of the political order itself or of the power struggle. The detached appraisal of a going system, the programmatic expression of discontent and aspiration, the organization of zealous men for sustained political activity: It is surely fair to say that these three together are aspects only of the modern, that is, the postmedieval political world. . . .

The idea that specially designated and organized bands of men might play a creative part in the political world, destroying the established order and reconstructing society according to the Word of God or the plans of their fellows – this idea did not enter at all into the thought of Machiavelli, Luther, or Bodin. In establishing the state, these three writers relied exclusively upon the prince, whether they imagined him as an adventurer, a Christian magistrate, or a hereditary bureaucrat. All other men remained subjects, condemned to political passivity. . . .

It was the Calvinists who first switched the emphasis of political thought from the prince to the saint (or the band of saints) and then constructed a theoretical justification for independent political action. What Calvinists said of the saint, other men would later say of the citizen: The same sense of civic virtue, of discipline and duty, lies behind the two names. Saint and citizen together suggest a new integration of private men (or rather, of *chosen* groups of private men, of proven holiness and virtue) into the political order, an integration based upon a novel view of

From Walzer, *The Revolution of the Saints: A Study in the Origins of Radical Politics*. Cambridge, Mass.: Harvard University Press, 1965. Excerpted by permission of the publisher from pp. 1–2, 27–9, 57–9, 63, 66, 92–4, 97–101, 103–4, 107–13 of *The Revolution of the Saints: A Study in the Origins of Radical Politics,* by Michael Walzer, Cambridge, Mass.: Harvard University Press, © 1965 by Michael Walzer.

politics as a kind of conscientious and continuous labor. This is surely the most significant outcome of the Calvinist theory of worldly activity, preceding in time any infusion of religious worldliness into the economic order. The diligent activism of the saints – Genevan, Huguenot, Dutch, Scottish, and Puritan – marked the transformation of politics into work and revealed for the first time the extraordinary conscience that directed the work. . . .

The permanent, inescapable estrangement of man from God is the starting point of Calvin's politics. Unlike Luther once again, he did not believe reconciliation to be possible and sought rather to cope with the secondary effects of Adam's Fall. He explored the social implications of human alienation and searched for a social remedy. Fearfulness and anxiety, distrust and war, he thought, were the key experiences of fallen men (they were the key experiences more particularly of sixteenth-century Europeans), cut off not only from God, but also from all stable and meaningful association with their fellows. Calvin used the old doctrine of the Fall to explain to his contemporaries the world around them. And because he firmly believed that the terrors of contemporary life could be politically controlled, he became an activist and an ecclesiastical politician. . . .

Calvin demanded of his fellows wholehearted participation in this activity. They presumably shared the anxiety and alienation; they must join in the work of reconstruction. It was this demand which established ideology as a new factor in the historical process. Although initially made only upon the king, it was subject to gradual extension until finally every man (or at least every saint) was called upon to do his share for the holy cause. This "devolution" (as Richard Hooker called it) was possible because Calvin was not searching, in the manner of medieval writers, for a moral king, but rather for a man, *any man,* ready to be God's instrument. . . .

That God rather than man must always be obeyed is probably the most significant platitude in the history of political thought. Like most platitudes it offers neither clear-cut definitions nor a program for action. Obedience to God may involve submissions to any number of well-established earthly authorities which claim to speak in God's name; it may also describe the spontaneous heroism of a conscientious individual who challenges the powers that be. It is certain only that the precept rests upon an appeal to conscience and that conscience, unless bound by an authoritative church, has no rules. . . .

The first Protestants relived in spirit the enthusiasm of the first Christmas. Obedience to God involved for them only passive resistance and a quick martyrdom or flight from their homeland and a weary exile. Both of these were individual responses to persecution. . . .

This was not the conclusion that Calvinists drew from the theory of God's sovereign power. For the view of political reality as the embodiment of divine will had this fundamental ambiguity: The divine will must be active also in any group of men actually in revolt, manifest in revolutionary organizations as much as in the institutions of government. And did not the Calvinist saints know themselves to be instruments of that will? God had put his mark upon them and that mark was conscience, a piece of divine willfullness implanted in man. Conscience would be the saint's warrant to free himself from political passivity and success would be the divine sign justifying whatever he did. . . .

Calvin's recourse to an avenging Providence was, of course, less a program for action than a rhetorical warning to tyrants, but the idea had a peculiar suggestiveness about it. God sometimes raised up "providential liberators," "public avengers," Calvin wrote; "let princes hear and fear." Such men, whenever they made their appearance, had a "legitimate commission" from the Lord; "being armed with authority from heaven, they punish an inferior power by a superior one. . . ."[1] It was hard to see how their legitimacy could be known, however, except by their success; Calvin had merely readmitted the tyrannicide under the cover of divinity. In so doing he revealed that the legality of resistance was at least in part a *post facto* ascription.

More interesting still was his discussion of the powers of religious office, that is, of the minister and the prophet. Both were presumably excluded from any political activity. But the Calvinist effort to enforce the moral law with secular and religious power altered the nature of their exclusion. Religious office involved the duty of moral censure – and it was surely not difficult to see that the denunciation of kings by prophets and ministers was a political matter.[2]

> Why are prophets and teachers sent? That they may reduce the
> world to order: they are not to spare their hearers, but freely
> to reprove them whenever there may be *need;* they are also to
> use threatenings when they find men perverse . . . prophets and
> teachers may take courage and thus boldly set themselves
> against kings and nations, when armed with the power of celestial truth.

Rulers must be obeyed, but certain of the saints have a special office to rebuke their evil doings. . . .

Men driven by the pressures of rapid social change or political defeat and persecution may adopt a new ideology with astonishing recklessness, cutting themselves off from a long intellectual tradition. In this manner

1. *Institutes,* IV, xx, 30–1.
2. Calvin, *Jeremiah,* lecture 2; I, 44.

the Marian exiles expounded Calvin's ideas with a logic and boldness that greatly disturbed the master himself. . . .

In the years after Catholic Queen Mary came to the throne, some 800 English Protestants went into exile on the continent. About 100 of these were men not very different from the exiles of previous ages, noblemen and their followers who fled upon the victory of one or another feudal faction. Mostly younger sons of gentry families, these most recent exiles traveled little farther than the coast of France; there they stayed to intrigue, spy upon one another, and play the pirate. They had been supporters of Northumberland, adherents of the unfortunate Queen Jane, Kentish companions of the rebel Wyatt. Their Protestantism was a function of their politics, and their politics of their familial and local interests. Intrigue at home and exile abroad led them to no generalized political viewpoint. . . .

The majority by far of the exiles were different men, separated by a great gulf from the times and manners of the banished feudal lord. They did not stop in France, a country receptive to English conspirators but not to English Protestants, but moved on instead to the reformed cities of south Germany and Switzerland. There they established self-governing religious communities, replacing the spying and intrigue of the adventurers with political and theological controversy. Perhaps half of these exiles were clergymen. . . .

In England the ministers had been nothing more than church officers, obedient to their bishop, to the convocation, and to the Supreme Head. Politically they were private persons, holding no office at all. . . .

But the men of Geneva, unlike the other exiles with their "English face" and law, could no longer pretend even to official status in a church – except that tiny religious commonwealth which was entirely their own creation. They had no legal or public calling to address Englishmen at all. Facing England from exile, then, they sought a new office and found it not in men's constitutions but in divine prophecy. They thus seized upon an aspect of Calvinist thought that never interested the Huguenots. In the person of the Old Testament prophet, the men of Geneva found their new public character. "I, a man sent of God" – thus did John Knox designate himself – "to call . . . this people . . . again to the true service of God."[3] They described prophecy as a Calvinist *office*, in which individual inadequacy and corruption were overcome by the discipline of duty and divinely ordained status. God's ministers, Knox wrote, "as they be the sons of men, of nature are they liars, unstable and vain; but His eternal World which He putteth in their

3. Knox, *The Appellation from the Sentence Pronounced by the Bishops and Clergy* (1558) in *Works*, IV, 474.

mouths and whereof they are made ambassadors is of . . . truth, stability and assurance."[4] . . .

In the world of religious office, conscience played a part very similar to its political role: It freed men from old loyalties, enforced a new sense of duty, and required obedience to a willful God. The prophet, Knox assured his readers – though they might well have had their doubts – does not relish the doom he foretells. . . .

In the polemic and prophecy of the exiles in Geneva, there appeared a steadily growing emphasis on the utter and total corruption of this world, of "men's wisdom," of tradition and law, of the opinion of the multitude. Every earthly authority was undermined, every merely human or rational justification of authority was called into doubt. Knox and the other prophets described what was almost a Manichean universe in which an earth corrupt "in all its estates" was ruled by a stalwart Satan: ". . . albeit it is contrary to our fantasy, yet we must believe it, for the devil is called prince and god of this world, because he reigneth and is honored by idolatry in it."[5]

Himself in "league with God," he defended a narrowly conceived divine truth against the sinfulness and ignorance of mankind and its governors. In more traditional thought, it was these governors who were called "gods of this world" – a title Knox gave to the devil. The magistrates were only fallen men; neither their reason nor their human nature would be any basis for a godly politics. "The true knowledge of God," wrote Knox, "is not born with man, neither yet cometh it unto him by natural power." Reason, education, study: All these brought men far short of that true knowledge which the prophet had in "the grace of his election."[6] True knowledge was thus identified with religious illumination (or, since the prophets were not mystics, with religious dedication) and the identity was also a restriction. Knox recognized the "daily delectations" that classical literature might bring; he condemned it nevertheless – indeed, all the more enthusiastically – because he saw no value except in the "perpetual repetition" of God's word.[7] In the writings of Knox, Goodman, and Whittingham, the wealth of classical reference so

4. Knox, *The Copy of an Epistle* (1559) in *Works*, V, 486. See also Edwin Muir, *John Knox: Portrait of a Calvinist* (London, 1939). This is the most interesting of the modern biographies of Knox; it attempts, not always successfully, a psychological examination of the tensions between man and "instrument."
5. Knox, *Faithful Admonition, Works*, III, 285. For Knox's theological difficulties with the problem of the effective power of Satan, see his tract on predestination, *An Answer to a Great Number of Blasphemous Cavillations, Works*, V, 35–6.
6. Knox, *Godly Letter, Works*, III, 204; *An Answer, Works*, V, 28.
7. Knox, *A Letter of Wholesome Counsel* (1556), *Works*, IV, 135.

common in the sixteenth century, so common even in the work of other Calvinists, virtually disappeared. Writing his tract against women, Knox dragged it all in again, presumably using the current handbooks, but classical learning was never a key element in his argument. Nor would his politics be based on such conventional knowledge as might also be available to magistrates and lords. His appeal was always to a special truth; tutored by the Holy Ghost, he boasted an understanding of what was "already appointed in the counsel of the eternal."[8]

Custom provided no surer evidence of this counsel than did reason. Knox recited the usual arguments by which men sought to justify their actions: "They are laudable, they are honest and decent, they have good significations, they pleased our fathers and the most part of the world used the same" – and he condemned them all. "And thus into idolatry the corrupt children follow the footsteps of their forefathers."[9] . . .

Denunciation made judgment a possibility: It had broken the link between divine command and earthly event. Although the theology of the Genevans remained strictly predestinarian, their rhetoric actually shifted the ground of argument. As is often the case with prophets, their polemical tongues and pens were bolder and more inventive than their theological minds. The prophet announced the effective and independent power of the devil. He could not, of course, fit such a power into his conception of God's omnipotence, but whatever the shifts to which he was driven, it was dramatically clear that with the devil in the field God's will was no longer revealed by what happened on earth. Instead earth acknowledged another sovereign and the divine law existed in sharp and radical contrast to what were called the abominations of the world. Knox returned to the simplest sort of theodicy – as if Job had never been. To say that iniquitous kings were ordained by God, he wrote, would be to make God the author of iniquity. Such a conclusion was impossible. Evil men might still be described as God's instruments, the whips and scorpions of divine punishment, but they were also God's enemies – a fact for which Knox found a novel corollary: "For all those that would draw us from God (be they kings or queens), being of the devil's nature, are enemies unto God, and therefore will God that we declare ourselves enemies unto them."[10]

8. "God shall always raise up some to whom the verity shall be revealed, and unto such ye shall give place . . . ," *First Blast of the Trumpet Against Monstrous Regiment of Women, Works,* IV, 379.

9. Knox, *Godly Letter, Works,* III, 180.

10. See Goodman's discussion, *Superior Powers,* pp. 110, 133ff. "And in disobeying and resisting [tyrants and idolators] we do not resist God's ordinance, but Satan's." This should be contrasted with the older Protestant view of Tyndale: "Let us receive all things of God whether it be good or bad . . . and submit ourselves unto his nurture and chastising. . . ." *Works of the English Reformers: Tyndale and Frith,* ed. Thomas Russel (London, 1851), I, 230–1.

The reality of Satan's power gave a new meaning to the usual Calvinist description of the warfare of saints and worldlings: It made the war a very immediate and practical matter. Indeed, the enlistment of soldiers became a prophetic task. "Our captain Christ Jesus and Satan his adversary are now at plain defiance. Their banners be displayed and the trumpets blow upon either party, for assembling of their armies. Our master calleth upon his own, and that with vehemence, that they depart from Babylon. . . ."[11] Here was no merely defensive struggle. The prophet's denunciation of the world had made defense irrelevant; what was there left that might legitimately be protected? It had set the stage, instead, for transformation, for an all-out attack upon Satan, for the imposition of a new order upon the corrupted world. . . .

Failing in their duty, rulers and noblemen would "be accounted no more for kings or lawful magistrates, but as private men: and to be examined, accused, condemned and punished by the law of God. . . ."[12] Goodman thus described what would become the key symbolic moment of revolution: the judicial murder of the king. The king would not be judged by his own laws, but by an entirely different law; nor would he recognize his judges, for they would be new men who became public at the same time as the king was "accounted" private. And at their first appearance, these new men justified their politics by pointing not to their human rights but to their divine duties. Like the prophet, the revolutionary viewed himself as an instrument of God; in Calvinist ideology, then, he found an identity fortifying enough to permit him to act in a world temporarily devoid of conventional authority and routine procedures. . . .

For a time, Knox offered the people only a limited revolutionary program. They were to work for reformation "according to the vocation of every man." But if the reformer thus paid tribute to the social hierarchy, he went on to overthrow it. "You, although you be but subjects, may lawfully require of your superiors . . . that they provide you true preachers. . . . And if your superiors be negligent . . . most justly may you provide true preachers for yourselves." Subjects might also withhold from their superiors "the fruits and profits which [they] most unjustly receive of you. . . ."[13] Goodman forsook even such lingering caution and gave warning of more violent things to come; he wrote a prophecy of Cromwell: "And though it appear at first sight a great disorder, that the people should take unto them the punishment of transgressions, yet when the

11. Knox, *The Appellation, Works*, IV, 496.
12. Knox, *Godly Letter, Works*, III, 193. These lines appear in the mss. but not in the published version of the *Letter*. See also p. 198: "We are persuaded that all which our adversaries do is diabolical."
13. Knox, "Letter to Mrs. Anna Loch" (1559), *Works*, IV, 11; see also *Copy of an Epistle, Works*, V. 478.

magistrates and other officers cease to do their duty, they are as it were without officers . . . and then God giveth the sword into the people's hand and he himself is become immediately their head. . . ."[14]

Revolution could not wait upon majorities; Knox described instead the political privileges of a small minority, a revolutionary elect "to whom God granteth knowledge."[15] Political right "devolved" only to the godly among the people: The prophet enlisted the saints.

For such men law and casuistry would have little application. They would not be bound by elaborate rules or careful, painstaking distinctions. The application of conscience to its cases was not for them a matter of endless debate and discussion, as it was for Huguenot intellectuals; it was a matter of practical activity. The self-confident saint, intimately acquainted with God's Word, legitimized his every act by his divine intention. Prophet and saint thus shared a special political character, summed up most dramatically by Knox. "God's word draweth his elect after it," he wrote in a discussion of the slaughter of the golden-calf worshippers in Exodus 32, "against worldly appearance, against natural affections and against civil statutes and constitutions."[16] The privileges of the saint thus extended as far as his power might reach. Later in his life, when Knox was asked whether godly subjects might overthrow an ungodly prince, he answered briefly, raising no legal or moral problems: *if they are able.*[17]

The saint was a new political man, different alike from the feudal officer and the "providential avenger." His duty did not stem from constitutional office nor from divine inspiration; his activity was neither resistance nor assassination. Resistance was a form of collective social defense by prescribed officials of recognized public and legal character. Assassination was the act of a private person, infused with grace, who sacrificed himself in a sudden, unpredictable burst of enthusiasm. The saint, however, was a revolutionary: a private man in the old order and according to the old conventions, who laid claim to public status upon the basis of a new law. He would not resist the king, but overthrow him; he would not assassinate the king, but put him on trial. His activity was systematic and organized; in some fashion he was already obedient to the discipline of the new order he envisioned.

In the old political order, the saint was a stranger. It was appropriate, then, that he be the creation of an intellectual in exile. The cleric, disillusioned with the old world, alienated from a conventional and routine obedience, turned upon England with his "spiritual hatred" – a hatred

14. Goodman, *Superior Powers,* p. 139. He advocated the execution (but not the assassination) of Mary Tudor, p. 99.
15. Knox, *Letter to the Commonality, Works,* IV, 534.
16. Goodman, *Superior Powers,* p. 185.
17. Knox, *Godly Letter, Works,* III, 199.

deepened and given intellectual form by Calvinist theology. Physically exiled, he had moved outside the world of political limitation and into the new world of self-control. His new freedom made radical aspiration and exploration possible; it also made fanaticism possible – and even necessary. An old-fashioned activity like piracy required only an adventurer, but revolution needed, perhaps, men made of "sterner stuff." By calling himself elect, the saint specified his exclusive allegiance to God's Word and (presumably) to the community of the future, when men would live in fellowship on the "Lord's hill." But for the present it was warfare and not fellowship, military order and ideological discipline, and not Christian love that occupied his mind. In order to produce a revolutionary, the prophet had set God against the devil's world and then the saints against the worldlings. Revolution in its origins was only a particular form of this eternal warfare, the continuation, it might be said, of religious activity by military means.

The rhetoric of opposition and struggle thus played an important part in the development of the idea of revolution. . . .

Resistance in the Middle Ages had usually been viewed as a defensive struggle against a tyrant guilty of acts of aggression upon the political order. Defense was a temporarily necessary form of legal violence, ending as soon as order was restored. But the permanent warfare of saints and worldlings set legality and order aside. The devil might be expected to use every imaginable form of wiliness and deception; the saints would continually test his power and rise up whenever they found him weak. They would obey him, as Goodman wrote, only "in captivity and thraldom," never willingly, passively, or in a routine fashion. They would disobey and rebel whenever it was possible, for it was their "bounden duty" to "maintain the cause of God with all [their] might."[18] In the history of political thought, this Calvinist idea of permanent warfare lies between the theory of resistance and that of revolution, and mediates the transition from one to the other. As Calvinism produced a new kind of army, so it discovered in warfare a new politics. The saints were soldiers, subject to an almost military discipline; the minister was "captain of the Lord's host"; together they fought in enemy territory where they were strangers, without earthly allegiance or sympathy.

18. Knox, *Faithful Admonition, Works,* III, 311–12. Exodus 32 was cited frequently during the English Revolution by preachers calling for a "purge" like the one which Moses carried out at the very foot of Sinai. It does not seem ever to have been cited by the leading Huguenot writers, though Calvin discusses the passage in a manner similar to Knox's; see *Sermons on the Fifth Book of Moses* (London, 1583), p. 1203.

12

French Catholicism and secular grace

Jesse R. Pitts

The problems that France has encountered in developing new economic and political structures for the twentieth century can scarcely be understood without studying the traditional values of the French society. My purpose is to offer a scheme for a better understanding of France's learning problems. . . . I go on the assumption that the terms of adaptation to conditions are not automatically given by some sort of hedonistic or *Realpolitik* utilitarianism; that one of the major elements of this adaptation is what a society wants, how it defines the good life; and that this varies from one nation to another, depending on their values. . . .

In analyzing the value system of any Western society one must refer to Christianity. In studying France we must look at Roman Catholicism. All religious systems contain internal tension, contradictions, and ambiguities; and how these are resolved depends in part upon cultural tradition and social structure. Hence one may speak of a French Catholicism as against a Spanish or an Italian or an Irish Catholicism. For example, in French Catholicism one does not find the emphasis on death and the dangers of damnation found in Spanish Catholicism, nor the puritanism found in Irish Catholicism. Although these differences seem to be important to the understanding of national cultures, we know very little about them. We do know, however, that Catholicism in general, as compared with Protestantism, especially of the Calvinist variety, is not interested in building the City of God upon this earth through the application of science (a combination of human reason and will) to Nature. In the eyes of Rome this is Protestant pride. Catholicism is more interested in increasing the power of the Church, which acts as the apostle of Christ on earth. Through sacraments and dogma a contact with the Divine is maintained which transcends human reason, human utility, and the sins of church

From Pitts, "Continuity and Change in Bourgeois France" in Stanley Hoffman, ed., *In Search of France*. Cambridge, Mass.: Harvard University Press, 1964. Excerpts from pp. 235–49. Excerpted by permission of the author and publishers from *In Search of France*, Cambridge, Massachusetts, Harvard University Press, copyright © 1963 by the President and Fellows of Harvard College.

members. It is as church members that human beings reach their highest
level of value achievement. *It is the organization that is divine,* and no
salvation can be gained outside this organization.

The power of the Church has a material aspect which involves it in the
world and an even more important spiritual aspect which is strengthened
by every act of faith accomplished by man. And this is where we meet one
of the main tensions in the Catholic value and idea system: Acts of faith
derive their meaning from man's freedom of choice in the face of temptation. This is the individualistic strain in Catholicism. The Church recognizes the possibility, even the desirability, of any Catholic's sharing contact with God directly through prayer, ecstasy, and special signs. But it is
only through membership in the Church that the individual has qualified
for this special grace, and he is supposed to use it to strengthen the
Church rather than strike out for salvation on his own, as the Puritan of
Pilgrim's Progress would be expected to do. This is the collectivistic
strain in Catholicism. Since the Church's wisdom is greater than that of
man, the act of faith will mean the choice to obey the commands of the
Church, a genuine contrition for sins, and a commitment to greater effort
to defeat the tempter. The Church prevents any individual from harming
the Church through sinful or uninformed action. The Church represents
the spiritual capital of mankind in a world of sin and is the intercessor,
the helper, the defender, the protector of the sinner who shows a true
desire to be saved, even if his flesh be too weak. The supreme value of free
choice and the sanctity of the *Church qua organization* create the crucial
Catholic dilemma.

Faced with this basic tension in Catholicism, French culture has
stressed the inner cohesion and perfection of doctrine rather than the
discipline of organization. In this doctrinaire direction the free will of
man has been interpreted more in the reflexive sense of reason and comprehension than as a force for systematic action upon the world. The
result has been to put upon the Church the burden of remaining intellectually meaningful on a sophisticated basis. The stress on doctrine and upon
rationalization has produced a remarkable array of theologians and dis-
senting movements which have given Rome many difficult moments.

Nevertheless there has been an effective commitment to the Church's
unity since the Church was a body that had a theological (doctrinaire)
and sacramental continuity with Christ. The effort is to influence the
consensus – the Church's doctrine – toward one's point of view, rather
than divide it.

We find here, in what could be called the "doctrinaire-hierarchical"
aspect of French Catholicism, a trait that seems fairly specific to French
culture. This trait is a commitment to a nexus of authoritative ideas
which incarnate the highest spirituality. In religious terms the nexus is the

Church, in secular terms the Nation. There is a conviction that all behavior should have a clear deductive connection to this spirituality through rules, principles, and regulations which ensure inherent value to the action. It is not necessary that the action be effective, or even altogether moral, as long as it demonstrates the link of the individual to the sacred tradition. Here we find the roots of French formalism, the demand for deductive chains of reasoning and hierarchy, the insistence upon the unity of the power center, and formulations where everything and everybody is *à sa place* (in its place). Individuality here means finding one's position in the hierarchy and using it as an anchor for one's thoughts and even for one's deviance. Aspects of French social structure that seem to implement this doctrinaire-hierarchical theme are the centralizing and formalistic features of the civil service and its technocratic tradition.

Another aspect of French Catholicism is the "aesthetic-individualistic" theme, which was strongly reinforced by the humanist "reform" of the Renaissance. Here the whole of Nature – which includes society – assumes a divine quality. The proper goal of man is to reveal this divine quality through understanding and aesthetic appreciation. He must become attuned to the spirituality that is incarnated in Nature. *In this process he is his own authority.*

This approach is still compatible with Catholic allegiance, although it is more sensitive to the artistic and supportive nature of the Holy Mother, the Church, than to the rigor of its doctrine. It sees in the pleasure of aesthetic experience, of ecstasy, the clearest signs of grace. Yet this grace is not accessible without a long period of preparation, realized usually, though not necessarily, by an exacting education and thorough familiarity with the basic principles and organic realities of one's existence such as family and community. This is *enracinement* (rootedness), which replaces the logical connection to the sacred body of ideas, so essential to the doctrinaire-hierarchical theme described above. *Enracinement* puts one in harmony with God's creation. Here the action of the individual is to reveal the sacred content of the world, rather than disturb the equilibrium of the world. This aesthetic-individualistic polarity in French Catholicism exists in aesthetic, deistic, or even orthodox Catholic varieties: In the latter case we have a sort of anticlerical Catholicism. If the doctrinaire-hierarchical polarity corresponds to the centralizing and logico-deductive aspects of French life, the aesthetic-individualistic polarity corresponds to its humanist and aristocratic tendencies.

Although there is a certain tension between the two polarities, they also complement each other. The aesthetic-individualistic polarity needs the framework of principles and the security of membership provided by the Church if its individualism is to be compatible with the order necessary for the maintenance of society. The doctrinaire-hierarchical polarity cannot but recognize the ethical value of the individual's freedom of choice and – on its own hierarchical grounds – the fact that the individual soul is closest to the problems of implementation raised by the Church's commands. Both stress communion with the Harmony of Ideas that defines the City of God. In one view this communion is reached by the aesthetic-intuitive methods of the autonomous individual, in the other by rational deductive methods within a holy organization (Church, State). But, in both views, communion with the Harmony of Ideas is the way to salvation, and both have been represented in either of the Right or Left ideologies which have divided Frenchmen.

The search for salvation – in secular terms, the search for success – is pressed in different ways according to whether the search is made in the hierarchical-doctrinaire direction or in the aesthetic-individualistic direction. In the first case we have the attempt to reach the higher levels of the hierarchy through encyclopedic knowledge, the discovery of universal solutions, and disciplined service to a valued organization. In the second case we have the phenomenon of *prouesse* (prowess). Of course, none of the structures nor any complex pattern of action will ever be a pure and exclusive expression of either one of these two value polarities. They will be syntheses where one or the other dominates. Prowess deserves special attention because it is a type of action which is less understood, and yet it is a greater component of behavior in France than in other European countries.

Prowess is a conspicuous act by which an individual signals his success in reaching, within particular circumstances, the highest possible level of value achievement attainable by man. What matters in prowess, though, is not success in terms of increased power or wealth for the community or for oneself. Prowess does not concern itself with utility. "Do what you must, happen what may" is an expression typical of the spirit of prowess. Another one is "All is lost but honor." Historically, *faire des prouesses* meant to perform a noteworthy act of valor, to perform it spontaneously and unpredictably, although the principles governing and limiting the act were clearly defined and well known. At Roncevaux, Roland by an act of faith in the principles of chivalry seized an opportunity to turn adverse circumstances into an occasion for the triumph of the spirit. Today, as earlier, prowess must be spontaneous: It is not a tormented surmounting of oneself, but rather the discovery and demonstration of a harmony between the self and the environment in the service of the divine. Here Nature provides man with the occasion of honoring God through demonstrating the primacy of the spirit. Man becomes leader of a rite in which Nature reveals the design of God.

Prowess depends for its formulation and evaluation upon canons of value which are given to it by the Church – or by the traditions of the

Nation-State. These are the *principes*. Prowess consists in the application of these *principes* to particular situations that result in elegant solutions where the immutability of principles, their sacred character, and the talent (grace) of the individual are clearly revealed. It is an "act of faith" and reinforces the commitment of its author and of his witnesses to the true faith.

The application of the principle is an element of individual decision, not reducible to rational components available to all. Rather it is a question of instinct, of intuition, and contingent opportunity. When knowledge intervenes as a variable, it is not so much systematic knowledge as it is insight.

Although the concept of prowess evokes the notion of an elite, prowess in fact is theoretically available to anyone who has deep enough roots in the locale of his action (*enracinement*) or, more generally, in the field of his prowess. For prowess is not a perfect solution for any problem at any time, but rather the concept of the conspicuously perfect – miraculous – solution by which one person triumphs over a unique situation. What can be imitated is the skill in finding the occasion when the individual can demonstrate his capacity. And prowess can be found at all levels. The creation of a piece of jewelry by a Parisian craftsman, the peasant's careful distillation of a liqueur, the civilian's stoicism in the face of Gestapo torture, Marcel Proust's suave gallantry in the salon of Madame de Guermantes – all are examples of prowess in modern France.

Prowess depends upon an opportunity and a capacity which cannot be predicted. It depends upon a gift of grace which can be withheld. The concept of prowess is not the Judaic-Protestant concept of election, which implies a commitment of God to the individual and which makes him "saved" forever. In French prowess there is little of the Protestant "calling" with its rationalization, systematization, and reliability of individual behavior.

In any society with an individualistic value system – whether of the aesthetic or puritan type – personalities are bound to have a problem of self-validation which is not raised so acutely by collectivistic value systems. In a society with puritan values this self-validation will be achieved through pragmatic success that is objectively measured: profit, buildings, discoveries, and so on. In the aesthetic-individualistic value system, self-validation cannot claim such objective tokens because the personal component of the actions is so important. Hence validation has to bear on the total personality. Is this a man of taste? Is this a man of honor? These questions are answered in the affirmative when the author of prowess wins unconditional support through some form of love. His act is validated in his own eyes when the spectator to it acknowledges the irresistible appeal of both the man and the deed. Thus the spectator of prowess is "seduced" by its author. In turn, the spectator shares the values the deed represents.

To illustrate this point let us take the example of the military. It is commonly said of a successful French officer that "his men adored him; they would do anything for him." The ideal group under these conditions is *la bande,* a group with minimum organization, where all members are equal in their common subordination to the leader and where the *bande* shares the superiority of the leader by protecting him. The relation between superior and inferior in this context has many of the aspects of romantic love. The leader seduces. The *bande* reciprocates with unconditional support. The gratuitousness of the support is all the more evident if the leader goes against generally recognized authority or traditional practice. Love in the context of prowess leadership must be gratuitous. Since there is no other aim in the relationship but to be with the leader, there is no uncertainty about the hero's validation.

The support the *bande* gives the leader is necessary to validate his action, but this support also validates the *bande*'s own behavior. In this type of leadership the author of prowess requires either enthusiastic passivity (the spectator's role) or an imitation of his goal for prowess. The leader's action lifts his followers beyond themselves. They partake of his essence; there is no more inequality. This is one of the major paradoxes of the aesthetic-individualistic value system and of its cult of prowess: It promotes a very jealous equalitarianism. First, everybody is capable of prowess, and second, prowess is created by the recognition of the spectator as much as by the actions of the hero.

A consequence of the stress upon prowess, with its equalitarianism and its contingencies, is that it raises very acutely the problem of order. This is solved in France by (1) the existence of a state that is immune to seduction because it follows a logic that is not of this world, this fact explaining all at once its strength, its legitimacy, and its unrealism; (2) the respect for any stable system of rights and duties such as the *positions acquises;* and (3) above all, the strong demand that is made upon individuals by that sense of proportion and appropriateness which is expressed in the familiar French ideal of *mesure.*

Mesure is an important ingredient in French classical thought, derived from the Greek idea that the unforgivable sin was defying the natural order according to which each man must keep to his proper place and function. *Mesure* requires that every author of prowess should avoid damaging the fabric of society and its network of *positions acquises.* *Mesure* is reason applied to human action, the result being that certain areas are considered legitimate and suitable for acts of prowess. In a relatively stable society the best fields for prowess must be those where unpredictability of performance can be high without endangering social order – for example, limited warfare (preferably in colonial lands); conspiracies that never succeed; contemplative religion; missionary activities; gratuitous personal relationships (love, friendship, *politesse*); craftsmanship; and elegant selection and use of consumer goods.

Thus, although prowess is intuitive, intensely individual, and unpredictable, the limitations necessary to maintain the stability of the social order are built into the *principes* on which prowess itself is based. The French do not have the cult of the tragic surmounting of self that is characteristic of the Germans. Prowess is above all the discovery of the predetermined harmony, rather than the imposition of a personal will.

The prestige of the aristocracy in classical France was based on its dedication to the values of aesthetic individualism and in particular to its expression of the concept of prowess. Because traditionally the aristocrat was free from the responsibility of saving money and earning a living, he could devote his full attention to performing deeds of prowess. Limited only by the necessity to act *comme il faut* and challenged to exhibit spontaneity and individuality, the French aristocrat developed models of elegance and taste. In matters of love, war, dress, housing, and conversation he showed the world how the application of the principle of prowess could affect these everyday concerns. . . .

Money, whatever its original source, opens up a possibility for prowess which is not as easily accessible when prowess depends upon specialized training or organizational support, such as prowess in war or in political administration. It is easier to show oneself a man of taste than to show oneself to be a brilliant officer, a clever diplomat, a saintly monk, or a dedicated Jesuit. Good taste means doing particularly well what must be done anyway; it is an art of everyday living and theoretically accessible to anyone. It is also a mode of living that is very expensive and thus creates in the French aristocracy a continuing demand for money. By the same token, when a nonaristocrat has wealth the possibilities for prowess are greatly increased. Because of the aristocracy's emphasis on education and talent rather than on the superiority of its blood, there is competition within its own circles and from those in other strata of society who accept aristocratic standards of taste. And because of its emphasis on elegant consumption the aristocracy has maintained close contacts with the professionals of the crafts that are most closely involved in problems of taste of universal reference: literature, fine arts, music. Almost anybody who could compete successfully with the aristocracy in conspicuous and tasteful expenditure or the creation of acceptable new fashions has been entertained by it. Money also opened the salons to those willing to subsidize the aristocrats by giving their own daughters big dowries and to follow aristocratic patterns. This has permitted many bourgeois families to attach themselves to the aristocracy through marriage and through the addition to their names of the particle "de."

The paradox of the aristocratic values of prowess is that they turn out to be the most democratic, because in one's little sphere where one has roots, it is always possible to reach the unique and perfect solution of prowess. The broad diffusion of aristocratic-aesthetic-individualistic values in French society is due to this, and also to the essential role played by the spectator to the aristocrat's deeds of prowess. As in the case of the officer and his soldiers, the aristocrat has been successful in exhibiting his prowess only when others have acknowledged it and thus shared in it. A further reason for the general acceptance of French aristocratic values is the strength of the bond the aristocracy has had to the literary world. Descriptions of upper-class behavior gave the bourgeoisie and middle classes the same vicarious pleasures they now find in the movies. Moreover the assumption of aristocratic symbols by bourgeois families eager to climb socially is not considered a heinous crime. Indeed, because of the universality and relative accessibility of the aristocratic values of consumption prowess, an intense current of upward mobility exists through all the French society.

What were some of the consequences of these values for the French economy prior to the Second World War?

As the industrial revolution gained headway in France, certain characteristics essential to its growth were seen to be incompatible with the aristocratic concept of the role of the consumer. In a bourgeois capitalist economy, economic action must be governed by the encouragement of sales, a concern for consumer demands, an acceptance of the need for specialization, and the necessity to keep costs as low as possible in order to increase profits. The aristocrat's tradition of devoting his life to proving himself through his prowess could not fit into this framework.

The aristocrat had traditionally been a consumer par excellence but there was no possibility of his becoming a salesman. Offering something for sale implies that it can be rejected; and this contradicts the theoretical irrelevance of the public in the realm of prowess (although in fact acceptance and recognition by the spectator were basic to the success of each individual's acts of prowess). In a way the aristocrat was a salesman, selling himself and his values while pretending not to care; but commercial selling would have violated the requirement for prowess both by subordinating the seller to the random customer and by denying the aristocrat's generalized superiority. To encourage sales, one must subject the value of the product to the judgment of anyone.

The value of goods produced for the market is determined by society's needs and wishes rather than by their value to the producer. Theoretically the reverse was true for the aristocrat; to *faire des prouesses* was its own reward. The aristocratic tradition was rather to direct craftsmen in the creation of objects according to individual taste and specifications.

Specialization implies the necessity of focusing on a limited area of problem solving and is therefore contrary to the aristocratic belief in a man's capacity for top performance in any area he may choose. The refusal to specialize is a favored theme in French education, which aims to create cultured gentlemen – the *honnetes hommes* of the seventeenth and eighteenth centuries. In refusing to specialize, the aristocrat also refused the dependency which goes with specialization.

Finally, the aristocrat could not accept the economic necessity of keeping down costs because for him perfection and not price was the *mesure* of the worth of an object or a deed. Costs were irrelevant; even the value of his own expended time could not be considered. To use economic terms, the aristocrat felt he must act as if the expenditure of his energy always produced the highest marginal utility.

These incompatibilities, of course, did not make the French nobility indifferent to the process of industrialization. But some activities were more acceptable than others. The aristocrat could enter an economic organization which had a political dimension as conspicuous as its purely economic one. Organizations which centralize savings and create credit fall in that category. Besides, the man wanting to buy ranking credit usually comes as a solicitor; thus there is no problem of being judged by inferiors. Firms which produce basic raw materials or which produce essential services such as railway transportation are in a position where the individual customer exercises little sanction power over them. In steel and mining the economic organization assumes the posture of a sort of benevolent purveyor to the nation or a direct retainer of the state. In fact, as David Landes points out, the prestige of industries varies in direct proportion to their distance from the random customer.

Once the economic organization was defined as a retainer of the state it was entitled to favored treatment from the state, which guaranteed opportunities for profit through monopolies, selective immunity for the violations of regulations, blocking of entry into the field, discouragement of foreign competition, and other props characteristic of what Max Weber calls "politically oriented capitalism." The history of French railroad building under the sponsorship of the state-financed Freycinet plan is a good example of political capitalism.

The man of aristocratic values, bringing to industry the attitudes which elsewhere win him prestige and power, is not primarily interested in the applied-science aspects of production or in the problems of adding value to the goods or services produced. He will visualize the firm as being superior to its customers, inferior to the state, and hostile toward the rest of the world. His executive function will be – through shrewd diplomacy – to neutralize the threats of competitors, the greed of the random customers, and the fickleness of the government. He will think of his remuneration more as tribute than as payment for a performance objectively measured. He assumes that "the world owes him a living." He represents for the whole society the rewards that must accrue to the exercise of certain values regardless of their contribution to the wealth of the nation.

The importance of this aristocratic point of view was the marked influence it had upon those groups which aspired to identify themselves with the aristocracy. Bourgeois families tried to assume as soon as possible a rentier relationship with the economy. Both capital and executive ability were therefore withdrawn from business pursuits, and the economic growth of France was slower than one would have expected from the human and material resources that existed.

I have been emphasizing the aesthetic-individualistic values held by the aristocracy and those groups which accepted its social leadership. The aristocracy, in its pattern of living, shows a higher concentration of aesthetic-individualistic values than of doctrinaire-hierarchical ones. On the other hand, the classical French bourgeoisie, whose center of gravity was to be found more among lawyers and civil servants than among merchants, showed a higher concentration of doctrinaire-hierarchical values. During the nineteenth century the two great value streams were combined in new, creative forms. This could be seen during the first Napoleonic period; and later the Saint-Simonian movement tried to give to the economy a prowess interpretation and yet at the same time to fit private enterprise into a general plan of social organization. But the two sets of values have been adapted and combined most successfully in institutions where there is a common attitude toward property, authority, and the terms under which a group is organized. The existence of these syntheses is responsible for the fact that industrialization did not fundamentally alter the social pattern inherited from the *ancien regime:* The industrialists merely became another set of notables combining many of the functions of the old rural aristocracy and of the traditional burgher.

APPROACHES TO CULTURE: DURKHEIMIAN

- Victor Turner, *Liminality and community*
- Mary Douglas, *Symbolic pollution*
- Carroll Smith-Rosenburg, *Sex as symbol in Victorian purity*

•

13

Liminality and community

Victor Turner

Van Gennep has shown that all rites of passage or "transition" are marked by three phases: separation, margin (or *limen,* signifying "threshold" in Latin), and aggregation. The first phase of separation comprises symbolic behavior signifying the detachment of the individual or group either from an earlier fixed point in the social structure, from a set of cultural conditions (a "state"), or from both. During the intervening "liminal" period, the characteristics of the ritual subject (the "passenger") are ambiguous; he passes through a cultural realm that has few or none of the attributes of the past or coming state. In the third phase (reaggregation or reincorporation), the passage is consummated. The ritual subject, individual or corporate, is in a relatively stable state once more and, by virtue of this, has rights and obligations vis-à-vis others of a clearly defined and "structural" type; he is expected to behave in accordance with certain customary norms and ethical standards binding on incumbents of social position in a system of such positions.

The attributes of liminality or of liminal personae ("threshold people") are necessarily ambiguous, since this condition and these persons elude or slip through the network of classifications that normally locate states and positions in cultural space. Liminal entities are neither here nor there; they are betwixt and between the positions assigned and arrayed by law, custom, convention, and ceremonial. As such, their ambiguous and indeterminate attributes are expressed by a rich variety of symbols in the many societies that ritualize social and cultural transitions. Thus, liminality is frequently likened to death, to being in the womb, to invisibility, to darkness, to bisexuality, to the wilderness, and to an eclipse of the sun or moon.

Liminal entities, such as neophytes in initiation or puberty rites, may be represented as possessing nothing. They may be disguised as monsters,

From Turner, *The Ritual Process.* Chicago: Aldine, 1969. Excerpts from pp. 94–113, 128–30. Reprinted with permission from Victor W. Turner, *The Ritual Process: Structure and Antistructure.* New York: Aldine de Gruyter. Copyright © 1969 by Victor W. Turner.

wear only a strip of clothing, or even go naked to demonstrate that as liminal beings they have no status, property, insignia, secular clothing indicating rank or role, position in a kinship system – in short, nothing that may distinguish them from their fellow neophytes or initiands. Their behavior is normally passive or humble; they must obey their instructors implicitly and accept arbitrary punishment without complaint. It is as though they are being reduced or ground down to a uniform condition to be fashioned anew and endowed with additional powers to enable them to cope with their new station in life. Among themselves, neophytes tend to develop an intense comradeship and egalitarianism. Secular distinctions or rank and status disappear or are homogenized. . . . In initiations with a long period of seclusion, such as the circumcision rites of many tribal societies or induction into secret societies, there is often a rich proliferation of liminal symbols.

What is interesting about the liminal phenomena for our present purposes is the blend they offer of lowliness and sacredness, of homogeneity and comradeship. We are presented, in such rites, with a "moment in and out of time," and in and out of secular social structure, which reveals, however fleetingly, some recognition (in symbol if not always in language) of a generalized social bond that has ceased to be and has simultaneously yet to be fragmented into a multiplicity of structural ties. These are the ties organized in terms either of caste, class, or rank hierarchies or of segmentary oppositions in the stateless societies beloved of political anthropologists. It is as though there are here two major "models" for human interrelatedless, juxtaposed and alternating. The first is of society as a structured, differentiated, and often hierarchical system of political-legal-economic positions with many types of evaluation, separating men in terms of "more" or "less." The second, which emerges recognizably in the liminal period, is of society as an unstructured or rudimentarily structured and relatively undifferentiated *comitatus,* community, or even communion of equal individuals who submit together to the general authority of the ritual elders.

I prefer the Latin term *communitas* to "community," to distinguish this modality of social relationship from an "area of common living." The distinction between structure and *communitas* is not simply the familiar one between "secular" and "sacred" or that, for example, between politics and religion. Certain fixed offices in tribal societies have many sacred attributes; indeed, every social position has some sacred characteristics. But this "sacred" component is acquired by the incumbents of positions during the *rites de passage,* through which they changed positions. Something of the sacredness of that transient humility and modelessness goes over, and tempers the pride of the incumbent of a higher position or office. This is not simply, as Fortes has cogently argued, a matter of giving a general stamp of legitimacy to society's structural positions.[1] It is rather a matter of giving recognition to an essential and generic human bond, without which there could be no society. Liminality implies that the high could not be high unless the low existed, and he who is high must experience what it is like to be low. No doubt something of this thinking, a few years ago, lay behind Prince Philip's decision to send his son, the heir apparent to the British throne, to a bush school in Australia for a time, where he could learn how "to rough it."

From all this I infer that, for individuals and groups, social life is a type of dialectical process that involves successive experience of high and low, *communitas* and structure, homogeneity and differentiation, equality and inequality. The passage from lower to higher status is through a limbo of statuslessness. In such a process, the opposites, as it were, constitute one another and are mutually indispensable. Furthermore, since any concrete tribal society is made up of multiple personae, groups, and categories, each of which has its own developmental cycle, at a given moment many incumbencies of fixed positions coexist with many passages between positions. In other words, each individual's life experience contains alternating exposure to structure and *communitas,* and to states and transitions.

One brief example from the Ndembu of Zambia of a *rite de passage* that concerns the highest status in that tribe, that of the senior chief Kanongesha, will be useful here. . . .

The liminal component of such rites begins with the construction of a small shelter of leaves about a mile away from the capital village. This hut is known as *kafu* or *kafwi,* a term Ndembu derive from *Ku-fwa,* "to die," for it is here that the chief-elect dies from his commoner state. Imagery of death abounds in Ndembu liminality. For example, the secret and sacred site where novices are circumcised is known as *ifwilu* or *chifwilu,* a term also derived from *ku-fwa.* The chief-elect, clad in nothing but a ragged waist-cloth, and a ritual wife, who is either his senior wife (*mwadyi*) or a special slave woman, known as *lukanu* (after the royal bracelet) for the occasion, similarly clad, are called by Kafwana to enter the *kafu* shelter just after sundown. The chief himself, incidentally, is also known as *mwadyi* or *lukanu* in these rites. The couple are led there as though they were infirm. There they sit crouched in a posture of shame (*nsonyi*) or modesty, while they are washed with medicines mixed with water brought from Katukang'onyi, the river site where the ancestral chiefs of the southern Lunda diaspora dwelt for a while on their journey from Mwantiyanvwa's capital before separating to carve out realms for them-

---

1. Meyer Fortes, "Ritual and Office," in Max Gluckman, ed., *Essays on the Ritual of Social Relations.* Manchester: University of Manchester Press. 1962, p. 86.

selves. The wood for this first must not be cut by an ax but found lying on the ground. This means that it is the product of the earth itself and not an artifact. Once more we see the conjunction of ancestral Lundahood and the chthonic powers.

Next begins the rite of *Kumukindyila*, which means literally "to speak evil or insulting words against him"; we might call this rite "The Reviling of the Chief-Elect." It begins when Kafwana makes a cut on the underside of the chief's left arm – on which the *lukanu* bracelet will be drawn on the morrow – presses medicine into the incision, and presses a mat on the upper side of the arm. The chief and his wife are then forced rather roughly to sit on the mat. The wife must not be pregnant, for the rites that follow are held to destroy fertility. Moreover, the chiefly couple must have refrained from sexual congress for several days before the rites.

Kafwana now breaks into a homily, as follows:

> Be silent! You are a mean and selfish fool, one who is bad-tempered! You do not love your fellows, you are only angry with them! Meanness and theft are all you have! Yet here we have called up and we say that you must succeed to the chief-tainship. Put away meanness, put aside anger, give up adulter-ous intercourse, give them up immediately! We have granted you chieftainship. You must eat with your fellow men, you must live well with them. Do not prepare witchcraft medicines that you may devour your fellows in their huts – that is forbid-den! We have desired you and you only for our chief. Let your wife prepare food for the people who come here to the capital village. Do not be selfish, do not keep the chieftainship to yourself! . . .
>
> > You must not bring partial judgments to bear on any law case involving your people, especially where your own children are involved. You must say: "If someone has slept with my wife, or wronged me, today I must not judge his case unjustly. I must not keep resentment in my heart."

After this harangue, any person who considers that he has been wronged by the chief-elect in the past is entitled to revile him and most fully express his resentment, going into as much detail as he desires. The chief-elect, during all this, has to sit silently with downcast head, "the pattern of all patience" and humility. Kafwana meanwhile splashes the chief with medicine, at intervals striking his buttocks against him (*kumubayisha*) insultingly. Many informants have told me that "a chief is just like a slave (*ndung'u*) on the night before he succeeds." . . .

The phase of reaggregation in this case comprises the public installation of the Kanongesha with all pomp and ceremony. While this would be of the utmost interest in [the] study of Ndembu chieftainship, and . . . an important trend in current British social anthropology, it does not concern us here. Our present focus is upon liminality and the ritual powers of the weak. These are shown under two aspects. First, Kafwana and the other Ndembu commoners are revealed as privileged to exert authority over the supreme authority figure of the tribe. In liminality, the underling comes uppermost. Second, the supreme political authority is portrayed "as a slave," recalling that aspect of the coronation of a pope in western Christendom when he is called upon to be the "*servus servorum Dei.*" Part of the rite has, of course, what Monica Wilson has called a "prophylactic function."[2] The chief has to exert self-control in the rites [so] that he may be able to have self-mastery thereafter in [the] face of the temptations of power. But the role of the humbled chief is only an extreme example of a recurrent theme of liminal situations. This theme is the stripping off of preliminal and postliminal attributes. . . .

The neophyte in liminality must be a *tabula rasa,* a blank slate, on which is inscribed the knowledge and wisdom of the group in those respects that pertain to the new status. The ordeals and humiliations, often of a grossly physiological character, to which neophytes are submitted represent partly a destruction of the previous status and partly a tempering of their essence in order to prepare them to cope with their new responsibilities and restrain them in advance from abusing their new privileges. They have to be shown that in themselves they are clay or dust, mere matter, whose form is impressed upon them by society. . . .

The pedagogics of liminality, therefore, represent a condemnation of two kinds of separation from the generic bond of *communitas.* The first kind is to act only in terms of the rights conferred on one by the incumbency of office in the social structure. The second is to follow one's psychobiological urges at the expense of one's fellows. A mystical character is assigned to the sentiment of humankindness in most types of liminality, and in most cultures this stage of transition is brought closely in touch with beliefs in the protective and punitive powers of divine or preterhuman beings or powers. . . .

Many of these properties constitute what we think of as characteristics of the religious life in the Christian tradition. Undoubtedly, Muslims, Buddhists, Hindus, and Jews would number many of them among their religious characteristics, too. What appears to have happened is that with the increasing specialization of society and culture, with progressive complexity in the social division of labor, what was in tribal society princi-

2. Monica Wilson, "Nyakyusa Ritual and Symbolism." *American Anthropologist* 56(2) (1954):46–54.

pally a set of transitional qualities betwixt and between defined states of culture, and society, has become itself an institutionalized state. But traces of the passage quality of the religious life remain in such formulations as "The Christian is a stranger to the world, a pilgrim, a traveler, with no place to rest his head." Transition has here become a permanent condition. Nowhere has this institutionalization of liminality been more clearly marked and defined than in the monastic and mendicant states in the great world religions. . . .

In most societies, there are other areas of manifestation to be readily recognized by the symbols that cluster around them and the beliefs that attach to them, such as "the powers of the weak," or, in other words, the permanently or transiently sacred attributes of low status or position. . . . We could also mention the role of structurally small and politically insignificant nations within systems of nations as upholders of religious and moral values, such as the Hebrews in the ancient Near East, the Irish in early medieval Christendom, and the Swiss in modern Europe. . . .

Folk literature abounds in symbolic figures, such as "holy beggars," "third sons," "little tailors," and "simpletons," who strip off the pretensions of holders of high rank and office and reduce them to the level of common humanity and mortality. Again, in the traditional "Western" we have all read of the homeless and mysterious "stranger" without wealth or name who restores ethical and legal equilibrium to a local set of political power relations by eliminating the unjust secular "bosses" who are oppressing the smallholders. Members of despised or outlawed ethnic and cultural groups play major roles in myths and popular tales as representatives or expressions of universal-human values. Famous among these are the good Samaritan, the Jewish fiddler Rothschild in Chekhov's tale "Rothschild's Fiddle," Mark Twain's fugitive Negro slave Jim in *Huckleberry Finn,* and Dostoevsky's Sonya, the prostitute who redeems the would-be Nietzchean "superman" Raskolnikov in *Crime and Punishment.*

Among the more striking manifestations of *communitas* are to be found the so-called millenarian religious movements. . . . It is noteworthy that many of these movements cut right across tribal and national divisions during their initial momentum. *Communitas,* or the "open society," differs in this from structure, or the "closed society," in that it is potentially or ideally extensible to the limits of humanity. In practice, of course, the impetus soon becomes exhausted, and the "movement" becomes itself an institution among other institutions – often one more fanatical and militant than the rest, for the reason that it feels itself to be the unique bearer of universal human truths.

In modern Western society, the values of *communitas* are strikingly present in the literature and behavior of what came to be known as the "beat generation," who were succeeded by the "hippies," who, in turn, have a junior division known as the "teeny-boppers." These are the "cool" members of the adolescent and young-adult categories – which do not have the advantages of national *rites de passage* – who "opt out" of the status-bound social order and acquire the stigmata of the lowly, dressing like "bums," itinerant in their habits, "folk" in their musical tastes, and menial in the casual employment they undertake. They stress personal relationships rather than social obligations, and regard sexuality as a polymorphic instrument of immediate *communitas* rather than as the basis for an enduring, structured social tie. The poet Allen Ginsberg is particularly eloquent about the function of sexual freedom. The "sacred" properties often assigned to *communitas* are not lacking here, either: This can be seen in their frequent use of religious terms, such as "saint," and "angel," to describe their congeners and in their interest in Zen Buddhism. The Zen formulation "all is one, one is none, none is all" well expresses the global, unstructured character earlier applied to *communitas*. The hippie emphasis on spontaneity, immediacy, and "existence" throws into relief one of the senses in which *communitas* contrasts with structure. *Communitas* is of the now; structure is rooted in the past and extends into the future through language, law, and custom. . . .

Communitas breaks in through the interstices of structure, in liminality; at the edge of structure, in marginality; and from beneath structure, in inferiority. It is almost everywhere held to be sacred or "holy," possibly because it transgresses or dissolves the norms that govern structured and institutionalized relationships and is accompanied by experiences of unprecedented potency.

The notion that there is a generic bond between men, and its related sentiment of "humankindness," are not epiphenomena of some kind of herd instinct but are products of "men in their wholeness wholly attending." Liminality, marginality, and structural inferiority are conditions in which are frequently generated myths, symbols, rituals, philosophical systems, and works of art. These cultural forms provide men with a set of templates or models which are, at one level, periodical reclassifications of reality and man's relationship to society, nature, and culture. But they are more than classifications, since they incite men to action as well as to thought. Each of these productions has a multivocal character, having many meanings, and each is capable of moving people at many psychobiological levels simultaneously.

There is a dialectic here, for the immediacy of *communitas* gives way to the mediacy of structure, while, in *rites de passage,* men are released from structure into *communitas* only to return to structure revitalized by their experience of *communitas*. What is certain is that no society can function adequately without this dialectic. Exaggeration of structure may well lead to pathological manifestations of *communitas* outside or against "the law." Exaggeration of *communitas,* in certain religious or political movements of the leveling type, may be speedily followed by despotism, overbureaucratization, or other modes of structural rigidification.

14

Symbolic pollution

Mary Douglas

Comparative religion has always been bedevilled by medical materialism. Some argue that even the most exotic of ancient rites have a sound hygienic basis. Others, though agreeing that primitive ritual has hygiene for its object, take the opposite view of its soundness. For them a great gulf divides our sound ideas of hygiene from the primitive's erroneous fancies. But both these medical approaches to ritual are fruitless because of a failure to confront our own ideas of hygiene and dirt. . . .

If we can abstract pathogenicity and hygiene from our notion of dirt, we are left with the old definition of dirt as matter out of place. This is a very suggestive approach. It implies two conditions: a set of ordered relations and a contravention of that order. Dirt, then, is never a unique, isolated event. Where there is dirt there is system. Dirt is the by-product of a systematic ordering and classification of matter in so far as ordering involves rejecting inappropriate elements. This idea of dirt takes us straight into the field of symbolism and promises a link-up with more obviously symbolic systems of purity.

We can recognize in our own notions of dirt that we are using a kind of omnibus compendium which includes all the rejected elements of ordered system. It is a relative idea. Shoes are not dirty in themselves, but it is dirty to place them on the dining-table; food is not dirty in itself, but it is dirty to leave cooking utensils in the bedroom or food bespattered on clothing; similarly, bathroom equipment in the drawing room; clothing lying on chairs; out-door things in-doors; upstairs things downstairs; under-clothing appearing where over-clothing should be, and so on. In short, our pollution behaviour is the reaction which condemns any object or idea likely to confuse or contradict cherished classifications.

We should not force ourselves to focus on dirt. Defined in this way it appears as a residual category, rejected from our normal scheme of classifications. In trying to focus on it we run against our strongest mental

From Douglas, *Purity and Danger*. London: Routledge and Kegan Paul, 1966. Excerpted from pp. 41–9, 114–19, 128–36, 158–9. Reprinted with permission.

habit. For it seems that whatever we perceive is organized into patterns for which we, the perceivers, are largely responsible. Perceiving is not a matter of passively allowing an organ – say of sight or hearing – to receive a ready-made impression from without, like a palette receiving a spot of paint. Recognizing and remembering are not matters of stirring up old images of past impressions. It is generally agreed that all our impressions are schematically determined from the start. As perceivers we select from all the stimuli falling on our senses only those which interest us, and our interests are governed by a pattern-making tendency, sometimes called schema. In a chaos of shifting impressions, each of us constructs a stable world in which objects have recognizable shapes, are located in depth, and have permanence. In perceiving we are building, taking some cues and rejecting those which fit most easily into the pattern that is being built up. Ambiguous ones tend to be treated as if they harmonized with the rest of the pattern. Discordant ones tend to be rejected. If they are accepted, the structure of assumptions has to be modified. As learning proceeds, objects are named. Their names then affect the way they are perceived next time: Once labelled they are more speedily slotted into the pigeon-holes in future.

As time goes on and experiences pile up, we make a greater and greater investment in our system of labels. So a conservative bias is built in. It gives us confidence. At any time we may have to modify our structure of assumptions to accommodate new experience, but the more consistent experience is with the past, the more confidence we can have in our assumptions. Uncomfortable facts, which refuse to be fitted in, we find ourselves ignoring or distorting so that they do not disturb these established assumptions. . . .

Granted that disorder spoils pattern; it also provides the materials of pattern. Order implies restriction; from all possible materials, a limited selection has been made and from all possible relations a limited set has been used. So disorder by implication is unlimited, no pattern has been realized in it, but its potential for patterning is indefinite. This is why, though we seek to create order, we do not simply condemn disorder. We recognize that it is destructive to existing patterns; also that it has potentiality. It symbolizes both danger and power. . . .

Consider beliefs about persons in a marginal state. These are people who are somehow left out in the patterning of society, who are placeless. They may be doing nothing morally wrong, but their status is indefinable. Take, for example, the unborn child. Its present position is ambiguous, equally its future. For no one can say what sex it will have or whether it will survive the hazards of infancy. It is often treated as both vulnerable and dangerous. The Lele regard the unborn child and its mother as in constant danger, but they also credit the unborn child with capricious ill-will which makes it a danger to others. When pregnant, a Lele woman tries to be considerate about not approaching sick persons lest the proximity of the child in her womb cause coughing or fever to increase.

Among the Nyakyusa a similar belief is recorded. A pregnant woman is thought to reduce the quantity of grain she approaches, because the foetus in her is voracious and snatches it. She must not speak to people who are reaping or brewing without first making a ritual gesture of goodwill to cancel the danger. They speak of the foetus "with jaws agape" snatching food, and explain it by the inevitability of the "seed within" fighting the "seed without."

> The child in the belly . . . is like a witch; it will damage food like witchcraft; beer is spoiled and tastes nasty, food does not grow, the smith's iron is not easily worked, the milk is not good.[1]

Even the father is endangered at war or in the hunt by his wife's pregnancy.

Levy-Bruhl noted that menstrual blood and miscarriage sometimes attract the same kind of belief. The Maoris regard menstrual blood as a sort of human being *manque*. If the blood had not flowed it would have become a person, so it has the impossible status of a dead person that has never lived. He [referred to] a common belief that a foetus born prematurely has a malevolent spirit, dangerous to the living. Levy-Bruhl did not generalize that danger lies in marginal states, but Van Gennep had more sociological insight. He saw society as a house with rooms and corridors in which passage from one to another is dangerous. Danger lies in transitional states; simply because transition is neither one state nor the next, it is undefinable. The person who must pass from one to another is himself in danger and emanates danger to others. The danger is controlled by ritual which precisely separates him from his old status, segregates him for a time, and then publicly declares his entry [into] his new status. . . .

To plot a map of powers and dangers in a primitive universe, we need to underline the interplay of ideas of form and formlessness. So many ideas about power are based on an idea of society as a series of forms contrasted with surrounding non-form. There is power in the forms and other power in the inarticulate area, margins, confused lines, and beyond the external boundaries. If pollution is a particular class of danger, to see where it belongs in the universe of dangers we need an inventory of all the possible sources of power. In a primitive culture the physical agency of misfortune is not so significant as the personal intervention to which it can be traced. The effects are the same the world over: Drought is

---

1. Monica Wilson, *Rituals and Kinship among the Nyakyusa*. London: Oxford University Press, 1967, pp. 138–9.

drought, hunger is hunger; epidemic, child labour, infirmity – most of the experiences are held in common. But each culture knows a distinctive set of laws governing the way these disasters fall. The main links between persons and misfortunes are personal links. So our inventory of powers must proceed by classifying all kinds of personal intervention in the fortunes of others. . . .

First consider the case of the man in a position of authority who abuses the secular powers of his office. If it is clear that he is acting wrongly, out of role, he is not entitled to the spiritual power which is vested in the role. Then there should be scope for some shift in the pattern of beliefs to accommodate his defection. He ought to enter the class of witches, exerting involuntary, unjust powers instead of intentionally controlled powers against wrongdoers. For the official who abuses his office is as illegitimate as a usurper, an incubus, a spanner in the works, a dead weight on the social system. Often we find this predicted shift in the kind of dangerous power he is supposed to wield.

In the Book of Samuel, Saul is presented as a leader whose divinely given powers are abused. When he fails to fill his assigned role and leads his men into disobedience, his charisma leaves him and terrible rages, depression, and madness afflict him. So when Saul abuses his office, he loses conscious control and becomes a menace even to his friends. With reason no longer in control, the leader becomes an unconscious danger. The image of Saul fits the idea that conscious spiritual power is vested in the explicit structure and uncontrolled unconscious danger vested in the enemies of the structure.

The Lugbara have another and similar way of adjusting their beliefs to abuse of power. They credit their lineage elders with special powers to invoke the ancestors against juniors who do not act in the widest interests of the lineage. Here again we have conscious controlled powers upholding the explicit structure. But if an elder is thought to be motivated by his own personal, selfish interests, the ancestors neither listen to him nor put their power at his disposal. So here is a man in a position of authority, improperly wielding the powers of office. His legitimacy being in doubt, he must be removed, and to remove him, his antagonists accuse him of having become corrupt and emanating witchcraft, a mysterious, perverted power which operates at night. The accusation is itself a weapon for clarifying and strengthening the structure. It enables guilt to be pinned on the source of confusion and ambiguity. So these two examples symmetrically develop the idea that conscious power is exerted from the key positions in the structure and a different danger from its dark, obscure areas. . . .

Pollution powers . . . inhere in the structure of ideas itself and . . . punish a symbolic breaking of that which should be joined or joining of that which should be separate. It follows from this that pollution is a type of danger which is not likely to occur except where the lines of structure, cosmic or social, are clearly defined.

A polluting person is always in the wrong. He has developed some wrong condition or simply crossed some line which should not have been crossed and this displacement unleashes danger for someone. Bringing pollution, unlike sorcery and witchcraft, is a capacity which men share with animals, for pollution is not always set off by humans. Pollution can be committed intentionally, but intention is irrelevant to its effect – it is more likely to happen inadvertently. . . .

The fact that pollution beliefs provide a kind of impersonal punishment for wrong-doing affords a means of supporting the accepted system of morality. . . .

1. When a situation is morally ill-defined, a pollution belief can provide a rule for determining post hoc whether infraction has taken place or not.
2. When moral principles come into conflict, a pollution rule can reduce confusion by giving a simple focus for concern.
3. When action that is held to be morally wrong does not provoke moral indignation, belief in the harmful consequences of a pollution can have the effect of aggravating the seriousness of the offence, and so of marshalling public opinion on the side of the right.
4. When moral indignation is not reinforced by practical sanctions, pollution beliefs can provide a deterrent to wrongdoers.

Some pollutions are too grave for the offender to be allowed to survive. But most pollutions have a very simple remedy for undoing their effects. There are rites of reversing, untying, burying, washing, erasing, fumigating, and so on, which at a small cost of time and effort can satisfactorily expunge them. The cancelling of a moral offence depends on the state of mind of the offended party and on the sweetness of nursing revenge. The social consequences of some offences ripple out in all directions and can never be reversed. Rites of reconciliation which enact the burial of the wrong have the creative effect of all ritual. They can help to erase the memory of the wrong and encourage the growth of right feeling. There must be an advantage for society at large in attempting to reduce moral offences to pollution offences which can be instantly scrubbed out by ritual. . . .

15

Sex as symbol in Victorian purity

Carroll Smith-Rosenberg

What is so compelling about the Victorians' ideological denial of their sexuality?

The answer lies, most probably, in the uniqueness of the Victorian purity ideology. At no other period in American history has such a sexually repressive belief system been so elaborately delineated. Appearing suddenly in the 1830s and 1840s, it contrasts sharply with the sexual permissiveness of either the 18th or the 20th century. What we chose to delineate as "Puritanism" began in America during the last stages of preindustrial commercial capitalism. . . .

Historians traditionally have used sexual prescription to hypothesize about sexual behavior. Prescription, however, is not behavior. Rather than seeing the arguments of the early male moral reformers as a dim and distorted window into Jacksonian bedrooms, I propose to examine them as a symbolic statement of values and concerns, as one of a number of ideologies produced by American society as it grew in social and economic complexity. Historians of religion study theology not to learn about the nature of God but about the nature of the culture that produced that theology. Let us seek to relate the sexual-purity arguments not to what people may or may not have done in bed but to conditions in American society and in the American family during this last stage of preindustrial development. . . .

Sexual purity began as a male reform movement. Its pamphlets and books were written exclusively by mature men. Without exception, they addressed a youthful male audience. Sylvester Graham's *Lectures to Young Men on Chastity*, S. B. Woodward's *Hints for the Young*, William Alcott's *Young Men's Guide* and *Physiology of Marriage* all implicitly or explicitly spoke to adolescent boys at boarding school or college and youthful clerks in towns and cities. This was the very audience Sylvester

From Smith-Rosenberg, *American Journal of Sociology* 84 Supplement (1978). Excerpted from pp. 212–47. Reprinted with permission of the author and the *American Journal of Sociology*.

Graham addressed in his luminous career as public lecturer in the 1830s and 1840s. Graham's audience consisted . . . not of older men, not of rural and agrarian youths, but of students in the new postrevolutionary colleges and of clerks attending the new urban lyceums. . . . The problems, anxieties, and temptations of the male adolescent dominate this literature. Brief histories detailing the terrible effects of uncontrolled adolescent sexuality repeatedly accost the reader. The purity advocates' protagonist was the male youth; his moral education and physical well-being were their espoused goals. . . . The future happiness and stability of American society rested upon his purity. As Graham stated in the opening paragraph of his *Lecture to Young Men:* "The wisest and best men of every age have manifested a deep interest in the welfare of youth; and have considered their intellectual, moral and physical education, character and condition of the utmost importance to the individual, social and civil welfare of mankind. . . . The proper education of youth . . . [is] the foundation of national prosperity and happiness."

Combining temperance and vegetarianism with pungent criticism of the regular medical profession, the male moral reformers constructed a physiological model that condemned male orgasm as the source of physical, mental, and social deterioration. Sexual activity for the purpose of personal pleasure, they argued, was physiologically disastrous and hence socially irresponsible. Male orgasm had only one justifiable purpose – reproduction. Continence should characterize most periods of a man's life – especially that of adolescence. Young men must remain virgins until they married in their late twenties and early thirties. . . .

Most importantly, young men must not masturbate. Fear of the classic sexual act of boyhood and youth dominated these writings. Masturbation was "the worst form of excessive and perverted amativeness," O. S. Fowler thundered, while John B. Newman condemned it as "a crime wholly unnatural and . . . pernicious. It is worthy only of brutes, like the dog-faced monkey" (Fowler 1856, p. 48; Newman 1856, p. 56). Masturbation sapped the vitality and innocence of America's youth, deforming minds and bodies. "In the young . . . its influence is much more seriously felt; . . . [they] cannot know how much their physical energy, mental vigor and moral sensibility have been affected by the indulgence." "The effects of this horrible vice are the more pernicious the earlier it is practiced," another doctor commented in the 1850s (Graham 1837, pp. 77–9; Alcott 1866, pp. 67–8, 72–4). It occurred in secret, outside the knowledge and control of the adult world. Fed by fantasy, it lay beyond the limits of reality. It was widespread. "I have never conversed with a lad of twelve years of age," Woodward remarked, "who did not know all about the practice and understand the language commonly used to describe it" (1856, p. 5). . . .

A deep-seated fear of male orgasm underlay these admonitions against marital coitus and masturbation. The male orgasm was overpowering, uncontrollable, raging. Rebellious and anarchical, it possessed vast potential for destruction. . . . Graham expressed the male reformers' fears: "The convulsive paroxysms attending venereal indulgence are connected with the most intense excitement and cause the most powerful agitation to the whole system that it is ever subject to. The brain, the heart, lungs, liver, skin and the other organs feel it sweeping over them with the tremendous violence of a tornado. The powerfully intoxicated and convulsed heart drives the blood, in fearful congestion, to the principal viscera, producing oppression, irritation, debility, rupture, inflammation, and sometimes disorganization. . . . These excesses, too frequently repeated, cannot fail to produce the most terrible effects" (1837, p. 49).

Feared as a physical force out of control, the male orgasm also threatened the body's hierarchy of functions. Male moral reformers, like most medical writers of the period, thought in terms of the body as a closed energy system. Individuals possessed limited amounts of nervous and nutritional energy which the body appropriated to the different organs according to their importance in man's overall metabolism. Sexual excitation and orgasm, the moral reformers argued, disrupted this natural order, drawing blood and energy to the lowest and least necessary of man's organs – his genitals. While the nobler organs – brain, heart, lungs, indeed all man's vital parts – were robbed of their strength, the genitals became engorged, "irritated and excited," and insatiable (Graham 1837, pp. 58, 74). . . .

To counter the instability and rashness they saw in all male sexual desire, male moral reformers sought to subject that desire to a rigid system of laws that lay beyond human volitional control. The moral reformers worked within a system of laws, not men; time and again they referred to the human body as a balanced constitution, a harmonious system. . . . The specific law governing male coitus was female ovulation. Intercourse should be limited to marriage, occurring only when a wife was fertile, a moment she alone instinctively knew. Husbands must wait for their wives' advances. Marital intercourse should, as a consequence, occur once a month until pregnancy ensued and not recommence until the child was weaned. Coitus during nonfertile periods caused a disastrous dislocation of the nervous energies of both men and women. It destroyed the masculinity of the one, the femininity of the other. . . .

Disease and death were not the only threats held before the youthful indulger. Male moral reformers predicted that the masturbator would lose not only his health but also his masculinity. Masturbation would force him into a liminal state, between masculinity and femininity. . . . "Whoever gives way to this passion proportionately impairs his manhood," phrenologist and reformer O. S. Fowler warned: "The man lays down his nobleness, dignity, honor and manhood and is no longer bold, resolute, determined, aspiring, dignified, but becomes deprecated, irresolute, undetermined, tamed . . . disheartened, uncertain in his plans . . . a drone to himself and society" (1856, pp. 28–9). The masturbator, Trall asserted, will be "timid, afraid of his own shadow, uncertain . . . nor will he walk erect or dignified as if conscious of his manhood and lofty in his aspirations, but will walk more with a diminutive, cringing, sycophantic, inferior, mean, self-debased manner. . . . This secret practice has impaired both his physical and mental manhood, and thereby effaced the nobleness and efficiency of the masculine and deteriorated his soul" (1856, pp. 55–7).

There is much evidence suggesting that male moral reformers might well have used masturbation as a code for homosexuality. The effeminate masturbator possessed all the stereotypic qualities of the male homosexual. Furthermore, women appeared to repulse him. Writer after writer accused masturbators of avoiding women and refusing to marry. . . .

What order can we, as historians, impose upon this system of physiological misunderstandings and sexual terrors? Such a belief system, built around bodily controls, concerned with purity regulations, with hierarchical order within a closed universe, and with acts of transgression against that order, is not unique to Victorian America. It has parallels in advanced and in traditional societies around the world and across time. Over the past 10 years anthropologists have begun to interpret such ideologies as symbolic systems expressive of social change and cultural tensions. They have found that the societies which produced them share a deep concern for social control and a desire to contain institutional and familial fragmentation. At the core of these ideologies lies a rigid system of regulations which fuses the moral and the physical, a system in which chance plays no role. No bodily detail is too small to weigh in the balance of an individual's, a family's, or a group's fate. No item of prohibited or approved food, no physical act passes unnoticed. An exact balance is struck between bodily input and output. Sickness and sin are linked; disease punishes sin (Douglas 1970, chap. 1 and pp. 111, 114, 124–5).

Such an interpretation is based upon a recognition of the emotional and symbolic logic that connects an individual's perception of his relation to his society, his family, and his body. This emotional logic underlies the formulation of cultural symbols. . . . Complex and ironic ties relate the physical body to the body politic. The physical body serves as both microcosm and counterpoint to the body of social structure and social arrangements. The physical body, while symbolizing the social body, at the same time incorporates carnal demands that threaten to disrupt – soil – the purity of the allegorical body (Douglas 1970, pp. 98, 99, 191).

To see the physical as symbolic of the nonphysical, however, is not to deny the carnality of bodily imagery. It is just this psychosexual component that transforms the body into symbol. Anthropologist Victor Turner has argued that all symbols are, in fact, bipolar, at once sensory and sociological. It is their sensory aspect incorporating the timeless affect of primitive emotions that social groups utilize, shaping the sensory and timeless into a socially shared experiential vocabulary expressive of concrete values (1967, pp. 28, 29–47). . . .

If the body is symbol, then a determination to control bodily functions, to legislate, and to punish indicates a desire to control or protect specific institutions and groups within that society. If the body is seen as endangered by uncontrollable forces, then presumably this is a society or social group which fears change – change which it perceives simultaneously as powerful and beyond its control. All society is built upon an assertion of order and the containment of disorder. Order within the world of symbol and metaphor, by its nature, is invested with power to maintain itself and contain the forces of disorder. But disorder also possesses its own wild, formless power. Order and disorder, Douglas argues, are pitted against each other in all cultures. . . . Formlessness will appear particularly threatening when a society, or specific groups within that society, experiences rapid change – a movement either toward less structure or to a new and untried structure.

This was true of American society during the last stages of preindustrial commercial capitalism. Much of the conflict intellectual and social historians have traditionally seen in Jacksonian society could well be described in terms of a never-ending struggle between form and formlessness. Those Jacksonians opposed to a ritualized, structured, and traditional order championed the creative power of "unrestrained" individualism, the potential and lure of the new western lands, the transportation revolution, the new and powerful cities, God's revivalistic grace descending like Pentecostal tongues on the poor, the ill educated, the young, the female. Conservatives feared this power, seeing in it an assault on the established structures of society, structures which possessed their own sources of power: constitutional checks and balances, wealth and influence, tradition, the patriarchal family, the established church, the educated ministry, a theology urging preparation and Christian nurture. Both dreaded the even less restrained power of the savage, of uncultivated and "wild" land, of "Promethean individualism," of rebellion, of "uncontrolled" nature. Thus all Jacksonians – Whigs and Democrats, frontiersmen and Brahmins – lived within a symbolic and emotional universe in which order had relentlessly to struggle against the power of disorder. Significantly, within the sexual system the Jacksonian male moral reformers had created, it was not the emission of sperm or the penetration of a woman's body that threatened but the orgasmic thrust itself, wild and unstructured, pulsing through the male body, stealing energy, disrupting order.

Inherent in a world view that pitted form against formlessness lay a suspicion of individuals who remained outside recognized structures or who were in flux between social categories. Two states are involved: marginality, defined as the lack of power, status, or centrality within a social structural complex of roles and responsibilities; and liminality, the quality of a person who is in movement between two states and consequently possesses the roles and responsibilities of neither (Turner 1967, pp. 93–111). . . . Marginal and liminal figures by their very nature lie outside and thus are alien to order and control. In cultures which perceive their traditional order as endangered, marginal and liminal figures appear particularly dangerous to themselves and to others. They lie on the margins, between form and formlessness. They embody the power of formlessness. They have *entrée* to the areas of form. They are potential Trojan horses.

But at the same time each of these terms embodies its own particular form of deviance – and danger. Marginality is a relatively permanent state and refers to an individual's or a group's location within a social structure. Douglas argues that "where the social system requires people to hold dangerously ambiguous roles these persons are credited with uncontrolled, unconscious, dangerous, disapproved powers" (1966, p. 99). They are seen as antisocial; "dirt, obscenity and lawlessness" characterize them.[1] The liminal figure is equally threatening. Liminality most frequently suggests the process of transition. The individual is contrasted not so much with others in her or his social structural system as with her or his own past and future state. The transition from one stage in the life cycle to another is the most classic example of liminality. Liminality thus refers to nature, marginality to location.

The pubescent male is the quintessential liminal figure. Rites of passage traditionally contain his danger. To such universal fears, Jacksonian America added its own specific economic and social complications. The unapprenticed adolescent was marginal as well as liminal. Apprenticeship in the 17th and 18th centuries had served two essential social functions. It had removed psychosexual adolescents from their parents' home, isolated them, and ritualistically confirmed their transitional status. The completion of their apprenticeship ritualistically marked their emergence into

1. When women began to attend academies and colleges in increasing numbers (especially beginning in the 1870s) similar arguments were made concerning the danger of education to women's health and morals. A very direct connection was made between disease and role change. Again we have an example of adult males treating male adolescents and women in similar ways – especially when role change was an issue (see Smith-Rosenberg and Rosenberg 1973).

sexual and social adulthood. But the apprenticeship system also served a central socioeconomic function, training unformed youth for a specific trade and hence a predictable rank and social responsibilities within a preindustrial hierarchical world. As the hierarchical and settled economic and social world of the 18th century disintegrated, apprenticeship as a sociosexual and socioeconomic institution disappeared. Male youths no longer could be prepared realistically and ritualistically for an ordered world. They became socially marginal at the very time that the institution (apprenticeship) that had structured their liminal phase died out. It cannot be coincidental that male purity advocates chose the Jacksonian youth as a symbol of their forces of disorder, change, and sexuality that they saw endangering the male body and thus their idealized and static 18th-century patriarchal world. In the Jacksonian youth, the dangers inherent in liminality and marginality intersected and fused. . . .

The Jacksonian youth was dangerous. He entailed a host of diseases upon himself and his progeny (Alcott 1866, p. 77). More alarmingly, unrestrained adolescent sexuality endangered the very order and structure of society. Male purity writers in the 1830s and 1840s saw young men as a potentially despotic power, cutting through civil and moral law, involved in illicit commerce, breaking down mercantile restrictions, ultimately engulfing and destroying social order. Older men were impotent to stop them: "Is it not then a matter of course . . . that young concupiscence should kindle into a passion of despotic power and compel the unwary youth either to break through the restraints of civil and moral law to find indulgence in illicit commerce, or more clandestinely to yield to the more degrading and destructive vice of self-pollution? To what avail, then, are moral laws, and civil legislation . . . ? As well might we attempt to prevent the eruption of volcanic mountains, when the internal fires were kindled . . . and roll back the burning tide, and save the world from dissolution" (Graham 1837, p. 63). . . .

Unapprenticed young men, united together in new educational institutions – boarding schools, high schools, or colleges – clerks in the cities, youths in boarding houses, all lived outside the nuclear family and outside the mercantile economic structure. These were the true liminal figures of the Jacksonian world order. It was their sexuality that threatened destruction. They were the men who in masturbating killed themselves and polluted their children.

Schools, especially boarding schools, the new high schools, and colleges posed a double threat to the male reformers. Institutional responses to the new commercial and urban world, such schools facilitated the movement of sons into that world. At the same time, by creating the institutional setting for a separate youth culture, they permitted youth to bond against age, liminal figures to organize against traditional order.

With the demise of apprenticeship systems, no adequate rite of passage purged the adolescent of his dangerous powers and led him back into organized society. Pathetically, the male moral reformers sought to resurrect the family as an institution to contain the adolescent's drive toward autonomy and maturity. . . .

The school endangered, the city ensnared. Young men could attend schools and live at home. Even at boarding school their youth and innocence – and the alert eye of the school master – could shield them. But in the city, living in boarding houses, associating day and night with other "loose" young men, the dangers of the school were magnified. Not only were patriarchal restraints weaker, the city itself allured, enticed, and corrupted. . . .

The city stimulated the senses. It was the source of a host of novel and alien foods – the accoutrements of the urban, commercial middle classes. Imported teas, coffees, and cocoa; rich gravies; novel spices; cordials; even richly prepared meats – all inflamed the blood and stimulated the sexual organs. Masturbation must ensue. "If we will train our offspring in the early and free use of flesh-meat, and accustom them to . . . richly prepared dishes and learn them to drink tea and coffee and wine and . . . other stimulants with which civic life is unwisely cursed, we effeminate their bodies with feather beds and enervating dress," Sylvester Graham thundered at indulgent and fashionable parents. "In short, if we will sedulously educate them to all the degenerating habits of luxury, indolence, voluptuousness and sensuality we shall be . . . indebted to their want of *opportunity to sin* . . . if, indeed, we escape the heart-rending anguish of seeing them the early victims of passions" (1837, p. 59). . . .

The physiological system of sin and punishment constructed by male moral reformers possessed all the components of a classic pollution taboo system. The ingestion of forbidden foods poisoned the system, corrupting the body and hence the morals and reason of the violator. Sexual fantasies, orgasms, and especially masturbation acted in a similar fashion. The blood of the masturbator became "enflamed," "corrupted," and "polluted" (Fowler 1844, p. xii; Trall 1856, pp. 25–6; Woodward 1856, p. 7). . . . Specific violations of a sexual and dietary code thus automatically produced a carefully defined physiological retribution. George R. Calhoun, in *Spermatorrhoea* (1858), described the pollution process. The mechanism was slow but implacable: "Self abuse . . . destroys the body . . . the destruction is not accomplished all at once; slowly but most certainly, the Onanist distills a poison into his frame that will inevitably, if not relieved by timely aid, lead to death" (p. 8). Spermatorrhoea was the disease specific to masturbation. The "secret vice" was punished by a disease itself secret, indeed invisible. . . . Within this Jacksonian system, liminal figures offended; liminal acts – nonreproductive orgasms, masturbation, homosexuality – were tabooed. A slow, barely perceived poison punished.

A pollution taboo system constitutes a fantasy system in which specified behavior is magically punished. . . . Yet if individual pleasures were sacrificed, the rewards to the young men, to their families, and to society would be unlimited. A physiological millennium in which pain, disease, and immorality were banished lay before the pure young man who observed the reformers' dietary and sexual taboos. Hereditarian thought during the early 19th century assumed much of the activism and optimism of its day. . . . By no means deterministic in its operations, it asserted that each individual had within his power the potential to either strengthen or weaken his constitution. Furthermore, these actions for good or evil were themselves passed on to all future generations; thus a man weak himself and predisposed to disease could both strengthen his own constitution and improve his hereditary potential by conforming to a reformed dietary and sexual regimen. His offspring and their world could attain perfection. . . . As O. S. Fowler stated in the introduction to his marriage guide, *Love and Parentage:* "When, but only when mankind properly LOVE and MARRY and then rightly generate, CARRY, NURSE, and EDUCATE their children, they will be indeed and in truth the holy and happy sons and daughters of the 'Lord Almighty,' compared with those miserable and depraved scapegoats of humanity which infest our earth. Oh! the boundless capabilities and perfections of our God-like nature! Alas, its deformities!" ". . . The virtuous youth, far from threatening disorder and damnation, became the new Christ. In the iconography of the Protestant 19th century, the continent youth replaced the Virgin, standing on the world, with his foot crushing the serpent's head." . . .

Women emerge in the male purity literature as whores or madonnas. The sexually assertive woman is the classic temptress and castrator. The danger inherent in her sexuality transcends any possible to men. She is an anathema. She seduces women as well as men. Indulging her own appetite, she initiate[s] her more innocent sisters into the pleasures of masturbating and solicit[s] and train[s] "virtuous . . . lovely worth" as prostitutes. "They scath and scourge wherever they are most fearfully," Alcott warned (1866, p. 51).[2] Significantly, male purity advocates believed that

2. Women as mothers seduce as well. Trall (1853, p. 29), who saw sexual impulses as the product of oral stimulation – that is, of the ingestion of illicit foods – also saw mothers as the initial and primary seducers of their children. "The mothers are grievously at fault. . . . They are continually depraving the appetites of their infants and young children, and tempting and stuffing them with various animal dishes, until they are absolutely forced to love and desire that which they by nature instinctively loathe and abhor." Trall's statement possesses significant meaning both on a psychoanalytic level in terms of male

American girls, pure by nature, were only corrupted by the importation of foreign degenerate practices. For instance, if a young girl unwisely emulated European women, leaving home in search of an advanced – and unnatural – education in one of the new female boarding schools or academies, then foreign corruptions, especially the habit of masturbation learned from and practiced with other girls, could debase her. "But Heaven forbid that . . . depraved customs of artificial life should ever make such a Sodom of our beloved land," Graham exclaimed, using an odd image to describe female sexuality – especially female homosexuality (1837, p. 20). Like the new male youth, the new female youth when associated with new social arrangements, in search of individual intellectual fulfillment, became endangered and dangerous. She no longer stood guardian of the patriarchal order of the past.

In contrast, the pure, frigid woman, devoted to her children, holding tightly to her traditional and home-bound role, served as the savior of home and society. Male purity writers granted such women absolute sexual power over men. Men were to assume a dependent sexual position, to obey women, the procreative force. . . . In return for this grant of sexual power, a woman was to limit her own sexual desires even more stringently than she did her husband's. She was expected, as well, to remain subservient to him and to her children in all other areas of life; she must narrow her horizons to the hearth and the nursery, be obedient, self-effacing, and nurturant within that sphere. . . . If the young man needed an example of righteous suffering, it would be his mother, his sister – his wife. . . . In the end, women and the family emerge as symbols of order, continuity, and harmony. Marriage "is . . . the golden chain that binds society together. . . . Marriage, regarded as duty, should be aimed at in all our education" (Alcott 1866, p. 14).

The images and symbols of the male moral reformers served multiple functions and addressed varied realities. On one level they expressed timeless fears of the power and uncontrollability of orgasms, of Oedipal conflict, of male fears and fascination with woman's sexuality and her reproductive powers. On the other hand, they provided an ideal sexual regimen for a newly urbanized middle class that had suddenly to reverse the procreational practices of the past two centuries. . . .

While important and accurate, however, these explanations remain partial. They fail to systematically deal with sexual purity arguments and images. . . . Popular beliefs, symbolic and metaphorical, while containing important universal components, must be seen and understood as part of the culture that formulated them.

> fear and hatred of women and on a more symbolic level, related to pollution taboos – the intake of forbidden, poisonous foods and their subsequent psychosexual toll.

They must also be analyzed as a coherent whole. Specific metaphors and arguments cannot be plucked out of the system and be analyzed in isolation. . . .

This was a cosmic system that pitted formlessness against form and saw danger as emanating from liminal figures. It was a pollution system created to guide the American family through the critical stage of adolescence – a process that threatened to destroy the family and society. Within this system, the bizarre transformations that the moral reformers made in traditional medical theories of disease etiology and therapeutics and the unreasonableness of their sexual prescription assume an emotional if not cognitive logic. Their function within their culture has become visible.

REFERENCES

Alcott, William. 1866. *The Physiology of Marriage*. Boston: Dinsmoor.
Calhoun, George R. 1858. *Report of the Consulting Surgeon on Spermatorrhoea or Sexual Weakness. Impotence, the Vice of Onanism, Masturbation, or Self-Abuse and the Diseases of the Sexual Organs*. Philadelphia: Howard.
Douglas, Mary. 1966. *Purity and Danger. An Analysis of Concepts of Pollution and Taboo*. New York: Praeger.
   1970. *Natural Symbols*. New York: Vintage.
Fowler, O. S. 1844. *Love and Parentage*. New York: Fowlers & Wells.
   1856. *Amativeness, or Evils and Remedies of Excessive and Perverted Sexuality*. New York: Fowlers & Wells.
Graham, Sylvester. (1834) 1837. *Lecture to Young Men on Chastity*. 3d ed. Boston: Light & Stearns.
Newman, J. B. 1856. *Philosophy of Generation: Its Abuses with Their Causes, Prevention and Cure*. New York: Fowlers & Wells.
Smith-Rosenberg, Carroll, and Charles Rosenberg. 1973. "The Female Animal: Medical and Biological Views of Women's Role in Nineteenth-Century America." *Journal of American History* 60 (September):332–56.
Trall, R. T. 1856. *Home-Treatment for Sexual Abuses. A Practice Treatise*. New York: Fowlers & Wells.
Turner, Victor. 1967. *The Forest of Symbols*. Ithaca, N.Y.: Cornell University Press.
Woodward, S[amuel] B[ayard]. (1838) 1856. *Hints for the Young in Relation to the Health of Mind and Body*. Boston: Light.

APPROACHES TO CULTURE: MARXIAN

- E. P. Thompson, *Rituals of mutuality*
- Paul Willis, *Masculinity and factory labor*

16

Rituals of mutuality

E. P. Thompson

Again and again the "passing of old England" evades analysis. We may see the lines of change more clearly if we recall that the Industrial Revolution was not a settled social context but a phase of transition between two ways of life. And we must see, not one "typical" community, but many different communities coexisting with each other. . . . In all of these communities there were a number of converging influences at work, all making towards discipline and the growth in working-class consciousness.

The working-class community of the early 19th century was the product neither of paternalism nor of Methodism, but in a high degree of conscious working-class endeavour. In Manchester or Newcastle the traditions of the trade union and the friendly society, with their emphasis upon self-discipline and community purpose, reach far back into the 18th century. Rules which survive of the Manchester small-ware weavers in the 1750s show already meticulous attention to procedure and to institutional etiquette. The committee members must sit in a certain order. The doors must be kept locked. There are careful regulations for the safe-keeping of the "box." Members are reminded that "Intemperance, Animosity and Profaneness are the Pest and Vermin that gnaw out the very Vitals of all Society."

> If we consider this Society, not as a Company of Men met to regale themselves with Ale and Tobacco, and talk indifferently on all Subjects: but rather as a Society sitting to Protect the Rights and Privileges of a Trade by which some hundreds of People . . . subsist . . . How awkward does it look to see its Members jumbled promiscuously one amongst another, talking differently on all Subjects.

From E. P. Thompson, *The Making of the Working Class*. New York: Vintage, 1963. Excerpts from pp. 418–29. Copyright © 1963 by E. P. Thompson. Reprinted by permission of Pantheon Books, a Division of Random House, Inc. and Victor Gollancz, Ltd.

"Decency and Regularity" are the watchwords; it is even hoped that when "Gentlemen and Magistrates" observe such order "they will rather revere than punish such a Society."

This represents the code of the self-respecting artisan, although the hope that such sobriety would win the favour of the authorities was to be largely disappointed. It was in a similar school that such men as Hardy and Place received their education in London. But as the Industrial Revolution advanced, it was this code (sometimes in the form of model rules) which was extended to ever-wider sections of working people. Small tradesmen, artisans, labourers – all sought to insure themselves against sickness, unemployment, or funeral expenses[1] through membership [in] "box clubs" or friendly societies. But the discipline essential for the safe-keeping of funds, the orderly conduct of meetings, and the determination of disputed cases involved an effort of self-rule as great as the new disciplines of work. An examination of rules and orders of friendly societies in existence in Newcastle and [other] district[s] during the Napoleonic Wars gives us a list of fines and penalties more exacting then those of a Bolton cotton-master. A General Society imposed fines for any member "reflecting upon" another member in receipt of sick money, being drunk on the Sabbath, striking another, "calling one another bye-names," coming into the clubroom in liquor, taking God's name in vain. The Brotherhood of Malsters added fines for drunkenness at any time, or for failure to attend the funerals of brothers or of their wives. The Glass-Makers (founded as early as 1755) added fines for failure in attending meetings or for those who refused to take their turn in the rota of officers; for failing to keep silence when ordered, speaking together, answering back the steward, betting in the club, or (a common rule) disclosing secrets outside the society. Futher:

> Persons that are infamous, of ill character, quarrelsome, or disorderly, shall not be admitted into this society. . . . No Pitman, Collier, Sinker, or Waterman to be admitted.

The Waterman, not to be outdone, added a rule excluding from benefits any brother sick through "any illness got by lying with an unclean woman, or is clap't or pox'd." Brothers were to be fined for ridiculing or provoking each other to passion. The Unanimous Society was to cut off benefits if any member in receipt of sick money was found "in ale-houses,

1. Working-people attached an exceptional valuation to the ceremony of funeral. A pauper funeral was the ultimate social disgrace. And ceremony bulked large in folk-lore and preoccupied dying men. "I could wish," wrote a condemned Luddite, "for John Rawson, John Roberts, and John Roper to be my bearers; dear wife, choose the other three thyself" (*The Surprising . . . History of "General Ludd"* [Nottingham, n.d.], p. 239).

gaming, or drunk." To maintain its unanimity there were fines for members proposing "discourse or dispute upon political or ecclesiastical matters, or government and governors." The Friendly Society of All Trades had a rule similar to "huffing" in draughts; there was a fine "if any member has an opportunity of fining his brother, and does not." The Cordwainers added fines for calling for drink or tobacco without leave of the stewards. The House-Carpenters and Joiners added a prohibition of "disloyal sentiments" or "political songs."

It is possible that some of these rules, such as the prohibition of political discourse and songs, should be taken with a pinch of salt. While some of these societies were select sick-clubs of as few as twenty or thirty artisans, meeting at an inn, others were probably covers for trade union activity; while at Newcastle, as at Sheffield, it is possible that after the Two Acts the formation of friendly societies was used as a cover for Jacobin organisation. (A "company" friendly society, in 1816, bore testimony to "the loyal, patriotic, and peaceable regulations" of many Newcastle societies, but complained that these regulations were often insufficient to prevent "warm debate and violent language.") The authorities were deeply suspicious of the societies during the war years, and one of the purposes of the rules was to secure registration with the local magistrates. But anyone familiar with procedure and etiquette in some trade unions and working-men's clubs today will recognise the origin of still-extant practices in several of the rules. Taken together, they indicate an attainment of self-discipline and a diffusion of experience of a truly impressive order.

Estimates of friendly society membership suggest 648,000 in 1793, 704,350 in 1803, 925,429 in 1815. Although registration with the magistrates, under the first Friendly Society Act of 1793, made possible the protection of funds at law in the event of defaulting officers, a large but unknown number of clubs failed to register, either through hostility to the authorities, parochial inertia, or through a deep secretiveness which, Dr. Holland found, was still strong enough to baffle his enquiries in Sheffield in the early 1840s. Nearly all societies before 1815 bore a strictly local and self-governing character, and they combined the functions of sick insurance with convivial club nights and annual "outings" or feasts. An observer in 1805 witnessed near Matlock –

> ... about fifty women preceded by a solitary fiddler playing a merry tune. This was a female benefit society, who had been to hear a sermon at Eyam, and were going to dine together, a luxury which our female benefit society at Sheffield does not indulge in, having tea only, and generally singing, dancing, smoking, and negus.

Few of the members of friendly societies had a higher social status than that of clerks or small tradesmen; most were artisans. The fact that each brother had funds deposited in the society made for stability in membership and watchful participation in self-government. They had almost no middle-class membership and, while some employers looked upon them favourably, their actual conduct left little room for paternalist control. Failures owing to actuarial inexperience were common, defaulting officers not infrequent. Diffused through every part of the country, they were (often heartbreaking) schools of experience.

In the very secretiveness of the friendly society, and in its opaqueness under upper-class scrutiny, we have authentic evidence of the growth of independent working-class culture and institutions. This was the subculture out of which the less stable trade unions grew, and in which trade union officers were trained.[2] Union rules, in many cases, were more elaborate versions of the same code of conduct as the sick club. Sometimes, as in the case of the Woolcombers, this was supplemented by the procedures of secret masonic orders:

> Strangers, the design of all our Lodges is love and unity,
> With self-protection founded on the laws of equity,
> And when you have our mystic rights gone through,
> Our secrets all will be disclosed to you.

After the 1790s, under the impact of the Jacobin agitation, the preambles to friendly society rules assume a new resonance; one of the strangest consequences of the language of "social man" of the philosophical Enlightenment is its reproduction in the rules of obscure clubs meeting in the taverns or "hush-shops" of industrial England. On Tyneside "Social" and "Philanthropic" societies expressed their aspirations in terms which ranged from throw-away phrases – "a sure, lasting, and loving society," "to promote friendship and true Christian charity," "man was not born for himself alone" – to more thundering philosophical affirmations:

> Man, by the construction of his body, and the disposition of his mind, is a creature formed for society. . . .
> We, the members of this society, taking it into our serious consideration, that man is formed a social being . . . in continual need of mutual assistance and support; and having interwoven in our constitutions those humane and sympathetic af-

2. It was a continual complaint of the authorities that friendly societies allowed members to withdraw funds when on strike. Macclesfield was described in 1812 as "a nest of illicit association, full of sick and burial societies which are the germ of revolution" (C. S. Davies, *History of Macclesfield* [*Manchester*, 1961], p. 180).

fections which we always feel at the distress of any of our
fellow creatures. . . .

The friendly societies, found in so many diverse communities, were a
unifying cultural influence. Although for financial and legal reasons they
were slow to federate themselves, they facilitated regional and national
trade union federation. Their language of "social man" also made towards the growth in working-class consciousness. It joined the language
of Christian charity and the slumbering imagery of "brotherhood" in the
Methodist (and Moravian) tradition with the social affirmations of
Owenite socialism. Many early Owenite societies and stores prefaced
their rules with the line from Isaiah (XLI, 6): "They helped every one his
neighbour; and every one said to his brother, be of good courage." By the
1830s there were in circulation a score of friendly society or trade union
hymns and songs which elaborated this theme.

Mr. Raymond Williams has suggested that "the crucial distinguishing
element in English life since the Industrial Revolution is . . . between
alternative ideas of the nature of social relationship." As contrasted with
middle-class ideas of individualism or (at their best) of service, "what is
properly meant by 'working-class culture' . . . is the basic collective idea,
and the institutions, manners, habits of thought, and intentions which
proceed from this." Friendly societies did not "proceed from" an idea;
both the ideas and the institutions arose in response to certain common
experiences. But the distinction is important. In the simple cellular structure of the friendly society, with its workaday ethos of mutual aid, we can
see many features which were reproduced in more sophisticated and
complex forms in trade unions, co-operatives, Hampden Clubs, Political
Unions, and Chartist lodges. At the same time the societies can be seen as
crystallising an ethos of mutuality very much more widely diffused in the
"dense" and "concrete" particulars of the personal relations of working
people, at home and at work. Every kind of witness in the first half of the
19th century – clergymen, factory inspectors, Radical publicists – remarked upon the extent of mutual aid in the poorest districts. In times of
emergency, unemployment, strikes, sickness, childbirth, then it was the
poor who "helped every one his neighbour." Twenty years after Place's
comment on the change in Lancashire manners, Cooke Taylor was as-
tounded at the way in which Lancashire working men bore "the extreme
of wretchedness":

> with a high tone of moral dignity, a marked sense of propriety,
> a decency, cleanliness, and order . . . which do not merit the
> intense suffering I have witnessed. I was beholding the gradual
> immolation of the noblest and most valuable population that
> ever existed in this country or in any other under heaven.

"Nearly all the distressed operatives whom I met north of Manchester . . . had a thorough horror of being forced to receive parish relief."

It is an error to see this as the only effective "working-class" ethic. The "aristocratic" aspirations of artisans and mechanics, the values of "self-help," or criminality and demoralisation, were equally widely dispersed. The conflict between alternative ways of life was fought out, not just between the middle and working classes, but within working-class communities themselves. But by the early years of the 19th century it is possible to say that collectivist values are dominant in many industrial communities; there is a definite moral code, with sanctions against the backleg, the "tools" of the employer or the un-neighbourly, and with an intolerance towards the eccentric or individualist. Collectivist values are consciously held and are propagated in political theory, trade union ceremonial, moral rhetoric. It is, indeed, this collective self-consciousness, with its corresponding theory, institutions, discipline, and community values which distinguishes the 19th-century working class from the 18th-century mob.

Political Radicalism and Owenism both drew upon and enriched this "basic collectivist idea." Francis Place may well have been right when he attributed the changed behaviour of Lancashire crowds in 1819 to the advance of political consciousness "spreading over the face of the country ever since the Constitutional and Corresponding Societies became active in 1792":

> Now 100,000 people may be collected together and no riot
> ensue, and why?. . . . The people have an object, the pursuit of
> which gives them importance in their own eyes, elevates them
> in their own opinion, and thus it is that the very individuals
> who would have been the leaders of the riot are the keepers of
> the peace.

Another observer attributed the changes in Lancashire to the influence both of Cobbett and of the Sunday schools and noted a "general and radical change" in the character of the labouring classes:

> The poor, when suffering and dissatisfied, no longer make a
> riot, but hold a meeting – instead of attacking their neigh-
> bours, they arraign the Ministry.

This growth in self-respect and political consciousness was one real gain of the Industrial Revolution. It dispelled some forms of superstition and of deference, and made certain kinds of oppression no longer tolerable. We can find abundant testimony as to the steady growth of the ethos of mutuality in the strength and ceremonial pride of the unions and trades clubs which emerged from quasi-legality when the Combination Acts were repealed. During the Bradford woolcombers' strike of 1825 we find that in Newcastle, where the friendly society was so well rooted, the unions contributing to the Bradford funds included smiths, mill-wrights, joiners, shoemakers, morocco leather dressers, cabinet-makers, ship-wrights, sawyers, tailors, wool-combers, hatters, tanners, weavers, pot-ters, and miners. Moreover, there is a sense in which the friendly society helped to pick up and carry into the trade union movement the love of ceremony and the high sense of status of the craftsman's guild. These traditions, indeed, still had a remarkable vigour in the early 19th century in some of the old Chartered Companies or Guilds of the masters and of master-craftsmen, whose periodical ceremonies expressed the pride of both the masters and of their journeymen in "the Trade." In 1802, for example, there was a great jubilee celebration of the Preston "Guilds." In a week of processions and exhibitions, in which the nobility, gentry, merchants, shopkeepers, and manufacturers all took part, the journey-men were given a prominent place:

> The Wool-Combers and Cotton Workers . . . were preceded by twenty-four young blooming handsome women, each bearing a branch of the cotton tree, then followed a spinning machine borne on men's shoulders, and afterwards a loom drawn on a sledge, each with work-people busily employed at them. . . .

At Bradford, on the eve of the great strike of 1825, the wool-combers' feast of Bishop Blaize was celebrated with extra-ordinary splendour:

> Twenty-four Woolstaplers on horseback, each horse caparisoned
> with a fleece.
> Thirty-eight Worsted-Spinners and Manufacturers on horse-back, in white stuff waiscoats [sic], with each a sliver of wool over his shoulder and a white stuff sash: the horses' necks covered with nests made of thick yarn.

And so on until we reach:

BISHOP BLAIZE
Shepherd and Shepherdess.
Shepherd-Swains.
One hundred and sixty Woolsorters on horseback, with ornamented
caps and various coloured slivers.
Thirty Comb-makers.
Charcoal Burners.
Combers' Colours.

Band.
Four hundred and seventy Wool-combers, with wool wigs, &c.
Band.
Forty Dyers, with red cockades, blue aprons, and crossed slivers
of red and blue.

After the great strike such a ceremony could not be repeated.

This passage from the old outlook of "the Trade" to the duality of the masters' organisations, on the one hand, and the trade unions on the other, takes us into the central experience of the Industrial Revolution. But the friendly society and trade union, not less than the organisations of the masters, sought to maintain the ceremonial and the pride of the older tradition; indeed, since the artisans (or, as they still are called, *tradesmen*) felt themselves to be the *producers* upon whose skill the masters were parasitic, they emphasised the tradition the more. With the repeal of the Combination Acts their banners moved openly through the streets. In London, in 1825, the Thames Ship Caulkers Union (founded in 1794) displayed its mottos: "Main et Coeur," "Vigeur, Verite, Concorde, Depeche," which reveal the pride of the medieval craft. The Ropemakers Union proceeded with a white banner on which was portrayed a swarm of bees around a hive: "Sons of Industry! Union gives Strength." (At the houses of masters who had granted them an increase, they stopped and gave a salute.) John Gast's Thames Shipwrights Provident Union, the pacemaker of the London "trades," outdid all with a blue silk banner: "Hearts of Oak Protect the Aged," a handsome ship drawn by six bay horses, three postillions in blue jackets, a band, the Committee, the members with more banners and flags, and delegations representing the trade from Shields, Sunderland, and Newcastle. The members wore blue rosettes and sprigs of oak, and in the ship were old shipwrights who lived in the union's alms-houses at Stepney. At Nantwich in 1832 the shoemakers maintained all the sense of status of the artisan's craft union, with their banner, "full set of secret order regalia, surplices, trimmed aprons . . . and a crown and robes for King Crispin." In 1833 the King rode on horseback through the town attended by train-bearers, officers with the "Dispensation, the Bible, a large pair of gloves, and also beautiful specimens of ladies' and gents' boots and shoes":

> Nearly 500 joined in the procession, each one wearing a white
> apron neatly trimmed. The rear was brought up by a
> shopmate in full tramping order, his kit packed on his back,
> and walking-stick in hand.

No single explanation will suffice to account for the evident alteration in manner of the working people. Nor should we exaggerate the degree of change. Drunkenness and uproar still often surged through the streets. But it is true that working men often appear most sober and disciplined, in the twenty years after the Wars, when most in earnest to assert their rights. Thus we cannot accept the thesis that sobriety was the consequence only, or even mainly, of the Evangelical propaganda. And we may see this, also, if we turn the coin over and look at the reverse. By 1830 not only the Established Church but also the Methodist revival was meeting sharp opposition in most working-class centres from free-thinkers, Owenites, and non-denominational Christians. In London, Birmingham, southeast Lancashire, Newcastle, Leeds, and other cities the Deist adherents of Carlile or Owen had an enormous following. The Methodists had consolidated their position, but they tended increasingly to represent tradesmen and privileged groups of workers, and to be morally isolated from working-class community life. Some old centres of revivalism had relapsed into "heathenism." In Newcastle's Sandgate, once "as noted for praying as for tippling, for psalm-singing as for swearing," the Methodists had lost any following among the poor by the 1840s. In parts of Lancashire, weaving communities as well as factory operatives became largely detached from the chapels and were swept up in the current of Owenism and free-thought:

> If it had not been for Sunday schools, society would have been in a horrible state before this time. . . . Infidelity is growing amazingly. . . . The writings of Carlile [sic] and Taylor and other infidels are more read than the Bible or any other book. . . . I have seen weeks after weeks the weavers assembled in a room, that would contain 400 people, to applaud the people who asserted and argued that there was no God. . . . I have gone into the cottages around the chapel where I worship, I have found 20 men assembled reading infidel publications. . . .

Owenite and secular movements often took fire "like whins [sic] on the common," as revivalism had done before.

Engels, writing from his Lancashire experience in 1844, claimed that "the workers are not religious, and do not attend church," with the exception of the Irish, "a few elderly people, and the half-bourgeois, the overlookers, foremen, and the like." "Among the masses there prevails almost universally a total indifference to religion, or at the utmost, some trace of Deism. . . ." Engels weakened his case by overstating it; but Dodd quoted a Stockport factory where nine out of ten did not attend any church, while Cooke Taylor, in 1842, was astonished at the vigour and knowledge of the Scriptures shown by Lancashire working men who contested Christian orthodoxies. "If I thought that the Lord was the cause of all the misery I see around me," one such man told a Methodist preacher, "I would quit his service, and say he was not the Lord I took him for." Similarly, in Newcastle in the Chartist years thousands of artisans and engineers were convinced free-thinkers. In one works employing 200 "there are not more than six or seven who attend a place of worship." "The working classes," said one working-man,

> are gathering knowledge, and the more they gather, the wider becomes the breach between them and the different sects. It is not because they are ignorant of the Bible. I revere the Bible myself . . . and when I look into it . . . I find that the prophets stood between the oppressor and the oppressed, and denounced the wrong doer, however rich and powerful. . . .
> When the preachers go back to the old book, I for one will go back to hear them, but not till then. . . .

The Sunday schools were bringing an unexpected harvest.

The weakening hold of the churches by no means indicated any erosion of the self-respect and discipline of class. On the contrary, Manchester and Newcastle, with their long tradition of industrial and political organisation, were notable in the Chartist years for the discipline of their massive demonstrations. Where the citizens and shopkeepers had once been thrown into alarm when the "terrible and savage pitmen" entered Newcastle in any force, it now became necessary for the coal-owners to scour the slums of the city for "candy-men" or rag-collectors to evict the striking miners. In 1838 and 1839 tens of thousands of artisans, miners, and labourers marched week after week in good order through the streets, often passing within a few feet of the military, and avoiding all provocation. "Our people had been well taught," one of their leaders recalled, "that it was not riot we wanted, but revolution."

17

Masculinity and factory labor

Paul Willis

In what sense can we link work with culture? It is one of the fundamental paradoxes of our social life that when we are at our most natural, our most *everyday,* we are also at our most cultural; that when we are in roles that look the most obvious and given, we are actually in roles that are constructed, learned, and far from inevitable. Whenever we are under pressure, late, worried; whenever there is little time for self-reflection, pretence; whenever we are pushed and thankful for any role, any role, to get us through time and the hour: then it seems we act in the obvious single way, the way dictated by "reality." So too with work – for many, *dead* time, human time sold for the possibility of a real life later: It seems the most obvious and self-evident category of human experience, the area where manners, culture, and artifice intervene least into our daily existence.

This view is wrong not because it mistakes the nature of work, but because it mistakes the nature of *culture.* Culture is not artifice and manners, the preserve of Sunday best, rainy afternoons, and concert halls. It is the very material of our daily lives, the bricks and mortar of our most commonplace understandings, feelings, and responses. We rely on cultural patterns and symbols for the minute, and unconscious, social reflexes that make us social and collective beings: We are therefore most *deeply* embedded in our culture when we are at our most natural and spontaneous: if you like, at our most work-a-day. As soon as we think, as soon as we see life as parts in a play, we are in a very important sense, already, one step away from our real and living culture.

Clearly this is a special use of the concept of culture. In part it can be thought of as an anthropological use of the term, where not only the special, heightened, and separate forms of experience, but *all* experiences, and especially as they lie around central life struggles and activities, are taken as the proper focus of a cultural analysis.

From Willis in John Clarke et al., eds., *Working Class Culture.* London: Hutchinson, 1979. Excerpts from pp. 185–98. Reprinted with permission.

Given this perspective, it should be clear that not only can work be analysed from a cultural point of view, but that it must occupy a *central* place in any full sense of culture. Most people spend their prime waking hours at work, base their identity on work activities, and are defined by others essentially through their relation to work. . . .

There is then no question, for me, of counterposing the "cultural" with the "productive" or the "real," as if the former had no actual constitutive role in the basic social relations which govern the form of our society. I am arguing against a *trivialization* of the notion of culture, of working-class culture, and especially of its central domain: cultural relations/ struggles/forms at the point of production. Culture is not simply a *response* to imposition which blinds or blunts a "proper" understanding, nor is it merely a compensation, an adjustment to defeat – these are essentially mechanized, reactive models. Cultural forms occupy precisely those same spaces and human potentialities which are fought over by capital to continue valorization and capital accumulation. There are different logics possible in the direct experience of production than are posed in the capital relation itself, for itself. Merely because capital would like to treat workers as robots does not mean they are robots. The direct experiences of production are worked through and over in the praxis of different cultural discourses. To be sure, these discourses do not arise purely on the basis of production, and many of their important contents and inner relationships arise from or in articulation with external forces and institutions: the family, state, labour organizations, etc. It is also clear that in this society, for the moment, the material consequences of these cultural forms are for continued production in the capitalist mode. But none of this should blind us to the complexities, struggles, and tensions on the shop floor even if they do not always call their name in a way which we can recognize. There are forms of praxis arising from definite human agency at the site of production which, in the very same moment, provide the conditions for capitalist relations and also partially penetrate and variably challenge those relationships.

It is also specifically working-class cultural forces from the place of production which help to mould the whole of the class culture. Production is not simply the engine house of the social totality producing, some- how, its "effects" elsewhere on the social plane. Production, and its rela- tions, is social and cultural to its very roots, to its very surface. It is the privileged site and generator of working-class culture both because of its massive presence and also because the struggle there fixes, organizes in a particular combination, those discourses and external influences which play over the place of work – helping to develop them in a particular way, clinching certain features, even when appearing manifestly outside of production. Work is where the demands of capital must be met, from the resources not simply of potential *abstract* labour but from concrete, cultural forms of labour power. Whatever "free" play there is in cultural forms articulates always around this most central point of reference. Non-work supplies many of the categories and meanings for work, but it can only be understood in relation to work and is finally shaped by it.

The system of capitalism still means essentially, despite its contemporary "human face," that labour is bought, detached from the individual, and directed towards the production of commodities for the profit of others. Labour is dispossessed from its owners. This labour is directed, emphatically, not for the satisfaction of its providers but for the profit of its new owners. If this requires work in inhuman and meaningless circumstances, then, there is nothing in the logic of capitalism to prevent this.

Although distinctions must be made for region and occupation, the absolutely central thing about the working-class culture of the shop floor is, however, that despite the dispossession, despite the bad conditions, despite the external directions, despite the subjective ravages, people do look for meaning, they do impose frameworks, they do seek enjoyment in activity, they do exercise their abilities. They repossess, symbolically and really, aspects of their experience and capacities. They do, paradoxically, thread through the dead experience of work a living culture which isn't simply a reflex of defeat. This culture is not the human remains of a mechanical depradation, but a positive transformation of experience and a celebration of shared values in symbols, artifacts, and objects. It allows people to recognize and even to develop themselves. For this working-class culture of work is not simply a foam padding, a rubber layer between humans and unpleasantness. It is an appropriation in its own right, an exercise of skill, a motion, an activity applied towards an end. It has this specifically human characteristic even in conditions of hardship and oppression.

What are the elements of this culture? In the first place, there is the sheer mental and physical bravery of surviving in hostile conditions and doing difficult work on intractable materials. It is easy to romanticize this element, of course, and in one way it is simply charting the degree of brutality a heavy work situation can inflict. But it another way it is the first and specifically human response – the holding of an apparently endless and threatening set of demands by sheer strength and brute skill. Already in this there is a stature and self-respect, a human stake on the table against the relentless pressure of work to be done. This is the vital precondition of more developed cultural forms and accomplishes the basic and primitive humanization of a situation: It marks a kind of limit of dispossession. It halts the rout of human meaning and takes a kind of control so that more specifically creative acts can follow. This primitivist base of work experience is also the material for a crude pride and, as will be developed much more fully later, for the mythology of masculine reputation – to be strong and to be known for it. Here is a retired steel-man describing the furnaces in a steel-making area of the west of Scotland as they were before World War II:

> They were the cold, metal, hand-charging sort and they ca-tered for strong men, only very strong men. About one steel worker in every ten could stand up to them successfully, which was one reason why the furnacemen were looked up to in the world of heavy industry. That they got the biggest pay packets was another reason. They also had the biggest thirsts and that too was a prideful possession in that part of the world [. . .] a legend grew up about the steel smelters [. . .] The whole dis-trict and for miles beyond it was a hotbed of steel works, iron puddling works and coal mines. It was a place given over to the worship of strength and durability. Indeed it needed strength to look at it, and durability to live in it.[1]

In a much less articulate way, but for that perhaps more convincing, the following extract shows the same elemental self-esteem in the doing of a hard job well. It also shows that in some respects the hard environment can become the most natural environment. There is also the grudging recognition of the profound change this kind of acclimatization can make on a normal social life, even at the same time that it is one of the major ways in which the hostile work environment is made habitable. This is a foundry man talking at home about his work:

> I work in a foundry . . . you know, drop forging . . . do you know anything about it . . . no . . . well you have the factory know the factory down down in Rolfe Street, with the noise . . . you can hear it in the street . . . I work there on the big hammer . . . it's a six-tonner. I've worked there twenty-four years now. It's bloody noisy but I've got used to it now . . . and its hot . . . I don't get bored . . . there's always new lines coming and you have to work out the best way of doing it. . . . You have to keep going . . . and it's heavy work, the managers couldn't do it, there's not many strong enough to keep lifting the metal . . . I earn eighty, ninety pounds a week, and that's not bad is it? . . . it ain't easy like . . . you can definitely say that I earn every penny of it . . . you have to keep it up you know. And the managing director, I'd say "hello" to him you know, and the progress manager . . . they'll come around and I'll go . . . "all right" [thumbs up] . . . and

1. R. Fraser (ed.) *Work 2* (London: Penguin, 1969), pp. 56–7.

they know you, you know . . . a group standing there watching you . . . working . . . I like that . . . there's something there . . . watching you like . . . working . . . like that . . . you have to keep going to get enough out . . . that place depends on what you produce [. . .]. You get used to the noise, they say I'm deaf and ignorant here, but it's not that I'm deaf like . . . it's that you can hold a conversation better, talk, hear what people say better at work . . . I can always hear what they say there. I can talk easy, it's easier . . . yet in the house here, you've got to make . . . pronunciations is it? Yeah, you've got to like, say the word, say it clearly, and that's hard sometimes . . . sometimes I can't hear straight away . . . they say, "you silly deaf old codger" . . . it's not that . . . it's just . . . well, it's just getting used to the noise. I can hear perfectly well in the factory. . . . If I see two managers at the end of the shop, I know, like I know just about what they're saying to each other.

It may be objected that the pattern of industrial work has changed: There are no rough jobs today. Besides, it can certainly be argued that there is nothing heroic about the elemental qualities of strength and pride. They are not only made anachronistic by today's technology but are insulting, oppressive, and right at the poisonous heart of male chauvinism and archaic machismo.

Be that as it may, two things are clear. Rough, unpleasant, demanding jobs do still exist in considerable numbers. A whole range of jobs from building work to furnace work to deep-sea fishing still involve a primitive confrontation with exacting physical tasks. Secondly, the basic attitudes and values developed in such jobs are still very important in the general working-class culture, and particularly the culture of the shop floor; this importance is vastly out of proportion to the number of people actually involved in such heavy work. Even in so-called light industries, or in highly mechanized factories with perhaps mixed-sex work forces, where the awkwardness of the physical task has long since been reduced, the metaphoric figures of strength and bravery *worked through* masculinity and reputation still move beneath the more varied, visible forms of workplace culture.

Let us go on from this general minimum proposition to look at some of the more specific and developed human patterns of the workplace. One of the marks of the lived and contemporary culture of the shop floor is a development of this half-mythical primitive confrontation with the *task*. It is a familiarity and experiential sense of control of technology, or at least sharing of its power. At the most positive and extreme this can be not merely a meeting of demands, but a strange kind of celebration. Here is a description from a toolmaker of his first day at work.[2] It inverts the usual middle-class account of the dark satanic mill:

> On every piece of open ground lay metal shapes; some mere bars and sheets straight from the steelworks: others gigantic welded constructs covered in a deep brown rust. . . . Then I entered the great main workshops. Each chamber, or aisle as they were called, was about 150 feet across and anything between 500 and 700 hundred yards long. Several of these great vulcan halls lay parallel to each other [. . .] Over head rolled the girded cranes capable of carrying weights of more than two hundred tons [. . .] one passed over my head. [. . .] My startled attitude to the crane's passage amused the men at work [. . .] a series of catcalls followed my passage down the aisle. Mostly the shouts were good-natured advice to get out of the plant while I had the youth to do so. Such advice never even penetrated my outer consciousness, for how could anyone abhor this great masculine domain with its endless overtones of power and violence?

Of course this is a special case of a skilled, elitist view of work. Changes in the labour process are no doubt squeezing out the space for such views. But we should not underestimate the surviving degree to which mechanical, sensuous, and concrete *familiarity* with the tools of production (despite the dispossession of labour) mediates the demands of the labour process, allowing, for instance, the possibility of an easy and confident mobility which at least brings alleviating changes in the *form* of particular work experience, if not in its deep structures.

Even, or perhaps especially, among the formally "un/semi/skilled" there is a process of obtaining skills as if by osmosis from the technical environment. There is a profound air of competence in the culture of the shop floor, a competence which always exists prior to the particular situation. It is not always based on strict ability, but mixed in with cheek and confidence; it is enough to pull a worker through any number of jobs and problems. Here is a man talking about his industrial career. He gives us a glimpse of the real paths beaten between different jobs and occupations: the paths, incidentally, which make it sensible to speak of the working class not only as an abstract group of those who share similar interests, but as at least something of a self-experienced organic whole with real and used inner connections:

2. Ibid., pp. 22–3.

Well, I've got four trades really, you know I've only been in this job seven weeks. I'm in a foundry now [. . .] on the track you know [. . .]. I was a metal polisher before. It's a dirty job, but it pays good money, and a skilled job, you know metal polishing.[. . .] Yes and I was a fitter down at drop forgings, as well, well I mean in the situation today, you've got to go where the money is. Polishing is the best money, but it's up and down, there was four or five months run of work and then it 'ud go dead [. . .] I got out of it didn't I. [. . .] Friend o'mine got me a job down at the MMC. [. . .] I've worked in a garage, er . . . I worked for the council paper-hanging and decorating, I worked for a fella . . . chimney sweeping in the winter, decorating and painting in the summer and all this but I've always took an interest in what I've been doing you know, I mean, I'm pretty adaptable, put it that way you know. [. . .] I've always had a motor of my own, and I've always done me own repairs, whenever I've broken me motor, only through experience doing it meself. [. . .] Paper hanging, decorating, I've got an in-law ain't I, that's a decorator, give me a lot of tips you know. [. . .] I bluffed me way in to decorating. I said I was a decorator you know, went to work for the council. Actually I subcontracted for the council, and they give an house to do, an empty house, and I done it see. Course the inspector come round from the council and they was satisfied with the work, you know, so you know if the inspector's satisfied, you're all right see. It's only common sense really.

In one sense this can be seen as a way of regaining some control over one's labour power and its disposition. This leads us to another important element in shop-floor culture: the massive attempt to gain informal control of the work process. Limitation of output or "systematic soldiering" and "gold bricking" have been observed from the particular perspective of management from Taylor onwards, but there is evidence now of a more concerted – though still informal – attempt to gain control. In many plants the men, themselves, to all intents and purposes actually control at least manning and the speed of production. Of course the downward limit for this possibility is set by the production of the costs of subsistence of the worker. If control is exerted on production it is indeed a control of minima as well as of maxima. Nevertheless the exertion towards control should not be minimized. Here is a man on track production of car engines:

Actually the foreman, the gaffer, don't run the place, the men run the place. See, I mean you get one of the chaps says, "All

right, you'm on so and so today." You can't argue with him.
The gaffer don't give you the job, the men on the track give
you the job, they swop each other about, tek it in turns. Ah,
but I mean the work's done. If the gaffer had gi'd you the job
you would. . . . They tried to do it one morning, gi'd a chap a
job you know, but he'd been on it, you know, I think he'd
been on all week, and they just downed tools.[. . .] There's
four hard jobs on the track and there's dozens that's . . . you
know, a child of five could do it, quite honestly, but everybody
has their turn. That's organized by the men.

This tendency rests on the social force most basically of the informal
group. It is the zone where strategies for wresting control of symbolic and
real space from official authority are generated and disseminated. It is the
massive presence of this informal organization which most decisively
marks off shop-floor culture from middle-class cultures of work.

Amongst workers it is also the basis for extensive bartering, "arranging
foreigners," and "fiddling." "Winning" materials is widespread on the
shop floor and is endorsed by implicit informal criteria. Ostracism is the
punishment for not maintaining the integrity of this world against the
persistent intrusions of the formal.

A foreman is like, you know what I mean, they're trying to
get on, they're trying to get up. They'd cut everybody's throat
to get there. You get people like this in the factory. Course
these people cop it in the neck off the workers, they do all the
tricks under the sun. You know what I mean, they don't like
to see anyone crawlin'.[. . .] Course instead of taking one pair
of glasses from the stores Jim had two, you see, and a couple
of masks and about six pairs o'gloves. Course this Martin was
watching and actually two days after we found out that he'd
told the foreman see. Had 'im, Jim, in the office about it, the
foreman did, and,[. . .] well I mean, his life hasn't been worth
livin has it? Eh, nobody speaks to him, they won't give him a
light, nobody'll give him a light for his fag or nothin'. . . .
Well, he won't do it again, he won't do it again. I mean he
puts his kettle on, on the stove of a morning, so they knock it
off, don't they, you know, tek all his water out, put sand in,
all this kind of thing [. . .] if he cum to the gaffer, "Some-
body's knocked me water over" or, er, "They put sand in me
cup," and all this business, "Who is it then? "I don't know
who it is." He'll never find out who it is.

Another clear aspect of shop-floor culture is the distinctive form of language use and a highly developed form of intimidatory humour. Many

verbal exchanges on the shop floor are not serious or about work activities. They are jokes, or "piss-takes," or "kiddings," or "windups." There is a real skill in being able to use this language with fluency: to identify the points on which you are being "kidded" and to have appropriate responses ready in order to avoid further baiting.

This badinage is necessarily difficult to record on tape or to represent, but the highly distinctive ambience it gives to shop-floor exchanges is widely recognized by those involved, and to some extent recreated in their accounts of it. Here is a foundry worker:

> Oh, there's all sorts, millions of them [jokes]. "Want to hear what he said about you," and he never said a thing, you know. Course you know the language at the work like. "What you been saying about me?" "I said nothing" "Oh you're a bloody liar," and all this.

Associated with this concrete and expressive verbal humour is a well developed physical humour: essentially the practical joke. These jokes are vigorous, sharp, sometimes cruel, and often hinge around prime tenets of the culture such as disruption of production or subversion of the boss's authority and status. Here is the track worker again:

> They play jokes on you, blokes knocking the clamps off the boxes, they put paste on the bottom of the hammer you know, soft little thing, puts his hammer down, picks it up, gets a handful of paste, you know, all this. So he comes up and gets a syringe and throws it in the big bucket of paste, and it's about that deep, and it goes right to the bottom, you have to put your hand in and get it out. . . . This is a filthy trick, but they do it. [. . .] They asked, the gaffers asked Charlie to make the tea. Well it's fifteen years he's been there and they say "go and make the tea." He goes up to toilet, he wets in the teapot, then makes the tea. I mean, you know, this is the truth this is you know. He says, you know, "I'll piss in it if I mek it, if they've asked me to mek it" [. . .] so he goes up, wees in the pot, then he puts the tea bag, then he puts the hot water in. [. . .] He was bad the next morning, one of the gaffers, "My stomach isn't half upset this morning." He told them after and they called him for everything, "You ain't makin' our tea no more." He says "I know I ain't not now."

Another important element of this culture is the massive feeling on the shop floor, and in the working class generally, that practice is more important than theory. As a big handwritten sign, borrowed from the back of a matchbox and put up by one of the workers, announces on one shop floor: "An ounce of keenness is worth a whole library of certificates." The shop floor abounds with apocryphal stories about the idiocy of purely theoretical knowledge. Practical ability always comes first and is a *condition* of other kinds of knowledge. Whereas in middle-class culture knowledge and qualifications are seen as a way of shifting upwards the whole mode of practical alternatives open to an individual, in working-class eyes theory is riveted to particular productive practices. If it cannot earn its keep there, it is to be rejected. Here is a man currently working as a metal polisher:

> In Toll End Road, there's a garage, and I used to work part time there and . . . there's an elderly fellow there, been a mechanic all his life, and he must have been seventy years of age then. He was an old Indconsville professional, been a professional boxer once, an elderly chap and he was a practical man, he was practical, right? . . . and he told me this. [. . .] I was talking to him, was talking about something like this, he says. [. . .] "This chap was all theory and he sends away for books about everything," and he says "Do you know," he says, "he sent away for a book once and it came in a wooden box, and it's still in that box 'cos he can't open it." Now that in't true, is it? But the point is true. That i'nt true, that didn't happen, but his point is right. He can't get at that book 'cos he don't know how to open the box! Now what's the good of that? . . .

Perhaps the most prosaic but actually startling element of shop-floor culture is the articulation of manual labour power – as it is concretely practised – with assertive male gender definitions. There is an infusion of assertive masculine style and meaning into the primitive, mythologized elements of confrontation with "the task." It is also a masculine *expressivity* which often delivers or makes possible some of the *concrete* revelatory or oppositional cultural practices we have considered: resistance to authority; control through the group; humour and language; distrust of theory. There are profound implications here for the *internal* (to production) disorganisation of a proper recognition of the nature and capitalist use of labour power and for *external* gender definitions and forms of family life. The conjunction of elements of manual labour power with certain kinds of masculine gender definitions in the culture of the shop floor is one of the truly essential features of the social organisations of the shop floor. Yet it is usually un- or misrecognised. The sexist attitudes of the male shop floor, the inevitable nubile pin-up over well-worked machinery, heavy sexual references and jokes in language are simply accepted as the natural form of shop-floor life. One of our central tasks must be to critically understand this relationship.

Manual labour is suffused with masculine qualities and given certain sensual overtones. The toughness and awkwardness of physical work and effort – for itself and in the division of labour, and for its strictly capitalist logic quite without intrinsic heroism or grandeur – takes on masculine lights and depths and assumes a significance beyond itself. Whatever the specific problems of the difficult task, they are always essentially masculine problems, requiring masculine capacities to deal with them. We may say that where the principle of general abstract labour has emptied work of significance from the inside, a transformed patriarchy has filled it with significance from the outside. Discontent with work is turned away from a political discontent and confused in its logic by a huge detour into the symbolic sexual realm.

The brutality of the working situation is partially reinterpreted into a heroic exercise of manly confrontation with "the task." Difficult, uncomfortable, or dangerous conditions are seen, not for themselves, but for their appropriateness to a masculine readiness and hardness. They are understood more through the toughness required to survive them than through the nature of the imposition which asks them to be faced in the first place.

Though it is difficult to obtain stature in work itself, both what work provides and the very sacrifice and strength required to do it provides the materials for an elemental self-esteem. This self-esteem derives from the achievement of a purpose which not all – particularly women – are held capable of achieving. The wage packet is the provider of freedom and independence; the particular prize of masculinity in work. This is the complement of, and what makes it possible, the fetishism of the wage packet. A trade is judged not for itself, nor even for its general financial return, but for its ability to provide the central, domestic, role for its incumbent. Clearly money is part of this – but as a measure, not the essence. "You can raise a family off polishing." The male wage packet is held to be central, not simply because of its size, but because it is won in a masculine mode in confrontation with the "real" world which is too tough for the woman. Thus the man in the domestic household is held to be the bread-winner, "the worker," while the wife works for the extras. Very often, of course, the material importance of her wage may be much greater than this suggests, and certainly her domestic labour is the lynchpin of the whole household economy. The wage packet as a kind of symbol of machismo dictates the domestic culture and economy and tyrannizes both men and women.

In the machismo of manual work the will to finish the job, the will to really work, is posited as a masculine logic, and not as the logic of exploitation. "It's a man's want to be finished when he starts a job." The very teleology of the process of work upon nature, and the material power involved in that, becomes, through the conflation of masculine and manual work, a property of masculinity and not of production. Masculinity is power in its own right, and if its immediate expression is in the completion of work for another, then what of it? It has to be expressed somewhere because it is a quality of being. That is the destiny which a certain kind of self-esteem and dignity seems naturally to bring. Where the intransigence and hardness of a task might bring weakness, or collective opposition, or questioning, an override of masculinity – a transferred teleology of production – can cut in to push back fatigue and rational assessment of purpose.

And if the nature of masculinity in work becomes a style of teleology, completion, and production, femininity is associated with a fixed state. Its labour power is considered as an ontological state of being, not a teleological process of becoming. Housework is not completion. It is rather maintenance of status. Cooking, washing, and cleaning reproduce what was there before. Female domestic work is simply subsumed under *being* "mum" or "housewife." Mum will always do it and should always be expected to do it. It is part of the definition of what she is, and the wage packet and the productive world of work is of what dad is.

Though this is speculation only, I pose the following concluding remarks just to explore the breaking open of the constructedness of cultural forms. The public and visible struggle of the labour movement too often renders invisible the ocean of what it moves through: shop-floor culture. This is not to minimize the historic importance of the trade unions, but it might be suggested that the type of masculine expression and identity we have considered influence the *form* of trade union struggle in the most profound ways. It has certainly been remarked that the acceptance of the wage form – and of the struggle delimited by that – has profoundly influenced British trade unionism. Can we add that both conscious and unconscious masculine structures have confirmed this and also helped to develop a characteristic trade union consciousness? And on both accounts we should not ignore the reverse shaping force of trade unions on cultural forms – or at least the significance of them to formally develop nascent forms not only of opposition but of repossession in shop-floor culture.

Certainly the union official or shop steward uses particular shop-floor cultural forms to mobilize "the lads" – the spectacle of bluff, or strong and combative language which are suffused with masculine feelings. This establishes a real expression of anger and opposition which may be very effective in the short term and is certainly a force to be reckoned with. This is, however, a selective working up and use of cultural forms, one which ominously corresponds with certain profound features of the wage form. It may be that longer-term objectives – which are at least partially expressed in other cultural forms – simply cannot be conceptualized in this way and are, to a certain extent, made inoperative by default at the face-to-face and grass-roots level. The masculine style of confrontation demands an appropriate and honourable resolution: visible and immediate concessions. If this is its price, however, it can be bought off in the most "concrete" of all forms: "hard cash." But the visibility of the concessions won in this way – the larger, masculine, fetishised, brown wage packet – may actually conceal longer-term defeats over the less visible issues of control and ownership. It is possible to satisfy violent and possibly even frightening demands by short-term, visible, and dramatic concessions without changing any of those basic arrangements which the violence might appear to threaten.

It may be the unholy interlocked grip of masculinity and the wage form which holds in check the other possibilities of shop-floor culture and settles, for the moment, the nature of its influence on other social regions.

APPROACHES TO CULTURE: POSTSTRUCTURALIST

- Michel Foucault, *Sexual discourse and power*
- Pierre Bourdieu, *Artistic taste and cultural capital*

18

Sexual discourse and power

Michel Foucault

The central issue . . . is not to determine whether one says yes or no to sex, whether one formulates prohibitions or permissions, whether one asserts its importance or denies its effects, or whether one refines the words one uses to designate it; but to account for the fact that it is spoken about, to discover who does the speaking, the positions and viewpoints from which they speak, the institutions which prompt people to speak about it and which store and distribute the things that are said. What is at issue, briefly, is the over-all "discursive fact," the way in which sex is "put into discourse." Hence, too, my main concern will be to locate the forms of power, the channels it takes, and the discourses it permeates in order to reach the most tenuous and individual modes of behavior, the paths that give it access to the rare or scarcely perceivable forms of desire, how it penetrates and controls everyday pleasure — all this entailing effects that may be those of refusal, blockage, and invalidation, but also incitement and intensification; in short, the "polymorphous techniques of power." . . .

Up to the end of the eighteenth century, three major explicit codes — apart from the customary regularities and constraints of opinion — governed sexual practices: canonical law, the Christian pastoral, and civil law. They determined, each in its own way, the division between licit and illicit. They were all centered on matrimonial relations: the marital obligation, the ability to fulfill it, the manner in which one complied with it, the requirements and violences that accompanied it, the useless or unwarranted caresses for which it was a pretext, its fecundity or the way one went about making it sterile, the moments when one demanded it (dangerous periods of pregnancy or breast-feeding, forbidden times of Lent or abstinence), its frequency or infrequency, and so on. It was this domain that was especially saturated with prescriptions. The sex of husband and wife was beset by rules and recommendations. The marriage relation was the most intense focus of constraints; it was spoken of more than anything else; more than any other relation, it was required to give a detailed accounting of itself. It was under constant surveillance: If it was found to be lacking, it had to come forward and plead its case before a witness. The "rest" remained a good deal more confused: One only has to think of the uncertain status of "sodomy" or the indifference regarding the sexuality of children.

Moreover, these different codes did not make a clear distinction between violations of the rules of marriage and of desires — and the life of Don Juan overturned them both. We shall leave it to psychoanalysts to speculate whether he was homosexual, narcissistic, or impotent.

Although not without delay and equivocation, the natural laws of matrimony and the immanent rules of sexuality began to be recorded on two separate registers. There emerged a world of perversion which partook of that of legal or moral infraction, yet was not simply a variety of the latter. An entire subrace was born, different — despite certain kinship ties — from the libertines of the past. From the end of the eighteenth century to our own, they circulated through the pores of society; they were always hounded, but not always by laws; were often locked up, but not always in prisons; were sick perhaps, but scandalous, dangerous victims, prey to a strange evil that also bore the name of vice and sometimes crime. They were children wise beyond their years, precocious little girls, ambiguous schoolboys, dubious servants and educators, cruel or maniacal husbands, solitary collectors, ramblers with bizarre impulses; they haunted the houses of correction, the penal colonies, the tribunals, and the asylums; they carried their infamy to the doctors and their sickness to the judges. This was the numberless family of perverts who were on friendly terms with delinquents and akin to madmen. In the course of the century they successively bore the stamp of "moral folly," "genital neurosis," "aberration of the genetic instinct," "degenerescence," or "physical imbalance."

What does the appearance of all these peripheral sexualities signify? Is the fact that they could appear in broad daylight a sign that the code had become more lax? Or does the fact that they were given so much attention testify to a stricter regime and to its concern to bring them under close supervision? In terms of repression, things are unclear. There was permissiveness, if one bears in mind that the severity of the codes relating to sexual offenses diminished considerably in the nineteenth century and that law itself often deferred to medicine. But an additional ruse of severity, if one thinks of all the agencies of control and all the mechanisms of surveillance that were put into operation by pedagogy or therapeutics. It may be the case that the intervention of the Church in conjugal sexuality and its rejection of "frauds" against procreation had lost much of their insistence over the previous two hundred years. But medicine made a forceful entry into the pleasures of the couple: It created an entire organic, functional, or mental pathology arising out of "incomplete" sexual practices; it carefully classified all forms of related pleasures; it incorporated them into the notions of "development" and instinctual "disturbances"; and it undertook to manage them.

Perhaps the point to consider is not the level of indulgence or the quantity of repression but the form of power that was exercised. When this whole thicket of disparate sexualities was labeled, as if to disentangle them from one another, was the object to exclude them from reality? It appears, in fact, that the function of the power exerted in this instance was not that of interdiction, and that it involved four operations quite different from simple prohibition.

1. Take the ancient prohibitions of consanguine marriages (as numerous and complex as they were) or the condemnation of adultery, with its inevitable frequency of occurrence; or, on the other hand, the recent controls through which, since the nineteenth century, the sexuality of children has been subordinated and their "solidarity habits" interfered with: It is clear that we are not dealing with one and the same power mechanism. Not only because in the one case it is a question of law and penality, and in the other, medicine and regimentation; but also because the tactics employed are not the same. On the surface, what appears in both cases is an effort at elimination that was always destined to fail and always constrained to begin again. But the prohibition of "incest" attempted to reach its objective through an asymptotic decrease in the thing it condemned, whereas the control machinery of power that focused on this whole alien strain did not aim to suppress it, but rather to give it an analytical, visible, and permanent reality: It was implanted in bodies, slipped in beneath modes of conduct, made into a principle of classification and intelligibility, established as a raison d'être and a natural order of disorder. Not the exclusion of these thousand aberrant sexualities, but the specification, the regional solidification of each one of them. The strategy behind this dissemination was to strew reality with them and incorporate them into the individual.

2. More than the old taboos, this form of power demanded constant, attentive, and curious presences for its exercise; it presupposed proximities; it proceeded through examination and insistent observation; it required an exchange of discourses, through questions that extorted admissions, and confidences that went beyond the questions that were asked. It implied a physical proximity and an interplay of intense sensations. The medicalization of the sexually peculiar was both the effect and the instrument of this. Embedded in bodies, becoming deeply characteristic of

individuals, the oddities of sex relied on a technology of health and pathology. And conversely, since sexuality was a medical and medicalizable object, one had to try and detect it – as a lesion, a dysfunction, or a symptom – in the depths of the organism, or on the surface of the skin, or among all the signs of behavior. The power which thus took charge of sexuality set about contacting bodies, caressing them with its eyes, intensifying areas, electrifying surfaces, dramatizing troubled moments. It wrapped the sexual body in its embrace. There was undoubtedly an increase in effectiveness and an extension of the domain controlled, but also a sensualization of power and a gain of pleasure. This produced a twofold effect: An impetus was given to power through its very exercise; an emotion rewarded the overseeing control and carried it further; the intensity of the confession renewed the questioner's curiosity; the pleasure discovered fed back to the power that encircled it. But so many pressing questions singularized the pleasures felt by the one who had to reply. They were fixed by a gaze, isolated and animated by the attention they received. Power operated as a mechanism of attraction; it drew out those peculiarities over which it kept watch. Pleasure spread to the power that harried it; power anchored the pleasure it uncovered.

The medical examination, the psychiatric investigation, the pedagogical report, and family controls may have the overall and apparent objective of saying no to all wayward or unproductive sexualities, but the fact is that they function as mechanisms with a double impetus: pleasure and power. The pleasure that comes of exercising a power that questions, monitors, watches, spies, searches out, palpates, brings to light; and on the other hand, the pleasure that kindles at having to evade this power, flee from it, fool it, or travesty it. The power that lets itself be invaded by the pleasure it is pursuing; and opposite it, power asserting itself in the pleasure of showing off, scandalizing, or resisting. Capture and seduction, confrontation and mutual reinforcement: Parents and children, adults and adolescents, educators and students, doctors and patients, the psychiatrist with his hysteric and his perverts, all have played this game continually since the nineteenth century. These attractions, these evasions, these circular incitements have traced around bodies and sexes, not boundaries to be crossed, but *perpetual spirals of power and pleasure.* . . .

Nineteenth-century "bourgeois" society – and it is doubtless still with us – was a society of blatant and fragmented perversion. And this was not by way of hypocrisy, for nothing was more manifest and more prolix, or more manifestly taken over by discourses and institutions. Not because, having tried to erect too rigid or too general a barrier against sexuality, society succeeded only in giving rise to a whole perverse outbreak and a long pathology of the sexual instinct. At issue, rather, is the type of power it brought to bear on the body and on sex. In point of fact, this power had neither the form of the law nor the effects of the taboo. On the contrary, it acted by multiplication of singular sexualities. It did not set boundaries for sexuality; it extended the various forms of sexuality, pursuing them according to lines of indefinite penetration. It did not exclude sexuality, but included it in the body as a mode of specification of individuals. It did not seek to avoid it; it attracted its varieties by means of spirals in which pleasure and power reinforced one another. It did not set up a barrier; it provided places of maximum saturation. It produced and determined the sexual mosaic. Modern society is perverse, not in spite of its puritanism or as if from a backlash provoked by its hypocrisy; it is in actual fact, and directly, perverse.

In actual fact. The manifold sexualities – those which appear with the different ages (sexualities of the infant or the child), those which become fixated on particular tastes or practices (the sexuality of the invert, the gerontophile, the fetishist), those which, in a diffuse manner, invest relationships (the sexuality of doctor and patient, teacher and student, psychiatrist and mental patient), those which haunt spaces (the sexuality of the home, the school, the prison) – all form the correlate of exact procedures of power. We must not imagine that all these things that were formerly tolerated attracted notice and received a pejorative determination when the time came to give a regulative role to the one type of sexuality that was capable of reproducing labor power and the form of the family. These polymorphous conducts were actually extracted from people's bodies and from their pleasures; or rather, they were solidified in them; they were drawn out, revealed, isolated, intensified, incorporated, by multifarious power devices. The growth of perversions is not a moralizing theme that obsessed the scrupulous minds of the Victorians. It is the real product of the encroachment of a type of power on bodies and their pleasures. It is possible that the West has not been capable of inventing any new pleasures, and it has doubtless not discovered any original vices. But it has defined new rules for the game of powers and pleasures. The frozen countenance of the perversions is a fixture of this game. . . .

We must therefore abandon the hypothesis that modern industrial societies ushered in an age of increased sexual repression. We have not only witnessed a visible explosion of unorthodox sexualities; but – and this is the important point – a deployment quite different from the law, even if it is locally dependent on procedures of prohibition, has ensured, through a network of interconnecting mechanisms, the proliferation of specific pleasures and the multiplication of disparate sexualities. It is said that no society has been more prudish; never have the agencies of power taken such care to feign ignorance of the thing they prohibited, as if they were determined to have nothing to do with it. But it is the opposite that has become apparent, at least after a general review of the facts: Never have there existed more centers of power; never more attention manifested and verbalized; never more circular contacts and linkages; never more sites where the intensity of pleasures and the persistency of power catch hold, only to spread elsewhere.

19

Artistic taste and cultural capital

Pierre Bourdieu

An act of deciphering unrecognized as such, immediate and adequate "comprehension," is possible and effective only in the special case in which the cultural code which makes the act of deciphering possible is immediately and completely mastered by the observer (in the form of cultivated ability or inclination) and merges with the cultural code which has rendered the work perceived possible. . . .

Whenever these specific conditions are not fulfilled, misunderstanding is inevitable: The illusion of immediate comprehension leads to an illusory comprehension based on a mistaken code. In the absence of perception that the works are coded, and coded in another code, one unconsciously applies the code which is good for everyday perception, for the deciphering of familiar objects, to works in a foreign tradition: There is no perception which does not involve an unconscious code and it is essential to dismiss the myth of 'the "fresh eye," considered as a virtue granted to artlessness and innocence. One of the reasons why the less educated beholders in our societies are so strongly inclined to demand realistic portrayal is that, being devoid of specific categories of perception, they cannot apply to works of scholarly culture any other code than that which enables them to apprehend, as having a meaning, objects of their everyday environment. Minimum, and apparently immediate, comprehension, accessible to the simplest observer and enabling him to recognize a house or a tree, still presupposes partial agreement (unconscious, of course) between artist and beholder concerning categories that define the representation of the real which a historic society holds to be "realistic."

The spontaneous theory of art perception is founded on experience of familarity and immediate comprehension – an unrecognized special case.

Educated people are at home with scholarly culture. They are conse-

From Pierre Bourdieu, "Outline of a Theory of Art Perception," *International Social Science Journal* (1968) 2 (4); excerpted from pp. 589–612. Reprinted with permission.

quently carried towards that kind of ethnocentrism which may be called class-centrism and which consists in considering as natural (in other words, both as a matter of course and based on nature) a way of perceiving which is but one among other possible ways and which is acquired through education that may be diffuse or specific, conscious or unconscious, institutionalized or noninstitutionalized. . . .

The work of art considered as a symbolic asset (and not as an economic asset, which it may also be) only exists as such for a person who has the means to appropriate it, or in other words, to decipher it.[1]

The degree of art competence of an agent is measured by the degree to which he masters the set of instruments for the appropriation of the work of art, available at a given time, that is to say the interpretation schemes which are the prerequisite for the appropriation of art capital or, in other words, the prerequisite for the deciphering of works of art offered to a given society at a particular time.

Art competence can be provisionally defined as the preliminary knowledge of the possible divisions into complementary classes of a universe of representations: A mastery of this kind of system of classification enables each element of the universe to be placed in a class necessarily determined in relation to another class, constituted itself by all the art representations consciously or unconsciously taken into consideration which do not belong to the class in question. . . .

Artistic competence is therefore defined as the previous knowledge of the strictly artistic principles of division which enable a representation to be located, through the classification of the stylistic indications which it contains, among the possibilities of representation constituting the universe of art and not among the possibilities of representation constituting the universe of everyday objects (or, more exactly, of implements) or the

---

1. The laws governing the reception of works of art are a special case of the laws of cultural diffusion: Whatever may be the nature of the message – religious prophecy, political speech, publicity image, technical object, etc. – reception depends upon the categories of perception, thought, and action of those who receive it. In a differentiated society, a close relationship is therefore established between the nature and quality of the information transmitted and the structure of the public, its "readability," and its effectiveness being all the greater when it meets as directly as possible the expectations, implicit or explicit, which the receivers owe chiefly to their family upbringing and social circumstances (and also, in the matter of scholarly culture at least, to their school education) and which the diffuse pressure of the reference group maintains, sustains, and reinforces by constant recalls to the norm. It is on the basis of this connexion between the level of transmission of the message and the structure of the public, treated as a reception level indicator, that it has been possible to construct the mathematical model of museum visiting.

universe of signs, which would amount to treating it as a mere monument, in other words, as a mere means of communication used to transmit a transcendental signification. The perception of the work of art in a truly aesthetic manner, that is to say as a significant which signifies nothing other than itself, does not consist, as is sometimes said, of considering it "without connecting it with anything other than itself, either emotionally or intellectually," in short, of giving oneself up to the work apprehended in its irreducible singularity, but of noting its *distinctive stylistic features* by relating it to the whole of the works forming the class to which it belongs, and to these works only. . . .

The art code as a system of possible principles of division into complementary classes of the universe of representations offered to a particular society at a given time is in the nature of a social institution.

Being an historically constituted system, founded on social reality, this set of instruments of perception whereby a particular society, at a given time, appropriates artistic wealth (and, more generally, cultural wealth) does not depend upon individual wills and consciousnesses and forces itself upon individuals, often without their knowledge, determining the distinctions which they can make and those which escape them. . . .

The inclination to appropriate cultural wealth is the product of general or specific education, institutionalized or not, which creates (or cultivates) art competence as a mastery of the instruments for appropriation of this wealth, and which creates the "cultural need" by giving the means to satisfy it.

The repeated perception of works of a certain style encourages the unconscious interiorization of the rules which govern the production of these works. Like rules of grammar, these rules are not apprehended as such, and are still less explicitly formulated and formulatable: For instance, a lover of classical music may have neither consciousness nor knowledge of the laws obeyed by the sound-making art to which he is accustomed, but his auditive education is such that, having heard a dominant chord, he is induced urgently to await the tonic which seems to him the "natural" resolution of this chord, and he has difficulty in apprehending the internal coherence of music founded on other principles. The unconscious mastery of the instruments of appropriation which are the basis of familiarity with cultural works is acquired by slow familiarization, a long succession of "little perceptions," in the sense in which Leibniz uses these words. Connoisseurship is an "art" which, like the art of thinking or the art of living, cannot be imparted entirely in the form of precepts or instruction, and apprenticeship to it presupposes the equivalent of prolonged contact between disciple and master in traditional education, that is to say repeated contact with the work (or with works of the same class). And, just as the student or disciple can unconsciously absorb the rules of the art – including those which are not explicitly known to the master himself – by giving himself up to it, excluding analysis and the selection of elements of exemplary conduct, so the art lover can, by abandoning himself in some way to the work, interiorize the principles and rules of its construction without their ever being brought to his consciousness and formulated as such, which makes all the difference between the art theorist and the connoisseur, who is usually incapable of explicating the principles on which his judgments are based. In this field as in others (learning the grammar of one's mother tongue, for instance), school education tends to encourage the conscious reflection of patterns of thought, perception, or expression which have already been mastered unconsciously by formulating explicitly the principles of the creative grammar, for example the laws of harmony and counterpoint or the rules of pictorial composition, and by providing the verbal and conceptual material essential in order to give a name to differences previously experienced in a purely intuitive way. The danger of academism is obviously inherent in any rationalized teaching which tends to mint, within one doctrinal body, precepts, prescriptions, and formulae, explicitly described and taught, more often negative than positive, which a traditional education imparts in the form of a *habitus,* directly apprehended *uno intuito,* as a global style not susceptible to analytical breakdown. . . .

Even when the educational institution makes little provision for art training proper (as is the case in France and many other countries), even when therefore it gives neither specific encouragement to cultural activities nor a body of concepts specifically adapted to plastic art works, it tends on the one hand to inspire a certain *familiarity* – conferring a feeling of belonging to the cultivated class – with the world of art, in which people feel at home and among themselves as the appointed addressees of works which do not deliver their message to the first-comer: On the other hand, they tend to inculcate (at least in France and in the majority of European countries, at the secondary education level) a *cultivated disposition* as a durable and generalized attitude which implies recognition of the value of works of art and ability to appropriate them by means of generic categories.[2] Although it deals almost exclusively with literary works, in-school learning tends to create, on the one hand, a transposable inclination to admire works approved by the school and a duty to admire and to love certain works or, rather, certain classes of works which gradually seem to become linked to a certain educational and social status; and, on the other hand, an equally generalized and transposable

2. School instruction always fulfills a function of legitimation, if only by giving its blessing to works which it sets up as worthy of being admired, and thus helps to define the hierarchy of cultural wealth valid in a particular society at a given time.

aptitude for categorizing by authors, by genres, by schools, and by periods, for the handling of educational categories of literary analysis and for the mastery of the code which governs the use of the different codes, giving at least a tendency to acquire equivalent categories in other fields and to store away the typical knowledge which, even though extrinsic and anecdotal, makes possible at least an elementary form of apprehension, however inadequate it might be. Thus, the first degree of strictly pictorial competence shows itself in the mastery of an arsenal of works, making it possible to name differences and to apprehend them while naming them: These are the proper names of famous painters – da Vinci, Picasso, Van Gogh – which function as generic categories, because one can say about any painting or non-figurative object "that suggests Picasso," or, about any work recalling nearly or distantly the manner of the Florentine painter, "that looks like a da Vinci"; there are also broad categories, like "the Impressionists" (a school commonly considered to include Gauguin, Cezanne, and Degas), the "Dutch School," "the Renaissance." It is particularly significant that the proportion of subjects who think in terms of schools is very clearly growing as the level of education rises and that, more generally, generic knowledge which is required for the perception of differences. . . .

To be able to form discerning or so-called personal opinions is again a result of the education received: Ability to throw off school constraints is the privilege of those who have sufficiently assimilated school education to make their own the free attitude towards scholastic culture taught by a school so deeply impregnated with the values of the ruling classes that it accepts the fashionable depreciation of school instruction. The contrast between accepted, stereotyped, and, as Max Weber would say "routinized" culture, and genuine culture, freed from school dissertations, has meaning only for an infinitely small minority of educated people for whom culture is second nature, endowed with all the appearances of talent, and the full assimilation of school culture is a prerequisite for going beyond it towards this "free culture" – freed, that is to say, from its school origins – which the bourgeois class and its school regard as the value of values.

But the best proof that the general principles for the transfer of training also hold for school training lies in the fact that the practices of one single individual and, a fortiori, of individuals belonging to one social catgory or having a specific level of education, tend to constitute a system, so that a certain type of practice in any field of culture very probably implies a corresponding type of practice in all the other fields; thus, frequent visits to museums are almost necessarily associated with an equal amount of theatre-going and, to a lesser degree, attendance at concerts. Similarly, everything seems to indicate that knowledge and preferences tend to form into constellations which are strictly linked to the level of education, so that a typical structure of preferences in painting is most likely to be linked to a structure of preferences of the same type in music or literature. . . .

Only an institution like the school, the specific function of which is methodically to develop or create the inclinations which produce an educated man and which lay the foundations, quantitatively and consequently qualitatively, of a constant and intense pursuit of culture, could offset (at least partially) the initial disadvantage of those who do not receive from their family circle the encouragement to undertake cultural activities and the competence presupposed in any dissertation on works, on condition and only on condition that it employs every available means to break down the endless series of cumulative processes to which any cultural education is condemned. For if the apprehension of a work of art depends, in its intensity, its modality, and in its very existence, on the beholder's mastery of the generic and specific code of the work, that is to say on his competence, which he owes partly to school training, the same thing applies to the pedagogic communication which is responsible, among other functions, for transmitting the code of works of scholarly culture (at the same time as the code according to which it effects this transmission), so that the intensity and modality of the communication are here again a function of culture (as a system of schemes of perception, expression, and historically constituted and socially conditioned thinking) which the receiver owes to his family circle and which is more or less close to scholarly culture and the linguistic and cultural models according to which the school effects the transmission of this culture. Considering that the direct experience of works of scholarly culture and the institutionally organized acquisition of culture which is a prerequisite for adequate experience of such works are subject to the same laws, it is obvious how difficult it is to break the sequence of the cumulative effects which cause cultural capital to attract cultural capital: In fact, the school has only to give free play to the objective machinery of cultural diffusion without working systematically to give to all, in and through the pedagogical message itself, what is given to some through family inheritance, that is to say the instruments which condition the adequate reception of the school message, for it to redouble and entrench by its approval the socially conditioned inequalities of cultural competence, by treating them as natural inequalities, or in other words as inequalities of gifts.

Charismatic ideology is based on parenthesizing the relationship, evident as soon as it is revealed, between art competence and education, which alone is capable of creating both the inclination to recognize a value in cultural wealth and the competence which gives a meaning to this inclination by making it possible to appropriate such wealth. Since their art competence is the product of an imperceptible familiarization and an automatic transferring of aptitudes, members of the privileged classes are naturally inclined to regard as a gift of nature a cultural heritage which is transmitted by a process of unconscious training. But, in addition, the contradictions and ambiguities of the relationship which the most cultured among them maintain with their culture are both encouraged and permitted by the paradox which defines the "realization" of culture as *becoming natural:* Culture being achieved only by negating itself as such, that is to say as artificial and artificially acquired, so as to become second nature, a *habitus,* a possession turned into being, the virtuosi of the judgment of taste seem to reach an experience of aesthetic grace so completely freed from the constraints of culture and so little marked by the long, patient training of which it is the product that any reminder of the conditions and the social conditionings which have rendered it possible seems to be at once obvious and shocking. It follows that the most experienced connoisseurs are the natural champions of charismatic ideology, which concedes to the work of art a magical power of conversion capable of awakening the potentialities latent in a few of the elect, and which contrasts authentic experience of a work of art as an "affection" of the heart or immediate enlightenment of the intuition with the laborious proceedings and cold comments of the intelligence, ignoring the social and cultural conditions underlying such an experience, and at the same time treating as a birthright the virtuosity acquired through long familiarization or through the exercises of a methodical training; silence concerning the social prerequisites for the appropriation of culture or, to be more exact, for the acquisition of art competence in the sense of mastery of all means for the specific appropriation of works of art is a self-seeking silence because it is what makes it possible to legitimatize a social privilege by pretending that it is a gift of nature.

To remember that culture is not what one is but what one has, or, rather what one has become; to remember the social conditions which render possible aesthetic experience and the existence of those beings – art lovers or "people of taste" – for whom it is possible; to remember that the work of art is given only to those who have received the means to acquire the means to appropriate it and who could not seek to possess it if they did not already possess it, in and through the possession of means of possession as an actual possibility of effecting the taking of possession; to remember, lastly, that only a few have the real possibility of benefiting by the theoretical possibility, generously offered to all, of taking advantage of the works exhibited in museums, all this is to bring to light the hidden mobile of the effects of the majority of culture's social uses.

The parenthesizing of the social conditions which render possible culture and culture become nature, cultivated nature, having all the appearances of grace or a gift and yet acquired, so therefore "deserved," is the condition precedent of charismatic ideology which makes it possible to confer on culture and in particular on "love of art" the all-important place which they occupy in middle-class "sociodicy." The bourgeoisie find naturally in culture as cultivated nature and culture that has become nature the only possible principle for the legitimation of their privilege: Being unable to invoke the right of birth (which their class, through the ages, has refused to the aristocracy) or Nature which, according to "democratic" ideology, represents universality, that is to say the ground on which all distinctions are abolished, or the aesthetic virtues which enabled the first generation of bourgeois to invoke their merit, they can resort to cultivated nature and culture become nature, to what is sometimes called "class," through a kind of telltale slip, to "education," in the sense of a product of education which seems to owe nothing to education, to *distinction,* grace which is merit and merit which is grace, an unacquired merit which justifies unmerited acquisitions, that is to say inheritance. To enable culture to fulfill its primary ideological function of class cooptation and legitimation of this mode of selection, it is necessary and enough that the link between culture and education, which is simultaneously obvious and hidden, be forgotten, disguised, and denied.

The unnatural idea of inborn culture, of a gift of culture, bestowed on certain people by Nature, is inseparable from blindness to the functions of the institution which insures the profitability of the cultural heritage and legitimizes its transmission while concealing that it fulfills this function: The school in fact is the institution which, through its outwardly irreproachable verdicts, transforms socially conditioned inequalities in regard to culture into inequalities of success, interpreted as inequalities of gifts which are also inequalities of merit. Plato records towards the end of *The Republic* that the souls who are to begin another life must themselves choose their lot among "patterns of life" of all kinds and that, when the choice has been made, they must drink of the water of the river Lethe before returning to earth. The function which Plato attributes to the water of forgetfulness devolves, in our societies, on the university which, in its impartiality, though pretending only to recognize students as equal in rights and duties, divided only by inequalities of gifts and of merit, in fact confers on individuals degrees judged according to their cultural heritage, and therefore according to their social status.

By symbolically shifting the essential of what sets them apart from other classes from the economic field to that of culture, or rather, by adding to strictly economic differences, namely those created by the simple possession of material wealth, differences created by the possession of symbolic wealth such as works of art, or by the pursuit of symbolic distinctions in the manner of using such wealth (economic or symbolic), in short, by turning into a fact of nature everything which determines their "value," or to take the word in the linguistic sense, their *distinction* – a mark of difference which, according to the Littre, sets people apart from the common herd "by the characteristics of elegance, nobility, and good form" – the privileged members of middle-class society replace the difference between two cultures, historic products of social conditions, by the essential difference between two natures, a naturally cultivated nature and a naturally natural nature. Thus, the sacralizing of culture and art fulfills a vital function by contributing to the consecration of the social order: To enable educated men to believe in barbarism and persuade their barbarians within the gates of their own barbarity, all they must and need do is to manage to conceal themselves and to conceal the social conditions which render possible not only culture as second nature in which society recognizes human excellence or "good form" as the "realization" in a *habitus* of the aesthetics of the ruling classes, but also the legitimized predominance (or, if you like, the legitimacy) of a particular definition of culture. And in order that the ideological circle may be completely closed, all they have to do is to find, in an essentialist representation of the bipartition of society into barbarians and civilized people, the justification of their right to conditions which produce the possession of culture and the dispossession of culture, an estate of "nature" destined to appear based on the nature of the men who are condemned to it.

If such be the function of culture and if it be love of art which really determines the choice which separates, as by an invisible and insuperable barrier, those to whom it is given from those who have not received this grace, it can be seen that museums betray, in the smallest details of their morphology and their organization, their true function, which is to strengthen the feeling of belonging in some and the feeling of exclusion in others.[3] Everything, in these civic temples in which bourgeois society deposits its most sacred possessions, that is to say relics inherited from a past which is not its own, in these holy places of art, in which the chosen few come to nurture a faith of virtuosi while conformists and bogus devotees come and perform a class ritual, old palaces or great historic

---

3. It is not infrequent that working-class visitors express explicitly the feeling of exclusion which, in any case, is evident in their whole behavior. Thus, they sometimes see in the absence of any indication which might facilitate the visit, arrows showing the direction to follow, explanatory panels, etc., the signs of a deliberate intention to exclude the uninitiated. The provision of teaching and didactic aids would not, in fact, really make up for the lack of schooling, but it would at least proclaim the right not to know, the right to be there in ignorance, the right of the ignorant to be there, a right which everything in the presentation of works and in the organization of the museum combines to challenge, as this remark overheard in the Chateau of Versailles testifies: "This chateau was not made for the people, and it has not changed."

homes to which the nineteenth century added imposing edifices, built often in the Graeco-Roman style of civic sanctuaries, everything combines to indicate that the world of art is as contrary to the world of everyday life as the sacred is to the profane: The prohibition to touch the objects, the religious silence which is forced upon visitors, the puritan asceticism of the facilities, always scarce and uncomfortable, the almost systematic refusal of any instruction, the grandiose solemnity of the decoration and the decorum, colonnades, vast galleries, decorated ceilings, monumental staircases, both outside and inside, everything seems done to remind people that the transition from the profane world to the sacred world presupposes, as Durkheim says, "a genuine metamorphosis," a radical spiritual change, that the bringing together of the worlds "is always, in itself, a delicate operation which calls for precaution and a more or less complicated initiation," that "it is not even possible unless the profane lose their specific characteristics, unless they themselves become sacred to some extent and to some degree."[4] Although the work of art, owing to its sacred nature, calls for particular dispositions or predispositions, it brings in return its consecration to those who satisfy its demands, to the small elite who are self-chosen by their aptitude to respond to its appeal.

The museum gives to all, as a public legacy, the monuments of a splendid past, instruments of the sumptuous glorification of the great figures of bygone ages: This is false generosity, because free entrance is also optional entrance, reserved for those who, endowed with the ability to appropriate the works, have the privilege of using this freedom and who find themselves consequently legitimized in their privilege, that is to say in the possession of the means of appropriating cultural wealth or, to borrow an expression of Max Weber, in the *monopoly* of the handling of cultural wealth and

4. E. Durkheim, *Les formes élémentaires de la vie réligieuse* (Paris: PUF, 1960, sixth edition), pp. 55–6. The holding of a Danish exhibition showing modern furniture and utensils in the old ceramic rooms of the Lille Museum brought about such a "conversion" in the visitors as can be summarized in the following contrasts, the very ones which exist between a store and a museum: noise – silence; touch – see; quick, haphazard exploration, in no particular order – leisurely, methodical inspection, according to a fixed arrangement; freedom – constraint; economic assessment of works which may be purchased – aesthetic appreciation of "priceless" works. However, despite these differences bound up with the things exhibited, the solemnizing (and distancing) effect of the museum no less continued to be felt, contrary to expectations, for the structure of the public at the Danish exhibition was more "aristocratic" (in respect of level of education) than the ordinary public of the museum. The mere fact that works are consecrated by being exhibited in a consecrated place is sufficient, in itself, profoundly to change their signification and, more precisely, to raise the level of their emission.

of the institutional signs of cultural salvation (awarded by the school). Being the keystone of a system which can function only by concealing its true function, the charismatic representation of art experience never fulfills its function of mystifying so well as when it resorts to a "democratic" language: to claim that works of art have power to awaken the grace of aesthetic enlightenment in anyone, however culturally uninitiated he may be, to presume in all cases to ascribe to the unfathomable accidents of grace or to the arbitrary bestowal of "gifts" aptitudes which are always the product of unevenly distributed education, and therefore to treat inherited aptitudes as personal virtues which are both natural and meritorious. Charismatic ideology would not be so strong if it were not the only outwardly irreproachable means of justifying the right of the heirs to the inheritance without being inconsistent with the ideal of formal democracy, and if, in this particular case, it did not aim at establishing in nature the sole right of the middle class to appropriate art treasures to itself, to appropriate them to itself *symbolically,* that is to say in the only legitimate manner, in a society which pretends to yield to all, "democratically," the relics of an aristocratic past.

Part II

Substantive debates: Moral order and social crisis – perspectives on modern culture

Steven Seidman

In his introduction Jeffrey Alexander has reviewed some conceptual difficulties involved in cultural analysis. Yet, the problem of understanding meaning is not only an analytical concern of social researchers. It is a practical everyday concern for each of us. The routines of daily life are maintained only by achieving mutual understanding. Interpretation is not only a specialized method of social science but a practical accomplishment that makes social life possible.[1]

There is, moreover, a peculiar relation between the interpretative effects of the researchers and those of ordinary people. Only by sharing the life-world of those the researcher is studying is scientific understanding possible. Researchers must share the meanings and conventions of their object domain in order to develop a second-order scientific interpretation.[2] Furthermore, scientific interpretations are built upon everyday meanings; they inevitably inform the presuppositions and categorical structure of science. From the reverse side, the interpretations of researchers may become constitutive of daily life.[3] Scientific interpretations of social events function as social forces. Like the symbolic configurations that researchers study, their own symbolic productions contribute to the construction of identities, the legitimation of institutions, the forging of forms of social solidarity, and so forth. The social or human sciences are, then, in the rather odd position of having to acknowledge that the knowledge they create contributes to producing the forms of life they study. I will draw on these observations to introduce some themes in the contemporary debate over modern culture.

1. See Hans-Georg Gadamer, *Truth and Method* (New York: Seabury, 1975).
2. See Jurgen Habermas, *The Theory of Communicative Action*, Vol. 1 (Boston: Beacon Press, 1984).
3. See Anthony Giddens, *Central Problems in Social Theory* (Berkeley: University of California Press, 1979).

The framing ideas: Millennial and apocalyptic constructions of modernity

The human sciences were born in the midst of a social crisis. Under the impact of modernizing processes, the material infrastructure of Western societies was changing. Existing symbolic frameworks that gave order, identity, and value to individual and group life were discordant with the emerging modern structures of institutional order and authority. Many contemporaries felt compelled to innovate new cognitive maps of reality, moral rhetorics, and expressive symbolism and to do so in a decidedly post-Christian language. By the late eighteenth century science or, more generally, a secular analytical reason had become the accepted language in terms of which claims about truth and moral norms assumed legitimacy.

The human sciences materialized as part of the effort by modernizing strata to shape a posttraditional order by fashioning new constructions of human nature, social institutions, and history.[4] From this perspective, the explosion of discourses on human nature and society in the eighteenth and nineteenth centuries (e.g., contract theory, classical economics, the "science of man," the new history of the German Historical school, communitarian and socialist theories, social Darwinism, sociology, and Marxism) must be understood, in part, as substitutes for Christian and Aristotelian cosmologies. They assumed the role of identifying an epoch by explaining its origin, defining its historical significance, and projecting possible futures. By locating modernity in relation to the history of humanity, the human sciences contributed to shaping its identity. The proliferation of grand social theories in the eighteenth and nineteenth centuries was not, then, simply a sign of the undeveloped state of social science. Instead, it was a response to personal and collective needs for symbolic order and meaning in the face of the enfeeblement of the Judeo-Christian tradition. They functioned as either secular cosmologies, providing an integrated picture of humanity, or as grand narratives explaining who we are, where we come from, what our place is in history, and our likely future. Contrary to the belief that the twentieth century has witnessed a transition from the age of social thought to the age of social science, we need only point out that "grand theory" or theories relating big stories of progress or decline are no less salient today.[5] Although I do not wish to

4. See Ernest Becker, *The Structure of Evil* (New York: Free Press, 1968); Michel Foucault, *The Order of Things* (New York: Vintage Books, 1973); Steven Seidman, *Liberalism and the Origins of European Social Theory* (Berkeley: University of California Press, 1983).
5. See Quentin Skinner (ed.), *The Return of Grand Theory* (Cambridge: Cambridge University Press, 1985).

discount the analytical or explanatory intent of these theories, they can correctly be viewed as mythic constructions. They offer comprehensive stories of our origins and present conditions that imbue our lives with meaning and dramatic moment.

The *philosophes* and their successors in the nineteenth century conceived of modernity within the framework of a secular, millennial myth of human progress.[6] For Enlighteners, the coming of modernity was of world historical importance. It marked the beginning of humankind's willful and rational self-creation. Released from primitive superstitions and metaphysical illusions by scientific reason, the modern era initiates humanity's mastery of the world. Modernity anticipates an unprecedented era of freedom and happiness. The discovery of universal truths about nature, humanity, and society and their global spread will eventuate in the advance of enlightenment, social progress, and human perfection. Modernity signifies, then, the beginning of the end of history, that is, the end of the recurring cycles of advance and decline that has characterized human history.

Secular millennial myths of progress are equally prominent in the social thought of the nineteenth and twentieth centuries. For all his antipathy to the *philosophes,* Auguste Comte conceived of human history as a story of social progress and human perfection. Indeed, his law of the three stages of mental development made human advancement an inevitability. Modernity, or the "Positive" stage, marked the culmination and endpoint of history. Henceforth, human events will follow the law of continuous incremental human progress in an orderly way. The other great nineteenth-century critic of the Enlightenment, Karl Marx, was no less passionate in imbuing modernity with millennial significance. Despite repudiating an idealist notion of history as the progress of reason, Marx discerned in the succession of socioeconomic formations a trajectory of social progress. The capitalist form of modernity will, Marx thought, inevitably evolve into a communist society. Like Comte's "Positive Polity," communism signifies a posthistorical epoch of freedom, social harmony, and human perfection. One heir to both Comte and Marx in the nineteenth century was Emile Durkheim. In *The Division of Labor in Society* Durkheim composed a narrative in which humanity passed from a "primitive" communitarian order to the early modern "individualistic" society.[7] In the concluding section of *Division,* Durkheim argued that this individualistic order,

6. See J. B. Bury, *The Idea of Progress* (New York: Dover, 1955); Robert Nisbet, *History of the Idea of Progress* (New York: Basic Books, 1980); Sidney Pollard, *The Idea of Progress* (New York: Penguin, 1968). For a slightly revisionist argument, see Peter Gay, *The Enlightenment,* 2 vols. (New York: Norton, 1977).
7. Emile Durkheim, *The Division of Labor in Society* (New York: Free Press, 1964).

with its endemic strains and discontents, is historically transitional. It will pass into what must be described as a posthistorical epoch in which individual freedom and social solidarity are reconciled in a social system that is egalitarian and just.

Neither two devastating world wars, a succession of revelations of massive human cruelty, nor the advancing scientization of twentieth-century culture has disabused us of the belief in the millennial importance of modernity. There is a direct line between Condorcet's *Sketch for a Historical Picture of the Progress of the Human Mind*, Herbert Spencer's *Evolution of Society*, and Talcott Parsons's *The Evolution of Modern Societies*. The common thread is a story of human events from the beginning of history to the present framed in terms of a metanarrative of progress. Whether Parsons is analyzing the "Christianization" of modernity or the successive political, economic, and educational revolutions of the past two centuries, he details a story of the steady advance of humanity. In particular, Parsons discovers in the United States the fullest realization of a "societal community" free from serious social conflicts and crises. Parsons's millennialism is not anachronistic in twentieth-century social thought. The theorists of a postideological, postindustrial age implicitly endorse a millennial myth of modernity as a posthistorical era. The end-of-ideology thesis suggests, after all, the end of all systemic social conflicts, leaving only particular, local social problems. In the postindustrial age, ideologists will be replaced by administrative-technical experts who merely fine-tune an already well-functioning social machine. To be sure, compared to Condorcet or Marx, these theorists of a postideological age are decidedly restrained. Displaying a similarly moderate millennialism is Habermas's recent defense of modernity. Taking issue with various anti- and postmodern critics, Habermas discovers in modernity conventions and forms of life that prefigure a rational society.[8]

The millennial view of modernity as issuing in an era of human rebirth and ceaseless progress has never been without its critics. In the currents of social thought affiliated with romanticism and philosophical conservatism, we find an antithetical "apocalyptic" image of modernity. The so-called counter-enlightenment viewed modernity as heralding the coming of an era of cultural entropy, social decline, and spiritual exhaustion.[9]

8. Jurgen Habermas, "Modernity versus Postmodernity," *New German Critique* 22 (Winter 1981), pp. 3–14.
9. See Isaiah Berlin, "The Counter-Enlightenment," in *Against the Current* (New York: Viking Press, 1980); Karl Mannheim, "Conservative Thought," in *From Karl Mannheim*, edited by Kurt Wolff (New York: Oxford University Press, 1971); Robert Nisbet, *The Sociological Tradition* (New York: Basic Books, 1966); Steven Seidman, *Liberalism and the Origins of European Social Theory*.

Such eighteenth-century luminaries of the counter-Enlightenment as Burke, Bonald, Maistre, and Savigny painted a bleak picture. The ascendancy of science brings in its wake cynicism and moral relativism; secularization engenders pathological strains of anomie and nihilism; individualism promotes egotism and social alienation; democratization fosters the "revolt of the masses," ushering in a culture of mediocrity and conformity. Central to counter-Enlightenment social thought is the claim that modernity entails a perpetual social crisis. Its origin is the failure of secular reason to fashion symbolic structures that can provide overarching and compelling values and orientations that can give coherence and purpose to our lives.

These counter-Enlightenment themes are salient in nineteenth-century social theory. For example, although a modernist in his values and politics, Max Weber articulates a powerful apocalyptic image of modernity. In his famous essay on Protestantism and capitalism, Weber deliberately substitutes apocalyptic expectations for the millennial ones of the Enlighteners:

> No one knows who will live in this cage in the future, or whether at the end of this tremendous development entirely new prophets will arise, or there will be a great rebirth of old ideas and ideals, or, if neither, mechanized petrification, embellished with a sort of convulsive self-importance. For of the last stage of this cultural development, it might well be truly said: "Specialists without spirit, sensualists without heart; this nullity imagines that it has attained a level of civilization never before achieved."[10]

Curiously, these antiutopian themes surface in the social theory of the Frankfurt School. Believing that fascism or some authoritarian variant, not socialism, was to be the successor to capitalism, the Frankfurt School steadily retreats from any millennial hope. From the 1940s on, their writings highlight the regressive and dehumanizing features of modernity. Indeed, in the *Dialectic of Enlightenment*, Horkheimer and Adorno relate a chilling tale of a coming era of darkness and decline promoted by the very rationality that Enlighteners believed could bring social renewal and progress.[11] Incorporating these counter-Enlightenment themes into his social criticism but retaining some millennial hope, Herbert Marcuse maintains that scientific-technological rationality has forged a totalitarian society in

10. Max Weber, *The Protestant Ethic and the Spirit of Capitalism* (New York: Free Press, 1958), p. 182.
11. Max Horkheimer and Theodor Adorno, *The Dialectic of Enlightenment* (New York: Herder & Herder, 1972).

which humanity is reduced to a state of one-dimensionality.[12] Paradoxically, this critique is joined to a radical millennialism as postmodernity appears to involve a virtual rebirth of humanity requiring a total civilizational transformation.[13]

Typically, contemporary social thinkers mix millennial and apocalyptic themes. For example, Peter Berger and Daniel Bell appear to endorse both the notions that modernity marks an epoch of unprecedented social progress and that secularization produces an ongoing cultural crisis. Indeed, they contend that this crisis originates not from insufficient or misdirected modernization — as Marx and Durkheim held — but from cultural modernization, which spreads a corrosive ethos of criticism, individualism, and egalitarianism. They repudiate the Enlightenment belief that reason can contribute to the construction of a rational and good society. Instead, they look to a religious revival to initiate sociocultural renewal.[14] Reflecting a similar apocalyptic standpoint, Robert Bellah turns cynical toward his earlier argument that national civil religions might function as socially cohering symbolic configurations. In *The Broken Covenant* and in subsequent writings, he relates a story of social crisis in the aftermath of the enfeeblement of the American civil religion and the failure of the new religions to move beyond sectarianism.[15] However, Bellah, like Habermas, traces the origins of our crisis to social structural dynamics, not to the inherently debilitating effects of secular critical reason. Moreover, Bellah and Habermas continue to defend the millennial possibilities of modernity.

These millennial and apocalyptic images of modernity define its meaning. They function as a metaframework, providing an ultimate standpoint toward modernity. They give coherence to more particular, local stories about modernity. It is to these smaller stories and polemics that I turn, although we need to remember that these local narratives often make big statements about the meaning of modernity. Following the organization of this anthology, I provide an overview of three major debates on modern culture.

12. Herbert Marcuse, *One-Dimensional Man* (Boston: Beacon Press, 1964).
13. See Joel Whitebook, "The Politics of Redemption," *Telos* 63 (Spring 1985), pp. 157–63.
14. Daniel Bell, *The Cultural Contradictions of Capitalism* (New York: Basic Books, 1978); Peter Berger, "From the Crisis of Religion to the Crisis of Secularity," in *Religion and America*, edited by Mary Douglas and Steven Tipton (Boston: Beacon Press, 1982).
15. Robert Bellah, *The Broken Covenant* (New York: Seabury Press, 1975) and "New Religious Consciousness and the Crisis in Modernity," in *The New Religious Consciousness*, edited by Charles Glock and Robert Bellah (Berkeley: University of California Press, 1976).

Is modern culture a secular or sacred order? The debate over religion

The concept of modernity is typically viewed – by both its defenders and its critics – as a post-Christian and even postreligious one. In their ideological struggle against the Catholic church, the *philosophes* proposed the thesis of the inevitable historical decline of religion. Adopting an evolutionary perspective, eighteenth-century Enlighteners conceived of religion as a transitional phase in human development. Religion would inevitably be superseded by a secular culture. Specifically, they argued that the Judeo-Christian tradition would forfeit its role of providing a unifying common culture. Science would take over the world-defining function of religion, and a secular moral theory would furnish standards of behavior. The power of Christianity to shape social conventions and practices would diminish greatly. A secular culture would not necessarily abolish religion, but would render it an exclusively personal and voluntary commitment of fewer and fewer people.

The notion of modernity as a secular order received powerful sociological formulations in the nineteenth century by Marx and Weber. Whereas the *philosophes* explained secularization as a consequence of the progress of reason, Marx pointed to social sources, in particular capitalism. The utilitarian spirit unleashed by the market and a labor process undergoing continuous rationalization under the whip of profit making push religion out of the public realm. In passages that are breathtaking in their vision and millennialism, Marx describes the secularizing impact of the bourgeoisie and an ascendant capitalist order: "The bourgeoisie cannot exist without constantly revolutionizing the . . . whole relations of society. . . . All fixed, fast-frozen relations, with their train of ancient and venerable prejudices and opinions, are swept away, all new-formed ones become antiquated before they can ossify. All that is solid melts into air, all that is holy is profaned, and man is at last compelled to face with sober senses, his real conditions of life. . . ."[16] In place of a religious culture, bourgeois capitalism builds a secular, international, and refined culture that will serve as the foundations of a communist society.

Although lacking Marx's millennial hope, Weber was no less adamant in insisting that modernity is a post-Christian epoch. Weber traced an autonomous religious rationalization process beginning with ancient Judaism's construction of a sacred world apart from earthly life and culminating in Protestantism's radical withdrawal of all sacred forces and

16. Karl Marx, "The Communist Manifesto," in *The Revolutions of 1848*, edited by David Fernbach (New York: Vintage Books, 1974), pp. 70–1.

magical rituals from the human world.[17] The Protestant image of a human world without supernatural forces was extended to its logical conclusion in modern science. The outcome of this religiously inspired dynamic is a disenchanted or secular modern culture – a cosmos of human purposes and events under the dominance of merely natural and mechanical dynamics.

The debate over religion has been a prominent feature of the post–World War II period. In this regard, Peter Berger's writings stand out as one of the major contemporary sociological statements of the secularization thesis.[18] Berger offers an original synthesis of Marx and Weber. From Weber he develops the theme that the Judeo-Christian tradition unleashed an immanent secularizing process. By removing God from the world and proscribing all magic, the way was open for the complete intellectualization of culture. Drawing on the Marxian analysis, Berger holds that the structural dynamics of a capitalist or advanced industrial and bureaucratic society, with its demands for efficiency, productivity, predictability, rational calculability, and control over the environment, promotes a secular public culture. As religion loses its public institutional base, it can no longer provide cultural unity. Furthermore, it now faces rivals from nonreligious symbolic forces, such as philosophical world views or political ideologies. Religion is not only pushed into the private realm but becomes a personal commitment with diminishing social support.

Building on the ideas of Berger, among others, Wolfgang Schluchter offers his own formulation of the secularization thesis:

> As far as the world views are concerned, largely completed secularization means that religious beliefs have become subjective as a result of the rise of alternative interpretations of life, which in principle can no longer be integrated into a religious world view. As far as the institutions are concerned, largely completed secularization means that institutional religion has been depoliticized as a result of a functional differentiation of society, which in principle can no longer be integrated through institutionalized religion.[19]

Religions have, of course, reacted against this narrowing of their social and cultural roles. Yet, movements toward countersecularization have not and, according to Schluchter, cannot succeed. There is an inescapable antagonism between religion and modernity. The differentiation of social spheres and their functionally specific norms produce a tension between

17. See Max Weber, *The Sociology of Religion* (New York: Free Press, 1956).
18. See Peter Berger, *The Sacred Canopy* (New York: Doubleday, 1968).
19. Wolfgang Schluchter, "The Future of Religion," in Douglas and Tipton, *Religion and America*.

institutional order and religion. Moreover, secular modes of thought are at odds with religion. The former is anthropocentric; it assumes a view of world history as a natural and cultural process involving a dialectic of human dependency and emancipation. The latter is theocentric; it assumes that world history is a process of salvation driven by a dialectic of sinfulness and redemption. Today secular world views are dominant. Religion is tolerated only as a specific institutional sphere and a particular ideology or cultural ideal.

The thesis of modern culture as a secular one has had its critics. Initially, the criticisms were principally philosophical or moral. For example, Burke argued that a religious culture is necessary on the grounds of the religious nature of humans. Like other philosophical conservatives, Burke assumed an implicit functionalism that held that only religion can provide moral and social order. Durkheim offered one of the first serious sociological alternatives to the secularization thesis. Arguing that religion implies symbolic systems that classify objects and events into a sacred or a profane realm, he held that modern societies have their own unique 'religious' culture. In particular, Durkheim interprets the modern "religion of humanity" as a transfiguration of the Judeo-Christian tradition, the former retaining the latter's transcendentalism, ethical universalism, individualism, and millennialism. In modern society the human person and the beliefs, rituals, and practices associated with the individual become the objects of religious practice. Indeed, Durkheim points to a historical link between Christianity and the modern deification of the individual:

> The originality of Christianity consisted precisely in a remarkable development of the individualistic spirit. Whereas the religion of the ancient city-states was quite entirely made of external practices, Christianity demonstrates in its inner faith, in the personal conviction of the individual, the essential condition of piety. . . . The very center of moral life was thus transported from the external to the internal, and the individual was thus elevated to be sovereign judge of his own conduct. . . . It is therefore a singular error to present the individualistic ethic as the antagonist of Christian morality. Quite the contrary – the former derived from the latter.[20]

In modern society, the human person and related beliefs about individualism and autonomy function as the core of a distinctively religious culture.

20. Emile Durkheim, "Individualism and the Intellectuals," in Emile Durkheim, *On Morality and Society,* edited by Robert Bellah (Chicago: University of Chicago Press, 1973).

Durkheim's notion of modern culture as sacred has found important sociological elaborations in the twentieth century.[21] The work of Robert Bellah is especially important. Bellah acknowledges secularization as a process involving the decline of Judeo-Christian social and cultural dominance. Yet he holds that modernity has generated its own configuration of religious beliefs and practices centered on our national experience. There are, he says, "certain common elements of religious orientation that the great majority of Americans share. These have played a crucial role in the development of American institutions and still provide a religious dimension for the whole fabric of American life. . . . This public religious dimension is expressed in a set of beliefs, symbols, and rituals I am calling the American Civil Religion."[22] The abiding belief of the American civil religion is that America is a chosen nation called upon to carry out God's will on earth. Millennial themes drawn from the Judeo-Christian tradition surface, for example, in the notion of America as having a world-historical mission to spread public virtue or democracy. Linked to these religious beliefs are sacred symbols. Those persons, places, and objects associated with "times of trial" in American history acquire a sacred status. National figures like Washington, Lincoln, or Roosevelt become religious or sacred figures; epochal events, like the founding of the nation or the Civil War, are surrounded with a sacred aura; objects and places associated with these sacred events become sacred objects or shrines. Bellah's ambivalence regarding the religious character of modern culture surfaces, however, in his subsequent writings. In *The Broken Covenant* he announces the erosion of the American civil religion. In "New Religious Consciousness and the Crisis in Modernity" he draws from the Frankfurt School to highlight the ascendancy of instrumental reason. Today, he argues, religion has lost its cultural vitality. Moreover, since secular utilitarian culture is unable to furnish a secular substitute, America finds itself in the midst of a "crisis of meaning."[23]

On one issue many defenders and critics of the secularization thesis seem to agree: Secular ideologies or secular cultural representations cannot provide compelling frameworks for establishing personal, moral, and social order. Bellah, for example, maintains that utilitarian individualistic ideologies cannot "provide a meaningful pattern of personal and social existence."[24] Peter Berger concludes that secularization inevitably generates a cultural crisis. In more recent writings, Berger underscores the failure of

21. See Steven Seidman, "Modernity and the Problem of Meaning: The Durkheimian Tradition," *Sociological Analysis* 46 (1985), pp. 109–30.
22. Robert Bellah, "Civil Religion in America," *Daedalus* 96 (Winter 1967), p. 24.
23. Bellah, "New Religious Consciousness and the Crisis in Modernity."
24. Ibid., p. 339.

secular reason to forge credible symbolic frameworks of identity and order.[25] Cultural renewal hinges on the resacralization of modern culture.
These arguments, however, push us beyond the debate over religion to the
question of the meaning and fate of secular reason in modernity.

Can secular reason create cultural order? The debate over the "end of ideology"

Enlightenment social thinkers believed that the decline of religion as a
major social force was a sign of social progress. Religion was taken as a
symbol of social backwardness and an unfree and inauthentic existence.
Many Enlighteners viewed religion as a fiction or illusion imposed upon
ordinary folks by clerical and secular elites. It was not a functional requirement of social and moral order. It was necessary only to maintain a
particular social and political hierarchy. The critique of religion was,
then, a key part of the modern project of advancing human autonomy
and happiness. Released from religious mystifications that keep us dependent and unhappy, humanity would be in a position to create itself in a
deliberate and independent way.

Central to this modern project is the expectation that secular reason
would stand in as a cultural substitute for religion. Modern people still
need, after all, intellectual and moral rationales to give coherence and
purpose to their lives. This task was now assigned to a type of thinking
that relied solely upon itself and the realities of the human and natural
worlds to construct a cultural order. Science would furnish beliefs about
the world: moral theory would provide a rational ethic; aesthetics would
supply standards of taste. Implicit in this agenda is a notion of the anticipated "end of ideology." Secular reason would furnish rational beliefs,
values, and aesthetic standards. As these structures of rationality penetrated modern institutions and rationalized daily life, there would emerge
a cultural consensus. Humanity would enter a postideological age where
conflicts would be local and nonideological, that is, not about foundational beliefs, values, and norms.

In the nineteenth century, the Enlightenment critique of religion was
extended to secular reason. Social and political thinkers turned the cynicism of the *philosophes* toward religion against secular reason. The analytical secular reason that the Enlighteners relied upon to supply rational
beliefs and moral ends was itself criticized as producing fictions that were
also implicated in relations of domination. The presumed rationality of
social science or moral theory (e.g., Kantianism or utilitarianism) was

25. Berger, "From the Crisis of Religion to the Crisis of Secularity."

shown to be burdend by particular social and political interests. Reason seemed to be as socially embedded in and saturated with bias as religion.

A shift occurred in nineteenth-century social thought. The focus of social critique passed from religion to secular reason or its products, for example, political, moral, aesthetic, or social scientific ideas. Yet, although secular reason was often viewed as ideological, many nineteenth-century Enlighteners continued to anticipate a postideological era – the end of ideology was projected into the future. For example, Marx juxtaposed the present age of ideology, which coincides with a class society, and a future classless and postideological society, which would be founded upon a cultural consensus.

Twentieth-century social thinkers have inherited both this suspicion toward the claims of reason and the hope for the eventual triumph of its redemptive and truth-producing powers. The interested nature of reason has, indeed, cast doubt upon the Enlightenment hope that reason can furnish an uncoerced cultural consensus. Reason always seems to bear particular social agendas. Yet, one form or another of the end of ideology theme persists. It surfaces, most prominently, in the debate over the fate of political ideology.

The debate over mass culture and mass society in the 1950s is a key site for the general discussion of modern culture. Curiously, the end of ideology theme was embraced in radically different versions by the two major opposing parties to this debate. On the one side, Frankfurt School theorists maintained that ideologies are losing their social credibility. This does not, however, signal the triumph of reason, but rather its destruction and the rise of new forms of coerced consensus. The integration of culture into the commercial nexus of capitalism undermines the credibility of ideologies that entail integrated world views centered on political agendas of social reconstruction. In its place, mass culture, or the "culture industry," creates a homogeneous culture consisting of a largely uniform set of discrete beliefs and values, highly stereotyped models of identity and behavior, and a small range of life-style options that focus on consumption patterns.[26] Mass society integrates individuals though the commodification of needs and desires.[27] It superimposes upon conflicting social interests a common debased consumerist culture that promises security, happiness, and fulfillment in the proliferation of consumer goods and higher levels of consumption. Social and ideological conflicts are submerged under the weight of the uniformity and subtle coercion of mass culture and mass society. In a word, the thesis of the end of ideology signifies, to the Frankfurt School, the retreat of rationality from modern social institutions and culture.

26. Horkheimer and Adorno, *The Dialectic of Enlightenment.*
27. Herbert Marcuse, *One-Dimensional Man.*

Taking issue with the Frankfurt School was a group of American theorists who gained social prominence in the period immediately following World War II. Social theorists like Daniel Bell, Martin Lipset, Edward Shils, and Talcott Parsons disputed the critique of mass society advanced by the Frankfurt School. Writing in the afterglow of the American war triumph, they argued that the major social divisions and conflicts in Western societies have disappeared. Furthermore, despite the current discord between Western capitalism and Eastern communism, their common technological-industrial infrastructure and commitment to economic growth pointed in the direction of a basic convergence toward a common postindustrial society. In a postindustrial society, ideologies such as socialism or fascism lose their socially compelling character. Social conflicts may persist, but they will be local affairs or defined as administrative problems that will not involve mass political mobilization. The decline of systemic social conflicts along with the social disillusionment toward revolutionary regimes will turn the public away from ideology to a more pragmatic, administratively oriented politics. The decline of ideology, according to these liberal theorists, does not reflect the ascendancy of a technocratic order but the reverse: the institutionalization of Enlightenment beliefs and norms concerning individual freedom and rights, equality, justice, and democracy. Thus, taking issue with those critics who describe modernity as a coercive order, Parsons underscores its voluntary and consensual nature:

> Contrary to the opinion among many intellectuals, American society – and most modern societies without dictatorial regimes – has institutionalized a broader range of freedoms than had previous societies. . . . Such freedoms begin with freedom from some of the exigencies of physical life: ill health, short life. . . . They include reduced exposure to violence . . . [and] freedom of choice in consumption. . . . There is freedom of marital choice, of occupation, of religious adherence, of political allegiance, of thought, of speech and expression. From a comparative and evolutionary perspective, the societies of the later twentieth century have successfully institutionalized the liberal values of a century ago.[28]

Indeed, Parsons believes that the advanced modern societies have realized, in a significant way, the Enlightenment ideal of society as an ongoing voluntary creation of free and equal individuals.

The debate over mass culture and society is embedded in a specific sociohistorical context. The European experience of fascism is the back-

28. Talcott Parsons, *The Evolution of Societies* (Englewood Cliffs, N.J.: Prentice-Hall, 1977).

drop to the Frankfurt School critique; the American war triumph and its postwar prosperity, along with the anticipation of detente, lie behind the liberal defense of mass society and the utopian hopes tied to the notion of a postindustrial society. The upsurge of radicalism in the 1960s challenged the end of ideology thesis in both its critical and affirmative versions. The rise of mass-based social movements pursuing an agenda of social reconstruction (e.g., the women's, gay, black, peace, and ecological movements) discredited both the Frankfurt School view that genuine opposition has disappeared in a totally administered, one-diminished society and the liberal presumption of a coming postindustrial society resting upon an unforced cultural consensus. This historical juncture made it possible to reformulate the debate over ideology.[29]

One effort to rethink the end of ideology theme in the aftermath of the renewal of ideological politics is offered by Alvin Gouldner.[30] He proposes a position intermediate between the Frankfurt School and the liberal consensus theorists. He argues that ideologies have lost their power of identity formation and political mobilization for most people in advanced capitalist societies. Legitimation is today lodged in mass consumption and in the state administrative safeguarding of peace, civil order, and prosperity. Personal identities are built up from the discrete blocks of meaning provided by mass culture. Yet, Gouldner suggests that a culture of critical discourse informed by Enlightenment values flourishes in our intellectual culture. This critical culture finds its principal institutional embodiment in the university but penetrates the public through a variety of public organizations and through the mass media. Within this critical culture ideological politics is alive and well. Contemporary society continues to be formed by political mobilization focusing on ideological struggle.

In more recent years, the debate over ideology has taken another turn. The suspicion regarding the power of reason to create an unforced cultural consensus has heightened, often leaving cynicism with little hope. Today reason appears to be inextricably embedded in social conventions and relations of power. The Enlightenment suspicion toward religion has come full circle, threatening to render reason simply politics by other means. As hope in the power of reason to rise above the battle of interests has waned, the very notion of modernity as involving a project of human liberation has been thrown into doubt. In the discourses of the poststructuralists, there is no anticipated end to the ordering of human affairs within structures and discourses that entail power relations and social

29. For a useful overview of recent efforts to theorize the concept of ideology, see John Thompson, *Studies in the Theory of Ideology* (Berkeley: University of California Press, 1984).
30. Alvin Gouldner, *The Dialectic of Ideology and Technology* (New York: Seabury Press, 1976).

conflict; there is no "humanity" to be emancipated or realized, as they have debunked the idea of an essential humanity in favor of assuming only selves, identities, and behaviors produced by structures, discourses, representations, and so on. Some social observers argue that this episte-mological change indicates a broader cultural shift in the West. The culture of modernism is being challenged, and, some say, the outlines of a postmodern culture can be glimpsed. It is, in any event, this issue that is currently at the center of much current debate over modern culture.

The dissolution or reconstruction of moral order: modernism/postmodernism debated

Although there has never been a consensus about the meaning of moder-nity, we can identify a dominant cultural understanding. Modernity sug-gests such notions as an evolutionary conception of history, with the West showing the future of humanity; social progress anchored in the develop-ment of the cultural spheres of high art, science, morality-jurisprudence; a unitary or substantialist notion of the individual; and a conception of human emancipation that anticipates self-realization and the end of domi-nation. Although these assumptions have been contested by counter-Enlightenment figures, their critique typically presupposed a premodern standpoint. It was not until the post–World War II period that there materialized a critique of modernity that was forward-looking or post-modern in its premises. In contrast to antimodernist criticisms, postmod-ernism presupposes modernity and draws upon some of its less salient tendencies to challenge it.

The debate about postmodernism can be precisely situated: It initially appeared in the late 1960s and became a focal point for cultural debate in the late 1970s and 1980s. In part, this discussion has concentrated on defining narrowly aesthetic features that differentiate modernism and postmodernism. Thus, in contrast to the formally sophisticated, aestheti-cally demanding, universalistic claims of modernism, postmodern art is typically associated with the collapse of the hierarchical distinction be-tween high art and popular art, an eclectic mixing of aesthetic codes, an acceptance of the differentiation of art and life, a nostalgia for past and local traditions, and a playfulness and irony instead of the moral serious-ness of modernism. Yet, most interpreters describe these aesthetic shifts as part of a broader set of changes in our social structure and culture. The focus of the selections in this anthology and this brief review is on post-modernism as a description of broad changes in our sensibilities, norms and values, epistemology, and politics.

Daniel Bell frames the relation between modernism and postmodernism as one of cultural continuity.[31] Modernism refers to a culture whose unifying theme is the quest of the individual for self-fulfillment and empowerment. Postmodernism extends this notion to celebrate the sheer willfulness and instinctual impulse of individual action.

Bell offers a critical perspective on contemporary modernity that connects the fate of capitalism with its cultural underpinnings. In the nineteenth century, capitalism was supported by a culture that valued individualism but linked it to an ethic of self-restraint and social responsibility. Today capitalism is in crisis. The antinomian and anarchistic individualism incited by a romantic culture in the nineteenth century has become dominant with the triumph of aesthetic modernism in the twentieth century. This modernist culture is an adversarial one: It attacks the liberal-bourgeois demand for rational order, discipline, and self-sacrifice. It glorifies the impulsive sources of behavior, the ceaseless search for experience and self-realization. Although Bell acknowledges its creative period (1850–1930), he argues that by the time it became a dominant cultural logic (1960s), modernism had exhausted all of its creative energies. Postmodernism represents the cultural logic of late modernism carried to its furthest reaches. The celebration of the self ends in extolling intellectual impulse, sensual immediacy, and eroticism. Its relentless rage against order, limits, and boundaries ends, says Bell, in nihilism.

> Thus, against the aesthetic justification for life, post-modernism has completely substituted instinctual. Impulse and pleasure alone are real and life-affirming; all else is neurosis and death. . . . Post-modernism tears open the boundaries and insists that *acting out,* rather than making distinctions, is the way to gain knowledge. The "happening" and the "environment," the "street" and the "scene," are the proper arena not for art but for life.[32]

Postmodernism is now solidly entrenched in the popular arts and in mass culture. Its cultural ascendancy signals not only a crisis of the middle class but a crisis of modernity as it erodes the psychological and moral bases of our liberal-capitalist order.

From a different vantage point, Jurgen Habermas proposes a leftist critique of postmodernism.[33] Whereas Bell, as a neoconservative, is critical of both late modernism and postmodernism for destabilizing capitalism, Habermas defends modernism against the postmodern critique. The latter, says Habermas, shares with neoconservatism the abandonment of the progressive Enlightenment heritage.

31. Daniel Bell, *Cultural Contradictions of Capitalism.*
32. Ibid., pp. 51–2.
33. Jurgen Habermas, "Modernity versus Postmodernity."

Habermas describes modernity less as an aesthetic or cultural movement than as a project for social reconstruction. From a cultural point of
view, modernity signifies the dissolution of unified world views into three
autonomous spheres of knowledge: science, moral-juridical theory, and
aesthetics. The "project of modernity" that Habermas believes is implied
in the Enlightenment is twofold: The first is to develop each type of
knowledge as a reflection on truth, moral goodness, and beauty. These
discourses serve as critical standards to judge human behavior and social
institutions. The second is to establish regular interchanges between these
three cultural spheres and daily life. This enriches and elevates daily life
by bringing to bear on it the structures of rationality elaborated by these
expert cultural spheres. The project of modernity, then, aims at promoting the intellectual, moral, and aesthetic development of humanity.

Postmodernism, says Habermas, represents a retreat from the emancipatory aspirations of modernity. Reacting to the psychological and social
dislocations that stem from the uncoupling of these cultural spheres from
daily life and the conquest of the latter by bureaucratic-administrative
modes of instrumental control, postmodernists have mistakenly assailed
modernity itself. The postmodern critique, Habermas believes, is misdirected. Our aim should not be the repudiation of the project of modernity
but its completion.

Bell and Habermas are critics of postmodernism. Bell criticizes it as a
continuation of the nihilistic spirit of late modernism. Habermas portrays
postmodernism as a retreat from the utopian hopes of modernity. These
criticisms reflect, to some extent, the neoconservative and neo-Marxist
standpoints, respectively, of Bell and Habermas. Postmodernism emerged,
after all, out of the new social movements that defined themselves in a two-
sided struggle against both capitalism and the Marxian critique. The most
insistent defenders of postmodernism have been post-Marxian leftists who
identify with these movements. For example, the three major postmodern
social theorists – Foucault, Baudrillard, and Lyotard – arrived at their
standpoint through their criticism of Marxism and their identification
with the new movements.

Lyotard's *The Postmodern Condition,* for example, bears the traces of
this origin.[34] He describes postmodernism as an attack on grand narratives
or all totalizing or foundational theorizing. Enlightenment myths of progress, the Marxian story of human liberation, and the philosophical effort
to provide rational grounds for science and culture are losing their social
authority and legitimating power. In place of these master theories, postmodernism defends the more local, particularlistic character of knowl-

34. Jean-Francois Lyotard, *The Postmodern Condition* (Minneapolis: University
of Minnesota Press, 1984).

edge. Postmodern science is oriented to discerning differences and analyzing heterogeneous forms of life; it is more accepting of theoretical incommensurabilities and pursues innovation and experimentation rather than theory building, integration, and consolidation. Paralleling its epistemological break from the foundationalism and theoretism of modernism, postmodernism stands for a political agenda that highlights diverse local struggles. Lyotard claims that power is not institutionally centralized in the state or in one class; rather, it is socially dispersed in institutions, in the mass media, and in the various discourses and disciplines. Accordingly, oppositional politics is today less class based and integrated; it is dispersed in struggles that go on at various social junctures. Finally, the modernist utopian ideal of a posthistorical epoch of a liberated humanity is replaced by an ideal of a more open, decentralized society that values differences and permits fluidity in desires, identity, and institutional order.

The effort to relate postmodernism in a positive way to the new social movements is evident in Andreas Huyssen's "Mapping the Postmodern."[35] Indeed, Huyssen joins postmodernism inextricably to the diverse currents of social rebellion and cultural experimentation that began in the 1960s and have continued into the present. Against neoconservative critics like Bell or Hilton Kramer, Huyssen defends postmodernism as a movment of cultural renewal in the face of the enfeeblement of cultural modernism. Against leftist critics like Frederic Jameson or Habermas, Huyssen maintains that the radical intent of postmodernism is exhibited in its critique of hierarchy, abstract universalism, sociocultural standardization, aesthetic functionalism, and so on.[36]

At the core of postmodernism is its revolt against an increasingly stagnant high modernist culture that has become an elite overrefined, institutionally dominant aesthetic. In its mixing of high and popular culture, intermingling of codes and genres, and decentering of aesthetic standards and productions, postmodernism represents a movement of cultural revitalization. Its social base is the demand for social inclusion and empowerment by marginal social groups (e.g., women, blacks, Hispanics, Asians, gays, and lesbians). These groups have sought not only political power but legitimation for their particular social conventions and cultural productions. Drawing on their specific local vernaculars and traditions, they have waged a war against the narrow standards of high modernist culture, standards that have been imposed by a white, upper-middle-class, primarily heterosexual male elite. The social dispersal of the arts and the defense of cultural heterogeneity coincide with the political decentering of

35. Andreas Huyssen, "Mapping the Postmodern," in *After the Great Divide* (Bloomington: Indiana University Press, 1986).
36. See Fredric Jameson, "Postmodernism of the Cultural Logic of Late Capitalism," *New Left Review* 146 (July–August 1984), pp. 53–92.

the left. Postmodern politics entails a shift away from a class-based, statist politics to a politics centered in diverse movements or groups that are engaged in myriad local, institutional, and cultural struggles.

These three debates do not, of course, exhaust contemporary cultural discussion. There are, for example, important discussions occurring over issues of sexuality, gender, or race and how they relate to personal identity or moral and civic order. Today culture has become a theoretically and politically contested terrain. The most significant intellectual movements of the last two decades – hermeneutics, symbolic anthropology, semiotics, structuralism and poststructuralism, critical theory, and feminism – have placed cultural analysis at the center of the human and literary disciplines. The most significant political and moral struggles of our time, at least in the industrial West, focus on cultural issues concerning personal identity, community building, social legitimation and inclusion, moral order, and everyday ethics. The aim of this anthology is to contribute to the centering of the intellectual and moral-practical debates on the relation between culture and society.

THE PLACE OF RELIGION: IS MODERNITY A SECULAR OR SACRED ORDER?

- Peter Berger, *Social sources of secularization*
- Wolfgang Schluchter, *The future of religion*
- Robert Bellah, *Civil religion in America*

20

Social sources of secularization

Peter Berger

The original "locale" of secularization . . . was in the economic area, specifically, in those sectors of the economy being formed by the capitalistic and industrial processes. Consequently, different strata of modern society [have] been affected by secularization differentially in terms of their closeness to or distance from these processes. Highly secularized strata emerged in the immediate proximity of these same processes. In other words, modern industrial society has produced a centrally "located" sector that is something like a "liberated territory" with respect to religion. Secularization has moved "outwards" from this sector into other areas of society. One interesting consequence of this has been a tendency for religion to be "polarized" between the most public and the most private sectors of the institutional order, specifically between the institutions of the state and the family. Even at a point of far-reaching secularization of everyday life as lived at work and in the relationships that surround work one may still find religious symbols attached to the institutions of state and family. For instance, at a point where everyone takes for granted that "religion stops at the factory gate," it may nevertheless be also taken for granted that one does not inaugurate either a war or a marriage without the traditional religious symbolizations.

A way of putting this in terms of common sociological parlance is to say that there has been a "cultural lag" between the secularization of the economy on the one hand and that of the state and the family on the other. As far as the state is concerned, this has meant the continuation in several countries of traditional religious legitimations of the political order at a time when those countries were already well on the way toward becoming modern industrial societies. This was certainly the case with England, the first country to embark on this journey. On the other hand, secularizing political forces have been at work in countries that still

Excerpt from *The Sacred Canopy* by Peter L. Berger. Reprinted by permission of Doubleday & Company, Inc. Also reprinted by permission of Faber and Faber, Ltd., from *The Social Reality of Religion* by Peter Berger.

lagged behind in terms of capitalistic industrial development, as in France in the late eighteenth century and in many of the underdeveloped countries today. The relationship between socioeconomic modernization and political secularization, therefore, is not a simple one. Nevertheless, we would contend that there is a tendency toward the secularization of the political order that goes naturally with the development of modern industrialism. Specifically, there is a tendency toward the institutional separation between the state and religion. Whether this is a practical matter originally unconnected with ideological anticlericalism, as in America, or is linked to an anticlerical or even antireligious *laicisme,* as in France, is dependent upon peculiar historical factors at work in different national societies. The global tendency seems to be in all cases the emergence of a state emancipated from the sway of either religious institutions or religious rationales of political action. This is also true in those "antiquarian" cases in which the same political secularization continues to be decorated with the traditional symbols of religio-political unity, as in England or Sweden. Indeed, the anachronism of the traditional symbols in these cases only serves to underline the actuality of the secularization that has taken place despite them.

One of the most important consequences of this is that the state no longer serves as an enforcement agency on behalf of the previously dominant religious institution. Indeed, this is one of the major tenets in the political doctrine of the separation of state and church, both in its American and French versions (whatever their other differences may be), and it is equally strongly expressed in the various doctrines of religious toleration and liberty even where these are not legitimated in terms of the separation of state and church, as in England, Germany, or the Scandinavian countries. The state now takes on a role vis-à-vis the competing religious groups that is strikingly reminiscent of its role in laissez-faire capitalism – basically, that of impartial guardian of order between independent and uncoerced competitors. As we shall see in a moment, this analogy between economic and religious "free enterprise" is far from accidental.

Of course, there are differences in the specific attitude taken by the state toward religion in different national societies. But if one keeps in mind the basic similarity of the cessation of coercion these differences appear as less than decisive. Thus there are obvious differences between the American situation, in which the state is most benign to religion and in which the different religious groups profit equally from the fiscal bonanza guaranteed to them by the tax exemption laws, and the situation in Communist Europe, in which the state, for its own ideological reasons, is hostile to religion in both theory and practice. It is important to keep in mind, though, that both these situations, if they are compared with traditional "Christian societies," are similar to the extent that the churches can no longer call upon the political arm to enforce their claims of allegiance. In both these situations the churches are "on their own" in having to enlist the voluntary adherence of their respective clienteles, though of course the American state facilitates their endeavor in the same measure as the communist state tries to hinder them. Equally interesting is the failure of attempts to replicate the traditional coercive support of religion by the state under conditions of modernization. Contemporary Spain and Israel serve as interesting examples of such attempts, it being safe to say in both cases that the attempts are in [the] process of failing. We would argue that the only chance of success in these countries would lie in the reversal of the modernization process, which would entail their remaking into preindustrial societies – a goal as close to the impossible as anything in the realm of history.

The dynamics behind this are far from mysterious. Their roots are in the processes of rationalization released by modernization (that is, by the establishment of, first, a capitalist, then an industrial socioeconomic order) in society at large and in the political institutions in particular. The aforementioned "liberated territory" of secularized sectors of society is so centrally "located," in and around the capitalistic-industrial economy, that any attempt to "reconquer" it in the name of religio-political traditionalism endangers the continued functioning of this economy. A modern industrial society requires the presence of large cadres of scientific and technological personnel, whose training and ongoing social organization presuppose a high degree of rationalization, not only on the level of infrastructure but also on that of consciousness. Any attempts at traditionalistic *reconquista* thus threaten to dismantle the rational foundations of modern society. Furthermore, the secularizing potency of capitalistic-industrial rationalization is not only self-perpetuating but self-aggrandizing. As the capitalistic-industrial complex expands, so do the social strata dominated by its rationales, and it becomes ever more difficult to establish traditional controls over them. Since the expansion of the same complex is international (today just about worldwide), it becomes increasingly difficult to isolate any particular national society from its rationalizing effects without at the same time keeping that society in a condition of economic backwardness. The impact of modern mass communications and mass transportation (both nicely concentrated in the phenomenon of tourism) on contemporary Spain may serve as an illustration. As the modern state is increasingly occupied with the political and legal requirements of the gigantic economic machinery of industrial production, it must gear its own structure and ideology to this end. On the level of structure, this means above all the establishment of highly rational bureaucracies; on the level of ideology, it means the maintenance of legitimations that are adequate for such bureaucracies. Thus, inevitably, there develops an affinity, both in structure and in "spirit," between the economic and the political spheres. Secularization then passes from the economic to the political sphere in a near-inexorable process of "diffusion." The religious legitimation[s] of the state are then either liquidated altogether or remain as rhetorical ornamentations devoid of social reality. It may be added that, given an advanced state of industrialization, it seems of little consequence in this respect whether the rationalization of the political order takes place under capitalist or socialist, democratic or authoritarian auspices. The decisive variable for secularization does not seem to be the institutionalization of particular property relations, nor the specifics of different constitutional systems, but rather the process of rationalization that is the prerequisite for any industrial society of the modern type.

While the presence of religion within modern political institutions is, typically, a matter of ideological rhetorics, this cannot be said about the opposite "pole." In the sphere of the family and of social relationships closely linked to it, religion continues to have considerable "reality" potential, that is, continues to be relevant in terms of the motives and self-interpretations of people in this sphere of everyday social activity. The symbolic liaison between religion and the family is, of course, of ancient lineage indeed, grounded in the very antiquity of kinship institutions as such. The continuation of this liaison may then, in certain cases, be simply looked upon as an institutional "survival." More interesting, though, is the reappearance of the religious legitimation of the family even in highly secularized strata, as for instance in the contemporary American middle classes. In these instances religion manifests itself in its peculiarly modern form, that is, as a legitimating complex voluntarily adopted by an uncoerced clientele. As such, it is located in the private sphere of everyday social life and is marked by the very peculiar traits of this sphere in modern society. One of the essential traits is that of "individualization." This means that privatized religion is a matter of the "choice" or "preference" of the individual or the nuclear family, ipso facto lacking in common, binding quality. Such private religiosity, however "real" it may be to the individuals who adopt it, cannot any longer fulfill the classical task of religion, that of constructing a common world within which all of social life receives ultimate meaning binding on everybody. Instead, this religiosity is limited to specific enclaves of social life that may be effectively segregated from the secularized sectors of modern society. The values pertaining to private religiosity are, typically, irrelevant to institutional contexts other than the private sphere. For example, a businessman or politician may faithfully adhere to the religiously legitimated norms of family life, while at the same time conducting his activities in the public sphere without any reference to religious values of any kind. It is not difficult to see that such segregation of religion within the private sphere is quite "functional" for the maintenance of the highly rationalized order of modern economic and political institutions. The fact that this privatization of the religious tradition poses a problem for the theoreticians of the institutions embodying this tradition need not concern us at the moment.

The over-all effect of the aforementioned "polarization" is very curious. Religion manifests itself as public rhetoric and private virtue. In other words, insofar as religion is common it lacks "reality," and insofar as it is "real" it lacks commonality. This situation represents a severe rupture of the traditional task of religion, which was precisely the establishment of an integrated set of definitions of reality that could serve as a common universe of meaning for the members of a society. The world-building potency of religion is thus restricted to the construction of subworlds, of fragmented universes of meaning, the plausibility structure of which may in some cases be no larger than the nuclear family. Since the modern family is notoriously fragile as an institution (a trait it shares with all other formations of the private sphere), this means that religion resting on this kind of plausibility structure is of necessity a tenuous construction. Put simply, a "religious preference" can be abandoned as readily as it was first adopted. This tenuousness can (indeed, must) be mitigated by seeking more broadly based plausibility structures. Typically, these are the churches or other wider religious groupings. By the very nature of their social character as voluntary associations "located" primarily in the private sphere, however, such churches can only augment the strength and durability of the required plausibility structures to a limited extent.

The "polarization" of religion brought about by secularization, and the concomitant loss of commonality and/or "reality," can also be described by saying that secularization ipso facto leads to a pluralistic situation. The term "pluralism," to be sure, has usually been applied only to those cases (of which the American one is prototypical) in which different religious groups are tolerated by the state and engage in free competition with each other. There is little point to arguments over terminology and there is nothing wrong with this limited use of the term. If, however, one looks at the underlying social forces producing even this limited kind of pluralism, the deeper linkage between secularization and pluralism becomes apparent. One may then say that, as we have seen, secularization brings about a demonopolization of religious traditions and thus, ipso facto, leads to a pluralistic situation. . . .

The key characteristic of all pluralistic situations, whatever the details of their historical background, is that the religious ex-monopolies can no longer take for granted the allegiance of their client populations. Allegiance is voluntary and thus, by definition, less than certain. As a result, the religious tradition, which previously could be authoritatively imposed, now has to be marketed. It must be "sold" to a clientele that is no longer constrained to "buy." The pluralistic situation is, above all, a market situation. In it, the religious institutions become marketing agencies and the religious traditions become consumer commodities. And at any rate a good deal of religious activity in this situation comes to be dominated by the logic of market economics.

It is not difficult to see that this situation will have far-reaching consequences for the social structure of the various religious groups. What happens here, quite simply, is that the religious groups are transformed from monopolies to competitive marketing agencies. Previously, the religious groups were organized as befits an institution exercising exclusive control over a population of retainers. Now, the religious groups must organize themselves in such a way as to woo a population of consumers, in competition with other groups having the same purpose. All at once, the question of "results" becomes important. In the monopolistic situation the socio-religious structures are under no pressure to produce "results" – the situation itself predefines the "results." Medieval France, for instance, was Catholic by definition. Contemporary France, however, can be so defined only in the teeth of overwhelming contrary evidence. It has become, indeed, a *pays de mission*. Consequently, the Catholic church must raise the question of its own social structure, precisely in order to make possible the achievement of missionary "results." The confrontation with this question accounts in large measure for the turmoil through which French Catholicism has passed in recent years.

The pressure to achieve "results" in a competitive situation entails a rationalization of the socio-religious structures. However these may be legitimated by the theologians, the men charged with the mundane welfare of the various religious groups must see to it that the structures permit the rational execution of the groups' "mission." As in other institutional spheres of modern society, such structural rationalization expresses itself primarily in the phenomenon of bureaucracy.

The spread of bureaucratic structures through the religious institutions has the consequence that these, irrespective of their various theological traditions, increasingly resemble each other sociologically. The traditional terminology pertaining to matters of "polity" usually obfuscates this fact. Thus a certain position, A, may carry out the same bureaucratic functions in two different religious groups, but it may be legitimated by theological formula B in one group and by formula C in the other, and indeed the two theological legitimations may be directly contradictory without affecting the functionality of the position in question. For instance, the control over investment funds may be in the charge of a bishop in one group and of the chairman of a laymen's committee in another, yet the actual bureaucratic activities necessitated by this position will have little if any connection with the traditional legitimations of the episcopate or of lay authority. To be sure, there are different models or *Leitbilder* of bureaucracy involved in this process. Thus European Protestant churches, with long experience in state–church situations, will tend toward political models of bureaucracy, while American Protestantism tends to emulate the bureaucratic structures of economic corporations. The central administration of the Catholic church, on the other hand, has its own bureaucratic tradition, which so far has shown itself highly resistant to modernizing modifications. But the demands of rationality are very similar in all these cases and exercise similarly strong pressure on the respective socio-religious structures.

The contemporary situation of religion is thus characterized by a progressive bureaucratization of the religious institutions. Both their internal and their external social relations are marked by this process. Internally, the religious institutions are not only administered bureaucratically, but their day-to-day operations are dominated by the typical problems and "logic" of bureaucracy. Externally, the religious institutions deal with other social institutions, as well as with each other, through the typical forms of bureaucratic interaction. "Public relations" with the consumer clientele, "lobbying" with the government, "fund raising" with both governmental and private agencies, multifaceted involvements with the secular economy (particularly through investment) – in all these aspects of their "mission" the religious institutions are compelled to seek "results" by methods that are, of necessity, very similar to those employed by other bureaucratic structures with similar problems. Very importantly, the same bureaucratic "logic" applies to the dealings of the several religious institutions with each other.

Bureaucracies demand specific types of personnel. This personnel is specific not only in terms of its functions and requisite skills, but also in terms of its psychological characteristics. Bureaucratic institutions both select and form the personnel types they require for their operation. This means that similar types of leadership emerge in the several religious institutions, irrespective of the traditional patterns in this matter. The requirements of bureaucracy override such traditional differentiations of religious leadership as "prophet" versus "priest," "scholar" versus "saint," and so forth. Thus it does not matter very much whether a certain bureaucratic functionary comes out of a Protestant tradition of "prophetic" ministry or a Catholic tradition of "priestly" one – in either case, he must above all adapt himself to the requirements of his bureaucratic role. Where possible, the traditional formulas will be retained to legitimate the new social-psychological types; where this is no longer possible, they will have to be modified in order to permit such legitimation. For example, [although] theological scholarship was traditionally central to the role of the Protestant minister, it has become increasingly irrelevant to the roles of the ministry both in "wholesale" (bureaucratic administration) and "retail" (local marketing) operations; Protestant educational institutions for the ministry have been accordingly modified, with concomitant modifications in their legitimating rationales. The social-psychological type emerging in the leadership of the bureaucratized religious institutions is, naturally, similar to the bureaucratic personality in other institutional contexts – activist, pragmatically oriented, not given to administrative irrelevant reflection, skilled in interpersonal relations, "dynamic" and conservative at the same time, and so forth. The individuals conforming to this type in the different religious institutions speak the same language and, naturally, understand each other and each other's problems. . . .

The effects of the pluralistic situation are not limited to the social-structural aspects of religion. They also extend to the religious contexts, that is, to the product of the religious marketing agencies. It should not be difficult to see why this should be so, in view of the preceding discussion of structural changes. As long as religious institutions occupied a monopoly position in society, their contents could be determined in accordance with whatever theological lore seemed plausible and/or convenient to the religious leadership. This does not mean, of course, that the leadership and its theological decisions were immune to forces originating in the larger society, for instance within the power centers of the latter. Religion has always been susceptible to highly mundane influences, extending even to its most rarified theoretical constructions. The pluralistic situation, however, introduces a novel form of mundane influences, probably more potent in modifying religious contents than such older forms as the wishes of kings or the vested interests of classes – the dynamics of consumer preference.

To repeat, the crucial sociological and social-psychological characteristic of the pluralistic situation is that religion can no longer be imposed but must be marketed. It is impossible, almost a priori, to market a commodity to a population of uncoerced consumers without taking their wishes concerning the commodity into consideration. To be sure, the religious institutions can still count on traditional ties holding back certain groups of the population from too drastic liberty in religious choice – in terms of the market, there still is strong "product loyalty" among certain groups of "old customers." Furthermore, the religious institutions can to a certain extent restrain disaffection among the same groups by means of their own promotional activities. All the same, the basic necessity of taking on a soliciting stance vis-à-vis a public means that consumer controls over the product being marketed are introduced.

This means, further, that a dynamic element is introduced into the situation, a principle of changeability if not change, that is intrinsically inimical to religious traditionalism. In other words, in this situation it becomes increasingly difficult to maintain the religious traditions as unchanging verity. Instead, the dynamics of consumer preference is introduced into the religious sphere. Religious contents become subjects of "fashion." This need not necessarily imply that there will be rapid change or that the principle of unchangeability will be surrendered theologically, but the possibility of change is introduced into the situation once and for all. Sooner or later, the chances are that the possibility will be realized and that the possibility will eventually be legitimated on the level of theological theorizing. This is obviously easier to admit for some religious groups than for others (for instance, for the Protestants than for the Catholics), but no group can escape this effect completely.

The dynamics of consumer preference does not, in itself, determine the substantive contents – it simply posits that, in principle, they are susceptible to change, without determining the direction of change. However, there are some other factors in the contemporary situation that have substantive influence on the character of this change. Insofar as the world of the consumers in question is secularized, their preference will reflect this. That is, they will prefer religious products that can be made consonant with secularized consciousness over those that cannot. This will, of course, vary with the strata that serve as clienteles for different religious institutions. Consumer demand in upper-middle-class suburbia in America, for instance, is different in this respect from consumer demand in the rural South. Given the variability in the degree of secularization of different strata, the secularizing influence of these strata as religious consumers will vary. But inasmuch as secularization is a global trend, there is a global tendency for religious contents to be modified in a secularizing direction. In the extreme cases (as in liberal Protestantism and Judaism) this may lead to the deliberate excision of all or nearly all "supernatural" elements from the religious tradition and a legitimation of the continued existence of the institution that once embodied the tradition in purely secular terms. In other cases it may just mean that the "supernatural" elements are de-emphasized or pushed into the background, while the institution is "sold" under the label of values congenial to secularized consciousness. For example, the Catholic church is obviously less ready to "demythologize" its contents than most of its Protestant competitors, but both traditional Catholicism and "progressive" Protestantism can be effectively advertised as strengthening the moral fiber of the nation or as supplying various psychological benefits ("peace of mind" and the like).

Another substantive influence comes from the institutional "location" of religion in contemporary society. Since the socially significant "relevance" of religion is primarily in the private sphere, consumer preference reflects the "needs" of this sphere. This means that religion can more easily be marketed if it can be shown to be "relevant" to private life than if it is advertised as entailing specific applications to the large public institutions. This is particularly important for the moral and therapeutic functions of religion. As a result, the religious institutions have accommodated themselves to the moral and therapeutic "needs" of the individual in his private life. This manifests itself in the prominence given to private problems in the activity and promotion of contemporary religious institutions – the emphasis on the family and neighborhood as well as on the psychological "needs" of the individual in his private life. This manifests itself in the prominence given to private problems in the activity and promotion of contemporary religious institutions – the emphasis on family and neighborhood as well as on the psychological "needs" of the private individual. It is in these areas that religion continues to be "relevant" even in highly secularized strata, while the application of religious perspectives to political and economic problems is widely deemed "irrelevant" in the same strata. This, incidentally, helps to explain why the churches have had relatively little influence on the economic and political views of even their own members, while continuing to be cherished by the latter in their existence as private individuals. . .

In this way the demonopolization of religion is a social-structural as well as a social-psychological process. Religion no longer legitimates "the world." Rather, different religious groups seek, by different means, to maintain their particular subworlds in the face of a plurality of competing subworlds. Concomitantly, this plurality of religious legitimations is internalized in consciousness as a plurality of possibilities between which one may choose. Ipso facto, any particular choice is relativized and less than certain. What certainty there is must be dredged up from within the subjective consciousness of the individual, since it can no longer be derived from the external, socially shared, and taken-for-granted world. This "dredging up" can then be legitimated as a "discovery" of some alleged existential or psychological data. The religious traditions have lost their character as overarching symbols for the society at large, which must find its integrating symbolism elsewhere. Those who continue to adhere to the world as defined by the religious traditions then find themselves in the position of cognitive minorities – a status that has social-psychological as well as theoretical problems.

21

The future of religion

Wolfgang Schluchter

Every scientific investigation must approach its subject not only pragmatically but also analytically. In my case this requires a definition of religion. From a sociological perspective religion is the product of that "world-forming" action of human beings through which they constitute a sphere of the sacred, which is at the same time a realm of superior power. Religious action establishes and reinforces the distinction between a sacred and a profane sphere. The sacred appears as a reality that exists beyond or above the profane but that also remains connected with it. This is demonstrated especially in individual and collective extremities. Then it becomes clear that individual and collective action depends on circumstances beyond control. For Max Weber, therefore, religion requires the construction of a world behind or above the world, which is usually populated by demons and gods. Ordering the relationship of demons and gods to human beings constitutes "the realm of religious action." After a certain developmental level has been reached, this realm is organized by religious associations. They administer external or internal, this-worldly or otherworldly goods of salvation. They protect their order through the application of psychic coercion. They grant or deny those very goods for which they are responsible. The structure and content of religious world views and of religious associations vary within and among religious traditions. A historical sociology of religion has the task of discovering these variations and their consequences. Its analytical subject, however, is religious action – that action which establishes or maintains a sacred cosmos by trying to control uncontrollable contingencies.

What is the constellation within which religious action takes place today? What are the most important characteristics of our contemporary religious situation? If we follow the familiar analyses of some theologians and of many sociologists, our present religious situation appears as the

From Schluchter, *Religion and America,* ed. Mary Douglas and Steven M. Tipton. Boston, Beacon Press, 1982. Reprinted by permission of *Daedalus,* Journal of the American Academy of Arts and Sciences, "Religion," Vol. 111, No. 1, Winter 1982, Cambridge, MA.

result of a process of secularization that has been going on for centuries. Secularization replaced religious values by secular values on the value level, an otherworldly by an inner-worldly orientation on the level of consciousness, and the primacy of the religious institutions by that of the political and economic ones on the institutional level. The concept of secularization, however, has a dubious analytical status, because for a long time it was not a scientific notion. Like many other concepts employed by sociologists, secularization was at first a concept with which historical actors attempted to define their situation. It was a battle cry in the war of ideas. In the nineteenth century, in particular, it was used to demand the abolition of the allegedly illegitimate clerical domination, but it was also used for the opposite purpose. Thus, secularization was one of the central slogans in the church–state conflicts of the time. At the turn of the century Ernst Troeltsch and Max Weber attempted to neutralize the word. Since then, secularization has denoted that dialectical historical process through which the Christian religion furthered the rise of modern industrial capitalism, of the modern state, and of modern science at the same time that it was increasingly weakened by these very inner-worldly powers. According to this definition, secularization is a historiographic and sociological category of a process, a summary term that describes a historical development that should be understood neither one-dimensionally nor one-sidedly. The concept refers to profound changes on the level of ideas and of the world views enveloping them, to basic changes on the level of material and ideal interests and of the attitudes corresponding to them, and to crucial institutional transformations within which individual and collective action takes place. Secularization, however, also refers to the fact that religion has lost its power not only for external but also for internal reasons. In Max Weber's view, secularization, which he terms a process of disenchantment, originated in the pre-exilic Torah and the pre-exilic prophecy of ancient Israel and found decisive support in ascetic Protestantism, as it developed in the northwestern corner of Europe from the Reformation to the Westphalian Peace.

I am using secularization in this neutralized sense when I ask: What is the function of Western Christian religion after secularization has largely run its course? In view of the desirable differentiation of the concept, I am primarily interested in two dimensions – the world views and the institutional arrangements. I would like to suggest two theses: (1) As far as the world views are concerned, largely completed secularization means that religious beliefs have become subjective as a result of the rise of alternative interpretations of life, which in principle can no longer be integrated into a religious world view. (2) As far as the institutions are concerned, largely completed secularization means that institutionalized religion has been depoliticized as a result of a functional differentiation of society, which in principle can no longer be integrated through institutionalized religion. I will draw on Max Weber's diagnosis of modern culture, mainly from his sociology of religion, to support the first thesis. I will use arguments of recent systems theory to justify the second thesis. Two questions can now be asked on the basis of the two theses. (1) Is there a legitimate religious resistance to secular world views that is more than a refusal to accept the consequences of the Enlightenment? (2) Is there a legitimate religious resistance to depoliticization, a resistance that is more than a clinging to inherited privileges? Both questions are linked to that of the messianic future of Western Christianity. Our answers should permit at least a rough estimate of the developmental tendencies in Western industrialized societies.

I now turn to the first thesis, the claim that the religious world view, in our case the Christian, is today confronted with alternative world views that it can no longer integrate, thus becoming a matter of subjective preference. This thesis is true of the relation of Christianity to the other great world religions. Ever since the disintegration of classical evolutionism, since the results produced by an empirically and historically oriented comparative study of religion, cultural anthropology, psychology, and sociology, it has become clear that these religions can no longer be ranked simply according to a sequence of stages. (Today the various versions of neo-evolutionism in social science contrast with those of comparative historical sociology according to the different assessment of the role played by stage schemes for the reconstruction of historical processes.) Our thesis applies, however, primarily to the relationship of Christianity and secular humanism, as it was shaped by Hellenism, the Renaissance, and the Enlightenment. It is true that Western Christianity has always lived in tension with the orders of the world and their values, especially with the economic, the political-legal, the aesthetic, and the sexual-erotic spheres, since it was a salvation religion based on the construct of a transcendental and personal creator God and a universalist ethic of brotherhood (both at least as tendencies). This tension grew the more the religious world view was intellectually rationalized and the more its claims were sublimated in the direction of an ethic of conviction, but also the more the "worldly" goods themselves were rationalized and sublimated by this religious development or for immanent reasons. This interpretation is central to Max Weber's comparative studies in the sociology of religion. He discusses the ways in which these tensions were dealt with, in principle, not only by Christianity but also by other great world religions. Weber emphasizes, however, that in the Christian case the rise of secular humanism adds a new dimension to the tension between salvation religion and the world. The Enlightenment is the high point at which the integrated religious world view is confronted with an integrated secular world view, the presuppositions of which are mutually exclusive. Whereas before it seemed possible to achieve a direct unity, well-founded mutual recognition, or at least indifference between religious and secular values and goods, now a fundamental tension prevails that can no longer be hidden by some compromise formula.

What are the reasons for this fundamental tension? Wherein lies the heterogeneity, the "inescapable disparity" of the ultimate presuppositions of Christianity and secular humanism? If we follow Weber – and I for one am ready to go a long way with him on this score – the Christian religion and the discipline that rationalizes it, theology, are forced to make two assumptions if they do not want to abandon themselves: The world is "willed by God and therefore somehow ethically meaningful," and its comprehension requires "certain revelations that must simply be accepted on faith as facts of salvation." Only the idea of God can justify meaningful Christian conduct. Its foundation is a belief not in a kind of knowledge but in a kind of possession, the charisma of "illumination" or inspiration. Only those human beings who have been transfused with this experience can be positively religious and adhere to a positive theology. In spite of the cognitive component that is part and parcel of the belief in religious salvation, this spiritual possession involves "at some point the credo non quod, sed quia absurdum, the 'sacrifice of the intellect.' " Secular humanism, too, and the disciplines rationalizing it – philosophy and the empirical sciences – are forced to make at least two assumptions if they want to remain true to themselves. The world is not merely in the grip of natural causality but also subject to ethical control, and for this purpose the continuous improvement of our knowledge about the world by means of the rational concept and the rational experiment is a necessary, if possibly insufficient, condition. Meaningful secular humanist conduct can be based only on the idea of humanity. Its foundation is a belief not in a kind of possession but in a kind of knowledge, "an ultimate intellectual knowledge about the is and the ought" – the charisma of reason. It is true that this charisma of reason, which proved its historical efficacy during the Enlightenment and the democratic revolutions of the eighteenth century, has in the meantime largely disappeared. For a long time the dialectic of [the] Enlightenment, and the paradox of the rationalization caused by it, [have] replaced the glorification of reason by disillusionment, indifference, and even hostility, and the idea of world mastery through empirical knowledge pursues us like a nightmare in view of the world's potential self-destruction with the means of science. Moreover, although the empirical disciplines depend on value presuppositions, they have turned away from the problem of the world's meaning. At any rate, no empirical science that is aware of its limitations tries to promise a way to true happiness. Philosophy, too, finds it difficult to interpret the value presuppositions of the individual sciences, to develop them systematically, and to integrate them into a coherent world view appropriate to the post-Enlightenment period. Thus, it is not surprising that some prefer to become trumpeters of the counter-Enlightenment instead of carrying on the no longer rosy heritage of the Enlightenment under the changed conditions. Furthermore, as in the past, we hear today not only the voices of the counter-Enlightenment but, especially among academic youth, the voices of those who search for the kind of experience ("kicks") that can be had only by turning against modern science. Nevertheless, the disenchantment of the world through modern science is an irreversible fact. Those who want to lead a secular humanist life must claim that modern science is for them "the only possible form of thinking about the world." In spite of the recognition of the paradox of unintended consequences of their own actions they must also believe that there "are in principle no mysterious unpredictable forces" and "that all things can in principle be controlled through calculation."[1] At the same time, secular humanism is committed to purely this-worldly individual or collective goals of perfection, which must be outright unacceptable to religion and even to that theology that has participated in the anthropological turn. Therefore, there must be a fundamental tension and conflict between a religious and a secular world view, between religious and secular humanist conduct, rather than unity, recognition, or indifference. This is true even if modern science, with its humanist orientation, largely abandons its interest in unmasking religion, which it pursued for a long time, in view of its recognition of its own historical preconditions and limitations. Among other reasons, this fundamental tension arises from the fact that secular humanism has pushed religion out of "the realm of the rational": Religion appears to it not necessarily as "the irrational or antirational" power, but as the nonrational power. Even more, secular humanism, with the support of some sectors of theology, helps to make religion subjective through its idea of a world that can in principle be controlled through calculation and is thus without surprises. Religion is translated from an external fact into a component of individual consciousness.

Thus, the religion and the secular world views confront one another today. Both claim to be total world views. Irrespective of all variations, the one can be called theocentric and the other anthropocentric. Both suggest an ultimate position through which they attribute meaning to the world with its value spheres and institutional realms. In the one case, the world is understood as a process of salvation driven by the dialectic of sinfulness

---

1. Max Weber, "Science as a Vocation," in Hans Gerth and C. Wright Mills eds., *From Max Weber: Essays in Sociology* (New York: Oxford University Press, 1958), p. 139.

and redemption; in the other, primarily as a natural and cultural process caught up in the dialectic of dependency and emancipation. If the carriers of these ultimate positions do not avoid each other, if they face one another without neutralizing their fundamental conflict on the level of idea through so-called liberal interpretations and on the level of action through opportunism, they will relativize each other. Each will define the other as the carrier of a partial world view, which at best can offer a limited interpretation of the world. In the struggle the secular world view has been on the offensive for a long time. In fact, it has displaced the religious world view as the dominant one. Of course, the dominant world view was never without competition, not even in the Middle Ages after the transition from the Carolingian to the Gregorian church. This transformation aimed not only at creating a culture controlled by the church but at a whole Christian society. But then and for a long time to come, the competition took place in a setting in which the religious world view was dominant and the religious institutions were dominant, that is, "regulatory agencies for both thought and action." This situation has changed radically. Although the two Christian churches in West Germany count the majority of the population among their members, the carriers of a religious world view are today a "cognitive minority." They represent no longer a dominant interpretation of the world, but at best a partial world view among many others. Apparently this partial world view does not modify and specify the dominant one but deviates from it and therefore is faced with special problems of legitimation. Of course, this is not merely a matter of changing relations among ideas on the level of world views but also among church, state, university, and the like on the institutional level.

This brings me to my second thesis: In a functionally differentiated society, institutionalized religion is depoliticized and society can no longer be integrated through it. Sociologists distinguish societies, among other criteria, according to the form of primary differentiation – whether it is segmental, stratified, or functional. In this sequence, transitions from one to the other form are related to processes of external and internal differentiation. In the first case (that of external differentiation), new tasks come into being or old ones are newly defined. This leads to changes in the kind and relationship of the social orders of a society. In the second case, new environmental conditions demand from the existing social orders as a rule a reorganization of their internal structure. Beginning with the Middle Ages, but definitely since the French Revolution, institutionalized religion has had to deal with the consequences of functional differentiation. Apparently it is very difficult for it to find a place in a society whose contexts of individual and collective action are shaped to a significant degree by functional differentiation.

How has functional differentiation affected the kind and position of the religious sphere in society? To answer this question, it is useful to describe very briefly the institutional constellation out of which the process arose – medieval society, which in ideal-typical simplification can be seen as a society with stratified differentiation. Medieval society already knew spheres characterized by selectivity, particularity, and specialization, but these were coordinated in such a manner that an all-inclusive hierarchical structure came into being, at least as a tendency. In this structure the church played a particularly important role. It monopolized the religious tasks and, in contrast to the ancient Christian church, endeavored to penetrate the whole world. It aimed to be a universal church and no longer to be a regional one. The goal of the medieval church was "to transfuse all of mankind with sacramental grace." To accomplish this, the church gave precedence, at the latest since the Gregorian reform, to the papal over the episcopal principle and strove to subordinate the secular to the sacred power. It was the duty of the church to mediate between God and the world, since it perpetuated God's incarnation in Christ. Through this mediation the church must protect as well as support the secular power (imperium). Political authority, too, was considered an instrument for the Christianization of the world. As the Investiture Conflict and its consequences show, the religious order did not succeed in imposing an unequivocally vertical coordination of universal church and empire, religious and political domination. But religious values and institutions were ranked above the secular ones. The actual institutional arrangements reinforced the dominance of the religious world view. In Ernst Troeltsch's sense, medieval society can be regarded as the institutional articulation of a "relatively unified Christian culture" embodied in both the universal church and the empire. It is true that next to the religious culture, which was primarily one of monks and priests, a secular culture arose, especially a knightly and courtly feudal culture and increasingly the culture of the urban citizenry. But, according to Troeltsch: "Only the church reigned supreme, not the state, economic production, science or art. The transcendental values of the Gospel might encounter worldliness, hedonism, sensuality and violence, but it was not confronted by competing ideals, a secular culture that would have been independent of the church and capable of creating an autonomous order."

The central position of the religious sphere in the hierarchical structure of medieval society and the dominance of its world view are reinforced by the internal organization of this very sphere. The claims to autonomy and autocephaly toward the outside are combined with a centralist and hierarchical organization, with a relatively advanced bureaucratic structure. The relatively unified Christian culture of the society at large rests on a relatively unified ecclesiastic culture of the religious sphere. For Max Weber, the institutional backbone of the religious sphere is the church as a bureaucratic organization that administers grace through priestly sacraments. Of course, this church had to contend long before the Reformation with heterodox religious movements, which challenged her religious monopoly of interpretation and organization. In particular, these movements opposed the ecclesiastical model of organization with the alternative model of the sect, which from the earliest Christian beginnings constituted part of the realization of the Gospel. The universal church absorbed many of these currents through internal differentiation, by recognizing special organizations in which religious virtuosi could act upon their heightened needs of salvation. This had positive consequences for the church and did not compel a basic reformation of its organization. Just as externally the church ranked above the empire and the other secular institutions, so internally the priest, who had the powers of the keys and the monopoly of the sacraments, took precedence over the laity, whereas the religious virtuoso, the monk, stood above the priest, who as mediator between the sacred and the profane was in closer touch with the this-worldly orders and their autonomous values. The externally and internally important ideal of a hierarchical structure was formulated in the most impressive manner in the Thomist ethic. "The architecture of instrumental stages" and the notion of a "crowning stage of ecclesiastic sacramental grace in which mankind is unified and finds its fulfillment" permitted this Thomist ethic to conceive of the unity of the system as a whole and yet to grant to every stage its relative autonomy."[2]

Medieval society, then, was a religious society dominated by a Christian world view and deeply influenced by a bureaucratic universal church, which successfully monopolized the dispensation of grace. In this society the individuals were not given the choice of whether they wanted to have religion. They must have it. The question was merely how much or how little religion they had. The answer was given not by the individual but by the church, which decided the salvation of every individual, since there is no salvation outside of it. Its most severe sanction was exclusion from the sacraments, excommunication, which involves not only the loss of "salvation chances" but also of worldly life chances. Although the religious sphere is differentiated from the other spheres to such an extent that the latter can develop varying degrees of internal differentiation, the laity cannot disengage the political from the religious role. Membership in society depends on belonging to a political and a religious association.

Modern society has broken this connection, since it is a society based primarily on functional differentiation. This form of differentiation for-

2. Ernst Troeltsch, *The Social Teaching of the Christian Churches and Sects* (New York: Macmillan, 1949), p. 273.

goes the integration of social spheres into a hierarchical whole and enormously increases the selectivity, particularity, and specialization of the spheres. The rigid and permanent hierarchy is replaced by the flexible and open competition of the spheres. Of course, a functionally differentiated society too must be integrated through the coordination of the social spheres. This is, however, a negative rather than a positive integration. The rules of coordination are not meant to establish a permanent rank order among the spheres, which would be legitimated through the "unity of a highest value or through a value system or value hierarchy." Rather, the rules are supposed to make it impossible "that the operations of a partial system lead to insoluble problems in another partial system." When difficulties arise, the regulatory needs are satisfied by recourse to secular values, especially political ones. The latter may have a religious origin, as George Jellinek showed with the example of the Rights of Man and of Citizens, but they themselves are not religious. The functional differentiation of the religious and political order[s] leads to the separation of church and state, to the transformation of the Christian state into the "free state." This change has been treated especially by the left Hegelian critique of religion in the nineteenth century as a political emancipation from religion. It has influenced the state–church conflicts until far into the twentieth century. Moreover, the functional differentiation of the religious and the political system[s] has also led to the privatization of religious life. As the state and bourgeois society are separated, religion is assigned to the latter and thus "depoliticized" for structural reasons. When religious freedom became a Right of Man, instituted in the wake of the democratic revolutions of the eighteenth century, this involved not only the right to adhere to one's own religion but also the right to be free of religion. For laypersons the religious role becomes a private role and their access to society is regulated through the secular role of citizenship.

The depoliticization of religion as a result of functional differentiation does not mean, of course, that religious associations forgo politics. As before, they attempt to make the political order instrumental for the religious world view. In comparison with other associations, religious associations also retain a number of institutional privileges in spite of advanced secularization. In sociological perspective, some religious associations appear today as "separatist" churches that try to retain their past role. But in spite of the importance that religion still has for political decisions, especially in matters of education and family life, it cannot be denied that outside of the religious sphere itself the areas subject to penetration by religious values continue to shrink. The European Christian parties, too, which endeavor to bridge the religious and the political sphere[s], must follow the imperatives of a functionally differentiated political order, which can no longer be exclusively oriented – in fact, not even primarily oriented – to religious values. Religion is today not only privatized, its claims are also considerably restricted by the relative autonomy of the other social spheres. This forces religion to be highly selective, particularized, and specialized. Given the state of the social environment, religious specialization cannot choose areas for which other spheres were differentiated, that is, the areas of politics, economics, science, art, and leisure. Although the mass churches tend to react today to their changed position in society through the assumption of tasks that belong in these areas, their specialization must focus on the three central functions of the Christian tradition: spiritual communication, charity, and the reflection on these internal and external functions, theology.

In contrast to medieval society, then, modern society has structurally changed the relation of the religious sphere to the other spheres and thus brought about a depoliticization and privatization of religion. But this is only one aspect that emerges with advanced secularization on the institutional level. Another is that the religious sphere itself has been differentiated segmentally. This process began with the Reformation, which broke the spiritual monopoly of the medieval church: internally through the new doctrine of the sacraments, which put a community of believers next to the church as a sacramental institution and the teacher of faith next to the priest as the dispenser of grace; and externally through the split of the church, which led to denominationalism. Therewith arose a religious pluralism that reinforced the depoliticization and privatization of institutionalized religion. The religious believer must cope not only with secular but also with other religious world views. This makes it difficult to regard one's own beliefs as the only road to salvation. Universal church and sect are replaced by partial or quasi-churches and denominations, which only claim to offer one road to salvation among others. It is true that the claims of universal church and sect persist and that religious pluralism can justify at least Christian ecumenism. But religious pluralism weakens the institutional position of the individual religious association, both in relation to other spheres as well as in relation to members by birth if not by conversion, who may come to feel that their membership is accidental.

Our contemporary religious situation is thus characterized by two tendencies that are part of advanced secularization. The first is the tendency of modern culture to treat the religious world view as a partial one and to make religion subjective, and the second is the tendency of modern society to depoliticize institutional religion, to privatize it, and to specify its social function in such a way that it serves the exclusive purpose of interpreting and organizing the relation of human beings to the sacred. Both tendencies have been directed against the traditional structure and position of religion and have forced a response. Catholicism replied primarily with the institutional strengthening of the universal church as a sacramental institution, Protestantism with a greater effort at theological reflection. There have been attempts at a countersecularization, but in the meantime the old front lines have largely crumbled. Religion and the secular world have reconciled themselves to one another. This is not accidental, for modern culture and modern society can tolerate religion as long as it limits itself to a specific sphere. The secular world view recognizes an open pluralism of individual and collective ideals of perfection, which can include religious goals; functional differentiation as the primary form of differentiation recognizes an open pluralism of functions, which includes also the religious function. In the last analysis, however, religion cannot accept this placement. It represents a total world view and must raise total, and hence also political, claims.

In conclusion, I can now answer my two questions: (1) Is there a justified religious resistance to the secular world view that is more than a denial of the Enlightenment? and (2) Is there a justified religious resistance to depoliticization that is more than a clinging to inherited privileges?

The secular world view grew out of the charismatic glorification of reason. It is based on the idea of the self-sufficiency of the intellect. The belief has waned, but the idea has remained and with it the ideal of inner-worldly self-perfection. This ideal lies at the root of the rationalism of world mastery, which shapes our lives. For religion this ideal must be meaningless, since it cannot come to terms with what is perhaps the most difficult problem of life – death, which negates the ideal of inner-worldly perfection. Death is, however, not the only uncontrollable contingency with which we are faced. It is true that today we can control some forces that appeared uncontrollable in the past; and some things that elude us today will become manageable in the future. Nevertheless, our lives will remain subject to inescapable contingencies. The secular world view reaches its limits when it asks for the meaning of these uncontrollable contingencies. The experience of this dependency is not yet a religious experience, but it reveals the reason for the existence of religion. As Hermann Lubbe has put it, speaking in religious terms means to realize the contingencies of the world and of our lives within it. Religious practice is the recognition of this fact, but only if it is linked up with the notion of salvation. Recognition of the fact of dependency and acceptance of a certain interpretation of it are two different steps. The second requires, in the case of religion, the sacrifice of the intellect. Whoever cannot take this step will remain unmusical in matters religious. But recognition of the fact of contingency may make a person feel friendly toward religion.

Thus, the carriers of religious world views have good reasons for resisting the secular view. The recognition of nonrational, transcendental powers, upon whom our lives depend, is not tantamount to denying the

Enlightenment. There are questions of meaning that cannot be answered without going beyond an inner-worldly attitude. This remains true even if the majority of human beings no longer tries to face these questions. It is the task of religion to transcend the existing world and to remind it of its contingency. Therefore, institutionalized religion also has good reasons to resist the depoliticization that results from its being pushed back into a sphere of its own. Still, if religion today insists on a total view, it can at best be politically relevant but no longer politically dominant.

Does such a religion, however, still have the power to transcend the existing world? Is it still capable of a turnabout that would be a precondition for not just complementing the secular life but for breaking out of it and with it? Is such a religion still able to offer the charisma of inspiration? Has not its bureaucratic constitution ruined its ability to change hearts? This is the opinion of Johann Baptist Metz and probably of other political theologians from both Catholicism and Protestantism. Metz sees a future for this religion only if it turns around and regains its messianic dimension. Metz regards the turnabout as a new understanding of salvation and of the life of the church. He thinks of salvation in terms of palpable, concrete, visible, and liberating grace and of the life of the church as a solidary community united around the eucharist, a group that is no longer necessarily guided by a permanent official. Metz therefore pleads for the transition from the tutelary church to the liberation church, a church that is no longer a church for the people but a church of the people.

What are the chances of institutionalized religion finding its way back to its messianic dimension? After all, this dimension has been largely lost. The path proposed by Metz might indeed [lead] to a new Reformation, but with consequences that cannot be intended by political theology. From a sociological perspective, Metz's proposal amounts to an abandonment of the church as a large-scale bureaucratic organization in favor of a small democratic group or even a charismatic community. This would be quite compatible with a functionally differentiated society, but also without much political importance. Similar to the family, such a "church" would likely become part of the background structure of society, a realm of perhaps private but hardly of political revolution. For in a functionally differentiated society, a sphere that wants to revolutionize not only itself but above all its social environment must resort to generalized media of exchange and complex organization. For this, Christian love and the small eucharistic group are insufficient. The proposal of such a political theology indirectly supports Max Weber's diagnosis of the present: The disenchantment of the world has deprived charisma and religious messianism of a good deal of their once revolutionary impetus.

Does this mean that Christianity has no messianic future? I do not doubt that the prospects for a new prophetic inspiration (*Pneuma*) that could revolutionize a functionally differentiated society are not good. We live in a culture and society that are in part a product of religion but that largely emancipated themselves from it. If they do not face it with hostility, they do so with indifference. It was once again Max Weber who in his famous study of the Protestant ethic and the spirit of capitalism penetratingly analyzed this connection with regard to the modern occupational culture. No one knows, Weber wrote, who will live in the housing of our technological and scientific civilization "or whether at the end of this tremendous development entirely new prophets will arise, or there will be a great rebirth of old ideas and ideals, or, if neither, mechanized petrification, embellished with a sort of convulsive self-importance." If this is the alternative, and much speaks for it, then we should wish religion a messianic future, even if we are unmusical in matters religious.

22

Civil religion in America

Robert Bellah

While some have argued that Christianity is the national faith, and others that church and synagogue celebrate only the generalized religion of "the American Way of Life," few have realized that there actually exists alongside of and rather clearly differentiated from the churches an elaborate and well-institutionalized civil religion in America. This [chapter] argues not only that there is such a thing, but also that this religion – or perhaps better, this religious dimension – has its own seriousness and integrity and requires the same care in understanding that any other religion does.

The Kennedy inaugural

John F. Kennedy's inaugural address of January 20, 1961, serves as an example and a clue with which to introduce this complex subject. That address began:

> We observe today not a victory of party but a celebration of freedom – symbolizing an end as well as beginning – signifying renewal as well as change. For I have sworn before you and Almighty God the same solemn oath our forebears prescribed nearly a century and three quarters ago.
>
> The world is very different now. For man holds in his mortal hands the power to abolish all forms of human poverty and to abolish all forms of human life. And yet the same revolutionary beliefs for which our forebears fought are still at issue around the globe – the belief that the rights of man come not from the generosity of the state but from the hand of God.

And it concluded:

> Finally, whether you are citizens of America or of the world, ask of us the same high standards of strength and sacrifice

From Bellah, *Beyond Belief.* New York: Seabury Press. Reprinted with permission.

that we shall ask of you. With a good conscience our only
sure reward, with history the final judge of our deeds, let us
go forth to lead the land we love, asking His blessing and His
help, but knowing that here on earth God's work must truly
be our own.

These are the three places in this brief address in which Kennedy mentioned the name of God. If we could understand why he mentioned God,
the way in which he did it, and what he meant to say in those three
references, we would understand much about American civil religion.

Considering the separation of church and state, how is a president justified in using the word "God" at all? The answer is that the separation of
church and state has not denied the political realm a religious dimension.
Although matters of personal religious belief, worship, and association are
considered to be strictly private affairs, there are, at the same time, certain
common elements of religious orientation that the great majority of Americans share. These have played a crucial role in the development of American institutions and still provide a religious dimension for the whole fabric
of American life, including the political sphere. This public religious dimension is expressed in a set of beliefs, symbols, and rituals that I am calling the
American civic religion. The inauguration of a president is an important
ceremonial event in this religion. It reaffirms, among other things, the
religious legitimation of the highest political authority.

Let us look more closely at what Kennedy actually said. First he said, "I
have sworn before you and almighty God the same solemn oath our
forebears prescribed nearly a century and three quarters ago." The oath is
the oath of office, including the acceptance of the obligation to uphold
the Constitution. He swears it before the people (you) and God. Beyond
the Constitution, then, the president's obligation extends not only to the
people but to God. In American political theory, sovereignty rests, of
course, with the people, but implicitly, and often explicitly, the ultimate
sovereignty has been attributed to God. This is the meaning of the motto
"In God we trust," as well as the inclusion of the phrase "under God" in
the pledge to the flag. What difference does it make that sovereignty
belongs to God? Though the will of the people as expressed in majority
vote is carefully institutionalized as the operative source of political authority, it is deprived of an ultimate significance. The will of the people is
not itself the criterion of right and wrong. There is a higher criterion in
terms of which this will can be judged; it is possible that the people may
be wrong. The president's obligation extends to the higher criterion.

When Kennedy says that "the rights of man come not from the generosity of the state but from the hand of God," he is stressing this point again.
It does not matter whether the state is the expression of the will of an

autocratic monarch or of the "people"; the rights of man are more basic than any political structure and provide a point of revolutionary leverage from which any state structure may be radically altered. That is the basis for his reassertion of the revolutionary significance of America.

But the religious dimension in political life as recognized by Kennedy not only provides a grounding for the rights of man that makes any form of political absolutism illegitimate, it also provides a transcendent goal for the political process. This is implied in his final words that "here on earth God's work must truly be our own." What he means here is, I think, more clearly spelled out in a previous paragraph, the wording of which, incidentally, has a distinctly biblical ring:

> Now the trumpet summons us again – not as a call to bear arms, though arms we need – not as a call to battle, though embattled we are – but a call to bear the burden of a long twilight struggle, year in and year out, "rejoicing in hope, patient in tribulation" – a struggle against the common enemies of man: tyranny, poverty, disease and war itself.

The whole address can be understood as only the most recent statement of a theme that lies very deep in the American tradition, namely the obligation, both collective and individual, to carry out God's will on earth. This was the motivating spirit of those who founded America, and it has been present in every generation since. Just below the surface throughout Kennedy's inaugural address, it becomes explicit in the closing statement that God's work must be our own. That this very activist and noncontemplative conception of the fundamental religious obligation, which has been historically associated with the Protestant position, should be enunciated so clearly in the first major statement of the first Catholic president seems to underline how deeply established it is in the American outlook. Let us now consider the form and history of the civil religious tradition in which Kennedy was speaking.

The idea of a civil religion

The phrase "civil religion" is, of course, Rousseau's. In chapter 8, book 4 of *The Social Contract,* he outlines the simple dogmas of the civil religion: the existence of God, the life to come, the reward of virtue and the punishment of vice, and the exclusion of religious intolerance. All other religious opinions are outside the cognizance of the state and may be freely held by citizens. While the phrase "civil religion" was not used, to the best of my knowledge, by the founding fathers, and I am certainly not arguing for the particular influence of Rousseau, it is clear that . . . religion, particularly the idea of God, played a constitutive role in the thought of the early American statesmen.

Kennedy's inauguration pointed to the religious aspect of the Declaration of Independence, and it might be well to look at that document a bit more closely. There are four references to God. The first speaks of the "Laws of Nature and of Nature's God" that entitle any people to be independent. The second is the famous statement that all men "are endowed by their Creator with certain inalienable Rights." Here Jefferson is locating the fundamental legitimacy of the new nation in a conception of "higher law" that is itself based on both classical natural law and biblical religion. The third is an appeal to "the Supreme Judge of the world for the rectitude of our intentions," and the last indicates "a firm reliance on the protection of divine Providence." In these last two references, a biblical God of history who stands in judgment over the world is indicated.

The intimate relation of these religious notions with the self-conception of the new republic is indicated by the frequency of their appearance in early official documents. For example, we find in Washington's first inaugural address of April 30, 1789:

> It would be peculiarly improper to omit in this first official act my fervent supplications that the Almighty Being who rules over the universe, who presides in the councils of nations, and whose providential aids can supply every defect, that His benediction may consecrate to the liberties and happiness of the people of the United States a Government instituted by themselves for these essential purposes. . . .
>
> No people can be bound to acknowledge and adore the invisible Hand which conducts the affairs of man more than those of the United States. Every step by which we have advanced to the character of an independent nation seems to have been distinguished by some token of providential agency. . . .

Nor did these religious sentiments remain merely the personal expression of the president. At the request of both Houses of Congress, Washington proclaimed on October 3 of that same first year as president that November 26 should be "a day of public thanksgiving and prayer," the first Thanksgiving Day under the Constitution.

The words and acts of the founding fathers, especially the first few presidents, shaped the form and tone of the civil religion as it has been maintained ever since. Though much is selectively derived from Christianity, this religion is clearly not itself Christianity. For one thing, neither Washington nor Adams nor Jefferson mentions Christ in his inaugural address; nor do any of the subsequent presidents, although not one of them fails to mention God.[1] The God of the civil religion is not only rather "unitarian," he is also on the austere side, much more related to order, law, and right than to salvation and love. Even though he is somewhat deist in cast, he is by no means simply a watchmaker God. He is actively interested and involved in history, with a special concern for America. Here the analogy has much less to do with natural law than with ancient Israel; the equation of America with Israel in the idea of the "American Israel" is not infrequent. What was implicit in the words of Washington already quoted becomes explicit in Jefferson's second inaugural when he said: "I shall need, too, the favor of that Being in whose hands we are, who led our fathers, as Israel of old, from their native land and planted them in a country flowing with all the necessaries and comforts of life." Europe is Egypt; America, the promised land. God has led his people to establish a new sort of social order that shall be a light unto all the nations.

This theme, too, has been a continuous one in the civil religion. We have already alluded to it in the case of the Kennedy inaugural. We find it again in President Johnson's inaugural address:

> They came here – the exile and the stranger, brave but frightened – to find a place where a man could be his own man. They made a covenant with this land. Conceived in justice, written in liberty, bound in union, it was meant one day to inspire the hopes of all mankind; and it binds us still. If we keep its terms, we shall flourish.

What we have, then, from the earliest years of the republic is a collection of beliefs, symbols, and rituals with respect to sacred things and institutionalized in a collectivity. This religion – there seems no other

1. God is mentioned or referred to in all inaugural addresses but Washington's second, which is a very brief (two paragraphs) and perfunctory acknowledgment. It is not without interest that the actual word "God" does not appear until Monroe's second inaugural, March 5, 1821. In his first inaugural, Washington refers to God as "that Almighty Being who rules the universe," "Great Author of every public and private good," "Invisible Hand," and "benign Parent of the Human Race." John Adams refers to God as "Providence," "Being who is supreme over all," "Patron of Order," "Fountain of Justice," and "Protector in all ages of the world of virtuous liberty." Jefferson speaks of "that infinite Power which rules the destinies of the universe" and "that Being in whose hands we are." Madison speaks of "that Almighty Being whose power regulates the destiny of nations" and "Heaven." Monroe uses "Providence" and "the Almighty" in his first inaugural and finally "Almighty God" in his second. See *Inaugural Addresses of the Presidents of the United States from George Washington 1789 to Harry S. Truman 1949*, 82d Congress, 2d Session, House Document No. 540, 1952.

word for it – while not antithetical to and indeed sharing much in common with Christianity, was neither sectarian nor in any specific sense Christian. At a time when the society was overwhelmingly Christian, it seems unlikely that this lack of Christian reference was meant to spare the feelings of the tiny non-Christian minority. Rather, the civil religion expressed what those who set the precedents felt was appropriate under the circumstances. It reflected their private as well as public views. Nor was the civil religion simply "religion in general." While generality was undoubtedly seen as a virtue by some . . . the civil religion was specific enough when it came to the topic of America. Precisely because of this specificity, the civil religion was saved from empty formalism and served as a genuine vehicle of national religious self-understanding.

But the civil religion was not, in the minds of Franklin, Washington, Jefferson, or other leaders, with the exception of a few radicals like Tom Paine, ever felt to be a substitute for Christianity. There was an implicit but quite clear division of function between the civil religion and Christianity. Under the doctrine of religious liberty, an exceptionally wide sphere of personal piety and voluntary social action was left to the churches. But the churches were neither to control the state nor to be controlled by it. The national magistrate, whatever his private religious views, operates under the rubrics of the civil religion as long as he is in his official capacity, as we have already seen in the case of Kennedy. This accommodation was undoubtedly the product of a particular historical moment and of a cultural background dominated by Protestantism of several varieties and by the Enlightenment, but it has survived despite subsequent changes in the cultural and religious climate[s].

Civil War and civil religion

Until the Civil War, the American civil religion focused above all on the event of the Revolution, which was seen as the final act of the Exodus from the old lands across the waters. The Declaration of Independence and the Constitution were the sacred scriptures and Washington the divinely appointed Moses who led his people out of the hands of tyranny. The Civil War, which Sidney Mead calls "the center of American history," was the second great event that involved the national self-understanding so deeply as to require expression in the civil religion. In 1835, Alexis de Tocqueville wrote that the American republic had never really been tried and that victory in the Revolutionary War was more the result of British preoccupation elsewhere and the presence of a powerful ally than of any great military success of the Americans. But in 1861 the time of testing had indeed come. Not only did the Civil War have the tragic intensity of fratricidal strife, but it was one of the bloodiest wars of the nineteenth century; the loss of life was far greater than any previously suffered by Americans.

The Civil War raised the deepest questions of national meaning. The man who not only formulated but in his own person embodied its meaning for Americans was Abraham Lincoln. For him the issue was not in the first instance slavery but "whether that nation, or any nation so conceived, and so dedicated, can long endure." He had said in Independence Hall in Philadelphia on February 22, 1861:

> All the political sentiments I entertain have been drawn, so far as I have been able to draw them, from the sentiments which originated in and were given to the world from this Hall. I have never had a feeling, politically, that did not spring from the sentiments embodied in the Declaration of Independence.

The phrases of Jefferson constantly echo in Lincoln's speeches. His task was, first of all, to save the Union – not for America alone but for the meaning of America to the whole world so unfogettably etched in the last phrase of the Gettysburg Address.

But inevitably the issue of slavery as the deeper cause of the conflict had to be faced. In his second inaugural, Lincoln related slavery and the war in an ultimate perspective:

> If we shall suppose that American slavery is one of those offenses which, in the providence of God, must needs come, but which, having continued through His appointed time, He now wills to remove, and that He gives to both North and South this terrible war as the woe due to those by whom the offense came, shall we discern therein any departure from those divine attributes which the believers in a living God always ascribe to Him? Fondly do we hope, fervently do we pray, that this mighty scourge of war may speedily pass away. Yet, if God wills that it continue until all the wealth piled by the bondsman's two hundred and fifty years of unrequited toil shall be sunk, and until every drop of blood drawn with the lash shall be paid by another drawn with the sword, as was said three thousand years ago, so still it must be said "the judgments of the Lord are true and righteous altogether."

But he closes on a note if not of redemption then of reconciliation – "With malice toward none, with charity toward all."

With the Civil War, a new theme of death, sacrifice, and rebirth enters the civil religion. It is symbolized in the life and death of Lincoln. Nowhere is it stated more vividly than in the Gettysburg Address, itself part of the Lincolnian "New Testament" among the civil scriptures. Robert Lowell has recently pointed out the "insistent use of birth images" in this speech explicitly devoted to "these honored dead": "brought forth," "conceived," "created," "a new birth of freedom". . . . The earlier symbolism of the civil religion had been Hebraic without in any specific sense being Jewish. The Gettysburg symbolism (". . . those who here gave their lives, that the nation might live") is Christian without having anything to do with the Christian church.

The new symbolism soon found both physical and ritualistic expression. The great number of the war dead required the establishment of a number of national cemeteries. Of these, the Gettysburg National Cemetery, which Lincoln's famous address served to dedicate, has been overshadowed only by the Arlington National Cemetery. Begun somewhat vindictively on the Lee estate across the river from Washington, partly with the end that the Lee family could never reclaim it, it has subsequently become the most hallowed monument of the civil religion. Not only was a section set aside for the Confederate dead, but it has received the dead of each succeeding American war. It is the site of the one important new symbol to come out of World War I, the Tomb of the Unknown Soldier; more recently it has become the site of the tomb of another martyred president and its symbolic eternal flame.

Memorial Day, which grew out of the Civil War, gave ritual expression to the themes we have been expressing. As Lloyd Warner has so brilliantly analyzed it, the Memorial Day observance, especially in the towns and smaller cities of America, is a major event for the whole community involving a rededication to the martyred dead, to the spirit of sacrifice, and to the American vision. Just as Thanksgiving Day, which incidentally was securely institutionalized as an annual national holiday only under the presidency of Lincoln, serves to integrate the family into the civil religion, so Memorial Day has acted to integrate the local community into the national cult. Together with the less overtly religious Fourth of July and the more minor celebrations of Veterans Day and the birthdays of Washington and Lincoln, these two holidays provide an annual ritual calendar for the civil religion. The public school system serves as a particularly important context for the cultic celebration of the civil rituals.

The civil religion today

. . . The civil religion at its best is a genuine apprehension of universal and transcendent religious reality as seen in or, one could almost say, as revealed through the experience of the American people. Like all religions, it has suffered various deformations and demonic distortions. At its best, it has neither been so general that it has lacked incisive relevance to the American scene nor so particular that it has placed American society above universal human values. . . .

It is certainly true that the relation between religion and politics in America has been singularly smooth. This is in large part due to the dominant tradition. As de Tocqueville wrote:

> The greatest part of British America was peopled by men who, after having shaken off the authority of the Pope, acknowledged no other religious supremacy: they brought with them into the New World a form of Christianity which I cannot better describe than by styling it a democratic and republican religion.[2]

The churches opposed neither the Revolution nor the establishment of democratic institutions. Even when some of them opposed the full institutionalization of religious liberty, they accepted the final outcome with good grace and without nostalgia for an *ancien regime*. The American civil religion was never anticlerical or militantly secular. On the contrary, it borrowed selectively from the religious tradition in such a way that the average American saw no conflict between the two. In this way, the civil religion was able to build up without any bitter struggle with the church powerful symbols of national solidarity and to mobilize deep levels of personal motivation for the attainment of national goals.

Such an achievement is by no means to be taken for granted. It would seem that the problem of a civil religion is quite general in modern societies and that the way it is solved or not solved will have repercussions in many spheres. One need only think of France to see how differently things can go. The French Revolution was anticlerical to the core and attempted to set up an anti-Christian civil religion. Throughout modern French history, the chasm between traditional Catholic symbols and the symbolism of 1789 has been immense.

American civil religion is still very much alive. Just three years ago we participated in a vivid reenactment of the sacrifice theme in connection with the funeral of our assassinated president. The American Israel theme is clearly behind both Kennedy's New Frontier and Johnson's Great Society. Let me give just one recent illustration of how the civil religion serves to mobilize support for the attainment of national goals. On March 15, 1965, President Johson went before Congress to ask for a strong voting-rights bill. Early in the speech he said:

2. Alexis de Tocqueville, *Democracy in America* Vol. 1 (New York: Doubleday, 1954), p. 311.

Rarely are we met with the challenge, not to our growth or abundance, or our welfare or our security – but rather to the values and the purposes and the meaning of our beloved nation.

The issue of equal rights for American Negroes is such an issue. And should we defeat every enemy, and should we double our wealth and conquer the stars and still be unequal to this issue, then we will have failed as a people and as a nation.

For with a country as with a person, "What is a man profited, if he shall gain the whole world, and lose his own soul?"

And in conclusion he said:

Above the pyramid on the great seal of the United States it says in Latin, "God has favored our undertaking."

God will not favor everything that we do. It is rather our duty to divine his will. I cannot help but believe that He truly understands and that He really favors the undertaking that we begin here tonight.

The civil religion has not always been invoked in favor of worthy causes. On the domestic scene, and American-Legion type of ideology that fuses God, country, and flag has been used to attack nonconformist and liberal ideas and groups of all kinds. Still, it has been difficult to use the words of Jefferson and Lincoln to support special interests and undermine personal freedom. The defenders of slavery before the Civil War came to reject the thinking of the Declaration of Independence. Some of the most consistent of them turned against not only Jeffersonian democracy but Reformation religion; they dreamed of a South dominated by medieval chivalry and divine-right monarchy. For all the overt religiosity of the radical right today, their relation to the civil religious consensus is tenuous, as when the John Birch Society attacks the central American symbol of Democracy itself.

With respect to America's role in the world, the dangers of distortion are greater and the built-in safeguards of the tradition weaker. The theme of the American Israel was used, almost from the beginning, as a justification for the shameful treatment of the Indians so characteristic of our history. It can be overtly or implicitly linked to the idea of manifest destiny that has been used to legitimate several adventures in imperialism since the early nineteenth century. Never has the danger been greater than today. The issue is not so much one of imperial expansion, of which we are accused, as of the tendency to assimilate all governments or parties in the world that support our immediate policies or call upon our help by invoking the notion of free institutions and democratic values. Those nations that are for the moment "on our side" become "the free world." A repressive and unstable military dictatorship in South Vietnam becomes "the free people of South Vietnam and their government." It is then part of the role of America as the New Jerusalem and "the last best hope of earth" to defend such governments with treasure and eventually with blood. When our soldiers are actually dying, it becomes possible to consecrate the struggle further by invoking the great theme of sacrifice. For the majority of the American people who are unable to judge whether the people in South Vietnam (or wherever) are "free like us," such arguments are convincing. Fortunately President Johnson has been less ready to assert that "God has favored our undertaking" in the case of Vietnam than with respect to civil rights. But others are not so hesitant. The civil religion has exercised long-term pressure for the humane solution of our greatest domestic problem, the treatment of the Negro American. It remains to be seen how relevant it can become for our role in the world at large, and whether we can effectively stand for "the revolutionary beliefs for which our forebears fought," in John F. Kennedy's words.

The civil religion is obviously involved in the most pressing moral and political issues of the day. But it is also caught in another kind of crisis, theoretical and theological, of which it is at the moment largely unaware. "God" has clearly been a central symbol in the civil religion from the beginning and remains so today. This symbol is just as central to the civil religion as it is to Judaism or Christianity. In the late eighteenth century this posed no problem; even Tom Paine, contrary to his detractors, was not an atheist. From left to right and regardless of church or sect, all could accept the idea of God. But today, as even <i>Time</i> has recognized, the meaning of "God" is by no means so clear or so obvious. There is no formal creed in the civil religion. We have had a Catholic president; it is conceivable that we could have a Jewish one. But could we have an agnostic president? Could a man with conscientious scruples about using the word "God" the way Kennedy and Johnson have used it be elected chief magistrate of our country? If the whole God symbolism requires reformulation, there will be obvious consequences for the civil religion, consequences perhaps of liberal alienation and of fundamentalist ossification that have not so far been prominent in this realm. The civil religion has been a point of articulation between the profoundest commitments of the Western religious and philosophical traditions and the common beliefs of ordinary Americans. It is not too soon to consider how the deepening theological crisis may affect the future of this articulation.

THE DEBATE OVER THE "END OF IDEOLOGY": CAN SECULAR REASON CREATE CULTURAL ORDER?

- Theodor W. Adorno, *Culture industry reconsidered*
- Herbert Marcuse, *From consensual order to instrumental control*
- Daniel Bell, *The end of ideology in the West*
- Talcott Parsons, *Beyond coercion and crisis: The coming of an era of voluntary community*
- Alvin Gouldner, *Ideology, the cultural apparatus, and the new consciousness industry*

23

Culture industry reconsidered

Theodor W. Adorno

The term "culture industry" was perhaps used for the first time in the book *Dialectic of Enlightenment,* which Horkheimer and I published in Amsterdam in 1947. In our drafts we spoke of "mass culture." We replaced that expression with "culture industry" in order to exclude from the outset the interpretation agreeable to its advocates: that it is a matter of something like a culture that arises spontaneously from the masses themselves, the contemporary form of popular art. From the latter the culture industry must be distinguished in the extreme. The culture industry fuses the old and familiar into a new quality. In all its branches, products which are tailored for consumption by masses, and which to a great extent determine the nature of that consumption, are manufactured more or less according to plan. The individual branches are similar in structure or at least fit into each other, ordering themselves into a system almost without a gap. This is made possible by contemporary technical capabilities as well as by economic and administrative concentration. The culture industry intentionally integrates its consumers from above. To the detriment of both it forces together the spheres of high and low art, separated for thousands of years. The seriousness of high art is destroyed in speculation about its efficacy; the seriousness of the lower perishes with the civilizational constraints imposed on the rebellious resistance inherent within it as long as social control was not yet total. Thus, although the culture industry undeniably speculates on the conscious and unconscious state of the millions towards which it is directed, the masses are not primary, but secondary; they are an object of calculation, an appendage of the machinery. The customer is not king, as the culture industry would like to have us believe, not its subject but its object. The very word "mass-media," specially honed for the culture industry, already shifts the accent onto harmless terrain. Neither is it a question of primary concern for the masses, nor of the techniques of communication

From Adorno; "Culture industry reconsidered," *New German Critique* 6 (1975): 12–19. Reprinted with permission of the author and *New German Critique.*

as such, but of the spirit which sufflates them, their master's voice. The culture industry misuses its concern for the masses in order to duplicate, reinforce, and strengthen their mentality, which it presumes is given and unchangeable. How this mentality might be changed is excluded throughout. The masses are not the measure but the ideology of the culture industry, even though the culture industry itself could scarcely exist without adapting to the masses.

The cultural commodities of the industry are governed, as Brecht and Suhrkamp expressed it thirty years ago, by the principle of their realization as value, and not by their own specific content and harmonious formation. The entire practice of the culture industry transfers the profit motive naked onto cultural forms. Ever since these cultural forms first began to make a living for their creators as commodities in the marketplace they had already possessed something of this quality. But then they sought after profit only indirectly, over and above their autonomous essence. New on the part of the culture industry is the direct and undisguised primacy of a precisely and thoroughly calculated efficacy in its most typical products. The autonomy of works of art, which of course rarely ever predominated in an entirely pure form, and was always permeated by a constellation of effects, is tendentially eliminated by the culture industry, with or without the conscious will of those in control. The latter include both those who carry out directives as well as those who hold the power. In economic terms they are or were in search of new opportunities for the realization of capital in the most economically developed countries. The old opportunities became increasingly . . . precarious as a result of the same concentration process which alone makes the culture industry possible as an omnipresent phenomenon. Culture, in the true sense, did not simply accommodate itself to human beings; but it always simultaneously raised a protest against the petrified relations under which they lived, thereby honoring them. Insofar as culture becomes wholly assimilated to and integrated in those petrified relations, human beings are once more debased. Cultural entities typical of the culture industry are no longer also commodities, they are commodities through and through. This quantitative shift is so great that it calls forth entirely new phenomena. Ultimately, the culture industry no longer even needs to directly pursue everywhere the profit interests from which it originated. These interests have become objectified in its ideology and have even made themselves independent of the compulsion to sell the cultural commodities which must be swallowed anyway. The culture industry turns into public relations, the manufacturing of "good will" per se, without regard for particular firms or saleable objects. Brought to bear is a general uncritical consensus, advertisements produced for the world, so that each product of the culture industry becomes its own advertisement.

Nevertheless, those characteristics which originally stamped the transformation of literature into a commodity are maintained in this process. More than anything in the world, the culture industry has its ontology, a scaffolding of rigidly conservative basic categories which can be gleaned, for example, from the commercial English novels of the late 17th and early 18th centuries. What parades as progress in the culture industry, as the incessantly new which it offers up, remains the disguise for an eternal sameness; everywhere the changes mask a skeleton which has changed just as little as the profit motive itself since the time it first gained its predominance over culture.

Thus, the expression "industry" is not to be taken literally. It refers to the standardization of the thing itself – such as that of the Western, familiar to every movie-goer – and to the rationalization of distribution techniques, but not strictly to the production process. Although in film, the central sector of the culture industry, the production process resembles technical modes of operation in the extensive division of labor, the employment of machines and the separation of the laborers from the means of production – expressed in the perennial conflict between artists active in the culture industry and those who control it – individual forms of production are nevertheless maintained. Each product affects an individual air; individuality itself serves to reinforce ideology, insofar as the illusion is conjured up that the completely reified and mediated is a sanctuary from immediacy and life. Now, as ever, the culture industry exists in the "service" of third persons, maintaining its affinity to the declining circulation process of capital, to the commerce from which it came into being. Its ideology above all makes use of the star system, borrowed from individualistic art and its commercial exploitation. The more dehumanized its methods of operation and content, the more diligently and successfully the culture industry propagates supposedly great personalities and operates with heart-throbs. It is industrial more in a sociological sense, in the incorporation of industrial forms of organization even where nothing is manufactured – as in the rationalization of office work – rather than in the sense of anything really and actually produced by technological rationality. Accordingly, the misinvestments of the culture industry are considerable, throwing those branches rendered obsolete by new techniques into crises, which seldom lead to changes for the better.

The concept of technique in the culture industry is only in name identical with technique in works of art. In the latter, technique is concerned with the internal organization of the object itself, with its inner logic. In contrast, the technique of the culture industry is, from the beginning, one of distribution and mechanical reproduction, and therefore always remains external to its object. The culture industry finds ideological support precisely insofar as it carefully shields itself from the full potential of the techniques contained in its products. It lives parasitically from the extra-artistic technique of the material production of goods, without regard for the obligation to the internal artistic whole implied by its functionality (*Sachlichkeit*), but also with concern for the laws of form demanded by aesthetic autonomy. The result for the physiognomy of the culture industry is essentially a mixture of streamlining, photographic hardness, and precision on the one hand, and individualistic residues, sentimentality, and an already rationally disposed and adapted romanticism on the other. Adopting Benjamin's designation of the traditional work of art by the concept of aura, the presence of that which is not present, the culture industry is defined by the fact that it does not strictly counterpose another principle to that of aura, but rather by the fact that it conserves the decaying aura as a foggy mist. By this means the culture industry betrays its own ideological abuses.

It has recently become customary among cultural officials as well as sociologists to warn against underestimating the culture industry while pointing to its great importance for the development of the consciousness of its consumers. It is to be taken seriously, without cultured snobbism. In actuality the culture industry is important as a moment of the spirit which dominates today. Whoever ignores its influence out of skepticism for what it stuffs into people would be naive. Yet there is a deceptive glitter about the admonition to take it seriously. Because of its social role, disturbing questions about its quality, about truth or untruth, and about the aesthetic niveau of the culture industry's emissions are repressed, or at least excluded from the so-called sociology of communications. The critic is accused of taking refuge in arrogant esoterica. It would be advisable first to indicate the double meaning of importance that slowly worms its way in unnoticed. Even if it touches the lives of innumerable people, the function of something is no guarantee of its particular quality. The blending of aesthetics with its residual communicative aspects leads art, as a social phenomenon, not to its rightful position in opposition to alleged artistic snobbism, but rather in a variety of ways to the defense of its baneful social consequences. The importance of the culture industry in the spiritual constitution of the masses is no dispensation for reflection on its objective legitimation, its essential being, least of all by a science which thinks itself pragmatic. On the contrary: Such reflection becomes necessary precisely for this reason. To take the culture industry as seriously as its unquestioned role demands means to take it seriously critically and not to cower in the face of its monopolistic character.

Among those intellectuals anxious to reconcile themselves with the phenomenon and eager to find a common formula to express both their reservations against it and their respect for its power, a tone of ironic toleration prevails unless they have already created a new mythos of the

20th century from the imposed regression. After all, those intellectuals maintain, everyone knows what pocket novels, films off the rack, family television shows rolled out into serials and hit parades, advice to the lovelorn, and horoscope columns are all about. All of this, however, is harmless and, according to them, even democratic since it responds to a demand, albeit a stimulated one. It also bestows all kinds of blessings, they point out, for example, through the assimilation of information, advice, and stress reducing patterns of behavior. Of course, as every sociological study measuring something as elementary as how politically informed the public is has proven, the formation is meager or indifferent. Moreover, the advice to be gained from manifestations of the culture industry is vacuous, banal, or worse, and the behavior patterns are shamelessly conformist.

The two-faced irony in the relationship of servile individuals to the culture industry is not restricted to them alone. It may also be supposed that the consciousness of the consumers themselves is split between the prescribed fun such as is supplied to them by the culture industry and a not particularly well-hidden doubt about its blessings. The phrase, the world wants to be deceived, becomes truer than had ever been intended. People are not only, as the saying goes, falling for the swindle; if it guarantees them even the most fleeting gratification they desire a deception which is nonetheless transparent to them. They force their eyes shut and voice approval, in a kind of self-loathing, for what is meted out to them, knowing fully the purpose for which it is manufactured. Without admitting it they sense that their lives would be completely intolerable as soon as they no longer clung to satisfactions which are none at all.

The most ambitious defense of the culture industry today celebrates its spirit, which might safely be called ideology, as an ordering factor. In a supposedly chaotic world it provides human beings with something like standards for orientation, and that alone seems worthy of approval. However, what its defenders imagine is preserved by the culture industry is in fact all the more thoroughly destroyed by it. The color film demolishes the genial old tavern to a greater extent than bombs ever could: The film exterminates its imago. No homeland can survive being processed by the films which celebrate it, and which thereby turn the unique character on which it thrives into an unchangeable sameness.

That which legitimately could be called culture attempted, as an expression of suffering and contradiction, to maintain a grasp on the idea of the good life. Culture cannot represent either that which merely exists or the conventional and no longer binding categories of order which the culture industry drapes over the idea of the good life as if existing reality were the good life, and as if those categories were its true measure. If the response of [the] culture industry's representatives is that it does not deliver art at all, this is the ideology with which they evade responsibility for that from which the business lives. No misdeed is ever righted by explaining it as such.

The appeal to order alone, without concrete specificity, is futile; the appeal to the dissemination of norms, without these ever proving themselves in reality or before consciousness, is equally futile. The idea of an objectively binding order, huckstered to people because it is so lacking for them, has no claims if it does not prove itself internally and in confrontation with human beings. But this is precisely what no product of the culture industry would engage in. The concepts of order which it hammers into human beings are always those of the status quo. They remain unquestioned, unanalyzed, and undialectically presupposed, even if they no longer have any substance for those who accept them. In contrast to the Kantian, the categorical imperative of the culture industry no longer has anything in common with freedom. It proclaims: You shall conform, without instruction as to what; conform to that which exists anyway, and to that which everyone thinks anyway as a reflex of its power and omnipresence. The power of the culture industry's ideology is such that conformity has replaced consciousness. The order that springs from it is never confronted with what it claims to be or with the real interests of human beings. Order, however, is not good in itself. It would be so only as a good order. The fact that the culture industry is oblivious to this and extols order in abstraction bears witness to the impotence and untruth of the messages it conveys. While it claims to lead the perplexed, it deludes them with false conflicts which they are to exchange for their own. It solves conflicts for them only in appearance, in a way that they can hardly be solved in their real lives. In the products of the culture industry human beings get into trouble only so that they can be rescued unharmed, usually by representatives of a benign collective; and then in empty harmony, they are reconciled with the general, whose demands they had experienced at the outset as irreconcilable with their interests. For this purpose the culture industry has developed formulas which even reach into such nonconceptual areas as light musical entertainment. Here too one gets into a "jam," into rhythmic problems, which can be instantly disentangled by the triumph of the basic beat.

Even its defenders, however, would hardly contradict Plato openly who maintained that what is objectively and intrinsically untrue cannot also be subjectively good and true for human beings. The connections of the culture industry are neither guides for a blissful life nor a new art of moral responsibility, but rather exhortations to toe the line, behind which stand the most powerful interests. The consensus which it propagates strengthens blind, opaque authority. If the culture industry is measured not by its own substance and logic, but by its efficacy, by its position in reality and its explicit pretensions; if the focus of serious concern is with the efficacy to which it always appeals, the potential of its effect becomes twice as weighty. This potential, however, lies in the promotion and exploitation of the ego weakness to which the powerless members of contemporary society, with its concentration of power, are condemned. Their consciousness is further developed retrogressively. It is no coincidence that cynical American film producers are heard to say that their pictures must take into consideration the level of the eleven-year-olds. In doing so they would very much like to make adults into eleven-year-olds.

It is true that thorough research has not, for the time being, produced an airtight case proving the regressive effects of particular products of the culture industry. No doubt an imaginatively designed experiment could achieve this more successfully than the powerful financial interests concerned would find comfortable. In any case, it can be assumed without hesitation that steady drops hollow the stone, especially since the system of the culture industry that surrounds the masses tolerates hardly any deviation and incessantly drills the same formulas of behavior. Only their deep unconscious mistrust, the last residue of the difference between art and empirical reality in the spiritual makeup of the masses, explains why they have not, to a person, long since perceived and accepted the world as it is constructed for them by the culture industry. Even if its messages were as harmless as they were made out to be, on countless occasions they are obviously not harmless. If an astrologer urges his readers to drive carefully on a particular day, that certainly hurts no one; they will, however, be harmed indeed by the stupefication which lies in the claim that advice which is valid every day and which is therefore idiotic needs the approval of the stars.

Human dependence and servitude, the vanishing point of the culture industry, could scarcely be more faithfully described than by the American interviewee who was of the opinion that the dilemmas of the contemporary epoch would end if people would simply follow the lead of prominent personalities. Insofar as the culture industry arouses a feeling of well-being that the world is precisely in that order suggested by the culture industry, the substitute gratification which it prepares for human beings cheats them out of the same happiness which it deceitfully projects. The total effect of the culture industry is one of anti-enlightenment, in which, as Horkheimer and I have noted, enlightenment, that is, the progressive technical domination of nature, becomes mass deception and is turned into a means for fettering consciousness. It impedes the development of autonomous, independent individuals who judge and decide consciously for themselves. These, however, would be the precondition for a democratic society which needs adults who have come of age in order to sustain itself and develop. If the masses have been unjustly reviled from above as masses, the culture industry is not among the least responsible for making them into masses and then despising them, while obstructing the emancipation for which human beings are as ripe as the productive forces of the epoch permit.

24

From consensual order to instrumental control

Herbert Marcuse

1. The new forms of control

A comfortable, smooth, reasonable, democratic unfreedom prevails in advanced industrial civilization, a token of technical progress. Indeed, what could be more rational than the suppression of individuality in the mechanization of socially necessary but painful performances; the concentration of individual enterprises in more effective, more productive corporations; the regulation of free competition among unequally equipped economic subjects; the curtailment of prerogatives and national sovereignties which impede the international organization of resources. That this technological order also involves a political and intellectual coordination may be a regrettable and yet promising development.

The rights and liberties which were such vital factors in the origins and earlier stages of industrial society yield to a higher stage of this society: They are losing their traditional rationale and content. Freedom of thought, speech, and conscience were – just as free enterprise, which they served to promote and protect – essentially critical ideas, designed to replace an obsolescent material and intellectual culture by a more productive and rational one. Once institutionalized, these rights and liberties shared the fate of the society of which they had become an integral part. *The achievement cancels the premises.*

To the degree to which freedom from want, the concrete substance of all freedom, is becoming a real possibility, the liberties which pertain to a state of lower productivity are losing their former content. (Independence of thought, autonomy, and the right to political opposition are being deprived of their basic critical function in a society which seems increasingly capable of satisfying the needs of the individuals through the way in which it is organized.) Such a society may justly demand acceptance of its principles and institutions, and reduce the opposition to the discussion and promotion of alternative policies within the status quo. In this respect, it seems to make little difference whether the increasing satisfaction of needs is accomplished by an authoritarian or a nonauthoritarian system. (Under the conditions of a rising standard of living, non-conformity with the system itself appears to be socially useless, and the more so when it entails tangible economic and political disadvantages and threatens the smooth operation of the whole.) Indeed, at least in so far as the necessities of life are involved, there seems to be no reason why the production and distribution of goods and services should proceed through the competitive concurrence of individual liberties.

Freedom of enterprise was from the beginning not altogether a blessing. As the liberty to work or to starve, it spelled toil, insecurity, and fear for the vast majority of the population. If the individual were no longer compelled to prove himself on the market, as a free economic subject, the disappearance of this kind of freedom would be one of the greatest achievements of civilization. The technological processes of mechanization and standardization might release individual energy into a yet uncharted realm of freedom beyond necessity. The very structure of human existence would be altered; the individual would be liberated from the work world's imposing upon him alien needs and alien possibilities. (The individual would be free to exert autonomy over a life that would be his own.) If the productive apparatus could be organized and directed toward the satisfaction of the vital needs, its control might well be centralized; such control would not prevent individual autonomy, but render it possible.

This is a goal within the capabilities of advanced industrial civilization, the "end" of technological rationality. *In actual fact, however, the contrary trend operates:* The apparatus imposes its economic and political requirements for defense and expansion on labor time and free time, on the material and intellectual culture. By virtue of the way it has organized its technological base, *contemporary industrial society tends to be totalitarian.* For totalitarian[ism] is not only a terroristic political coordination of society, but also a nonterroristic economic–technical coordination which operates through the manipulation of needs by vested interests. It thus precludes the emergence of an effective opposition against the whole. Not only a specific form of government or party rule makes for totalitarianism, but also a specific system of production and distribution which may well be compatible with a "pluralism" of parties, newspapers, "countervailing powers," etc.

Today political power asserts itself through its power over the machine process and over the technical organization of the apparatus. (The government of advanced and advancing industrial societies can maintain and secure itself only when it succeeds in mobilizing, organizing, and exploiting the technical, scientific, and mechanical productivity available to industrial civilization.) And this productivity mobilizes society as a whole, above and beyond any particular individual or group interests. The brute fact that the machine's physical (*only physical?*) power surpasses that of the individual, and of any particular group of individuals, makes the machine the most effective political instrument in any society whose basic organization is that of the machine process. But the political trend may be reversed; essentially the power of the machine is only the stored-up and projected power of man. To the extent to which the work world is conceived of as a machine and mechanized accordingly, it becomes the potential basis of a new freedom for man.

The more rational, productive, technical, and total the repressive administration of society becomes, the more unimaginable the means and ways by which the administered individuals might break their servitude and seize their own liberation. To be sure, to impose Reason upon an entire society is a paradoxical and scandalous idea – although one might dispute the righteousness of a society which ridicules this idea while making its own population into objects of total administration. All liberation depends on the consciousness of servitude, and the emergence of this consciousness is always hampered by the predominance of needs and satisfactions which, to a great extent, have become the individual's own. The process always replaces one system of preconditioning by another; the optimal goal is the replacement of false needs by true ones, the abandonment of repressive satisfaction – false needs.

The distinguishing feature of advanced industrial society is its effective suffocation of those needs which demand liberation – liberation also from that which is tolerable and rewarding and comfortable – while it sustains and absolves the destructive power and repressive function of the affluent society. Here, the social controls exact the overwhelming need for the production and consumption of waste; the need for stupefying work where it is no longer a real necessity; the need for modes of relaxation which soothe and prolong this stupefication; the need for maintaining such deceptive liberties as free competition at administered prices, a free press which censors itself, free choice between brands and gadgets.

Under the rule of a repressive whole, liberty can be made into a powerful instrument of domination. The range of choice open to the individual is not the decisive factor in determining the degree of human freedom, but what can be chosen and what is chosen by the individual. The criterion for free choice can never be an absolute one, but neither is it entirely relative. (*Free election of masters does not abolish the masters or the slaves.* Free choice among a wide variety of goods and services does not signify freedom if these goods and services sustain social controls over a life of toil and fear – that is, if they sustain alienation.) And the spontaneous reproduction of superimposed needs by the individual does not establish autonomy; it only testifies to the efficacy of the controls.

Our insistence on the depth and efficacy of these controls is open to the objection that we overrate greatly the indoctrinating power of the "media," and that by themselves the people would feel and satisfy the needs which are now imposed upon them. The objection misses the point. The preconditioning does not start with the mass production of radio and television and with the centralization of their control. The people enter this stage as preconditioned receptacles of long standing; the decisive difference is in the flattening out of the contrast (or conflict) between the given and the possible, between the satisfied and the unsatisfied needs. Here, the so-called equalization of class distinctions reveals its ideological function. If the worker and his boss enjoy the same television program and visit the same resort places, if the typist is as attractively made up as the daughter of her employer, if the Negro owns a Cadillac, if they all read the same newspaper, then this assimilation indicates not the disappearance of classes, but the extent to which the needs and satisfactions that serve the preservation of the Establishment are shared by the underlying population.

Indeed, in the most highly developed areas of contemporary society, the transplantation of social into individual needs is so effective that the difference between them seems to be purely theoretical. Can one really distinguish between the mass media as instruments of information and entertainment, and as agents of manipulation and indoctrination? Between the automobile as nuisance and as convenience? Between the horrors and the comforts of functional architecture? Between the work for national defense and the work for corporate gain? Between the private pleasure and the commercial and political utility involved in increasing the birth rate?

We are again confronted with one of the most vexing aspects of advanced industrial civilization: the rational character of its irrationality. Its productivity and efficiency, its capacity to increase and spread comforts, to turn waste into need and destruction into construction, the extent to which this civilization transforms the object world into an extension of man's mind and body make the very notion of alienation questionable. The people recognize themselves in their commodities; they find their soul in their automobile, hi-fi set, split-level home, kitchen equipment. (The very mechanism which ties the individual to his society has changed, and social control is anchored in the new needs which it has produced.)

The prevailing forms of social control are technological in a new sense. To be sure, the technical structure and efficacy of the productive and destructive apparatus has [sic] been a major instrumentality *for subjecting the population to the established social division of labor throughout* the modern period. Moreover, such integration has always been accompanied by more obvious forms of compulsion: loss of livelihood, the administration of justice, the police, the armed forces. It still is. But in the contemporary period, *the technological controls* appear to be the very of Reason for the *benefit* of all social groups and interests – to such an extent that all contradiction seems irrational and all counteraction impossible.

No wonder then that, in the most advanced areas of this civilization, the social controls have been introjected to the point where even *individual protest is affected at its roots.* The intellectual and emotional refusal "to go along" appears neurotic and impotent. This is the socio-psychological aspect of the political event that marks the contemporary period: the passing of the historical forces which, at the preceding stage of industrial society, seemed to represent the possibility of new forms of existence.

But the term "introjection" perhaps no longer describes the way in which the individual by himself reproduces and perpetuates the external controls exercised by his society. Introjection suggests and reconciles the opposition. The impact of progress turns Reason into submission to the facts of life, and to the dynamic capability of producing more and bigger facts of the same sort of life. The efficiency of the system blunts the individuals' recognition that it contains no facts which do not communicate the repressive power of the whole. If the individuals find themselves in the things which shape their life, they do so, not by giving, but by accepting the law of things – not the law of physics but the law of their society.

I have just suggested that the concept of alienation seems to become questionable when the individuals identify themselves with the existence which is imposed upon them and have in it their own development and satisfaction. This identification is not illusion but reality. However, the reality constitutes a more progressive stage of alienation. The latter has become entirely objective; the subject which is alienated is swallowed up by its alienated existence. There is only one dimension, and it is everywhere and in all forms. The achievements of progress defy ideological indictment as well as justification; before their tribunal, the "false consciousness" of their rationality becomes the true consciousness.

This absorption of ideology into reality does not, however, signify the "end of ideology." On the contrary, in a specific sense advanced industrial culture is more ideological than its predecessor, inasmuch as today the ideology is in the process of production itself. In a provocative form, this proposition reveals the political aspects of the prevailing technological rationality. The variety of relatively spontaneous processes by which a Self (*Ego*) *transposes the "outer" into the "inner."* (Thus introjection implies the existence of an inner dimension distinguished from and even antagonistic to the external exigencies – an individual consciousness and an individual unconscious[ness] apart from public opinion and behavior. The idea of "inner freedom" here has its reality: It designates the *private space* in which man may become and remain "himself.")

Today this *private space has been invaded and whittled down by technological reality. Mass production and mass distribution claim the entire individual,* and industrial psychology has long since ceased to be confined to the factory. The manifold processes of introjection seem to be ossified in almost mechanical reactions. The result is, not adjustment but mimesis: an immediate identification of the individual with his society and, through it, with the society as a whole.

This immediate, automatic identification (which may have been characteristic of primitive forms of association) reappears in high industrial civilization; its new "immediacy," however, is the product of a sophisticated, scientific management and organization. In this process, the "inner" dimension of the mind in which opposition to the status quo can take root is whittled down. The *loss of* this dimension, in which the power of *negative thinking* – the critical power of *Reason* – is at home, is the ideological counterpart to the very material process in which advanced industrial society silences productive apparatus and the goods and services which it produces "sell" or impose the social system as a whole. The means of mass transportation and communication, the commodities of lodging, food, and clothing, the irresistible output of the entertainment and information industry carry with them prescribed attitudes and habits, certain intellectual and emotional reactions which bind the consumers more or less pleasantly to the producers and, through the latter, to the whole. The products indoctrinate and manipulate; they promote a false consciousness which is immune against its falsehood. And as these beneficial products become available to more individuals in more social classes, the indoctrination they carry ceases to be publicity; it becomes a way of life. It is a good way of life – much better than before – and as a good way of life, it militates against qualitative change. Thus emerges a pattern of one-dimensional thought and behavior in which ideas, aspirations, and objectives that, by their content, transcend the established universe of discourse and action are either repelled or reduced to terms of this universe. They are redefined by the rationality of the given system and of its quantitative extension. . . .

Today's fight against this historical alternative finds a firm mass basis in the underlying population, and finds its ideology in the rigid orientation of thought and behavior to the given universe of facts. Validated by the accomplishments of science and technology, justified by its growing productivity, the status quo defies all transcendence. Faced with the possibility of pacification on the grounds of its technical and intellectual achievements, the mature industrial society closes itself against this alternative. Operationalism in theory and practice becomes the theory and practice of *containment*. Underneath its obvious dynamics, this society is a thoroughly static system of life: self-propelling in its oppressive productivity and in its beneficial coordination. Containment of technical progress goes hand in hand with its growth in the established direction. In spite of the political fetters imposed by the status quo, the more technology appears capable of creating the conditions for pacification, the more are the minds and bodies of man organized against this alternative.

The most advanced areas of industrial society exhibit throughout these two features: a trend toward consummation of technological rationality, and intensive efforts to contain this trend within the established institutions. Here is the internal contradiction of this civilization: the irrational element in its rationality. It is the token of its achievements. The industrial society which makes technology and science its own is organized for the ever-more-effective domination of man and nature, for the ever-more-effective utilization of its resources. It becomes irrational when the success of these efforts opens new dimensions of human realization. Organization for peace is different from organization for war; the institutions which served the struggle for existence cannot serve the pacification of existence. Life as an end is qualitatively different from life as a means.

"Progress" is not a neutral term; it moves toward specific ends, and these ends are defined by the possibilities of ameliorating the human condition. Advanced industrial society is approaching the stage where continued progress would demand the radical subversion of the prevailing direction and organization of progress. This stage would be reached when material production (including the necessary services) becomes automated to the extent that all vital needs can be satisfied while necessary labor time is reduced to marginal time. From this point on, technical progress would transcend the realm of necessity, where it served as the instrument of domination and exploitation which thereby limited its rationality; technology would become subject to the free play of faculties in the struggle for the pacification of nature and of society.

25

The end of ideology in the West

Daniel Bell

There have been few periods in history when man felt his world to be durable, suspended surely, as in Christian allegory, between chaos and heaven. In an Egyptian papyrus of more than four thousand years ago, one finds: ". . . impudence is rife . . . the country is spinning round and round like a potter's wheel . . . the masses are like timid sheep without a shepherd . . . one who yesterday was indigent is now wealthy and the sometime rich overwhelm him with adulation." The Hellenistic period as described by Gilbert Murray was one of a "failure of nerve"; there was "the rise of pessimism, a loss of self-confidence, of hope in this life and of faith in normal human effort." And the old scoundrel Talleyrand claimed that only those who lived before 1789 could have tasted life in all its sweetness.

This age, too, can add appropriate citations – made all the more wry and bitter by the long period of bright hope that preceded it – for the two decades between 1930 and 1950 have an intensity peculiar in written history: worldwide economic depression and sharp class struggles; the rise of fascism and racial imperialism in a country that had stood at an advanced stage of human culture; the tragic self-immolation of a revolutionary generation that had proclaimed the finer ideals of man; destructive war of a breadth and scale hitherto unknown; the bureaucratized murder of millions in concentration camps and death chambers.

For the radical intellectual who had articulated the revolutionary impulses of the past century and a half, all this has meant an end to chiliastic hopes, to millenarianism, to apocalyptic thinking – and to ideology. For ideology, which once was a road to action, has come to be a dead end.

Whatever its origins among the French *philosophes*, ideology as a way of translating ideas into action was given its sharpest phrasing by the left Hegelians, by Feuerbach, and by Marx. For them, the function of philosophy was to be critical, to rid the present of the past. ("The tradition of all the dead generations weighs like a nightmare on the brain of the living," wrote Marx.) Feuerbach, the most radical of all the left Hegelians, called himself Luther II. Man would be free, he said, if we could demythologize region. The history of all thought was a history of progressive disenchantment, and if finally, in Christianity, God had been transformed from a parochial deity to a universal abstraction, the function of criticism — using the radical tool of alienation, or self-estrangement — was to replace theology by anthropology, to substitute Man for God. Philosophy was to be directed at life, man was to be liberated from the "specter of abstractions" and extricated from the bind of the supernatural. Religion was capable only of creating "false consciousness." Philosophy would reveal "true consciousness." And by placing Man, rather than God, at the center of consciousness, Feuerbach sought to bring the "infinite into the finite."

If Feuerbach "descended into the world," Marx sought to transform it. And where Feuerbach proclaimed anthropology, Marx, reclaiming a root insight of Hegel, emphasized History and historical contexts. The world was not generic Man, but men; and of men, classes of men. Men differed because of their class position. And truths were class truths. All truths, thus, were masks, or partial truths, but the real truth was the revolutionary truth. And this real truth was rational.

Thus a dynamic was introduced into the analysis of ideology, and into the creation of a new ideology. By demythologizing religion, one recovered (from God and sin) the potential in man. By the unfolding of history, rationality was revealed. In the struggle of classes, true consciousness, rather than false consciousness, could be achieved. But if truth lay in action, one must act. The left Hegelians, said Marx, were only *littérateurs*. (For them a magazine was "practice.") For Marx, the only real action was in politics. But action, revolutionary action as Marx conceived it, was not mere social change. It was, in its way, the resumption of all the old millenarian, chiliastic ideas of the Anabaptists. It was, in its new vision, a new ideology. . . .

Ideology is the conversion of ideas into social levers. Without irony, Max Lerner once entitled a book *Ideas Are Weapons*. This is the language of ideology. It is more. It is the commitment to the consequences of ideas. When Vissarion Belinsky, the father of Russian criticism, first read Hegel and became convinced of the philosophical correctness of the formula "what is, is what ought to be," he became a supporter of the Russian autocracy. But when it was shown to him that Hegel's thought contained the contrary tendency, that dialectically the "is" evolves into a different form, he became a revolutionary overnight. "Belinsky's conversion," comments Rufus W. Mathewson, Jr., "illustrates an attitude toward ideas which is both passionate and myopic, which responds to them on the basis of their immediate relevances alone, and inevitably reduces them to tools."[1]

What gives ideology its force is its passion. Abstract philosophical inquiry has always sought to eliminate passion, and the person, to rationalize all ideas. For the ideologue, truth arises in action, and meaning is given to experience by the "transforming moment." He comes alive not in contemplation, but in "the deed." One might say, in fact, that the most important, latent, funcion of ideology is to tap emotion. Other than religion (and war and nationalism), there have been few forms of channelizing emotional energy. Religion symbolized, drained away, dispersed emotional energy from the world onto the litany, the liturgy, the sacraments, the edifices, the arts. Ideology fuses these energies and channels them into politics.

But religion, at its most effective, was more. It was a way for people to cope with the problem of death. The fear of death – forceful and inevitable – and more, the fear of violent death, shatters the glittering, imposing, momentary dream of man's power. The fear of death, as Hobbes pointed out, is the source of conscience; the effort to avoid violent death is the source of law. When it was possible to believe, really believe, in heaven and hell, then some of the fear of death could be tempered or controlled; without such belief, there is only the total annihilation of the self.

It may well be that with the decline in religious *faith* in the last century and more, this fear of death as total annihilation, unconsciously expressed, has probably increased. One may hypothesize, in fact, that here is a cause of the breakthrough of the irrational, which is such a marked feature of the changed moral temper of our time. Fanaticism, violence, and cruelty are not, of course, unique in human history. But there was a time when such frenzies and mass emotions could be displaced, symbolized, drained away, and dispersed through religious devotion and practice. Now there is only this life, and the assertion of self becomes possible – for some even necessary – in the domination over others. One can challenge death by emphasizing the omnipotence of a movement (as in the "inevitable" victory of communism), or overcome death (as did the "immortality" of Captain Ahab) by bending others to one's will. Both paths are taken, but politics, because it can institutionalize power, in the way that religion once did, becomes the ready avenue for domination. The modern effort to transform the world chiefly or solely through politics (as meant that all other religious transformation of the self) has meant that all other institutional ways of mobilizing emotional energy

1. Rufus W. Mathewson, Jr., *The Positive Hero in Russian Literature* (New York, 1958), p. 6.

would necessarily atrophy. In effect, sect and church became party and social movement.

A social movement can rouse people when it can do three things: simplify ideas, establish a claim to truth, and, in the union of the two, demand a commitment to action. Thus, not only does ideology transform ideas, it transforms people as well. The nineteenth-century ideologies, by emphasizing inevitability and by infusing passion into their followers, could compete with religion. By identifying inevitability with progress, they linked up with the positive values of science. But more important, these ideologies were linked, too, with the rising class of intellectuals, which was seeking to assert a place in society.

The differences between the intellectual and the scholar, without being invidious, are important to understand. The scholar has a bounded field of knowledge, a tradition, and seeks to find his place in it, adding to the accumulated, tested knowledge of the past as to a mosaic. The scholar, qua scholar, is less involved with his "self." The intellectual begins with *his* experience, *his* individual perceptions of the world, *his* privileges and deprivations, and judges the world by these sensibilities. Since his own status is of high value, his judgments of the society reflect the treatment accorded him. In a business civilization, the intellectual felt that the wrong values were being honored, and rejected the society. Thus there was a "built-in" compulsion for the free-floating intellectual to become political. The ideologies, therefore, which emerged from the nineteenth century had the force of the intellectuals behind them. They embarked upon what William James called "the faith ladder," which in its vision of the future cannot distinguish possibilities from probabilities, and converts the latter into certainties.

Today, these ideologies are exhausted. The events behind this important sociological change are complex and varied. Such calamities as the Moscow Trials, the Nazi–Soviet pact, the concentration camps, the suppression of the Hungarian workers form one chain; such social changes as the modification of capitalism, the rise of the Welfare State, another. In philosophy, one can trace the decline of simplistic, rationalistic beliefs and the emergence of new stoic-theological images of man, e.g., Freud, Tillich, Jaspers, etc. This is not to say that such ideologies as communism in France and Italy do not have a political weight, or a driving momentum from other sources. But out of all this history, one simple fact emerges: For the radical intelligentsia, the old ideologies have lost their "truth" and their power to persuade.

Few serious minds believe any longer that one can set down "blueprints" and through "social engineering" bring about a new utopia of social harmony. At the same time, the older "counter-beliefs" have lost their intellectual force as well. Few "classic" liberals insist that the State should play no role in the economy, and few serious conservatives, at least in England and on the Continent, believe that the Welfare State is "the road to serfdom." In the Western world, therefore, there is today a rough consensus among intellectuals on political issues: the acceptance of a Welfare State; the desirability of decentralized power; a system of mixed economy and of political pluralism. In that sense, too, the ideological age has ended.

And yet, the extraordinary fact is that while the old nineteenth-century ideologies and intellectual debates have become exhausted, the rising states of Asia and Africa are fashioning new ideologies with a different appeal for their own people. These are the ideologies of industrialization, modernization, Pan-Arabism, color, and nationalism. In the distinctive difference between the two kinds of ideologies lies the great political and social problems of the second half of the twentieth century. The ideologies of the nineteenth century were universalistic, humanistic, and fashioned by intellectuals. The mass ideologies of Asia and Africa are parochial, instrumental, and created by political leaders. The driving forces of the old ideologies were social equality and, in the largest sense, freedom. The impulsions of the new ideologies are economic development and national power.

And in this appeal, Russia and China have become models. The fascination these countries exert is no longer the old idea of the free society, but the new one of economic growth. And if this involves the wholesale coercion of the population and the rise of new elites to drive the people, the new repressions are justified on the ground that without such coercions economic advance cannot take place rapidly enough. And even for some of the liberals of the West, "economic development" has become a new ideology that washes away the memory of old disillusionments.

It is hard to quarrel with an appeal for rapid economic growth and modernization, and few can dispute the goal, as few could ever dispute an appeal for equality and freedom. But in this powerful surge – and its swiftness is amazing – any movement that instates such goals risks the sacrifice of the present generation for a future that may see only a new exploitation by a new elite. For the newly-risen countries, the debate is not over the merits of communism – the content of that doctrine has long been forgotten by friends and foes alike. The question is an older one: whether new societies can grow by building democratic institutions and allowing people to make choices – and sacrifices – voluntarily, or whether the new elites, heady with power, will impose totalitarian means to transform their countries. Certainly in these traditional and old colonial societies where the masses are apathetic and easily manipulated, the answer lies with the intellectual classes and their conceptions of the future.

Thus one finds, at the end of the fifties, a disconcerting caesura. In the

West, among the intellectuals, the old passions are spent. The new generation, with no meaningful memory of these old debates, and no secure
tradition to build upon, finds itself seeking new purposes within a framework of political society that has rejected, intellectually speaking, the old
apocalyptic and chiliastic visions. In the search for a "cause," there is a
deep, desperate, almost pathetic anger. The theme runs through a remarkable book, *Convictions,* by a dozen of the sharpest young Left Wing
intellectuals in Britain. They cannot define the content of the "cause"
they seek, but the yearning is clear. In the United States too there is a
restless search for a new intellectual radicalism. Richard Chase, in his
thoughtful assessment of American society, *The Democratic Vista,* insists
that the greatness of nineteenth-century America for the rest of the world
consisted in its radical vision of man (such a vision as Whitman's) and
calls for a new radical criticism today. But the problem is that the old
politico-economic radicalism (preoccupied with such matters as the socialization of industry) has lost its meaning, while the stultifying aspects of
contemporary culture (e.g., television) cannot be redressed in political
terms. At the same time, American culture has almost completely accepted the avant-garde, particularly in art, and the older academic styles
have been driven out completely. The irony, further, for those who seek
"causes" is that the workers, whose grievances were once the driving
energy for social change, are more satisfied with the society than the
intellectuals. The workers have not achieved utopia, but their expectations were less than those of the intellectuals, and the gains correspondingly larger.

The young intellectual is unhappy because the "middle way" is for the
middle-aged, not for him; it is without passion and is deadening. Ideology,
which by its nature is an all-or-none affair, and temperamentally the thing
he wants, is intellectually devitalized, and few issues can be formulated
anymore, intellectually, in ideological terms. The emotional energies – and
needs – exist, and the question of how one mobilizes these energies is a
difficult one. Politics offers little excitement. Some of the younger intellectuals have found an outlet in science or university pursuits, but often at the
expense of narrowing their talent into mere technique; others have sought
self-expression in the arts, but in the wasteland the lack of content has
meant, too, the lack of the necessary tension that creates new forms and
styles.

Whether the intellectuals in the West can find passions outside of politics is moot. Unfortunately, social reform does not have any unifying
appeal, nor does it give a younger generation the outlet for "self-
expression" and "self-definition" that it wants. The trajectory of enthusiasm has curved East, where, in the new ecstasies for economic utopia, the
"future" is all that counts.

The end of ideology is not – should not be – the end of utopia as well. If anything, one can begin anew the discussion of utopia only by being aware of the trap of ideology. The point is that ideologists are "terrible simplifiers." Ideology makes it unnecessary for people to confront individual issues on their individual merits. One simply turns to the ideological vending machine, and out comes the prepared formulae. And when these beliefs are suffused by apocalyptic fervor, ideas become weapons, and with dreadful results.

There is now, more than ever, some need for utopia, in the sense that men need – as they have always needed – some vision of their potential, some manner of fusing passion with intelligence. Yet the ladder of the City of Heaven can no longer be a "faith ladder," but an empirical one: A utopia has to specify *where* one wants to go, *how* to get there, the costs of the enterprise, and some realization of and justification for the determination of *who* is to pay.

The end of ideology closes the book, intellectually speaking, on an era, the one of easy "left" formulae for social change. But to close the book is not to turn one's back upon it. This is all the more important now when a "new Left," with few memories of the past, is emerging. This "new Left" has passion and energy, but little definition of the future. Its outriders exult that it is "on the move." But where it is going, what it means by socialism, how to guard agains bureaucratization, what one means by democratic planning or workers' control – any of the questions that require hard thought are only answered by bravura phrases.

It is in attitudes toward Cuba and the new states in Africa that the meaning of intellectual maturity, and of the end of ideology, will be tested. For among the "new Left," there is an alarming readiness to create a *tabula rasa*, to accept the word "Revolution" as an absolution for outrages, to justify the suppression of civil rights and opposition – in short, to erase the lessons of the last forty years with an emotional alacrity that is astounding. The fact that many of these emerging social movements are justified in their demands for freedom, for the right to control their own political and economic destinies, does not mean they have a right to a blank check for everything they choose to do in the name of their emancipation. Nor does the fact that such movements take power in the name of freedom guarantee that they will not turn out to be as imperialist, as grandeur-concerned (in the name of Pan-Africanism or some other ideology) as demanding their turn on the stage of History, as the states they have displaced.

If the end of ideology has any meaning, it is to ask for the end of rhetoric, and rhetoricians, of "revolution" of the day when the young French anarchist Vaillant tossed a bomb into the Chamber of Deputies and the literary critic Laurent Tailhade declared in his defense: "What do a few human lives matter; it was a *beau geste*." (A *beau geste* that ended, one might say, in a mirthless jest: Two years later, Tailhade lost an eye when a bomb was thrown into a restaurant.) Today, in Cuba, as George Sherman, reporting for the *London Observer* summed it up: "The Revolution is law today although nobody has said clearly what that law is. You are expected to be simply for or against it and judge and be judged accordingly. Hatred and intolerance are wiping out whatever middle ground may have existed."

The problems which confront us at home and in the world are resistant to the old terms of ideological debate between "left" and "right," and if "ideology" by now, and with good reason, is an irretrievably fallen word, it is not necessary that "utopia" suffer the same fate. But it will if those who now call loudest for new utopias begin to justify degrading *means* in the name of utopian or revolutionary *end*, and forget the simple lessons that if the old debates are meaningless, some old verities are not – the verities of free speech, free press, the right of opposition and of free inquiry.

And if the intellectual history of the past hundred years has any meaning – and lesson – it is to reassert Jefferson's wisdom (aimed at removing the dead hand of the past, but which can serve as a warning against the heavy hand of the future as well) that "the present belongs to the living." This is the wisdom that revolutionists, old and new, who are sensitive to the fate of their fellow men, rediscover in every generation. "I will never believe," says a protagonist in a poignant dialogue written by the gallant Polish philosopher Leszek Kolakowski, "that the moral and intellectual life of mankind follows the law of economics, that is by saying today we can have more tomorrow; that we should use lives now so that truth will triumph or that we should profit by crime to pave the way for nobility."

And these words, written during the Polish "thaw," when the intellectuals had asserted, from their experience with the "future," the claims of humanism, echo the protest of the Russian writer Alexander Herzen, who, in a dialogue a hundred years ago, reproached an earlier revolutionist who would sacrifice the present mankind for a promised tomorrow: "Do you truly wish to condemn all human beings alive today to the sad role of caryatids . . . supporting a floor for others some day to dance on? . . . This alone should serve as a warning to people: An end that is infinitely remote is not an end, but, if you like, a trap; an end must be nearer – it ought to be, at the very least, the labourer's wage or pleasure in the work done. Each age, each generation, each life has its own fullness. . . ."

26

Beyond coercion and crisis: The coming of an era of voluntary community

Talcott Parsons

The industrial and democratic revolutions were transformations by which the institutional bulwarks of the early modern system were weakened. European monarchies survived only where they have become constitutional. Aristocracy still twitches but mostly in the informal aspects of stratification systems – nowhere is it structurally central. There are still established churches, but only on the less modern peripheries like Spain and Portugal is there restriction on religious freedom. The trend is toward the separation of church and state and denominational pluralism (except for the Communist countries). The industrial revolution shifted economic organization from agriculture and the commerce and handicrafts of small urban communities; it also extended markets.

The emergence of full modernity thus weakened the ascriptive framework of monarchy, aristocracy, established churches, and an economy circumscribed by kinship and localism to the point where ascription no longer exercises decisive influence. Modern components had already developed by the eighteenth century, particularly a universalistic legal system and secular culture, which had been diffused through Western society by the Enlightenment. Further developments in the political aspects of societal community emphasized the associational principle, nationalism, citizenship, and representative government. In the economy differentiated markets developed for the factors of production, primarily labor. Occupational services were increasingly performed in employing organizations structurally differentiated from households. New patterns of effectively organizing specific functions arose, especially administration (centering in government and the military) and the new economy. The democratic revolution stimulated efficient administration, the industrial revolution the new economy. Weber saw that in a later phase the two tend to fuse in the bureaucratization of the capitalist economy.

Reprinted with permission of Prentice-Hall, from *The Evolution of Societies* by Talcott Parsons.

The modern structural pattern crystallized in the northwest corner of Europe, and a secondary pattern subsequently emerged in the northeast corner, centering in Prussia. A parallel development took place in the second phase of modernization. The United States, the "first new nation," has come to play a role comparable to that of England in the seventeenth century. America was ripe for the democratic and industrial revolutions and for combining them more intimately than had been possible in Europe. By the time of Tocqueville's visit, a synthesis of the French and English revolutions had been achieved: The United States was as democratic a society as all but the extreme wing of the French Revolution had wished for, and its level of industrialization was to surpass that of England. We shall therefore concentrate in the following discussion upon the United States. . . .

The United States' new type of *societal community,* more than any other factor, justifies assigning it the lead in the latest phase of modernization. It attains fairly successfully the equality of opportunity stressed in socialism. It presupposes a market system, a legal order relatively independent of government, and a nation-state emancipated from religious and ethnic control. The educational revolution was a crucial innovation, with its emphasis on the associational pattern as well as on openness of opportunity. American society has gone farther than any comparable large-scale society in its dissociation from the older ascriptive inequalities and the institutionalization of an egalitarian pattern. Contrary to the opinion among many intellectuals, American society – and most modern societies without dictatorial regimes – has institutionalized a broader range of freedoms than had previous societies. This range is not greater that that enjoyed by small privileged groups [such] as eighteenth-century European aristocracy, but it is broader than ever before for large masses of people.

Such freedoms begin with freedom from some of the exigencies of physical life: ill health, short life, and geographical circumscription. They include reduced exposure to violence for most of the population most of the time. Higher incomes and extensive markets enhance freedom of choice in consumption. There is also general access to services like education and public accommodations. There is freedom of marital choice, of occupation, of religious adherence, of political allegiance, of thought, of speech and expression. From a comparative and evolutionary perspective, the more privileged societies of the later twentieth century have successfully institutionalized the liberal values of a century ago.

There are flaws. One, surely, is war and the danger of war. . . . The deficiencies of the new societal community type do not lie mainly in the older grievances against the tyranny of authoritarian regimes, especially of the monarchical variety, or the privileges of aristocracies. Nor do they lie in class antagonism and exploitation in the Marxian sense. The problems of inequality and social justice remain, but framing these problems in terms of bourgeoisie versus proletariat is no longer justified.

There is one context in which equality-justice complaints are justified in the United States: the existence of substantial poverty in combination with the large Negro minority that has suffered a long history of discrimination originating in slavery. Poverty is not exclusively a Negro problem. By most criteria the majority of the American poor is white, and a substantial nonwhite population is not poor. There is, however, a coincidence of the two aspects of the problem among ghetto blacks in the central cities. The older view of these problems stresses absolute deprivation, malnutrition, and disease. The conviction that *relative* deprivation is more important, that what hurts most is the sense of *exclusion* from full participation in the societal community, has been growing among social scientists. In our paradigm of social change we have stressed the connection between inclusion and adaptive upgrading – through rising income – but they are not identical. The connection does help to explain why, considering the recent reduction of legal and political discrimination, tensions over the race problem have intensified, not subsided. That mitigation of feelings of relative deprivation through inclusion is in a sense symbolic does not make it the less urgent.

In a second context, the problem of equality and social justice is more difficult to assess. The old grievances of tyranny, privilege, and class in the Marxian sense are less central than they once were. But there remains a sense that advantaged groups use their positions illegitimately to promote their interests at the expense of the common interest. In an earlier generation these grievances were defined in economic terms, as in Franklin D. Roosevelt's reference to "malefactors of great wealth." The tendency now is to invoke the symbol of power – in C. W. Mills' phrase, a "power elite" is now held responsible for our social ills. Members of the power elite are less likely to be defined as office holders than as sinister wire-pullers behind the scenes. Ideological complexes with paranoid themes are old, but the question of what lies behind this one nevertheless arises.

Indignation over the economic privileges of the rich does not seem to be a major source of the moral malaise in modern society; indeed, indignation seems less than at the turn of the century. There is consensus that those elements below the poverty line should be brought above it. Beyond that consensus, the problem of economic inequality becomes complicated. The trend has been one of reduction in conspicuous consumption among elite groups. Though not much has happened for a generation, the future trend will be toward greater equality.

In terms of power and authority, society has become more decentralized and associational rather than more concentrated. This trend again suggests an explanation of discontent in terms of relative rather than absolute deprivation. Bureaucracy has become a negative symbol, implying centralized control through rigid rules and authority. The trend is actually not toward increased bureaucracy, even if bureaucracy were not in [the] process of transformation, but toward associationism. But many sensitive groups *feel* that bureaucracy has been increasing. This sense is also related to accusations against the "military-industrial complex" in the United States, which is associated with a pervasive sense of limitation on freedom; in extreme groups, recent gains in freedoms are denied.

In the expression of relative deprivation two symbols are prominent. One is community, widely alleged to have deteriorated in the course of modern developments. The residential community has allegedly been privatized and many relationships have been shifted to the context of large formal organizations. However, bureaucratization is not actually sweeping all before it. Furthermore, the system of mass communications is a functional equivalent of features of *Gemeinschaft* society; it enables an individual selectively to participate according to his own standards and desires. A second symbol is "participation," especially in the formula of "participatory democracy." Demands for it are stated as if power were the main desideratum, but the diffuseness of these demands casts doubt on this conclusion. The demands are actually another manifestation of the desire for inclusion, for full acceptance as members of solidary groups. Similar considerations seem applicable to the fear of *illegitimate* power. What form participation can take compatible with the exigencies of effective organization is a difficult problem.

This interpretation is compatible with the recent prominence throughout modern societies of student unrest associated with the development of mass higher education. The themes stressed by student radicals have resonance in society at large. Both negatively and positively power is a potent symbol; the wrong kind of power allegedly explains what is wrong in society, and "student power" is among the remedies advocated. Bureaucracy and related themes are associated with the wrong kind of power. A new concept of community, with respect to which participation is urged, is endowed with magical virtues.

I have stressed the importance in modern society of three revolutions. Each has been a center of tension, producing radical groups that opposed features of the existing social structure as well as revolutionary changes. The French Revolution, a phase of the early democratic revolution, spawned the Jacobins, the absolutists of Rousseauean democracy. The industrial revolution generated conflicts about which I have had a good deal to say; the socialists were the radicals of this phase. The student radicals of the New Left have begun to play an analogous role in the educational revolution.

We face a paradox. Revolutionaries resent hearing that they share any values with those whose immoral systems they seek to overthrow. As I have used the concept of values in analysis, however, it is legitimate to raise the question whether or not the basic value *patterns* of modern society, and especially of the United States, are being fundamentally challenged. Are the institutional achievements associated with the progressive values of the nineteenth century no longer relevant? Have they been repudiated by the new generation? In my opinion these values are taken for granted, not repudiated. Modern society is indicted for not living up to its professed values, as demonstrated by the existence of poverty and racial discrimination and the persistence of war and imperialism. On the other hand, there is insistence that society should not be content with these value implementations but should introduce new ones.

Egalitarian themes suggest what the next phases may be; the two symbols of community and participation point a direction. The modern system, particularly in the United States, completed one phase of institutional consolidation, but it is also undergoing the ferment that accompanies the emergence of new phases. The strategic significance of the societal community to new phases seems clear. The emergence of important features of this community is recent. Furthermore, the United States has led the change, but its features will spread through all modern societies. A description of these features is therefore in order.

The principle of equality is being applied more pervasively than ever before. A societal community *basically* composed of equals seems to be the final development in the process of undermining the legitimacy of older, more particularistic and ascriptive bases of membership, such as religion (in pluralistic society), ethnic affiliation, region or locality, and hereditary in social status (in the aristocracy but also in more recent versions of class status). This theme of equality has many antecedents but first crystallized in conceptions of natural rights under the Enlightenment and found expression in the Bill of Rights of the American Constitution. The Bill of Rights has proved to be a time bomb; some of its consequences emerged long after its official adoption, dramatically through Supreme Court action but also more generally. Concern over poverty and race problems in the United States reflects the moral repugnance that the conception of an inherently lower class or an inferior race arouses in modern societies.

Some radical ideologies claim that genuine equality requires abolition of all hierarchical status distinctions. This version of community has been a persistently recurring ideal for many centuries. Such approximations to realistic institutionalization as have occurred, however, have always been on a small scale and of short duration. Too intensive a drive in this direction would disrupt larger-scale institutions of modern societies as law, markets, effective government, and competent creation and use of advanced knowledge. It would shatter society into primitive small communities. The direction of modern societal development is toward a new pattern of stratification. The historical bases of legitimate inequality have been ascriptive. The value base of the new egalitarianism requires a different basis of legitimation. In general terms, this basis must be *functional* to society conceived of as a system. Differential outcomes of the competitive education process must be legitimatized in terms of societal interest in the contributions of especially competent people; special competence is a function of both native ability and good training. A societal interest in economic productivity (with no presumption that every individual or collective unit that participates will be equally productive) implies special rewards for the economically more productive units. Similarly, effective organization is a functional necessity of complex collectivities and one of the factors in such effectiveness is the institutionalization of power, which has an inherently differential aspect.

Two modes of reconciliation exist between the value imperative of basic equality and the functional needs for competence, productivity, and collective effectiveness – all of which intersect in concrete areas of the social structure. The first is the institutionalization of *accountability,* one example of which is the accountability of elected officials to their constituencies. Economic markets perform analogous functions, though imperfectly, as do mechanisms for certifying competence in the academic world, the professions, and other fiduciary bodies. The second mode is the institutionalization of equality of opportunity so that no citizen shall, for ascriptive reasons (race, social class, religion, ethnic affiliation), be barred from equal access to opportunities for performance, as in employment, or to opportunities for making effective performance possible, like health and education. This ideal is far from full realization, but the view, so prevalent today, that equality of opportunity is sheer mockery suggests that the ideal actually is being taken seriously. In earlier times the lower classes, or individuals disadvantaged on other ascriptive bases, took for granted that opportunities open to their betters were not for them, and they did not protest. The volume of protest is not a simple function of the magnitude of the evil.

Balancing value commitments to equality against inequalities implied in functional effectiveness presents integrative problems to modern societies because many of the historic bases of hierarchical legitimation are no longer available. This difficulty is compounded by the appearance of the problem not in one overarching sphere but in many different spheres. There are many bases for functional inequality; the classification competence–economic efficiency–collective effectiveness constitutes only an elementary framework. There must be integration not only between claims to special prerogatives and the principles of equality but also among different kinds of claims to special prerogatives in a pluralistic social system.

This integration is the focus of emerging institutions of stratification. None of the inherited formulas purporting to describe modern stratification is satisfactory. The basis is not, except in special instances, national or ethnic membership. It is neither aristocracy in the older sense nor class in the Marxian sense. It is still incompletely developed and essentially new. The integration of such a societal community must depend upon mechanisms that center around the attachment of generalized prestige to specific groups and to the statuses that they occupy, including the office of bearers of authority in collectivities. The prestige of such groups and statuses must be rooted in combinations of factors rather than in any one, like wealth, political power, or even moral authority. *Prestige* is the communication node through which factors essential to the integration of the societal community can be evaluated, balanced, and integrated in an output, *influence.* The exercise of influence by one unit or set of units can help to bring other units into consensus by justifying allocations of rights and obligations, expected performances, and rewards in terms of their contributions to a common interest. The common interest is that of the society conceived as a community.

The concentration on the societal community that has characterized this book as a whole and the present chapter in particular should be balanced by a recognition that values potentially transcend any particular community. That is why this book has been concerned with the *system* of modern societies rather with any one society. The processes that transformed the societal community of the United States and promise to continue to transform it are not peculiar to this society but permeate the modern – and modernizing – system. Only on such an assumption of commonality is it understandable that European societies with no racial problems of their own can feel justified in taunting Americans about their callousness in the treatment of blacks or small independent countries in raising outcries of imperialism. From the vantage point of common membership in the modern system, the *intersocietal* institutionalization of a new value system, including its relevance to stratification, is worth studying.

The foci of conflict and thus of creative innovation in the modern system are not mainly economic in the sense of the nineteenth-century controversy over capitalism and socialism, nor do they seem political in the sense of the problem of the justice of the distribution of power, though both these conflicts are present. A cultural focus, especially in the wake of the educational revolution, is nearer the mark. The indications are that the storm center is the societal community. There is the relative obsolescence of many older values like hereditary privilege, ethnicity, and class. There are also unsolved problems of integrating the normative structure of community with the motivational basis of solidarity, which remains more problematic. The new societal community, conceived as an integrative institution, must operate at a level different from those familiar in our intellectual traditions; it must go beyond command of political power and wealth and of the factors that generate them to value commitments and mechanisms of influence.

27

Ideology, the cultural apparatus, and the new consciousness industry

Alvin Gouldner

There is a special connection, we have said, between the spread of modern ideologies with their historically special rationality, on the one side, and the unimodality and lineality of printed materials, on the other. Writing, and especially printed communication, then, is a basic grounding of "modern" ideologies, at least as we have come to know them. The future prospect of ideology will thus depend, in part, on the future of writing; on the production of writing and printed objects; on the consumption of writing and written objects; and, also, on the reproduction of audiences and markets for writings – "readers." Writers produce writings for readers. Hence anything that affects the production of writing, and the competition of printed objects for audiences, necessarily impinges on the role of ideology in the modern world. The position and structural character of ideologies [are] affected by changes in reading behavior and by the changing interest in (or time available for) reading. We shall thus attempt to explore, with great tentativeness, some of the ways in which the recent, full-scale emergence of modern communication technologies, and of the consciousness industry of which it is a part, may impinge on ideology and its prospect.

Hitherto, the fundamental symbolic means of ideology has been conceptual and linguistic. The relationship between ideology and society was mediated by the enormous development of printed matter. Ideology did not "reflect" society in a direct way but mediated the news and newspapers while, correspondingly, much of ideology's reciprocal impact on society was through its publication. Modern ideologies were made available, first, to readers, a relatively well-educated but small sector of the society – the "reading public" nucleated by a literate intelligentsia – and then through them to a larger public. Ideology was diffused via a relatively highly educated reading elite and spread to a larger public through written interpretations of "popularizations" of the ideology in newspa-

From Gouldner, *The Dialectic of Ideology and Technology*. New York: Seabury Press, 1976. Reprinted with permission.

pers, magazines, pamphlets, or leaflets, and through face-to-face oral communication in conversations, coffee shops, classrooms, lecture halls, or mass meetings.

In this "two step" model of communication, the dense information of complex ideologies is transmitted or "filtered down" to mass audiences by the media and, in particular, through a mediating intelligentsia. The mediating intelligentsia, then, serve partly as interpreters and partly as proprietors of those printed objects in which an ideology is defined as authoritatively exhibited. An intelligentsia may be said to have a proprietary relation to the printed object when (and to the extent that) they can certify readings of it as correct or incorrect, and certify others as possessing competent knowledge of it.

In contrast to the conventional printed objects central to ideologies, the modern communication media have greatly intensified the nonliguistic and iconic component, and hence the multimodal character of public communication. The communication breakthrough in the twentieth century begins with the spread of the radio and the cinema and is now coming to a culmination in the spread of television. The worldwide diffusion of television marks the end of one and the beginning of a new stage in the communications revolution – the development of a computerized mass information system. We are presently at the early stages of a radically new communications era in which computerized information storage and retrieval systems will be integrated with "cable" television. The computer console will control the computer's information storage and order it to produce selective bits of information, making them directly available in offices and homes via television scanning through cable television or through specially ordered printouts.

Television is not just an experience substitute or merely another experience; it is both, and hence is an historically new mass experience. Such ideologies as the television watchers accept must be successful in integrating and resonating the residual iconic imagery – "pictures-in-the-head" – generated by media-transmitted films as well as by their own "personal experience." In effect, this residual iconic imagery is a new, technologically implanted paleosymbolism; a type II paleosymbolism directly affecting, resonating, and reworking the type I paleosymbolism residual of early childhood experience. In brief, things people could not normally speak about are now being affected by other things they cannot speak about, in ways and with results they cannot speak about. To that extent, the characterological grounding of ideologies, normally changed only slowly and in the course of life experience, is being impinged upon and changed in new ways and, quite likely, at far more rapid rates. Television has instituted a new modality and tempo of experience.

If we can think of ideology and history as connected by the "black box" of personal experience, that black box has now been technologically amplified and we may therefore expect a decline in the manifest connection between ideologies and history, or people's social position in historical processes. In one way, this may be experienced as an "end of ideology," as the "irrelevance" of ideology, or as the "meaninglessness" or "absurdity" of life, of society, and culture. As the paleosymbolic materials of persons' character are now technologically touchable by six hours of television watching per day, which is to say, almost 40% of the person's waking day, the disjunction grows between the "personal" and the sociohistorical.

With such a technologically induced mass transformation of the paleosymbolic elements of character, changes will have to be made in the mass belief systems available, including the ideological. But it is not simply that different ideologies, ideologies having different public projects and appealing to different audiences, become necessary but, rather, that the entire lineal and activistic rationality of any kind of ideology – the very grammar of ideology – may be undermined. Television is a "you-are-there" participatory and consummatory activity. One is not commonly left with a sense that one needs to do something actively after a viewing. The viewing is an end in itself.

As a participatory experience, the viewers' sense of critical distance, one basis for the rationality premised by normal ideology, has been diminished. If there is residual tension after a viewing, it does not necessarily call for intellectual clarification of the kind provided for by ideology but for a "resolution" in the sense that a drama or piece of music may be "resolved." Ideology always implies a measure of rational social criticism, which is the specification of a social target and the readying of the self to change it. A viewer's participatory experience, when intellectualized at all, implies a dramaturgical criticism of an object to be consumed and experienced. Dramaturgical criticism does not prod a viewer to do something or change something, but simply to "appreciate" something in its givenness. The viewer presented with a negative dramaturgical criticism of something is not expected to produce a better showing, but to better "understand" it, to recommend others view or avoid viewing it, and to look forward to or avoid the next production by the same dramaturgist. Ideology implies rational criticism as preparation for action; dramaturgy implies the cultivation of the viewer's sensibility as the passive spectator of events as presented.

With the shift from a conceptual to an iconic symbolism, then, the very fundamentals shared by any ideology may be attenuated. The response prepared by the transition from a newspaper- to a television-centered system of communication may not take the form of ideological performances that vary around a common grammar of ideology, but of altogether differently structured symbol systems: of analogic rather than digital, of synthetic rather than analytic systems, of occult belief systems, new religious myths, the "discovery" of Oriental and other non-Western religions. In this, however, there is no "end" to ideology, for it continues among some groups, in some sites, and at some semiotic level, but it ceases to be as important a mode of consciousness of masses; remaining a dominant form of consciousness among some elites, ideology loses ground among the masses and lower strata. In consequence of television, it may be that the traditional undermining of "restricted" speech variants by the public school system is counterbalanced by television's reinforcement of it, and that "elaborated" speech variants become increasingly limited to an elite.

The "end of ideology" thesis of the 1950s was rooted in a kind of optimism and in a tacit myth of progress. The idea was that ideology would be replaced by the victory of technological, scientific, and rational-pragmatic modes of consciousness; in short, by a "higher" mode of consciousness. The view suggested here is that the mode of consciousness likely to compete with ideology among the masses, at any rate, may not be more rationalism but less, not a higher rationalism but a lower. Ideology and the critics of ideology both remained rooted in the Enlightenment. The critics of ideology overlooked the fact that, when ideology faded, it need not be replaced by something more rational but by something that they — as Enlighteners — might regard as regressive and irrational. This is not to say that there were no limits to the Enlightenment's rationality that needed transcending, nor even that the Western drift to occultism and Oriental religions does not rest on certain irrationalities of present societies. It is, rather, to doubt that occultism and Oriental religions successfully surmount these irrationalities.

People who do not read can have only a kind of secondhand relationship to ideologies and ideological movements. If they are to be convinced, they must be convinced by other means or in some other way. Since there has been a profound change in the symbolic environment with the emergence of radio, cinema, and television, there must also be an important change in the role of ideology as a spur to, interpreter and director of, public projects. Correspondingly, certain places — such as schools and universities — or certain social strata — such as the relatively well-educated — remain structurally advantaged with respect to opportunities for ideological production and consumption.

With the growth of the system of mass education, the consciousness of the population of advanced industrialized countries becomes profoundly split: There is an intensification among some "elites" of the consumption and production of ideological objects; but at exactly the same time, there is also a growth of "masses." "Masses" are here defined as those to whom ideology is less central because their consciousness is now shaped more by radio, cinema, and television – being influenced more by the "consciousness industry" than by the ideological products of the "cultural apparatus."

In industrial countries there is considerable tension between the "cultural apparatus," largely influenced by the intelligentsia and academicians, and the "consciousness industry," largely run by technicians within the framework of profit-maximization and now increasingly integrated with political functionaries and the state apparatus. For that reason, such technicians may seek to avoid overt political acts, lest they offend potential markets as well as offend the political preferences of the industry's owners and managers, or political leaders and state functionaries. This is not at all to say, of course, that the content of the "entertainment" produced by the consciousness industry is apolitical. Far from it.

"The cultural apparatus" was a term that C. Wright Mills first used in a BBC broadcast in 1959 to refer to "all the organizations and milieux in which artistic, intellectual, and scientific work goes on, and to the means by which such work is made available to circles, publics, and masses. In the cultural apparatus art, science, and learning, entertainment, malarkey, and information are produced and distributed and consumed. It contains an elaborate set of institutions: of schools and theaters, newspapers and census bureaus, studios, laboratories, museums, little magazines, radio networks."

This formulation tends to conflate two different things whose separation repays analysis. One is the sources, the creative persons, circles, or milieux, in which or by whom critical reason is displayed and exercised, in which science and technologies are developed, and in which sensibility is symbolically evoked and explored. These sources, however, are quite distinct from the media through which they are conveyed to audiences and publics. If this distinction between sources and media is not made clearly, there is a tendency to blur the social marginality of the cultural apparatus, their ideological isolation, and their political powerlessness. Correspondingly, to emphasize such a distinction is to indicate systematically that the producers of "culture" in modern society cannot communicate their work to mass audiences except by passing through a route controlled by media, and those who control the mass media, the consciousness industry.

This is not to say that the cultural apparatus is altogether devoid of its own media or has no control whatsoever over these. It does control certain magazines, theaters, and radio stations which are relatively small and, especially so, in the audience reached and in the influence exerted. The media directly under the influence of the cultural apparatus allows its members to communicate internally with one another, and thus to constitute themselves to some extent as a community; but it allows them little routine access to mass audiences. Often, they convey only elaborated codes.

Mills' discussion of the three stages through which, he held, modern culture was publicly supported essentially culminates in the consciousness industry. The first stage was the aristocratic patronage system, especially in Europe. The second was the bourgeois public for whom the cultural workman worked via the mediation of an anonymous market. The third was the one in which "commercial agencies or political authorities support culture, but unlike older patrons, they do not form its sole public." It is in this last state that (following Hans Enzensberger) what is called here the consciousness industry becomes the dominant force, as the medium of public communication.

Mills stresses that the earlier system in which cultural workers and buyers were integrated was unified only indirectly and as the unwitting product of the common taste of patrons or bourgeois publics. In contrast, however, in the third period now dominated by the consciousness industry, Mills notes that the definitions of reality, values, and taste once diffusely shaped by a cultural apparatus are now, however, "subject to official management and, if need be, backed up by coercion . . . the terms of debate, the terms in which the world may be seen, the standards and lack of standards by which men judge of their accomplishments, of themselves or of other men – these terms are officially or commercially determined, inculcated, enforced." Much the same point had been made (in 1954) by the dean of critical communications studies in the United States, Dallas W. Smythe, who remarked: ". . . as our culture has developed it has built into itself increasing concentrations of authority, and nowhere is this more evident than in our communications activities."

Written at the end of the so-called "silent decade" of the 1950s, Mills' analysis minimized the conflict between the cultural apparatus and the consciousness industry. Mills then emphasized the subordination of American academicians and intellectuals to business values of usefulness and efficiency, and their gratitude for business philanthropy. "Joseph Schumpeter's notion that under capitalism intellectuals generally tend to erode its foundations," declared Mills, "does not generally hold true of the United States." Mills was more nearly correct, if we take the focus of his remarks to be American intellectuals rather than Europeans. But, for the most part, however, we shall argue that it was Schumpeter who was correct.

There was a tendency on Mills' part to underestimate the alienation long felt by American cultural establishments from the society's dominant values. This alienation was fully visible at least as early as the American transcendentalists; it was an alienation that became more pronounced after World War I, as symbolized by Randolph Bourne's rejection of John Dewey's pragmatism; it was an alienation plainly visible during the Depression and the Marxism of the 1930s; and it was an alienation that would once again be evident only a few years after Mills' own talk on the cultural apparatus, a talk which, in itself, exhibited the very alienation whose absence it decried.

Speaking a decade after Mills, Herbert Gans remarked that "the most interesting phenomenon in America . . . is the political struggle between taste cultures over whose culture is to predominate in the major media, and over whose culture will provide society with its symbols, values, and world view." Gans also called attention to the continuing tensions "between the distributors and creators of culture,"[1] another expression of the conflict between the cultural apparatus and the consciousness industry.

The tensions between the cultural apparatus and the consciousness industry are, in part, derived from the tensions that arise between any kind of sellers and buyers. Here, however, there is the additional problem that those in the cultural apparatus are essentially small scale, handicraft workers who are ever in danger of domination by a narrowing circle of enormously powerful buyers. The buyers in the consciousness industry can establish prices and create political blacklists, exert continual economic and ideological pressure on the cultural workers, and violate the latter's sense of autonomy – of craftsmanship, of artistic or scientific integrity.

It is in part the very control exerted by the consciousness industry, on behalf of values opposed by cultural workers, that generates the latter's continuing critique of "mass culture." This bitterness is accentuated by the vulgarity of the standards that the consciousness industry is felt to impose. The relations between the two are also strained by the widespread feeling in the cultural apparatus that sheer contact with the consciousness industry is threatening to their deepest values. The consciousness industry is often viewed as a "dirty" business threatening the "purity" or authenticity of the cultural apparatus. Hans Enzensberger has noted sympathetically that, considering the nature of the consciousness industry, it is no wonder that "the temptation to withdraw is great." He adds, however, that "fear of handling this is a luxury a sewer-man cannot necessarily afford."[2]

An essential characteristic of the modern communication system is that it is a mass media system, which means that it can make an increasing number of low-cost messages available to an increasing proportion of the members of any society, and to an increasing number of societies throughout the world. This, in turn, has largely been a function of the technological

1. Herbert J. Gans, "The Politics of Culture in America," in Denis McQuail, ed., *The Sociology of Mass Communication* (London: Penguin, 1972), p. 378.
2. Hans Magnus Enzensberger, *The Consciousness Industry* (New York: Seabury Press, 1974), p. 105.

innovation, the invention of printing, with which the communication revolution began. Enzensberger recently formulated a list of technological innovations in the last 20 years or so in communication: new satellites, color television, cable relay television, cassettes, videotape, videotape recorder, video phones, stereophony, laser techniques, electrostatic reproduction processes, electronic high-speed printing, composing, and learning machines, microfiches with electronic access, printing by radio, time-sharing computers, data banks. "All these new forms of media are constantly forming new connections both with each other and with older media like printing, radio, film, television, telephone, radar, and so on. They are clearly coming together to form a universal system." In the next forty years, the symbolic environment and political systems of the world will, once again, be revolutionized by this newest communications revolution.

Both the cultural apparatus and [the] consciousness industry parallel the schismatic character of the modern consciousness: its highly unstable mixture of cultural pessimism and technological optimism. The cultural apparatus is more likely to be the bearer of the "bad news" concerning – for example – ecological crisis, political corruption, class bias; while the consciousness industry becomes the purveyors of hope, the professional lookers-on-the-bright-side. The very political impotence and isolation of the cadres of the cultural apparatus grounds their pessimism in their own everyday life, while the technicians of the consciousness industry are surrounded by and have use of the most powerful, advanced, and expensive communications hardware, which is the everyday grounding of their own technological optimism.

Cultural apparatus and consciousness industry thus each define the world quite differently and are, as a result, in a tense if somewhat one-sided relation with one another; one-sided in that the former worries more about the latter than the reverse. Clearly, the largest section of the populace in advanced industrial societies is now under the direct and immediate influence of the consciousness industry, while the cultural apparatus has little if any direct contact with this great public. In short, the cultural apparatus is largely without direct access to or influence on the rural peasantry or farmers, the poor, the blue-collar working classes, blacks, and women.

The differences between the cultural apparatus and the consciousness industry do not exactly parallel [the] differences between the politically involved and the apolitical, or between the "left" and the "right" ideologies in politics. There are some tendencies in that direction, but they could be overstated. For example, there are some involved in the cultural apparatus whose fastidiousness makes politics boring or offensive to their sensibilities. Correspondingly, the consciousness industry, perhaps particularly in its pop-music sectors, often fosters a deviant subculture isolated from mainstream consciousness. As we suggested earlier, it sometimes generates a counterculture that unwittingly undermines the very characterological and cultural requisites of the hegemonic class and the institutions that sustain it. It does so, of course, not because its personnel harbor a deliberate intent to sabotage, but from the most "respectable" of motives – to produce and sell whatever turns a profit – regardless of its consequences.

The cultural apparatus largely organizes itself in and around the modern university and its supporting facilities; it is therefore constantly threatened with isolation from the larger society and from any politically consequential following. In effect, the elites of the cultural apparatus surrender the mass of the populace to the consciousness industry, so long *as the elites continue to conceive of influencing others via ideology and ideological discourse.* For now, with the split between consciousness industry and cultural apparatus, ideology continues to ground an elite politics but loses effective influence over the masses.

Those who are ideologically mobilized and ready – the people of the cultural apparatus – are thus vulnerable to increasing political frustration, isolation, and impotence. The sense of self-identity and achievement implicit in and reinforced by ideology is here threatened. Even the ideologically mobilized are now, under the conditions of this split, tempted toward the rejection of ideology itself. They, too, are tempted toward a politics increasingly open to the irrational, in order somehow to make contact with the mass public from whom they have been cut off, and who do not respond to the conventional ideological appeals. Something of this was exhibited in what may be called the "Weatherman Syndrome," which is an impotence of the ideological? that generates "days of rage," of violence and trashing, as a way of suppressing a sense of ineffectuality and of overcoming inclinations to passivity. In the Weatherman Syndrome – and in terrorism more generally – discourse ceases and ideology collapses into the propaganda of the deed. If the growth of the consciousness industry and its tensions with the cultural apparatus did not produce an "end to ideology" it certainly fostered a crisis for ideological discourse, making the limits on ideology's traditional modes of discourse all to evident.

There is now a growing mass of the populace in advanced industrial countries who are incapable of being reached by ideological appeals and who are insulated from ideological discourse of any political persuasion. It no longer seems merely mistaken, but is more nearly archaic, to think of the proletariat as an "historical agent" with true political initiatives in societal transformation. With the rise of the consciousness industry the inability of the proletariat to play such a role may now be beyond remedy. As E. P. Thompson has suggested: "So long as any ruling group . . . can reproduce itself or manufacture social consciousness there will be no inherent logic of process within the system which . . . will work power-fully to bring about its overthrow."[3] The conclusion is sound, however, only if we omit discussions of the contradictions of the consciousness industry itself.

Thus one may not conclude that the working class remains reliably controllable, even if it is continually vulnerable to the consciousness in-dustry. Indeed, the proletariat in various countries, Italy, for example, may yet serve as the clean-up men of history, picking up power in the streets as their society's hegemonic class fumbles and collapses in the face of some abrupt crisis. But that is a far cry from being an historical agent with initiative and with a consciousness of its role.

The great and successful revolutions of the twentieth century, in Russia and China, occurred in societies that were not only behind in general industrial development but, also, in the development of their communica-tions technology. To this day, the Chinese Cultural Revolutions make important use of wall posters to mobilize their forces. Indeed, one might add that the Cultural Revolutions themselves seem to have been precipi-tated when Mao lost control over (and routine access to) Peking newspa-pers, which refused to print his criticisms of Peking's mayor.

In countries with an extensive development of the consciousness indus-try, talk of "revolutionary solutions" is primarily indicative of ideological rage at political impotence and of the fear of personal passivity. In other words, it is a symptom. At the same time, however, neither the continual readiness of the cultural apparatus for ideological arousal and mobiliza-tion, on the one side, nor the growth of deviant and countercultures among masses, on the other, can allow one to assume any persisting social stability and equilibrium. A potentially mobilizable mass coexists alongside of an easily arousable ideological elite. Presently, the "stability" of modern society results in some large part from the mutual isolation of these sectors. Indeed, one should think of the present not as any sort of stable equilibrium but simply as a temporary "inertness." But whether that coexistence of mass and elite – an inert adjacency without much interaction and mutual influence – can long persist remains to be seen. Nevertheless, revolutionary solutions remain mythical so long as ideologi-cal elites and their cultural apparatus can reach masses only by going through the consciousness industry.

The paradoxical character of the present becomes even more visible if it is noticed that the managers of the consciousness industry, as of others, are also likely to be among the relatively well-educated, university-trained persons most extensively exposed to the cultural apparatus. Their

3. E. P. Thompson, "An Open Letter to Leszek Kolakowski," *Socialist Register* (London: Merlin Press, 1973), p. 75.

ambiguous social role must yield an inevitable measure of ideological ambivalence. They cannot easily be dismissed by the cultural apparatus as philistine, illiberal, enemies of the mind. Indeed, the hegemonic elites have recently taken to accusing some in the consciousness industry of favoring the "left" and of being class traitors. This was, to some extent, the import of the Nixon-Agnew accusations against the press and of Daniel Patrick Moynihan's suggestion that university-trained journalists are one-sidedly critical of the status quo.

The tension between the consciousness industry and the cultural apparatus can become a center for a politics sensitive to the importance of the media and of the modern communications revolution. In one part, this will entail a struggle for public control and access to the burgeoning new communication's technology. In another part, this politics will concern itself with the cultural apparatus' isolation from the mass media and the public it reaches. The tension between the two exists in some measure because the consciousness industry has socially isolated the cultural apparatus and has successfully imposed an institutionalized form of tacit censorship on it. The political struggle between the two will, in part, concern itself with the maintenance or relaxation of this censorship.

But this is not a conflict in which the consciousness industry will be unambivalently opposed and solidary in its response to the cultural apparatus. The reliability and controllability of the technicians of the consciousness industry and even of some of its managers is, indeed, in question. For, as we have noted, they too have been exposed to the perspectives of the cultural apparatus and share its hostility to censorship. Moreover, to the extent that the cultural apparatus can produce products that capture and hold attention, and can be sold or used as a vehicle to sell other things, then the cultural apparatus will be given access to the media and publics controlled by the consciousness industry. A media-centered politics, then, will amplify the common values and hostility toward censorship shared by the consciousness industry and the cultural apparatus, building alliances around these. It will, at the same time, exploit the contradictions of the consciousness industry that dispose it to publicize any cultural outlook that helps maintain its own profitability.

MODERNISM OR POSTMODERNISM: DISSOLUTION OR RECONSTRUCTION OF MORAL ORDER?

- Daniel Bell, *Modernism, postmodernism, and the decline of moral order*
- Jean-François Lyotard, *The postmodern condition*
- Jurgen Habermas, *Modernity versus postmodernity*
- Andreas Huyssen, *Mapping the postmodern*

28

Modernism, postmodernism, and the decline of moral order

Daniel Bell

In the broader sense, the theme of this book is not just the cultural contradictions of capitalism as such, but of bourgeois society: that new world created by the mercantile and fabricating guilds, the middle or bourgeois class that revolutionized modern society after the sixteenth century by making economic activity, rather than military or religious concerns, the central feature of society.

Capitalism is a socioeconomic system geared to the production of commodities by a rational calculus of cost and price, and to the consistent accumulation of capital for the purposes of reinvestment. But this singular new mode of operation was fused with a distinctive culture and character structure. In culture, this was the idea of self-realization, the release of the individual from traditional restraints and ascriptive ties (family and birth) so that he could "make" of himself what he willed. In character structure, this was the norm of self-control and delayed gratification, of purposeful behavior in the pursuit of well-defined goals. It is the interrelationship of this economic system, culture, and character structure which comprised bourgeois civilization. It is the unraveling of this unity and its consequences which are the threads of this book.

I read the contradictions through two prisms: The first, a synthetic construct, is an "ideal type." It is "ahistorical" and treats the phenomena as a closed system. Thus it can be "hypothetical deductive" and specify the limits of the phenomena. Its virtue as an ideal type is the possibility of identifying the essential lineaments – what I call the axial principles and axial structures – of the circumscribed social realms which the flux of historical change sometimes obscures. Being static, however, the ideal type does not account for origins or future directions. For that, one needs the second prism of history and the detailed empirical complexity which is its content.

Using the ideal type, I see the contradictions of capitalism in the antagonistic principles that underlie the technical-economic, political, and cultural structures of the society. Now, the technical-economic realm, which became central in the beginning of capitalism, is, like all industrial society today, based on the axial principle of economizing: the effort to achieve efficiency through the breakdown of all activities into the smallest components of unit cost, as defined by the systems of financial accounting. The axial structure, based on specialization and hierarchy, is one of bureaucratic coordination. Necessarily, individuals are treated not as persons but as "things" (in the sociological jargon their behavior regulated by the role requirements), as instruments to maximize profit. In short, individuals are dissolved into their function.

The political realm, which regulates conflict, is governed by the axial principle of equality: equality before the law, equal civil rights, and, most recently, the claims of equal social and economic rights. Because these claims become translated into entitlements, the political order increasingly intervenes in the economic and social realms (in the affairs of corporations, universities, and hospitals) in order to redress the positions and rewards generated in the society by the economic system. The axial structure of the polity is representation and, more recently, participation. And the demands for participation, as a principle, now are carried over into all other realms of the society. The tensions between bureaucracy and equality frame the social conflicts of the day.

Finally, the cultural realm is one of self-expression and self-gratification. It is anti-institutional and antinomian in that the individual is taken to be the measure of satisfaction, and his feelings, sentiments, and judgments, not some objective standard of quality and value, determine the worth of cultural objects. At its most blatant, this sentiment asks of a poem, a play, or a painting, not whether it is good or meretricious, but "What does it do for me?" In this democratization of culture, every individual, understandably, seeks to realize his full "potential," and so the individual "self" comes increasingly into conflict with the role requirements of the technical-economic order.

A number of critics have objected to these formulations on the ground that "power" still lies primarily in the economic realm, principally in the hands of the large corporations, and that the impulses to self-expression in the culture have been "co-opted" by the capitalist system and converted into commodities, i.e., objects for sale.

Such questions are empirical ones that test particular assumptions, not whether this mode of analysis, i.e., the idea of the disjunction between the realms, is useful or not. The answers lie in the court of history, and I shall return to them at the close of my historical exposition, the second thread of my analysis.

Much of the prevailing view of capitalism (that of the last thirty years) was shaped by Max Weber through his emphasis on Calvinism and the Protestant ethic – the role of methodical work and the legitimation of the pursuit of wealth – as the doctrines that facilitated the rise of the distinctive Western organization of rational production and exchange. But the origins of capitalism were twofold. If one source was the asceticism which Weber emphasized, the other was acquisitiveness, a central theme of Werner Sombart, whose work was almost completely neglected in that period of time.

Whatever the exact locations of early capitalism, it is clear that, from the start, the two impulses of asceticism and acquisitiveness were yoked together. One was the bourgeois prudential spirit of calculation; the other, the restless Faustian drive which, as expressed in the modern economy and technology, took as its motto "the endless frontier" and, as its goal, the complete transformation of nature. The intertwining of the two impulses shaped the modern conception of rationality. The tension between the two imposed a moral restraint on the sumptuary display that had characterized earlier periods of conquest. What is also evident – and it is one of the arguments in this book – is that the ascetic element, and with it one kind of moral legitimation of capitalist behavior, has virtually disappeared.

On the level of philosophical justification, the major attack on asceticism was mounted by Jeremy Bentham, who argued that asceticism ("miseries" inflicted by sectarians on unwilling others) violated the "natural" hedonism which rules men – the search for pleasure and the avoidance of pain. Its "mischief" is that, whatever its pure intention, asceticism leads to "despotism" over men. The principle of utility alone could serve as the regulating instrument of men's search to satisfy their diverse ends. Thus the notion of common ends was dissolved into individual preferences.

On the plane of history, the "economic impulse" had been constrained earlier by the rules of custom and tradition, to some extent by the Catholic moral principle of the just price, and later by the Puritan emphasis on frugality. As the religious impulses diminished, a complex history in its own right, so did the restraints. What became distinctive about capitalism – its very dynamic – was its boundlessness. Propelled by the dynamo of technology, there were to be no asymptotes to its exponential growth. No limits. Nothing was sacred. Change became the norm. By the middle of the nineteenth century, this was the trajectory of the economic impulse. It was, as well, the trajectory of the culture.

The realm of culture is the realm of meanings, the effort in some imaginative form to make sense of the world through the expressiveness of art and ritual, particularly those "incomprehensions" such as tragedy and death that arise out of the existential predicaments which every self-conscious human being must confront at some point in his life. In these encounters, one becomes aware of the fundamental questions – what Goethe called *Urphanomen* – which frame all others. Religion, as the oldest effort to comprehend these "mysteries," has historically been the source of cultural symbols.

If science is the search for the unity of nature, religion has been the quest for the unity of culture in the different historical periods of civilizations. To close that circle, religion has woven tradition as the fabric of meaning and guarded the portals of culture by rejecting those works of art which threatened the moral norms of religion.

The modern movement disrupts that unity. It does so in three ways: by insisting on the autonomy of the aesthetic from moral norms; by valuing more highly the new and experimental; and by taking the self (in its quest for originality and uniqueness) as the touchstone of cultural judgment.

The most aggressive outrider of the movement is the self-proclaimed avant-garde which calls itself Modernism. The discussion of Modernism is the inner thread of this book, for I see Modernism as the agency for the dissolution of the bourgeois world view and, in the past half-century, as gaining hegemony in the culture.

The difficulties of defining Modernism are notorious. Schematically, I would specify three different dimensions:

1. Thematically Modernism has been a rage against order, and in particular, bourgeois orderliness. The emphasis is on the self, and the unceasing search for experience. If Terence once said, "Nothing human is alien to me," the Modernist could say with equal fervor, "Nothing inhuman is alien to me." Rationalism is seen as devitalizing; the surge to creativity is propelled by an exploration of the demonic. In that exploration, one cannot set aesthetic limits (or even moral norms) to this protean reach of the imagination. The crucial insistence is that experience is to have no boundaries to its cravings, that there be "nothing sacred."

2. Stylistically, there is a common syntax in what I have called "the eclipse of distance." This is the effort to achieve immediacy, impact, simultaneity, and sensation by eliminating aesthetic and psychic distance. In diminishing aesthetic distance, one annihilates contemplation and envelops the spectator in the experience. By eliminating psychic distance, one emphasizes (in Freudian terms) the "primary process" of dream and hallucination, of instinct and impulse. In all this, Modernism rejects the "rational cosmology" that was introduced into the arts during the Renaissance and codified by Alberti: of foreground and background in pictorial space; of beginning, middle, and end, or sequence, in time, and the distinction of genres and the modes of work appropriate to each genre. This eclipse of distance, as a formal syntax, cuts across all the arts: in literature, the "stream of consciousness"; in painting, the elimination of the interior distance" within the canvas; in music, the upset of the balance of

melody and harmony; in poetry, the disruption of the ordered meter. In the broadest sense, this common syntax repudiates mimesis as a principle of art.[1]

3. The preoccupation with the medium. In all periods of cultural history, artists have been conscious of the nature and complexity of the medium as a formal problem in transmuting the "prefigured" into the "figured" result. In the last twenty-five years, we have seen a preoccupation not with the content or form (i.e., style and genre), but with the medium of art itself: with the actual texture of paint and materials in painting, with the abstract "sounds" in music, with phonology or even "breath" in poetry, and with the abstract properties of language in literature – often to the exclusion of anything else. Thus it is the encaustic surface, not the image, that generates excitement in the paintings of Jasper Johns; the aleatory or chance factors in the music of John Cage; the aspirate rather than the syllable, as a measure of line in [the] poetry of Robert Creeley – all of these as expressions of the self, rather than formal explorations of the limits and nature of the medium itself.

Modernism has, beyond dispute, been responsible for one of the great surges of creativity in Western culture. The period from 1850 to 1930 probably saw more varied experiments in literature, poetry, music, and painting – if not more great masterpieces – than any previous period we have known. Much of this arose out of the creative tension of culture, with its adversary stance, against the bourgeois social structure. Yet there has been a price. One cost has been the loss of coherence in culture, particularly in the spread of an antinomian attitude to moral norms and even to the idea of cultural judgment itself. The greater price was exacted when the distinction between art and life became blurred so that what was once permitted in the imagination (the novels of murder, lust, perversity) has often passed over into fantasy, and is acted out by individuals who want to make their "lives" a work of art, and when, with the "democratization" of criticism, the touchstone of judgment is no longer some consensual agreement on standards, but each "self's" judgment as to how art enhances that "self."

Changes in culture interact with a social structure in complicated ways. Where there is a patronage system, the patron – be it prince, or Church, or State – commissions a work of art, and the cultural needs of the institu-

1. Clearly not all Modernist writers are "anti-bourgeois" in any overt sense. T. S. Eliot was a High-Church Anglican and William Faulkner a traditionalist in his Southern politics. Yet both men were great "experimenters" in poetry and in novel. Despite their specific political or cultural *beliefs*, one of the effects of their "modernist styles" was to disrupt the "rational cosomology" which underlay the bourgeois world view of an ordered relationship of space and time.

tion, such as the Church, or the tastes of the prince, or the demands for glorification by the State, will shape the regnant style of the time. But where art is bought and sold, the market is where culture and social structure cross. One would expect that where culture has become a "commodity" the bourgeois taste would prevail. But in extraordinary historical fact, this has not been the case.

The phrase "cultural hegemony" – identified with the Italian Marxist Antonio Gramsci – signifies the dominance of a single group in shaping the prevailing world view which gives a people an interpretation of the age. There have been many times where a single world view, growing out of and serving a dominant class, has prevailed. In the twelfth century – the "Age of Faith" symbolized by Innocent III – we see the apotheosis of Church control over society not in the uniformity of devotion, but, as Bryan Wilson has put it, "because the imprint of faith and order demanded by ecclesiastical authority dominated the social framework." The closest analogue today – in the regulation of daily life, the heavy-handed control of production and distribution, and the restraint of impulse and the glorification of authority – is the Soviet world, where the Party exercises complete cultural hegemony. It is an ideologically prescribed social order.

Marxists have assumed that under capitalism there has also been a single cultural hegemony – the ideas of the "ruling class." Yet the astonishing fact is that in the last hundred years, if there has been a dominant influence – in the high culture at least – it has been the avowed enemy of that class, Modernism.

At the start, the capitalist economic impulse and the cultural drive of modernity shared a common source, the ideas of liberty and liberation, whose embodiments were "rugged individualism" in economic affairs and the "unrestrained self" in culture. Though the two had a common origin in the repudiation of tradition and the authority of the past, an adversary relation between them quickly developed. One can say, as Freud would, that the discipline required by work was threatened by the libidinal energies diverted to culture. This may perhaps be true, but it is abstract. What would seem to be the more likely historical explanation is that the bourgeois attitudes of calculation and methodical restraint came into conflict with the impulsive searchings for sensation and excitement that one found in Romanticism, and which passed over into Modernism. The antagonism deepened as the organization of work and production became bureaucratized and individuals were reduced to roles, so that the norms of the workplace were increasingly at variance with the emphasis on self-exploration and self-gratification. The thread connecting Blake to Byron to Baudelaire – who is the avatar of Modernism – may not be literal, but it is a figurative symbolic lineage.

So long as work and wealth had a religious sanction, they possessed a transcendental justification. But when that ethic eroded, there was a loss of legitimation, for the pursuit of wealth alone is not a calling that justifies itself. As Schumpeter once shrewdly remarked: The stock exchange is a poor substitute for the Holy Grail.

The central point is that – at first, for the advanced social groups, the intelligentsia and the educated social classes, and later for the middle class itself – the legitimations of social behavior passed from religion to modernist culture. And with it here was a shift in emphasis from "character," which is the unity of moral codes and disciplined purpose, to an emphasis on "personality," which is the enhancement of self through the compulsive search for individual differentiation. In brief, not work but the "life style" became the source of satisfaction and criterion for desirable behavior in the society.

Yet paradoxically, the life style that became the imago of the free self was not that of the businessman, expressing himself through his "dynamic drive," but that of the artist defying the conventions of the society. And, as I have tried to show, increasingly, it is the artist who begins to dominate the audience, and to impose his judgment as to what is to be desired and bought. The paradox is completed when the bourgeois ethic, having collapsed in the society, finds few defenders in the culture (do any writers defend any institutions?) and Modernism, as an attack on orthodoxy, has triumphed and become the regnant orthodoxy of the day.

Any tension creates its own dialectic. Since the market is where social structure and culture cross, what has happened is that in the last fifty years the economy has been geared to producing the life styles paraded by the culture. Thus, not only has there been a contradiction between the realms, but that tension has produced a further contradiction within the economic realm itself. In the world of capitalist enterprise, the nominal ethos in the spheres of production and organization is still one of work, delayed gratification, career orientation, devotion to the enterprise. Yet, on the marketing side, the sale of goods, packaged in the glossy images of glamour and sex, promotes a hedonistic way of life whose promise is the voluptuous gratification of the lineaments of desire. The consequence of this contradiction, as I put it in these pages, is that a corporation finds its people being straight by day and swingers by night.

What has happened in society in the last fifty years – as a result of the erosion of the religious ethic and the increase in discretionary income – is that the culture has taken the initiative in promoting change, and the economy has been geared to meeting these new wants.

In this respect, there has been a significant reversal in the historical pattern of social change. During the rise of capitalism – in the "modernization" of any traditional society – one could more readily change the

economic structure of a society: by forcing people off the land into factories, by imposing a new rhythm and discipline of work, by using brutal
means or incentives (e.g., the theory of interest as the reward for "abstinence" from consumption) to raise capital. But the "superstructure" –
the patterns of family life, the attachements to religion and authority, the
received ideas that shaped people's perceptions of a social reality – was
more stubbornly resistant to change.

Today, by contrast, it is the economic structure that is the more difficult
to change. Within the enterprise, the heavy bureaucratic layers reduce
flexible adaptation, while union rules inhibit the power of management
to control the assignment of jobs. In the society, the economic enterprise
is subject to the challenges of various veto groups (e.g., on the location of
plants or the use of the environment) and subject more and more to
regulation by government.

But in the culture, fantasy reigns almost unconstrained. The media are
geared to feeding new images to people, to unsettling traditional conventions, and the highlighting of aberrant and quirky behavior which becomes imagos for other to imitate. The traditional is stodgy, and the
"orthodox" institutions such as family and church are on the defensive
about their inability to change.

Yet if capitalism has been routinized, Modernism has been trivialized.
After all, how often can it continue to shock if there is nothing shocking
left? If experiment is the norm, how original can anything new be? And
like all bad history, Modernism has repeated its end, once in the popgun
outbursts of Futurism and Dadaism, the second time in the phosphores-
cent parodies of Pop paintings and the mindless minimalism of conceptual art. The exclamation points that end each sentence of the Manifes-
toes have simply become four dots that trail away in the tedium of endless
repetition. And what is there in the end? As Beckett summed it up in his
sad dialogue:

VLADIMIR: Say you are, even if it's not true.
ESTRAGON: What am I to say?
VLADIMIR: Say, I am happy.
ESTRAGON: I am happy.
VLADIMIR: So am I.
ESTRAGON: So am I.
VLADIMIR: We are happy.
ESTRAGON: We are happy. (Silence.) What do we do now, now that we
          are happy?
VLADIMIR: Wait for Godot.

In the revelation of wisdom, the Owl of Minerva flies at dusk because
life had become gray on gray. In the victorious apocalypse of Modernism,

the dawn is a series of gaudy colors whirling in strobismic light. Today, Modernism has become not the work of serious artists but the property of the culturati, the "cultural mass," the distribution sector of cultural production, for whom the shock of the old has become the chic of the new. The culturati have carried over, in rhetoric, the adversary stance against bourgeois orderliness and sobriety, yet they impose a conformity of their own on those who deviate from its guarded canons.

In the 1960s, one beheld the "new" phenomenon of the counterculture. Yet the very name was a conceit. The "adversary culture" was concerned with art, the use of the imagination to transfigure recalcitrant memory or intractible materials into a work that could, in its power, transcend its time. It existed in the realm of culture. The so-called counter-culture was a children's crusade that sought to eliminate the line between fantasy and reality and act out in life its impulses under a banner of liberation. It claimed to mock bourgeois prudishness, when it was only flaunting the closet behavior of its liberal parents. It claimed to be new and daring when it was only repeating in more raucous form – its rock noise amplified in the electronic echo-chamber of the mass media – the youthful japes of a Greenwich Village bohemia of a half century before. It was less a counter-culture than a counterfeit culture.

In this double contradiction of capitalism, what has been established in the last thirty years has been the tawdry rule of fad and fashion: of "multiples" for the culturati, hedonism for the middle classes, and pornotopia for the masses. And in the very nature of fashion, it has trivialized the culture.

Has Modernism been "co-opted," as Herbert Marcuse suggests? In one dimension, yes. It has been converted into a commodity for promotion and profit. But in the deeper transformations of structure, that process can only undermine the foundations of capitalism itself. The sociological truism is that a societal order is shored up by its legitimations, which provide the defenses against its despisers. But the legitimation of the culture, as I have argued, is the quest for self-gratification and the expression of "personality." It attacks established orthodoxy in the name of personal autonomy and heterodoxy. Yet what modern culture has failed to understand is that orthodoxy is not the guardian of an existent order, but is itself a judgment on the adequacy and moral character of beliefs from the standpoint of "right reason." The paradox is that "heterodoxy" itself has become conformist in liberal circles, and exercises that conformity under the banner of an antinomian flag. It is a prescription, in its confusions, for the dissolution of a shared moral order.

Does power still lie in the economic realm, and largely in the hands of the giant corporations? To a considerable extent this is still so in Western society, yet such an argument misreads the nature of societal change today.

A capitalist order had historical strength when it fused property with power through a set of ruling families to maintain the continuity of the system. The first deep, internal structural change in capitalism was the divorce of family and property from managerial power and the loss of continuity through the chain of elites. Economic power today lies in institutions whose chiefs cannot pass along their power to their heirs and who, increasingly – since property is not private (but corporate), and technical skill, not property, is the basis of managerial positions – no longer have the traditional natural rights, justifications, and legitimacy in the exercise of that power, and feel it keenly. The larger fact is that a modern society multiplies the number of constituencies and, given the increasing interdependence of economic and social effects, the political order becomes the place where power is wielded in order to manage the systemic problems arising out of that interdependence and the increasing competition of other, state-directed economies. The major consequence . . . is the expansion of State power, and the fact that the State budget, not the division of profits within the enterprise, becomes the major arbiter of economic decisions (including the formation of capital), and that competition not between capitalist and workers, but between the multiple constituencies (where corporations still exercise a large degree of influence), is the mode of allocating power in the society.

A final word on religion, which for me is the fulcrum of the book. I do not (*pace* Durkheim) see religion as a "functional necessity" for society, or that without religion a society will dissolve. I do not believe in religion as a patch for the unraveled seams of society. Nor do societies "dissolve," though in periods of extreme crises (like times of war) the loss of legitimation may sap the will to resist. Religions cannot be manufactured. Worse, if they were, the results would be spurious and soon vanish in the next whirl of fashion.

My concern with religion goes back to what I assume is the constitutive character of culture: the wheel of questions that brings one back to the existential predicaments, the awareness in men of their finiteness and the inexorable limits to their power (the transgression of which is bamartia), and the consequent effort to find a coherent answer to reconcile them to the human condition. Since that awareness touches the deepest springs of consciousness, I believe that a culture which has become aware of the limits in exploring the mundane will turn, at some point, to the effort to recover the sacred.

We stand, I believe, with a clearing ahead of us. The exhaustion of Modernism, the aridity of Communist life, the tedium of the unrestrained self, and the meaninglessness of the monolithic political chants all indicate that a long era is coming to a slow close. The impulse of Modernism was to leap beyond: beyond nature, beyond culture, beyond tragedy – to explore the aperion, the boundless, driven by the self-infinitizing spirit of the radical self.

We are groping for a new vocabulary whose keyword seems to be limits: a limit to growth, a limit to the spoliation of the environment, a limit to arms, a limit to the tampering with biological nature. Yet if we seek to establish a set of limits in the economy and technology, will we also set a limit to the exploration of those cultural experiences which go beyond moral norms and embrace the demonic in the delusion that all experience is "creative"? Can we set a limit to *hubris?* The answer to that question could resolve the *cultural* contradiction of capitalism and its deceptive double, *semblable et frère,* the culture of modernity. It would leave only the economic and political mundane to be tamed.

29

The postmodern condition

Jean-François Lyotard

I define postmodern as incredulity toward metanarratives. This incredulity is undoubtedly a product of progress in the sciences: But that progress in turn presupposes it. To the obsolescence of the metanarrative apparatus of legitimation corresponds, most notably, the crisis of metaphysical philosophy and of the university institution which in the past relied on it. The narrative function is losing its functors, its great hero, its great dangers, its great voyages, its great goal. It is being dispersed in clouds of narrative language elements – narrative, but also denotative, prescriptive, descriptive, and so on. Conveyed within each cloud are pragmatic valencies specific to its kind. Each of us lives at the intersection of many of these. However, we do not necessarily establish stable language combinations, and the properties of the ones we do establish are not necessarily communicable.

Thus the society of the future falls less within the province of a Newtonian anthropology (such as structuralism or systems theory) than a pragmatics of language particles. There are many different language games – a heterogeneity of elements. They only give rise to institutions in patches – local determinism.

The decision makers, however, attempt to manage these clouds of sociality according to input/output matrices, following a logic which implies that their elements are commensurable and that the whole is determinable. They allocate our lives for the growth of power. In matters of social justice and of scientific truth alike, the legitimation of that power is based on its optimizing the system's performance – efficiency. The application of this criterion to all of our games necessarily entails a certain level of terror, whether soft or hard: be operational (that is, commensurable) or disappear.

The logic of maximum performance is no doubt inconsistent in many ways, particularly with respect to contradiction in the socio-economic

Excerpted from Lyotard, *The Postmodern Condition*. Minneapolis: University of Minnesota Press, 1984. Reprinted with permission.

field: It demands both less work (to lower production costs) and more (to lessen the social burden of the idle population). But our incredulity is now such that we no longer expect salvation to rise from these inconsistencies, as did Marx.

Still, the postmodern condition is as much a stranger to disenchantment as it is to the blind positivity of delegitimation. Where, after the metanarratives, can legitimacy reside? The operativity criterion is technological; it has no relevance for judging what is true or just. Is legitimacy to be found in consensus obtaining through discussion, as Jurgen Habermas thinks? Such consensus does violence to the heterogeneity of language games. And invention is always born of dissension. Postmodern knowledge is not simply a tool of the authorities; it refines our sensitivity to differences and reinforces our ability to tolerate the incommunsurable. Its principle is not the expert's homology, but the inventor's paralogy. . . .

In contemporary society and culture – postindustrial society, postmodern culture – the question of the legitimation of knowledge is formulated in different terms. The grand narrative has lost its credibility, regardless of what mode of unification it uses, regardless of whether it is a speculative narrative or a narrative of emancipation.

The decline of narrative can be seen as an effect of the blossoming of techniques and technologies since the Second World War, which has shifted emphasis from the ends of action to its means; it can also be seen as an effect of the redeployment of advanced liberal capitalism after its retreat under the protection of Keynesianism during the period 1930–60, a renewal that has eliminated the communist alternative and valorized the individual enjoyment of goods and services.

Anytime we go searching for causes in this way we are bound to be disappointed. Even if we adopted one or the other of these hypotheses, we would still have to detail the correlation between the tendencies mentioned and the decline of the unifying and legitimating power of the grand narratives of speculation and emancipation.

It is, of course, understandable that both capitalist renewal and prosperity and the disorienting upsurge of technology would have an impact on the status of knowledge. But in order to understand how contemporary science could have been susceptible to those effects long before they took place, we must first locate the seeds of "delegitimation" and nihilism that were inherent in the grand narratives of the nineteenth century.

First of all, the speculative apparatus maintains an ambiguous relation to knowledge. It shows that knowledge is only worthy of that name to the extent that it reduplicates itself ("lifts itself up," *hebt sich auf;* is sublated) by citing its own statements in a second-level discourse (autonomy) that functions to legitimate them. This is as much as to say that, in its immediacy, denotative discourse bearing on a certain referent (a living organism, a chemical property, a physical phenomenon, etc.) does not really know what it thinks it knows. Positive science is not a form of knowledge. And speculation feeds on its suppression. The Hegelian speculative narrative thus harbors a certain skepticism toward positive learning, as Hegel himself admits.

A science that has not legitimated itself is not a true science; if the discourse that was meant to legitimate it seems to belong to a prescientific form of knowledge, like a "vulgar" narrative, it is demoted to the lowest rank, that of an ideology or instrument of power. And this always happens if the rules of the science game that discourse denounces as empirical are applied to science itself.

Take for example the speculative statement: "A scientific statement is knowledge if and only if it can take its place in a universal process of engendering." The question is: Is this statement knowledge as it itself defines it? Only if it can take its place in a universal process of engendering. Which it can. All it has to do is to presuppose that such a process exists (the Life of spirit) and that it is itself an expression of that process. This presupposition, in fact, is indispensable to the speculative language game. Without it, the language of legitimation would not be legitimate; it would accompany science in a nosedive into nonsense, at least if we take idealism's word for it.

But this presupposition can also be understood in a totally different sense, one which takes us in the direction of postmodern culture: We could say, in keeping with the perspective we adopted earlier, that this presupposition defines the set of rules one must accept in order to play the speculative game. Such an appraisal assumes first that we accept that the "positive" sciences represent the general mode of knowledge and second that we understand this language to imply certain formal and axiomatic presuppositions that it must always make explicit. This is exactly what Nietzsche is doing, though with a different terminology, when he shows that "European nihilism" resulted from the truth requirement of science being turned back against itself.

There thus arises an idea of perspective that is not far removed, at least in this respect, from the idea of language games. What we have here is a process of delegitimation fueled by the demand for legitimation itself. The "crisis" of scientific knowledge, signs of which have been accumulating since the end of the nineteenth century, is not born of a chance proliferation of sciences, itself an effect of progress in technology and the expansion of capitalism. It represents, rather, an internal erosion of the legitimacy principle of knowledge. There is erosion at work inside the speculative game, and by loosening the weave of the encyclopedic net in which each science was to find its place, it eventually sets them free.

The classical dividing lines between the various fields of science are thus called into question – disciplines disappear, overlappings occur at the borders between sciences, and from these new territories are born. The speculative hierarchy of learning gives way to an immanent and, as it were, "flat" network of areas of inquiry, the respective frontiers of which are in constant flux. The old "faculties" splinter into institutes and foundations of all kinds, and the universities lose their function of speculative legitimation. Stripped of the responsibility for research (which was stifled by the speculative narrative), they limit themselves to the transmission of what is judged to be established knowledge, and through didactics they guarantee the replication of teachers rather than the production of researchers. This is the state in which Nietzsche finds and condemns them.

The potential for erosion intrinsic to the other legitimation procedure, the emancipation apparatus flowing from the *Aufklarung,* is no less extensive than the one at work within speculative discourse. But it touches a different aspect. Its distinguishing characteristic is that it grounds the legitimation of science and truth in the autonomy of interlocutors involved in ethical, social, and political praxis. As we have seen, there are immediate problems with this form of legitimation: The difference between a denotative statement with cognitive value and a prescriptive statement with practice value is one of relevance, therefore of competence. There is nothing to prove that if a statement describing a real situation is true, it follows that a prescriptive statement based upon it (the effect of which will necessarily be a modification of that reality) will be just.

Take, for example, a closed door. Between "The door is closed" and "Open the door" there is no relation of consequence as defined in propositional logic. The two statements belong to two autonomous sets of rules defining different kinds of relevance, and therefore of competence. Here, the effect of dividing reason into cognitive or theoretical reason on the one hand, and practical reason on the other, is to attack the legitimacy of the discourse of science; not directly, but indirectly, by revealing that it is a language game with its own rules (of which the a priori conditions of knowledge in Kant provide a first glimpse) and that it has no special calling to supervise the game of praxis (nor the game of aesthetics, for that matter). The game of science is thus put on a par with the others.

If this "delegitimation" is pursued in the slightest and if its scope is widened (as Wittgenstein does in his own way, and thinkers such as Martin Buber and Emmanuel Levinas in theirs) the road is then open for an important current of postmodernity: Science plays its own game; it is incapable of legitimating the other language games. The game of prescription, for example, escapes it. But above all, it is incapable of legitimating itself, as speculation assumed it could.

The social subject itself seems to dissolve in this dissemination of language games. The social bond is linguistic, but is not woven with a single thread. It is a fabric formed by the intersection of at least two (and in reality an indeterminate number of) language games, obeying different rules. Wittgenstein writes: "Our language can be seen as an ancient city: a maze of little streets and squares, of old and new houses, and of houses with additions from various periods; and this surrounded by a multitude of new boroughs with straight regular streets and uniform houses." And to drive home that the principle of unitotality – or synthesis under the authority of a metadiscourse of knowledge – is inapplicable, he subjects the "town" of language to the old sorites paradox by asking: "how many houses or streets does it take before a town begins to be a town?"

New languages are added to the old ones, forming suburbs of the old town: "the symbolism of chemistry and the notation of the infinitesimal calculus." Thirty-five years later we can add to the list: machine languages, the matrices of game theory, new systems of musical notation, systems of notation for nondenotative forms of logic (temporal logics, deontic logics, modal logics), the language of the genetic code, graphs of phonological structures, and so on.

We may form a pessimistic impression of this splintering: Nobody speaks all of those languages, they have no universal metalanguage, the project of the system-subject is a failure, the goal of emancipation has nothing to do with science, we are all stuck in the positivism of this or that discipline of learning, the learned scholars have turned into scientists, the diminished tasks of research have become compartmentalized and no one can master them all. Speculative or humanistic philosophy is forced to relinquish its legitimation duties, which explains why philosophy is facing a crisis wherever it persists in arrogating such functions and is reduced to the study of systems of logic or the history of ideas where it has been realistic enough to surrender them.

Turn-of-the-century Vienna was weaned on this pessimism: not just artists such as Musil, Kraus, Hofmannsthal, Loos, Schonberg, and Broch, but also the philosophers Mach and Wittgenstein. They carried awareness of and theoretical and artistic responsibility for delegitimation as far as it could be taken. We can say today that the mourning process has been completed. There is no need to start all over again. Wittgenstein's strength is that he did not opt for the positivism that was being developed by the Vienna Circle, but outlined in his investigation of language games a kind of legitimation not based on performativity. That is what the postmodern world is all about. Most people have lost the nostalgia for the lost narrative. It in no way follows that they are reduced to barbarity. What saves them from it is their knowledge that legitimation can only spring from their own linguistic practice and communicational interaction. Science "smiling into its beard" at every other belief has taught them the harsh austerity of realism. . . .

Legitimation by paralogy

Let us say at this point that the facts we have presented concerning the problem of the legitimation of knowledge today are sufficient for our purposes. We no longer have recourse to the grand narratives – we can resort neither to the dialectic of Spirit nor even to the emancipation of humanity as a validation for postmodern scientific discourse. But as we have just seen, the little narrative [*petit recit*] remains the quintessential form of imaginative invention, most particularly in science. In addition, the principle of consensus as a criterion of validation seems to be inadequate. It has two formulations. In the first, consensus is an agreement between men, defined as knowing intellects and free wills, and is obtained through dialogue. This is the form elaborated by Habermas, but his conception is based on the validity of the narrative of emancipation. In the second, consensus is a component of the system, which manipulates it in order to maintain and improve its performance. It is the object of administrative procedures, in Luhmann's sense. In this case, its only validity is as an instrument to be used toward achieving the real goal, which is what legitimates the system – power.

The problem is therefore to determine whether it is possible to have a form of legitimation based solely on paralogy. Paralogy must be distinguished from innovation: The latter is under the command of the system, or at least used by it to improve its efficiency; the former is a move (the importance of which is often not recognized until later) played in the pragmatics of knowledge. The fact that it is in reality frequently, but not necessarily, the case that one is transformed into the other presents no difficulties for the hypothesis.

Returning to the description of scientific pragmatics . . . it is now dissension that must be emphasized. Consensus is a horizon that is never reached. Research that takes place under the aegis of a paradigm tends to stabilize; it is like the exploitation of a technological, economic, or artistic "idea." It cannot be discounted. But what is striking is that someone always comes along to disturb the order of "reason." It is necessary to posit the existence of a power that destabilizes the capacity for explanation, manifested in the promulgation of new norms for understanding or, if one prefers, in a proposal to establish new rules circumscribing a new field of research for the language of science. This, in the context of scientific discussion, is the same process Thom calls morphogenesis. It is not without rules (there are classes of catastrophes), but it is always locally determined. Applied to scientific discussion and placed in temporal framework, this property implies that "discoveries" are unpredictable. In terms of the idea of transparency, it is a factor that generates blind spots and defers consensus.

This summary makes it easy to see that systems theory and the kind of legitimation it proposes have no scientific basis whatsover; science itself does not function according to this theory's paradigm of the system, and contemporary science excludes the possibility of using such a paradigm to describe society.

In this context, let us examine two important points in Luhmann's argument. On the one hand, the system can only function by reducing complexity, and on the other, it must induce the adaptation of individual aspirations to its own ends. The reduction in complexity is required to maintain the system's power capability. If all messages could circulate freely among all individuals, the quantity of the information that would have to be taken into account before making the correct choice would delay decisions considerably, thereby lowering performativity. Speed, in effect, is a power component of the system.

The objection will be made that these molecular opinions must indeed be taken into account if the risk of serious disturbances is to be avoided. Luhmann replies – and this is the second point – that it is possible to guide individual aspirations through a process of "quasi-apprenticeship," "free of all disturbance," in order to make them compatible with the system's decisions. The decisions do not have to respect individuals' aspirations: The aspirations have to aspire to the decisions, or at least to their effects. Administrative procedures should make individuals "want" what the system needs in order to perform well. It is easy to see what role telematics technology could play in this.

It cannot be denied that there is persuasive force in the idea that context control and domination are inherently better than their absence. The performativity criterion has its "advantages." It excludes in principle adherence to a metaphysical discourse; it requires the renunciation of fables; it demands clear minds and cold wills; it replaces the definition of essences with the calculation of interactions; it makes the "players" assume responsibility not only for the statements they propose, but also for the rules to which they submit those statements in order to render them acceptable. It brings the pragmatic functions of knowledge clearly to light, to the extent that they seem to relate to the criterion of efficiency: the pragmatics of argumentation, of the production of proof, of the transmission of learning, and of the apprenticeship of the imagination.

It also contributes to elevating all language games to self-knowledge, even those not within the realm of canonical knowledge. It tends to jolt everyday discourse into a kind of metadiscourse: Ordinary statements are now displaying a propensity for self-citation, and the various pragmatic posts are tending to make an indirect connection even to current messages concerning them. Finally, it suggests that the problems of internal communication experienced by the scientific community in the course of its work of dismantling and remounting its languages are comparable in nature to the problems experienced by the social collectivity when, deprived of its narrative culture, it must reexamine its own internal communication and in the process question the nature of the legitimacy of the decisions made in its name.

At [the] risk of scandalizing the reader, I would also say that the system can count severity among its advantages. Within the framework of the power criterion, a request (that is, a form of prescription) gains nothing in legitimacy by virtue of being based on the hardship of an unmet need. Rights do not flow from hardship, but from the fact that the alleviation of hardship improves the system's performance. The needs of the most underprivileged should not be used as a system regulator as a matter of principle: Since the means of satisfying them is already known, their actual satisfaction will not improve the system's performance, but only increase its expenditures. The only counterindication is that not satisfying them can destabilize the whole. It is against the nature of force to be ruled by weakness. But it is in its nature to induce new requests meant to lead to a redefinition of the norms of "life." In this sense, the system seems to be a vanguard machine dragging humanity after it, dehumanizing it in order to rehumanize it at a different level of normative capacity. The technocrats declare that they cannot trust what society designates as its needs; they "know" that society cannot know its own needs since they are not variables independent of the new technologies. Such is the arrogance of the decision makers – and their blindness.

What their "arrogance" means is that they identify themselves with the social system conceived as a totality in quest of its most performative unity possible. If we look at the pragmatics of science, we learn that such an identification is impossible: In principle, no scientist embodies knowledge or neglects the "needs" of a research project, or the aspirations of a researcher, on the pretext that they do not add to the performance of "science" as a whole. The response a researcher usually makes to a request is: "We'll have to see, tell me your story." In principle, he does not prejudge that a case has already been closed or that the power of "science" will suffer if it is reopened. In fact, the opposite is true.

Of course, it does not always happen like this in reality. Countless scientists have seen their "move" ignored or repressed, sometimes for decades, because it too abruptly destabilized the accepted positions, not only in the university and scientific hierarchy, but also in the problematic.

The stronger the "move," the more likely it is to be denied the minimum consensus, precisely because it changes the rules of the game upon which consensus had been based. But when the institution of knowledge functions in this manner, it is acting like an ordinary power center whose behavior is governed by a principle of homeostasis.

Such behavior is terrorist, as is the behavior of the system described by Luhmann. By terror I mean the efficiency gained by eliminating, or threatening to eliminate, a player from the language game one shares with him. He is silenced or consents, not because he has been refuted, but because his ability to participate has been threatened (there are many ways to prevent someone from playing). The decision makers' arrogance, which in principle has no equivalent in the sciences, consists in the exercise of terror. It says: "Adapt your aspirations to our ends – or else."

Even permissiveness toward the various games is made conditional on performativity. The redefinition of the norms of life consists in enhancing the system's competence for power. That this is the case is particularly evident in the introduction of telematics technology: The technocrats see in telematics a promise of liberalization and enrichment in the interactions between interlocutors; but what makes this process attractive for them is that it will result in new tensions in the system, and these will lead to an improvement in its performativity.

To the extent that science is differential, its pragmatics provides the antimodel of a stable system. A statement is deemed worth retaining the moment it marks a difference from what is already known, and after an argument and proof in support of it has been found. Science is a model of an "open system," in which a statement becomes relevant if it "generates ideas," that is, if it generates other statements and other game rules. Science possesses no general metalanguage into which all other languages can be transcribed and evaluated. This is what prevents its identification with the system and, all things considered, with terror. If the division between decision makers and executors exists in the scientific community (and it does), it is a fact of the socioeconomic system and not of the pragmatics of science itself. It is in fact one of the major obstacles to the imaginative development of knowledge.

The general question of legitimation becomes: What is the relationship between the antimodel of the pragmatics of science and society? Is it applicable to the vast clouds of language material constituting a society? Or is it limited to the game of learning? And if so, what role does it play with respect to the social bond? Is it an impossible ideal of an open community? Is it an essential component for the subset of decision makers, who force on society the performance criterion they reject for themselves? Or, conversely, is it a refusal to cooperate with the authorities, a move in the direction of counterculture, with the attendant risk that all possibility for research will be foreclosed due to lack of funding?

From the beginning of this study, I have emphasized the differences (not only formal, but also pragmatic) between the various language games, especially between denotative, or knowledge, games and prescriptive, or action, games. The pragmatics of science is centered on denotative utterances, which are the foundation upon which it builds institutions of learning (institutes, centers, universities, etc.). But its postmodern development brings a decisive "fact" to the fore: Even discussions of denotative statements need to have rules. Rules are not denotative but prescriptive utterances, which we are better off calling metaprescriptive utterances to avoid confusion (they prescribe what the moves of language games must be in order to be admissible). The function of the differential or imaginative or paralogical activity of the current pragmatics of science is to point out these metaprescriptives (science's "presuppositions") and to petition the players to accept different ones. The only legitimation that can make this kind of request admissible is that it will generate ideas, in other words, new statements.

Social pragmatics does not have the "simplicity" of scientific pragmatics. It is a monster formed by the interweaving of various networks of heteromorphous classes of utterances (denotative, prescriptive, performative, technical, evaluative, etc.). There is no reason to think that it would be possible to determine metaprescriptives common to all of these language games or that a revisable consensus like the one in force at a given moment in the scientific community could embrace the totality of metaprescriptions regulating the totality of statements circulating in the social collectivity. As a matter of fact, the contemporary decline of narratives of legitimation – be they traditional or "modern" (the emancipation of humanity, the realization of the Idea) – is tied to the abandonment of this belief. It is its absence for which the ideology of the "system," with its pretensions to totality, tries to compensate and which it expresses in the cynicism of its criterion of performance.

For this reason, it seems neither possible, nor even prudent, to follow Habermas in orienting our treatment of the problem of legitimation in the direction of a search for universal consensus through what he calls *Diskurs,* in other words, a dialogue of argumentation.

This would be to make two assumptions. The first is that it is possible for all speakers to come to agreement on which rules or metaprescriptions are universally valid for language games, when it is clear that language games are heteromorphous, subject to heterogeneous sets of pragmatic rules.

The second assumption is that the goal of dialogue is consensus. But as

I have shown in the analysis of the pragmatics of science, concensus is only a particular state of discussion, not its end. Its end, on the contrary, is paralogy. This double observation (the heterogeneity of the rules and the search for dissent) destroys a belief that still underlies Habermas's research, namely, that humanity as a collective (universal) subject seeks its common emancipation through the regularization of the "moves" permitted in all language games and that the legitimacy of any statement resides in its contributing to that emancipation.

It is easy to see what function this recourse plays in Habermas's argument against Luhmann. *Diskurs* is his ultimate weapon against the theory of the stable system. The cause is good, but the argument is not. Consensus has become an outmoded and suspect value. But justice as a value is neither outmoded nor suspect. We must thus arrive at an idea and practice of justice that is not linked to that of consensus.

A recognition of the heteromorphous nature of language games is a first step in that direction. This obviously implies a renunciation of terror, which assumes that they are isomorphic and tries to make them so. The second step is the principle that any consensus on the rules defining a game and the "moves" playable within it *must* be local, in other words, agreed on by its present players and subject to eventual cancellation. The orientation then favors a multiplicity and finite meta-arguments, by which I mean argumentation that concerns metaprescriptives and is limited in space and time.

This orientation corresponds to the course that the evolution of social interaction is currently taking; the temporary contract is in practice supplanting permanent institutions in the professional, emotional, sexual, cultural, family, and international domains, as well as in political affairs. This evolution is of course ambiguous: The temporary contract is favored by the system due to its greater flexibility, lower cost, and the creative turmoil of its accompanying motivations – all of these factors contribute to increased operativity. In any case, there is no question here of proposing a "pure" alternative to the system: We all now know, as the 1970s come to a close, that an attempt at an alternative of that kind would end up resembling the system it was meant to replace. We should be happy that the tendency toward the temporary contract is ambiguous: It is not totally subordinated to the goal of the system, yet the system tolerates it. This bears witness to the existence of another goal within the system: knowledge of language games as such and the decision to assume responsibility for their rules and effects. Their most significant effect is precisely what validates the adoption of rules – the quest for paralogy.

We are finally in a position to understand how the computerization of society affects this problematic. It could become the "dream" instrument for controlling and regulating the market system, extended to include knowledge itself and governed exclusively by the performativity principle. In that case, it would inevitably involve the use of terror. But it could also aid groups discussing metaprescriptives by supplying them with the information they usually lack for making knowledgeable decisions. The line to follow for computerization to take the second of these two paths is, in principle, quite simple: Give the public free access to the memory and data banks. Language games would then be games of perfect information at any given moment. But they would also be non-zero-sum games, and by virtue of that fact discussion would never risk fixating in a position of minimax equilibrium because it had exhausted its stakes. For the stakes would be knowledge (or information, if you will), and the reserve of knowledge – language's reserve of possible utterances – is inexhaustible. This sketches the outline of a politics that would respect both the desire for justice and the desire for the unknown.

30

Modernity versus postmodernity

Jurgen Habermas

Last year, architects were admitted to the Biennial in Venice, following painters and filmmakers. The note sounded at this first Architecture Biennial was one of disappointment. I would describe it by saying that those who exhibited in Venice formed an avant-garde of reversed fronts. I mean that they sacrificed the tradition of modernity in order to make room for a new historicism. Upon this occasion, a critic of the German newspaper *Frankfurter Allgemeine Zeitung* advanced a thesis whose significance reaches beyond this particular event; it is a diagnosis of our times: "Postmodernity definitely presents itself as Antimodernity." This statement describes an emotional current of our times which has penetrated all spheres of intellectual life. It has placed on the agenda theories of postenlightenment, postmodernity, even of posthistory.

From history we know the phrase:

"The ancients and the moderns"

Let me begin by defining these concepts. The term "modern" has a long history, one which has been investigated by Hans Robert Jauss. The word "modern" in its Latin form *modernus* was used for the first time in the late 5th century in order to distinguish the present, which had become officially Christian, from the Roman and pagan past. With varying content the term "modern" again and again expresses the consciousness of an epoch that relates itself to the past of antiquity in order to view itself as the result of a transition from the old to the new.

Some writers restrict this concept of "modernity" to the Renaissance, but this is historically too narrow. People considered themselves modern during the period of Charles the Great, in the 12th century, as well as in France of the late 17th century, at the time of the famous "Querelle des

From Habermas; "Modernity versus Postmodernity," *New German Critique* 22 (1981): 3–14. Reprinted with permission of the author and *New German Critique*.

Anciens et des Modernes." This is to say, the term "modern" appeared and reappeared exactly during those periods in Europe when the consciousness of a new epoch formed itself through a renewed relationship to the ancients – whenever, moreover, antiquity was considered a model to be recovered through some kind of imitation.

The spell which the classics of the ancient world cast upon the spirit of later times was first dissolved with the ideals of the French Enlightenment. Specifically, the idea of being "modern" by looking back to the ancients changed with the belief, inspired by modern science, in the infinite progress of knowledge and in the infinite advance towards social and moral betterment. Another form of modernist consciousness was formed in the wake of this change. The romantic modernist sought to oppose the antique ideals of the classicists; he looked for a new historical epoch and found it in the idealized Middle Ages. However, this new ideal age, established early in the 19th century, did not remain a fixed ideal. In the course of the 19th century, there emerged out of this romantic spirit that radicalized consciousness of modernity which freed itself from all specific historical ties. This most recent modernism simply makes an abstract opposition between tradition and the present; and we are, in a way, still the contemporaries of that kind of aesthetic modernity which first appeared in the midst of the 19th century. Since then, the distinguishing mark of works which count as modern is the "new." The characteristic of such works is "the new" which will be overcome and made obsolete through the novelty of the next style. But, while that which is merely "stylish" will soon become out-moded, that which is modern preserves a secret tie to the classical. Of course, whatever can survive time has always been considered to be a classic. But the emphatically modern document no longer borrows this power of being a classic from the authority of a past epoch; instead, a modern work becomes a classic because it has once been authentically modern. Our sense of modernity creates its own self-enclosed canons of being classic. In this sense we speak, e.g., in view of the history of modern art, of classical modernity. The relation between "modern" and "classical" has definitely lost a fixed historical reference.

The discipline of aesthetic modernity

The spirit and discipline of aesthetic modernity assumed clear contours in the work of Baudelaire. Modernity then unfolded in various avant-garde movements, and finally reached its climax in the Cafe Voltaire of the Dadaists and in Surrealism. Aesthetic modernity is characterized by attitudes which find a common focus in a changed consciousness of time.

This time consciousness expresses itself through metaphors of the vanguard and the avant-garde. The avant-garde understands itself as invading unknown territory, exposing itself to the dangers of sudden, of shocking encounters, conquering an as yet unoccupied future. The avant-garde must find a direction in a landscape into which no one seems to have yet ventured.

But these forward gropings, this anticipation of an undefined future and the cult of the new, mean in fact the exaltation of the present. The new time consciousness, which enters philosophy in the writings of Bergson, does more than express the experience of mobility in society, acceleration in history, of discontinuity in everyday life. The new value placed on the transitory, the elusive, and the ephemeral, the very celebration of dynamism discloses the longing for an undefiled, an immaculate and stable present.

This explains the rather abstract language in which the modernist temper has spoken of the "past." Individual epochs lose their distinct forces. Historical memory is replaced by the heroic affinity of the present with the extremes of history: a sense of time wherein decadence immediately recognizes itself in the barbaric, the wild, and the primitive. We observe the anarchistic intention of blowing up the continuum of history, and we can account for it in terms of the subversive force of this new aesthetic consciousness. Modernity revolts against the normalizing functions of tradition; modernity lives on the experience of rebelling against all that is normative. This revolt is one way to neutralize the standards of both morality and utility. This aesthetic consciousness continuously stages a dialectical play between secrecy and public scandal; it is addicted to the fascination of that horror which accompanies the act of profaning, and is yet always in flight from the trivial results of profanation.

On the other hand, the time consciousness articulated in avant-garde art is not simply ahistorical; it is directed against what might be called a false normativity in history. The modern, avant-garde spirit has sought, instead, to use the past in a different way; it disposes over those pasts which have been made available by the objectifying scholarship of historicism, but it opposes at the same time a neutralized history, which is locked up in the museum of historicism.

Drawing upon the spirit of surrealism, Walter Benjamin constructs the relationship of modernity to history in what I would call a post-historicist attitude. He reminds us of the self-understanding of the French Revolution: "The Revolution cited ancient Rome, just as fashion cites an antiquated dress. Fashion has a scent for what is current, whenever this moves within the thicket of what was once." This is Benjamin's concept of the *Jetztzeit*, of the present as a moment of revelation; a time in which splinters of a messianic presence are enmeshed. In this sense, for Robespierre, the antique Rome was a past laden with momentary revelations.

Now, this spirit of aesthetic modernity has recently begun to age. It has been recited once more in the 1960s; after the 1970s, however, we must admit to ourselves that this modernism arouses a much fainter response today than it did fifteen years ago. Octavio Paz, a fellow traveler of modernity, noted already in the middle of the 1960s that "the avant-garde of 1967 repeats the deeds and gestures of those of 1917. We are experiencing the end of the idea of modern art." The work of Peter Burger has since taught us to speak of "post-avant-garde" art; this term is chosen to indicate the failure of the surrealist rebellion. But, what is the meaning of this failure? Does it signal a farewell to modernity? Thinking more generally, does the existence of a post-avant-garde mean there is a transition to that broader phenomenon called postmodernity?

This is in fact how Daniel Bell, the most brilliant of the American neoconservatives, interprets matters. In his book, *The Cultural Contradictions of Capitalism*, Bell argues that the crises of the developed societies of the West are to be traced back to a split between culture and society. Modernist culture has come to penetrate the values of everyday life; the life-world is infected by modernism. Because of the forces of modernism, the principle of unlimited self-realization, the demand for authentic self-experience, and the subjectivism of a hyperstimulated sensitivity have come to be dominant. This temperament unleashes hedonistic motives irreconcilable with the discipline of professional life in society, Bell says. Moreover, modernist culture is altogether incompatible with the moral basis of a purposive rational conduct of life. In this manner, Bell places the burden of responsibility for the dissolution of the Protestant ethic (a phenomenon which has already disturbed Max Weber) on the "adversary culture." Culture, in its modern form, stirs up hatred against the conventions and virtues of an everyday life, which has become rationalized under the pressures of economic and administrative imperatives.

I would call your attention to a complex wrinkle in this view. The impulse of modernity, we are told on the other hand, is exhausted; anyone who considers himself avant-garde can read his own death warrant. Although the avant-garde is still considered to be expanding, it is supposedly no longer creative. Modernism is dominant but dead. For the neoconservative, the question then arises: How can norms arise in society which will limit libertinism, reestablish the ethic of discipline and work? What new norms will put a brake on the leveling caused by the social welfare state, so that the virtues of individual competition for achievement can again dominate? Bell sees a religious revival to be the only solution. Religious faith tied to a faith in tradition will provide individuals with clearly defined identities and with existential security.

Cultural modernity and societal modernization

One can certainly not conjure up by magic the compelling beliefs which command authority. Analyses like Bell's, therefore, only result in an attitude which is spreading in Germany no less than here in the States: an intellectual and political confrontation with the carriers of cultural modernity. I cite Peter Steinfels, an observer of the new style which the neoconservatives have imposed upon the intellectual scene in the 1970s.

> The struggle takes the form of exposing every manifestation of what could be considered an oppositionist mentality and tracing its "logic" so as to link it to various forms of extremism: drawing the connection between modernism and nihilism . . . between government regulation and totalitarianism, between criticism of arms expenditures and subservience to communism, between Women's liberation or homosexual rights and the destruction of the family . . . between the Left generally and terrorism, anti-semitism, and fascism. . . .[1]

The *ad hominem* approach and the bitterness of these intellectual accusations have also been trumpeted loudly in Germany. They should not be explained so much in terms of the psychology of neoconservative writers; rather, they are rooted in the analytical weaknesses of neoconservative doctrine itself.

Neoconservatism shifts onto cultural modernism the uncomfortable burdens of a more or less successful capitalist modernization of the economy and society. The neoconservative doctrine blurs the relationship between the welcome process of societal modernization on the one hand, and the lamented cultural development on the other. The neoconservative does not uncover the economic and social causes for the altered attitudes towards work, consumption, achievement, and leisure. Consequently, he attributes all of the following – hedonism, the lack of social identification, the lack of obedience, narcissism, the withdrawal from status and achievement competition – to the domain of "culture." In fact, however, culture is intervening in the creation of all these problems in only a very indirect and mediated fashion.

In the neoconservative view, those intellectuals who still feel themselves committed to the project of modernity are then presented as taking the

1. Peter Steinfels, *The Neoconservatives* (New York: Simon and Schuster, 1979), p. 65.

place of those unanalyzed causes. The mood which feeds neocon-servatism today in no way originates from the discontents about the antinomian consequences of a culture breaking from the museums into the stream of ordinary life. These discontents have not been called into life by modernist intellectuals. They are rooted in deep-seated reactions against the process of societal modernization. Under the pressures of the dynamics of economic growth and the organizational accomplishments of the state, this social modernization penetrates deeper and deeper into previous forms of human existence. I would describe this subordination of the life-worlds under [the] system's imperatives as a matter of disturb-ing the communicative infrastructure of everyday life.

Thus, for example, neopopulist protests only bring to expression in pointed fashion a widespread fear regarding the destruction of the ur-ban and natural environment[s] and of forms of human sociability. There is a certain irony about these protests in terms of neocon-servatism. The tasks of passing on a cultural tradition, of social integra-tion, and of socialization require the adherence to a criterion of commu-nicative rationality. The occasions for protest and discontent originate exactly when spheres of communicative action, centered on the repro-duction and transmission of values and norms, are penetrated by a form of modernization guided by standards and economic and administrative rationality; however, those very spheres are dependent on quite different standards of rationalization – on the standards of what I would call communicative rationality. But, neoconservative doctrines turn our at-tention precisely away from such societal processes: They project the causes, which they do not bring to light, onto the plane of a subversive culture and its advocates.

To be sure, cultural modernity generates its own aporias as well. Inde-pendently from the consequences of societal modernization, and from within the perspective of cultural development itself, there originate mo-tives for doubting the project of modernity. Having dealt with a feeble kind of criticism of modernity – that of neoconservatism – let me now move our discussion of modernity and its discontents into a different domain that touches on these aporias of cultural modernity, issues which often serve only as a pretense for those positions (which either call for a postmodernity, or recommend a return to some form of premodernity, or . . . throw modernity radically overboard).

The project of enlightenment

The idea of modernity is intimately tied to the development of European art; but what I call "the project of modernity" comes . . . into focus

[only] when we dispense with the usual concentration upon art. Let me start a different analysis by recalling an idea from Max Weber. He characterized cultural modernity as the separation of the substantive reason expressed in religion and metaphysics into three autonomous spheres. They are: science, morality, and art. These came to be differentiated because the unified world conceptions of religion and metaphysics fell apart. Since the 18th century, the problems inherited from these older world-views could be rearranged so as to fall under specific aspects of validity: truth, normative rightness, authenticity, and beauty. They could then be handled as questions of knowledge, or of justice and morality, or of taste. Scientific discourse, theories of morality, jurisprudence, the production and criticism of art, could in turn be institutionalized. Each domain of culture could be made to correspond to cultural professions, in which problems could be dealt with as the concern of special experts. This professionalized treatment of the cultural tradition brings to the fore the intrinsic structures of each of the three dimensions of culture. There appear the structures of cognitive-instrumental, moral-practical, and aesthetic-expressive rationality, each of these under the control of specialists who seem more adept at being logical in these particular ways than other people are. As a result, the distance has grown between the culture of the experts and that of the large public. What accrues to culture through specialized treatment and reflexion does not immediately and necessarily become the property of everyday praxis. With cultural rationalization of this sort, the threat increases that the life-world, whose traditional substance has already been devalued, will become more and more impoverished.

The project of modernity formulated in the 18th century by the philosophers of the Enlightenment consisted in their efforts to develop objective science, universal morality and law, and autonomous art according to their inner logic. At the same time, this project intended to release the cognitive potentials of each of these domains to set them free from their esoteric forms. The Enlightenment philosophers wanted to utilize this accumulation of specialized culture for the enrichment of everyday life, that is to say, for the rational organization of everyday social life.

Enlightenment thinkers of the cast of mind of Condorcet still had the extravagant expectation that the arts and the sciences would not only promote the control of natural forces, but would also further understanding of the world and of the self, would promote moral progress, the justice of institutions, and even the happiness of human beings. The 20th century has shattered this optimism. The differentiation of science, morality, and art has come to mean the autonomy of the segments treated by the specialist and at the same time letting them split off from the hermeneutics of everyday communication. This splitting off is the problem that has given rise to those efforts to "negate" the culture of expertise. But the problem won't go away: Should we try to hold on to the intentions of the Enlightenment, feeble as they may be, or should we declare the entire project of modernity a lost cause? I now want to return to the problem of artistic culture, having explained why, historically, that aesthetic modernity is a part only of cultural modernity in general.

The false programs of the negation of culture

Greatly oversimplifying, I would say [that] in the history of modern art one can detect a trend toward ever greater autonomy in the definition and practice of art. The category of "beauty" and the domain of beautiful objects were first constituted in the Renaissance. In the course of the 18th century, literature, the fine arts, and music were institutionalized as activities independent from sacred and courtly life. Finally, around the middle of the 19th century an aestheticist conception of art emerged, which encouraged the artist to produce his work according to the distinct consciousness of art for art's sake. The autonomy of the aesthetic sphere could then become a deliberate project: The talented artist could lend authentic expression to those experiences he had in encountering his own de-centered subjectivity, detached from the constraints of routinized cognition and everyday action.

In the mid-19th century, in painting and literature, a movement began which Octavio Paz finds epitomized already in the art criticism of Baudelaire. Color, lines, sounds, and movement ceased to serve primarily the cause of representation; the media of expression and the techniques of production themselves became the aesthetic object. Theodor W. Adorno could therefore begin his *Aesthetic Theory* with the following sentence: "It is now taken for granted that nothing which concerns art can be taken for granted any more: neither art itself, nor art in its relationship to the whole, nor even the right of art to exist." And this is what surrealism then denied: *das Existenzrecht der Kunst als Kunst.* To be sure, surrealism would not have challenged the right of art to exist if modern art no longer had advanced a promise of happiness concerning its own relationship "to the whole" of life. For Schiller, such a promise was delivered by aesthetic intuition but not fulfilled by it. Schiller's *Letters on the Aesthetic Education of Man* speak to us of a utopia reaching beyond art itself. But by the time of Baudelaire, who repeated this *promesse de bonheur,* via art, the utopia of reconciliation with society had gone sour. A relation of opposites had come into being; art had become a critical mirror, showing the irreconcilable nature of the aesthetic and the social world. This modernist transformation was all the more painfully realized the more art alienated itself from life and withdrew into the untouchableness of complete autonomy. Out of such emotional currents finally gathered those explosive energies which unloaded themselves in the surrealist attempt to blow up the autarkical sphere of art and to force a reconciliation of art and life.

But all those attempts to level art and life, fiction and praxis, appearance and reality to one plane; the attempts to remove the distinction between artifact and object of use, between conscious staging and spontaneous excitement; the attempts to declare everything to be art and everyone to be artist, to retract all criteria and to equate aesthetic judgement with the expression of subjective experiences – all these undertakings have proved themselves to be sort of nonsense experiments. These experiments have served to bring back to life, and to illuminate all the more glaringly, exactly those structures of art which they were meant to dissolve. They gave a new legitimacy, as an end in itself, to appearance as the medium of fiction, to the transcendence of the art work over society, to the concentrated and planned character of artistic production as well as to the special cognitive status of judgements of taste. The radical attempt to negate art has ended up ironically by giving due exactly to these categories through which Enlightenment aesthetics had circumscribed its object domain. The surrealists waged the most extreme warfare, but two mistakes in particular destroyed their revolt. First, when the containers of an autonomously developed cultural sphere are shattered, the contents get dispersed. Nothing remains from a desublimated meaning or a destructured form; an emancipatory effect does not follow.

Their second mistake has more important consequences. In everyday communication, cognitive meanings, moral expectations, subjective expressions and evaluations must relate to one another. Communciation processes need a cultural tradition covering all spheres – cognitive, moral-practical, and expressive. A rationalized everyday life, therefore, could hardly be saved from cultural impoverishment through breaking open a single cultural sphere – art – and so providing access to just one of the specialized knowledge complexes. The surrealist revolt would have replaced only one abstraction.

In the sphere of theoretical knowledge and morality as well, there are parallels to this failed attempt of what we might call the false negation of culture. Only they are less pronounced. Since the days of the Young Hegelians, there has been talk about the negation of philosophy. Since Marx, the question of the relationship of theory and practice has been posed. However, Marxist intellectuals joined a social movement; and only at its peripheries were there sectarian attempts to carry out a program of the negation of philosophy similar to the surrealist program to negate art. A parallel to the surrealist mistakes becomes visible in these programs when one observes the consequences of dogmatism and of moral rigorism.

A reified everyday praxis can be cured only by creating unconstrained interaction of the cognitive with the moral-practical and the aesthetic-expressive elements. Reification cannot be overcome by forcing just one of those highly stylized cultural spheres to open up and become more accessible. Instead, we see under certain circumstances a relationship emerge between terroristic activities and the overextension of any one of these spheres into other domains: Examples would be tendencies to aestheticize politics, or to replace politics by moral rigorism, or to submit it to the dogmatism of a doctrine. These phenomena should not lead us, however, into denouncing the intentions of the surviving Enlightenment tradition as intentions rooted in a "terroristic reason." Those who lump together the very project of modernity with the state of consciousness and the spectacular action of the individual terrorist are no less short-sighted than those who would claim that the incomparably more persistent and extensive bureaucratic terror practiced in the dark, in the cellars of the military and secret police, and in camps and institutions, is the raison d'être of the modern state, only because this kind of administrative terror makes use of the coercive means of modern bureaucracies.

Alternatives

I think that instead of giving up modernity and its project as a lost cause, we should learn from the mistakes of those extravagant programs which have tried to negate modernity. Perhaps the types of reception of art may offer an example which at least indicates the direction of a way out.

Bourgeois art had two expectations at once from its audiences. On the one hand, the layman who enjoyed art should educate himself to become an expert. On the other hand, he should also behave as a competent consumer who uses art and relates aesthetic experiences to his own life problems. This second, and seemingly harmless, manner of experiencing art has lost its radical implications, exactly because it had a confused relation to the attitude of being expert and professional.

To be sure, artistic production would dry up if it were not carried out in the form of a specialized treatment of autonomous problems, and if it were to cease to be the concern of experts who do not pay so much attention to esoteric questions. Both artists and critics accept thereby the fact that such problems fall under the spell of what I earlier called the "inner logic" of a cultural domain. But this sharp delineation, this exclusive concentration on one aspect of validity alone, and the exclusion of aspects of truth and justice, breaks down as soon as aesthetic experience is drawn into an individual life history and is absorbed into ordinary life. The reception of art by the layman, or by the "everyday expert," goes in a rather different direction than the reception of art by the professional critic.

Albrecht Wellmer has drawn my attention to one way that an aesthetic experience which is not framed around the experts' critical judgements of taste can have its significance altered: As soon as such an experience is used to illuminate a life-historical situation and is related to life problems, it enters into a language game which is no longer that of the aesthetic critic. The aesthetic experience then not only renews the interpretation of our needs in whose light we perceive the world. It permeates as well our cognitive significations and our normative expectations and changes the manner in which all these moments refer to one another. Let me give an example of this process.

This manner of receiving and relating to art is suggested in the first volume of the work *The Aesthetics of Resistance* by the German-Swedish writer Peter Weiss. Weiss describes the process of reappropriating art by presenting a group of politically motivated, knowledge-hungry workers in 1937 in Berlin. These were young people who, through an evening high school education, acquired the intellectual means to fathom the general and the social history of European art. Out of the resilient edifice of the objective mind, embodied in works of art which they saw again and again in the museums in Berlin, they started removing their own chips of stone, which they gathered together and reassembled in the context of their own milieu. This milieu was far removed from that of traditional education as well as from the then existing regime. These young workers went back and forth between the edifice of European art and their own milieu until they were able to illuminate both.

In examples like this which illustrate the reappropriation of the expert's culture from the standpoint of the life-world, we can discern an element which does justice to the intentions of the hopeless surrealist revolts, perhaps even more to Brecht's and Benjamin's interests in how art works, which lost their aura, could yet be received in illuminating ways. In sum, the project of modernity has not yet been fulfilled. And the reception of art is only one of at least three of its aspects. The project aims at a differentiated relinking of modern culture with an everyday praxis that still depends on vital heritages but would be impoverished through mere traditionalism. This new connection, however, can only be established under the condition that societal modernization will also be steered in a different direction. The life-world has to become able to develop institutions out of itself which set limits to the internal dynamics and to the imperatives of an almost autonomous economic system and its administrative complements.

If I am not mistaken, the chances for this today are not very good. More or less in the entire Western world, a climate has developed that furthers capitalist modernization processes as well as trends critical of cultural modernism. The disillusionment with the very failures of those programs that called for the negation of art and philosophy has come to serve as a pretense for conservative positions. Let me briefly distinguish the antimodernism of the young conservatives from the postmodernism of the neoconservatives.

The *Young Conservatives* recapitulate the basic experience of aesthetic modernity. They claim as their own the revelations of a decentered subjectivity, emancipated from the imperatives of work and usefulness, and with this experience they step outside the modern world. On the basis of modernistic attitudes, they justify an irreconcilable antimodernism. They remove into the sphere of the far away and the archaic the spontaneous powers of imagination, of self-experience, and of emotionality. To instrumental reason, they juxtapose in manichean fashion a principle only accessible through evocation, be it the will to power or sovereignty, Being, or the dionysiac force of the poetical. In France this line leads from Bataille via Foucault to Derrida.

The *Old Conservatives* do not allow themselves to be contaminated by cultural modernism. They observe the decline of substantive reason, the differentiation of science, morality, and art, the modern world view and its merely procedural rationality with sadness and recommend a withdrawal to a position anterior to modernity. Neo-Aristotelianism, in particular, enjoys a certain success today. In view of the problematic of ecology, it allows itself to call for a cosmological ethic. As belonging to this school, which originates with Leo Strauss, one can count for example the interesting works of Hans Jonas and Robert Spaemann.

Finally, the *Neoconservatives* welcome the development of modern science, as long as this only goes beyond its sphere to carry forward technical progress, capitalist growth, and national administration. Moreover, they recommend a politics of defusing the explosive content of cultural modernity. According to one thesis, science, when properly understood, has become irrevocably meaningless for the orientation of the life-world. A further thesis is that politics must be kept as far aloof as possible from the demands of moral-practical justification. And a third thesis asserts the pure immanence of art, disputes that it has a utopian content, and points to its illusory character in order to limit the aesthetic experience to privacy. One could name here the early Wittgenstein, Carl Schmitt of the middle period, and Gottfried Benn of the late period. But with the decisive confinement of science, morality, and art to autonomous spheres separated from the life-world and administered experts, what remains from the project of cultural modernity is only what we would have if we were to give up the project of modernity altogether. As a replacement one points to traditions, which, however, are held to be immune to demands of (normative) justification and validation.

This typology is like any other, of course, a simplification; but it may not prove totally useless for the analysis of contemporary intellectual and political confrontations. I fear that the ideas of antimodernity, together with an additional touch of premodernity, are becoming popular in the circles of alternative culture. When one observes the transformations of consciousness within political parties in Germany, a new ideological shift (*Tendenzwende*) becomes visible. And this is the alliance of postmodernists with premodernists. It seems to me that there is no party in particular that monopolizes the abuse of intellectuals and the position of neoconservatism. I therefore have good reason to be thankful for the liberal spirit in which the city of Frankfurt offers me a prize bearing the name of Theodor Adorno. Adorno, a most significant son of this city, who as philosopher and writer has stamped the image of the intellectual in our country in incomparable fashion; even more, who has become the very image of emulation for the intellectual.

31

Mapping the postmodern

Andreas Huyssen

The problem

While the recent media hype about postmodernism in architecture and the arts has propelled the phenomenon into the limelight, it has also tended to obscure its long and complex history. Much of my ensuing argument will be based on the premise that what appears on one level as the latest fad, advertising pitch, and hollow spectacle is part of a slowly emerging cultural transformation in Western societies, a change in sensibility for which the term "postmodernism" is actually, at least for now, wholly adequate. The nature and depth of that transformation are debatable, but transformation it is. I don't want to be misunderstood as claiming that there is a wholesale paradigm shift of the cultural, social, and economic orders; any such claim clearly would be overblown. But in an important sector of our culture there is a noticeable shift in sensibility, practices, and discourse formations which distinguishes a postmodern set of assumptions, experiences, and propositions from that of a preceding period. What needs further exploration is whether this transformation has generated genuinely new aesthetic forms in the various arts or whether it mainly recycles techniques and strategies of modernism itself, reinscribing them into an altered cultural context.

I will not attempt here to define what postmodernism *is*. The term "postmodernism" itself should guard us against such an approach as it positions the phenomenon as relational. Modernism as that from which postmodernism is breaking away remains inscribed into the very word with which we describe our distance from modernism. Thus keeping in mind postmodernism's relational nature, I will simply start from the *Selbstverstandnis* of the postmodern as it has shaped various discourses since the 1960s. What I hope to provide in this chapter is something like a large-scale map of the postmodern which surveys several territories and

From Huyssen, "Mapping the Postmodern," *New German Critique* 33 (1984). Reprinted with permission of *New German Critique*.

on which the various postmodern artistic and critical practices could find their aesthetic and political place. Within the trajectory of the postmodern in the United States I will distinguish several phases and directions. My primary aim is to emphasize some of the historical contingencies and pressures that have shaped recent aesthetic and cultural debates but have either been ignored or systematically blocked out in critical theory *à l'americaine*. While drawing on developments in architecture, literature, and the visual arts, my focus will be primarily on the critical discourse about the postmodern: postmodernism in relation to, respectively, modernism, the avantgarde, neoconservatism, and poststructuralism. Each of these constellations represents a somewhat separate layer of the postmodern and will be presented as such. And, finally, central elements of the *Begriffsgeschichte* of the term will be discussed in relation to a broader set of questions that have arisen in recent debates about modernism, modernity, and the historical avantgarde. A crucial question for me concerns the extent to which modernism and the avantgarde as forms of an adversary culture were nevertheless conceptually and practically bound up with capitalist modernization and/or with communist vanguardism, that modernization's twin brother. As I hope this chapter will show, postmodernisms's critical dimension lies precisely in its radical questioning of those presuppositions which linked modernism and the avantgarde to the mindset of modernization.

The exhaustion of the modernist movement

Let me begin, then, with some brief remarks about the trajectory and migrations of the term "postmodernism." In literary criticism it goes back as far as the late 1950s when it was used by Irving Howe and Harry Levin to lament the leveling off of the modernist movement. Howe and Levin were looking back nostalgically to what already seemed like a richer past. "Postmodernism" was first used emphatically in the 1960s by literary critics such as Leslie Fiedler and Ihab Hassan, who held widely divergent views of what a postmodern literature was. It was only during the early and mid-1970s that the term gained a much wider currency, encompassing first architecture, then dance, theater, painting, film, and music. While the postmodern break with classical modernism was fairly visible in architecture and the visual arts, the notion of a postmodern rupture in literature has been much harder to ascertain. At some point in the late 1970s, "postmodernism," not without American prodding, migrated to Europe via Paris and Frankfurt. Kristeva and Lyotard took it up in France, Habermas in Germany. In the United States, meanwhile, critics had begun to discuss the interface of postmodernism with French poststructuralism in its peculiar American adaptation, often simply on the assumption that the avantgarde in theory somehow had to be homologous to the avantgarde in literature and the arts. While skepticism about the feasibility of an artistic avantgarde was on the rise in the 1970s, the vitality of theory, despite its many enemies, never seemed in serious doubt. To some, indeed, it appeared as if the cultural energies that had fueled the art movements of the 1960s were flowing during the 1970s into the body of theory, leaving the artistic enterprise high and dry. While such an observation is at best of impressionistic value and also not quite fair to the arts, it does seem reasonable to say that, with postmodernism's big-bang logic of expansion irreversible, the maze of the postmodern became ever more impenetrable. By the early 1980s the modernism/postmodernism constellation in the arts and the modernity/postmodernity constellation in social theory had become one of the most contested terrains in the intellectual life of Western societies. And the terrain is contested precisely because there is so much more at stake than the existence or nonexistence of a new artistic style, so much more also than just the "correct" theoretical line.

Nowhere does the break with modernism seem more obvious than in recent American architecture. Nothing could be further from Mies van der Rohe's functionalist glass curtain walls than the gesture of random historical citation which prevails on so many postmodern facades. Take, for example, Philip Johnsons's AT&T highrise, which is appropriately broken up into a neoclassical mid-section, Roman colonnades at the street level, and a Chippendale pediment at the top. Indeed, a growing nostalgia for various life forms of the past seems to be a strong undercurrent in the culture of the 1970s and 1980s. And it is tempting to dismiss this historical eclecticism, found not only in architecture, but in the arts, in film, in literature, and in the mass culture of recent years, as the cultural equivalent of the neoconservative nostalgia for the good old days and as a manifest sign of the declining rate of creativity in late capitalism. But is this nostalgia for the past, the often frenzied and exploitative search for usable traditions, and the growing fascination with premodern and primitive cultures – is all of this rooted only in the cultural institutions' perpetual need for spectacle and frill, and thus perfectly compatible with the status quo? Or does it perhaps also express some genuine and legitimate dissatisfaction with modernity and the unquestioned belief in the perpetual modernization of art? If the latter is the case, which I believe it is, then how can the search for alternative traditions, whether emergent or residual, be made culturally productive without yielding to the pressures of conservatism which, with a vise-like grip, lays claim to the very concept of tradition? I am not arguing here that all manifestations of the postmodern recuperation of the past are to be welcomed because somehow they are in tune with the *Zeitgeist*. I also don't want to be misunderstood as arguing that postmodernism's fashionable repudiation of the high modernist aesthetic and its boredom with the propositions of Marx and Freud, Picasso and Brecht, Kafka and Joyce, Schonberg and Stravinsky are somehow marks of a major cultural advance. Where postmodernism simply jettisons modernism it just yields to the cultural apparatus' demands that it legitimize itself as radically new, and it revives the philistine prejudices modernism faced in its own time.

But even if postmodernism's own propositions don't seem convincing – as embodied, for example, in the buildings by Philip Johnson, Michael Graves, and others – that does not mean that continued adherence to an older set of modernist propositions would guarantee the emergence of more convincing buildings or works of art. The recent neoconservative attempt to reinstate a domesticated version of modernism as the only worthwhile truth of 20th-century culture – manifest for instance in the 1984 Beckmann exhibit in Berlin and in many articles in Hilton Kramer's *New Criterion* – is a strategy aimed at burying the political and aesthetic critiques of certain forms of modernism which have gained ground since the 1960s. But the problem with modernism is not just the fact that it can be integrated into a conservative ideology of art. After all, that already happened once on a major scale in the 1950s. The larger problem we recognize today, it seems to me, is the closeness of various forms of modernism in its own time to the mindset of modernization, whether in its capitalist or communist version. Of course, modernism was never a monolithic phenomenon, and it contained *both* the modernization euphoria of futurism, constructivism, and *Neue Sachlichkeit* and some of the starkest critiques of modernization in the various modern forms of "romantic anti-capitalism." The problem I address in this chapter is not what modernism *really was,* but rather how it was perceived retrospectively, what dominant values and knowledge it carried, and how it functioned ideologically and culturally after World War II. It is a specific image of modernism that had become the bone of contention for the postmoderns, and that image has to be reconstructed if we want to understand postmodernism's problematic relationship to the modernist tradition and its claim to difference.

Architecture gives us the most palpable example of the issues at stake. The modernist utopia embodied in the building programs of the Bauhaus, of Mies, Gropius, and Le Corbusier, was part of a heroic attempt after the Great War and the Russian Revolution to rebuild a war-ravaged Europe in the image of the new and to make building a vital part of the envisioned renewal of society. A new Enlightenment demanded rational design for a rational society, but the new rationality was overlaid with a utopian fervor which ultimately made it veer back into myth – the myth of modernization. Ruthless denial of the past was as much an essential component of the modern movement as its call for modernization through standardization and rationalization. It is well-known how the modernist utopia shipwrecked on its own internal contradictions and, more importantly, on politics and history. Gropius, Mies, and others were forced into exile; Albert Speer took their place in Germany. After 1945, modernist architecture was largely deprived of its social vision and became increasingly an architecture of power and representation. Rather than standing as harbingers and promises of the new life, modernist housing projects became symbols of alienation and dehumanization, a fate they shared with the assembly line, that other agent of the new which had been greeted with exuberant enthusiasm in the 1920s by Leninists and Fordists alike.

Charles Jencks, one of the most well-known popularizing chroniclers of the agony of the modern movement and spokesman for a postmodern architecture, dates modern architecture's symbolic demise [to] July 15, 1972, at 3:32 p.m. At that time several slab blocks of St. Louis' Pruitt-Igoe Housing (built by Minoru Yamaski in the 1950s) were dynamited, and the collapse was dramatically displayed on the evening news. The modern machine for living, as Le Corbusier had called it with the technological euphoria so typical of the 1920s, had become unlivable, the modernist experiment, so it seemed, obsolete. Jencks takes pains to distinguish the initial vision of the modern movement from the sins committed in its name later on. And yet, on balance he agrees with those who, since the 1960s, have argued against modernism's hidden dependence on the machine metaphor and the production paradigm, and against its taking the factory as the primary model for all buildings. It has become commonplace in postmodernist circles to favor a reintroduction of multivalent symbolic dimensions into architecture, a mixing of codes, an appropriation of local vernaculars and regional traditions. Thus Jencks suggests that architects look two ways simultaneously, "towards the traditional slow-changing codes and particular ethnic meanings of a neighborhood, and toward the fast-changing codes of architectural fashion and professionalism." Such schizophrenia, Jencks holds, is symptomatic of the postmodern moment in architecture; and one might well ask whether it does not apply to contemporary culture at large, which increasingly seems to privilege what Bloch called *Ungleichzeitigkeiten* (nonsynchronisms), rather than favoring only what Adorno, the theorist of modernism par excellence, described as *der fortgeschrittenste Materialstand der Kunst* (the most advanced state of artistic material). Where such postmodern schizophrenia is creative tension resulting in ambitious and successful buildings, and where, conversely, it veers off into an incoherent and arbitrary shuffling of styles, will remain a matter of debate. We should also not forget that the mixing of codes, the appropriation of regional traditions, and the uses of symbolic dimensions other than the machine were never entirely unknown to the architects of the International Style. In order to arrive at his postmodernism, Jencks ironically had to exacerbate the very view of modernist architecture which he persistently attacks.

One of the most telling documents of the break of postmodernism with the modernist dogma is a book coauthored by Robert Venturi, Denise Scott-Brown, and Steven Izenour and entitled *Learning from Las Vegas*. Rereading this book and earlier writings by Venturi from the 1960s today, one is struck by the proximity of Venturi's strategies and solutions to the pop sensibility of those years. Time and again the authors use pop art's break with the austere canon of high modernist painting and pop's uncritical espousal of the commercial vernacular of consumer culture as an inspiration for their work. What Madison Avenue was for Andy Warhol, what the comics and the Western were for Leslie Fiedler, the landscape of Las Vegas was for Venturi and his group. The rhetoric of *Learning from Las Vegas* is predicated on the glorification of the billboard strip and of the ruthless shlock of casino culture. In Kenneth Frampton's ironic words, it offers a reading of Las Vegas as "an authentic outburst of popular phantasy." I think it would be gratuitous to ridicule such odd notions of cultural populism today. While there is something patently absurd about such propositions, we have to acknowledge the power they mustered to explode the reified dogmas of modernism and to reopen a set of questions which the modernism gospel of the 1940s and 1950s had largely blocked from view: questions of ornament and metaphor in architecture, of figuration and realism in painting, of story and representation in literature, of the body in music and theater. Pop in the broadest sense was the context in which a notion of the postmodern first took shape, and from the beginning until today, the most significant trends within postmodernism have challenged modernism's relentless hostility to mass culture.

Postmodernism in the 1960s: An American avantgarde?

I will now suggest a historical distinction between the postmodernism of the 1960s and that of the 1970s and early 1980s. My argument will roughly be this: 1960s' and 1970s' postmodernism both rejected or [sic] criticized a certain version of modernism. Against the codified high modernism of the preceding decades, the postmodernism of the 1960s tried to revitalize the heritage of the European avantgarde and to give it an American form along what one could call in short-hand the Duchamp–Cage–Warhol axis. By the 1970s, that avantgardist postmodernism of the

1960s had in turn exhausted its potential, even though some of its manifestations continued well into the new decade. What was new in the 1970s was, on the one hand, the emergence of a culture of eclecticism, a largely affirmative postmodernism which had abandoned any claim to critique, transgression, or negation; and, on the other hand, an alternative postmodernism in which resistance, critique, and negation of the status quo were redefined in nonmodernist and nonavantgardist terms, which match the political developments in contemporary culture more effectively than the older theories of modernism. Let me elaborate.

What were the connotations of the term "postmodernism" in the 1960s? Roughly since the mid-1950s literature and the arts witnessed a rebellion of a new generation of artists such as Rauschenberg and Jasper Johns, Kerouac, Ginsberg, and the Beats, Burroughs and Barthelme against the dominance of abstract expressionism, serial music, and classical literary modernism. The rebellion of the artists was soon joined by critics such as Susan Sontag, Leslie Fiedler, and Ihab Hassan, who all vigorously, though in very different ways and to a different degree, argued for the postmodern. Sontag advocated camp and a new sensibility, Fielder sang the praise of popular literature and genital enlightenment, and Hassan – closer than the others to the moderns – advocated a literature of silence, trying to mediate between the "tradition of the new" and postwar literary developments. By that time, modernism had of course been safely established as the canon in the academy, the museums, and the gallery network. In that canon of New York School of abstract expressionism represented the epitome of that long trajectory of the modern which had begun in Paris in the 1850s and 1860s and which had inexorably led to New York – the American victory in culture following on the heels of the victory on the battlefields of World War II. By the 1960s artists and critics alike shared a sense of a fundamentally new situation. The assumed postmodern rupture with the past was felt as a loss: Art and literature's claim to truth and human value seemed exhausted, the belief in the constitutive power of the modern imagination just another delusion. Or it was felt as a breakthrough toward an ultimate liberation of instinct and consciousness, into the global village of McLuhancy, the new Eden of polymorphous perversity, Paradise Now, as the Living Theater proclaimed it on stage. Thus critics of postmodernism such as Gerald Graff have correctly identified two strains of the postmodern culture of the 1960s: the apocalyptic desperate strain and the visionary celebratory strain, both of which, Graff claims, already existed within modernism. While this is certainly true, it misses an important point. The ire of the postmodernists was directed not so much against modernism as such, but rather against a certain austere image of "high modernism," as advanced by the New Critics and other custodians of modernist culture. Such a view, which avoids the false dichotomy of choosing either continuity or discontinuity, is supported by a retrospective essay by John Barth. In a 1980 piece in *The Atlantic,* entitled "The Literature of Replenishment," Barth criticizes his own 1968 essay "The Literature of Exhaustion," which seemed at the time to offer an adequate summary of the apocalyptic strain. Barth now suggests that what his earlier piece was really about "was the effective 'exhaustion' not of language or of literature but of the aesthetic of high modernism." And he goes on to describe Beckett's *Stories and Texts for Nothing* and Nabokov's *Pale Fire* as late modernist marvels, distinct from such postmodernist writers as Italo Calvino and Gabriel Marquez. Cultural critics like Daniel Bell, on the other hand, would simply claim that the postmodernism of the 1960s was the "logical culmination of modernist intentions," a view which rephrases Lionel Trilling's despairing observation that the demonstrators of the 1960s were practicing modernism in the streets. But my point here is precisely that high modernism had never seen fit to be in the streets in the first place, that its earlier undeniably adversary role was superseded in the 1960s by a very different culture of confrontation in the streets *and* in art works, and that this culture of confrontation transformed inherited ideological notions of style, form, and creativity, artistic autonomy, and the imagination to which modernism had by then succumbed. Critics like Bell and Graff saw the rebellion of the late 1950s and the 1960s as continuous with modernism's earlier nihilistic and anarchic strain; rather than seeing it as a postmodernist revolt against classical modernism, they interpreted it as a profusion of modernist impulses into everyday life. And in some sense they were absolutely right, except that this "success" of modernism fundamentally altered the terms of how modernist culture was to be perceived. Again, my argument here is that the revolt of the 1960s was never a rejection of modernism per se, but rather a revolt against that version of modernism which had been domesticated in the 1950s, become part of the liberal–conservative consensus of the times, and which had even been turned into a propaganda weapon in the cultural-political arsenal of Cold War anticommunism. The modernism against which artists rebelled was no longer felt to be an adversary culture. It no longer opposed a dominant class and its world view, nor had it maintained its programmatic purity from contamination by the culture industry. In other words, the revolt sprang precisely from the success of modernism, from the fact that in the United States, as in West Germany and France, for that matter, modernism had been perverted into a form of affirmative culture.

I would go on to argue that the global view which sees the 1960s as part of the modern movement extending from Manet and Baudelaire, if not from romanticism, to the present is not able to account for the specifically American character of postmodernism. After all, the term accrued its emphatic connotations in the United States, not in Europe. I would even claim that it could not have been invented in Europe at the time. For a variety of reasons, it would not have made any sense there. West Germany was still busy rediscovering its own moderns who had been burnt and banned during the Third Reich. If anything, the 1960s in West Germany produced a major shift in evaluation and interest from one set of moderns to another: from Benn, Kafka, and Thomas Mann to Brecht, the left expressionists, and the political writers of the 1920s, from Heidegger and Jaspers to Adorno and Benjamin, from Schonberg and Webern to Eisler, from Kirchner and Beckmann to Grosz and Heartfield. It was a search for alternative cultural traditions within modernity and as such directed against the politics of a depoliticized version of modernism that had come to provide much needed cultural legitimation for the Adenauer restoration. During the 1950s, the myths of "the golden twenties," the "conservative revolution," and universal existentialist *Angst* all helped block out and suppress the realities of the fascist past. From the depths of barbarism and the rubble of its cities, West Germany was trying to reclaim a civilized modernity and to find a cultural identity tuned to international modernism which would make others forget Germany's past as predator and pariah of the modern world. Given this context, neither the variations on modernism of the 1950s nor the struggle of the 1960s for alternative democratic and socialist cultural traditions could have possibly been construed as *postmodern*. The very notion of postmodernism has emerged in Germany only since the late 1970s, and then not in relation to the culture of the 1960s, but narrowly in relation to recent architectural developments and, perhaps more importantly, in the context of the new social movements and their radical critique of modernity.

In France, too, the 1960s witnessed a return to modernism rather than a step beyond it, even though for different reasons than in Germany, some of which I will discuss in the later section on poststructuralism. In the context of French intellectual life, the term "postmodernism" was simply not around in the 1960s, and even today it does not seem to imply a major break with modernism, as it does in the United States.

I would now like to sketch four major characteristics of the early phase of postmodernism which all point to postmodernism's continuity with the international tradition of the modern, yes, but which – and this is my point – also establish American postmodernism as a movement *sui generis*.

First, the postmodernism of the 1960s was characterized by a temporal imagination which displayed a powerful sense of the future and of new frontiers, of rupture and discontinuity, of crisis and generational conflict, an imagination reminiscent of earlier continental avantgarde movements such as Dada and surrealism rather than of high modernism. Thus the revival of Marcel Duchamp as godfather of 1960s postmodernism is no historical accident. And yet, the historical constellation in which the postmodernism of 1960s played itself out (from the Bay of Pigs and the civil rights movement to the campus revolts, the antiwar movement and the counter-culture) makes this avantgarde specifically American, even where its vocabulary of aesthetic forms and techniques was not radically new.

Secondly, the early phase of postmodernism included an iconoclastic attack on what Peter Burger has tried to capture theoretically as the "institution art." By that term Burger refers first and foremost to the ways in which art's role in society is perceived and defined, and secondly, to [the] ways in which art is produced, marketed, distributed, and consumed. In his book *Theory of the Avantgarde* Burger has argued that the major goal of the historical European avantgarde (Dada, early surrealism, the postrevolutionary Russian avantgarde) was to undermine, attack, and transform the bourgeois institution art and its ideology of autonomy rather than only changing artistic and literary modes of representation. Burger's approach to the question of art as institution in bourgeois society goes a long way toward suggesting useful distinctions between modernism and the avantgarde, distinctions which in turn can help us place the American avantgarde of the 1960s. In Burger's account the European avantgarde was primarily an attack on the highness of high art and on art's separateness from everyday life as it had evolved in nineteenth-century aestheticism and its repudiation of realism. Burger argues that the avantgarde attempted to reintegrate art and life or, to use his Hegelian–Marxist formula, to sublate art into life, and he sees this reintegration attempt, I think correctly, as a major break with the aestheticist tradition of the later nineteenth century. The value of Burger's account for contemporary American debates is that it permits us to distinguish different stages and different projects within the trajectory of the modern. The usual equation of the avantgarde with modernism can indeed no longer be maintained. Contrary to the avantgarde's intention to merge art and life, modernism always remained bound up with the more traditional notion of the autonomous art work, with the construction of form and meaning (however estranged or ambiguous, displaced, or undecidable such meaning might be), and with the specialized status of the aesthetic. The politically important point of Burger's account for my argument about the 1960s is this: The historical avantgarde's iconoclastic attack on cultural institutions and on traditional modes of representation presupposed a society in which high art played an essential role in legitimizing hegemony, or, to put it in more neutral terms, to support a cultural establishment and its claims to aesthetic knowledge. It had been the achievement of the historical avantgarde to demystify and to undermine the legitimizing discourse of high art in European society. The various modernisms of this century, on the other hand, have neither maintained nor restored versions of high culture, a task which was certainly facilitated by the ultimate and perhaps unavoidable failure of the historical avantgarde to reintegrate art and life. And yet, I would suggest that it was this specific radicalism of the avantgarde, directed against the institutionalization of high art as a discourse of hegemony and a machinery of meaning, that recommended itself as a source of energy and inspiration to the American postmodernists of the 1960s. Perhaps for the first time in American culture an avantgardist revolt against a tradition of high art and what was perceived as its hegemonic role made political sense. High art had indeed become institutionalized in the burgeoning museum, gallery, concert, record, and paperback culture of the 1950s. Modernism itself had entered the mainstream via mass reproduction and the culture industry. And, during the Kennedy years, high culture even began to take on functions of political representation with Robert Frost and Pablo Casals, Malraux and Stravinsky at the White House. The irony in all of this is that the first time the United States had something resembling an "institution art" in the emphatic European sense, it was modernism itself, the kind of art whose purpose had always been to resist institutionalization. In the form of happenings, pop vernacular, psychedelic art, acid rock, alternative and street theater, the postmodernism of the 1960s was groping to recapture the adversary ethos which had nourished modern art in its earlier stages, but which it seemed no longer able to sustain. Of course, the "success" of the pop avantgarde, which itself had sprung full-blown from advertising in the first place, immediately made it profitable and thus sucked it into a more highly developed culture industry than the earlier European avantgarde ever had to contend with. But despite such cooption through commodification the pop avantgarde retained a certain cutting edge in proximity to the 1960s culture of confrontation. No matter how deluded about its potential effectiveness, the attack on the institution art was always also an attack on hegemonic social institutions, and the raging battles of the 1960s over whether or not pop was legitimate art prove the point.

Thirdly, many of the early advocates of postmodernism shared the technological optimism of segments of the 1920s avantgarde. What photography and film had been to Vertov and Tretyakov, Brecht, Heartfield, and Benjamin in that period, television, video, and the computer were for the prophets of a technological aesthetic in the 1960s. McLuhan's cybernetic and technocratic media eschatology and Hassan's praise for "runaway technology," the "boundless dispersal by media," "the computer as substitute consciousness" – all of this combined easily with euphoric vi-

sions of a postindustrial society. Even if compared to the equally exuberant technological optimism of the 1920s, it is striking to see in retrospect
how uncritically media technology and cybernetic paradigm were espoused in the 1960s by conservatives, liberals, and leftists alike.

The enthusiasm for the new media leads me to the fourth trend within
early postmodernism. There emerged a vigorous, though again largely
uncritical, attempt to validate popular culture as a challenge to the canon
of high art, modernist or traditional. This "populist" trend of the 1960s
with its celebration of rock 'n' roll and folk music, of the imagery of
everyday life and of the multiple forms of popular literature gained much
of its energy in the context of the counter-culture and by a next to total
abandonment of an earlier American tradition of a critique of modern
mass culture. Leslie Fiedler's incantation of the prefix "post" in his essay
"The New Mutants" had an exhilarating effect at the time. The postmodern harbored the promise of a "postwhite," "postmale," posthumanist,"
"post-Puritan" world. It is easy to see how all of Fiedler's adjectives aim
at the modernist dogma and at the cultural establishment's notion of
what Western Civilization was all about. Susan Sontag's camp aesthetic
did much the same. Even though it was less populist, it certainly was as
hostile to high modernism. There is a curious contradiction in all this.
Fiedler's populism reiterates precisely that adversarial relationship between high art and mass culture which, in the accounts of Clement Greenberg and Theodore W. Adorno, was one of the pillars of the modernist
dogma Fiedler had set out to undermine. Fiedler just takes his position on
the other shore, opposite Greenberg and Adorno, as it were, validating
the popular and pounding away at "elitism." And yet, Fiedler's call to
cross and border and close the gap between high art and mass culture as
well as his implied political critique of what later came to be called
"eurocentrism" and "logocentrism" can serve as an important marker
for subsequent developments within postmodernism. A new creative relationship between high art and certain forms of mass culture is, to my
mind, indeed one of the major marks of difference between high modernism and the art and literature which followed it in the 1970s and 1980s
both in Europe and the United States. And it is precisely the recent self-
assertion of minority cultures and their emergence into public consciousness which has undermined the modernist belief that high and low culture
have to be categorically kept apart; such rigorous segregation simply does
not make much sense *within* a given minority culture which has always
existed outside in the shadow of the dominant high culture.

In conclusion, I would say that from an American perspective the
postmodernism of the 1960s had some of the makings of a genuine
avantgarde movement, even if the overall political situation of 1960s

America was in no way comparable to that of Berlin or Moscow in the early 1920s when the tenuous and short-lived alliance between avant-gardism and vanguard politics was forged. For a number of historical reasons the ethos of artistic avantgardism as iconoclasm, as probing reflection upon the ontological status of art in modern society, as an attempt to forge another life was culturally not yet as exhausted in the United States of the 1960s as it was in Europe at the same time. From a European perspective, therefore, it all looked like the endgame of the historical avantgarde rather than like the breakthrough to new frontiers it claimed to be. My point here is that American postmodernism of the 1960s was both: an American avantgarde *and* the endgame of international avantgardism. And I would go on to argue that it is indeed important for the cultural historian to analyze such *Ungleichzeitigkeiten* within modernity and to relate them to the very specific constellations and contexts of national and regional cultures and histories. The view that the culture of modernity is essentially internalist – with its cutting edge moving in space and time from Paris in the later nineteenth and twentieth centuries to Moscow and Berlin in the 1920s and to New York in the 1940s – is a view tied to a teleology of modern art whose unspoken subtext is the ideology of modernization. It is precisely this teleology and ideology of modernization which has become increasingly problematic in our postmodern age, problematic not so much perhaps in its descriptive powers relating to past events, but certainly in its normative claims.

Postmodernism in the 1970s and 1980s

In some sense, I might argue that what I have mapped so far is really the prehistory of the postmodern. After all, the term "postmodernism" only gained wide currency in the 1970s, while much of the language used to describe the art, architecture, and literature of the 1960s was still derived – and plausibly so – from the rhetoric of avantgardism and from what I have called the "ideology of modernization." The cultural developments of the 1970s, however, are sufficiently different to warrant a separate description. One of the major differences, indeed, seems to be that the rhetoric of avantgardism has faded fast in the 1970s so that one can speak perhaps only now of a genuinely postmodern and postavantgarde culture. Even if, with the benefit of hindsight, future historians of culture were to opt for such a usage of the term, I would still argue that the adversary and critical element in the notion of postmodernism can only be grasped if one takes the late 1950s as the starting point of a mapping of the postmodern. If we were to focus only on the 1970s, the adversary moment of the postmodern would be much harder to work out precisely because of the shift within the trajectory of postmodernism that lies somewhere in the fault lines between "the '60s" and "the '70s."

By the mid-1970s, certain basic assumptions of the preceding decade had either vanished or been transformed. The sense of a "futurist revolt" (Fiedler) was gone. The iconoclastic gestures of the pop, rock, and sex avantgardes seemed exhausted since their increasingly commercialized circulation had deprived them of their avantgardist status. The earlier optimism about technology, media, and popular culture had given way to more sober and critical assessments: television as pollution rather than panacea. In the years of Watergate and the drawn-out agony of the Vietnam war, of the oil-shock and the dire predictions of the Club of Rome, it was indeed difficult to maintain the confidence and exuberance of the 1960s. Counter-culture, New Left, and antiwar movements were ever more frequently denounced as infantile aberrations of American history. It was easy to see that the 1960s were over. But it is more difficult to describe the emerging cultural scene which seemed much more amorphous and scattered than that of the 1960s. One might begin by saying that the battle against the normative pressures of high modernism waged during the 1960s had been successful – too successful, some would argue. While the 1960s could still be discussed in terms of a logical sequence of styles (pop, op, kinetic, minimal, concept) or in equally modernist terms of art versus antiart and nonart, such distinctions have increasingly lost ground in the 1970s.

The situation in the 1970s seems to be characterized rather by an ever wider dispersal and dissemination of artistic practices all working out of the ruins of the modernist edifice, raiding it for ideas, plundering its vocabulary, and supplementing it with randomly chosen images and motifs from premodern and non-modern cultures as well as from contemporary mass culture. Modernist styles have actually not been abolished, but, as one art critic recently observed, continue "to enjoy a kind of half-life in mass culture," for instance in advertising record cover design, furniture and household items, science fiction illustration, window displays, etc. Yet another way of putting it would be to say that all modernist and avantgardist techniques, forms, and images are now stored for instant recall in the computerized memory banks of our culture. But the same memory also stores all of premodernist art as well as the genres, codes, and image worlds of popular cultures and modern mass culture. How precisely these enormously expanded capacities for information storage, processing, and recall have affected artists and their work remains to be analyzed. But one thing seems clear: The great divide that separated high modernism from mass culture and that was codified in the various classical accounts of modernism no longer seems relevant to postmodern artistic or critical sensibilities.

Since the categorical demand for the uncompromising segregation of high and low has lost much of its persuasive power, we may be in a better position now to understand the political pressures and historical contingencies which shaped such accounts in the first place. I would suggest that the primary place of what I am calling the great divide was the age of Stalin and Hitler when the threat of totalitarian control over all culture forged a variety of defensive strategies meant to protect high culture in general, not just modernism. Thus conservative culture critics such as Ortega y Gasset argued that high culture needed to be protected from the "revolt of the masses." Left critics like Adorno insist[ed] that genuine art resist its incorporation into the capitalist culture industry, which he defined as the total administration of culture from above. And even Lukacs, the left critic of modernism par excellence, developed his theory of high bourgeois realism not in unison with but in antagonism to the Zhdanovist dogma of socialist realism and its deadly practice of censorship.

It is surely no coincidence that the Western codification of modernism as canon of the twentieth century took place during the 1940s and 1950s, preceding and during the Cold War. I am not reducing the great modernist works, by way of a simple ideology critique of their function, to a ploy in the cultural strategies of the Cold War. What I am suggesting, however, is that the age of Hitler, Stalin, and the Cold War produced specific accounts of modernism, such as those of Clement Greenberg and Adorno, whose aesthetic categories cannot be totally divorced from the pressures of that era. And it is in this sense, I would argue, that the logic of modernism advocated by those critics has become an aesthetic dead end to the extent that it has been upheld as rigid guideline for further artistic production and critical evaluation. As against such dogma, the postmodern has indeed opened up new directions and new visions. As the confrontation between "bad" socialist realism and the "good" art of the free world began to lose its ideological momentum in an age of detente, the whole relationship between modernism and mass culture as well as the problem of realism could be reassessed in less reified terms. While the issue was already raised in the 1960s, e.g., in pop art and various forms of documentary literature, it was only in the 1970s that artists increasingly drew on popular or mass cultural forms and genres, overlaying them with modernist and/or avantgardist strategies. A major body of work representing this tendency is the New German cinema, and here especially the films of Rainer Werner Fassbinder, whose success in the United States can be explained precisely in those terms. It is also no coincidence that the diversity of mass culture was now recognized and analyzed by critics who increasingly began to work themselves out from under the modernist dogma that all mass culture is monolithic *Kitsch,* psychologically regressive and mind-destroying. The possibilities for experimental meshing and mixing of mass culture and modernism seemed promising and produced some of the most successful, ambitious art and literature of the 1970s. Needless to say, it also produced aesthetic failures and fiascos, but then modernism itself did not only produce masterworks.

It was especially the art, writing, film-making, and criticism of women and minority artists, with their recuperation of buried and mutilated traditions, their emphasis on exploring forms of gender- and race-based subjectivity in aesthetic productions and experiences, and their refusal to be limited to standard canonizations, which added a whole new dimension to the critique of high modernism and to the emergence of alternative forms of culture. Thus, we have come to see modernism's imaginary relationship to African and Oriental art as deeply problematic, and will approach, say, contemporary Latin American writers other than by praising them for being good modernists, who, naturally, learned their craft in Paris. Women's criticism has shed some new light on the modernist canon itself from a variety of different feminist perspectives. Without succumbing to the kind of feminine essentialism which is one of the more problematic sides of the feminist enterprise, it just seems obvious that were it not for the critical gaze of feminist criticism, the male determinations and obsessions of Italian futurism, Vorticism, Russian constructivism, *Neue Sachlichkeit,* or surrealism would probably still be blocked from our view; and the writings of Marie Luise Fleisser and Ingeborg Bachmann, the paintings of Frida Kahlo, would still be known only to a handful of specialists. Of course, such new insights can be interpreted in multiple ways, and the debate about gender and sexuality, male and female authorship, and reader/spectatorship in literature and the arts is far from over, its implications for a new image of modernism not yet fully elaborated.

In light of these developments it is somewhat baffling that feminist criticism has so far largely stayed away from the postmodernism debate which is considered not to be pertinent to feminist concerns. The fact that to date only male critics have addressed the problem of modernity/ postmodernity, however, does not mean that it does not concern women. I would argue – and here I am in full agreement with Craig Owens – that women's art, literature, and criticism are an important part of the postmodern culture of the 1970s and 1980s and indeed a measure of the vitality and energy of that culture. Actually, the suspicion is in order that the conservative turn of these past years has indeed something to do with the sociologically significant emergence of various forms of "otherness" in the cultural sphere, all of which are perceived as a threat to the stability and sanctity of canon and tradition. Current attempts to restore a 1950s

version of high modernism for the 1980s certainly point in that direction.
And it is in this context that the question of neoconservatism becomes
politically central to the debate about the postmodern. . . .

Whither postmodernism?

The cultural history of the 1970s still has to be written, and the various
postmodernisms in art, literature, dance, theater, architecture, film,
video, and music will have to be•discussed separately and in detail. All I
want to do now is to offer a framework for relating some recent cultural
and political changes to postmodernism, changes which already lie outside the conceptual network of "modernism/avantgardism" and have so
far rarely been included in the postmodernism debate.

   I would argue that the contemporary arts – in the widest possible
sense, whether they call themselves postmodernist or reject that label –
can no longer be regarded as just another phase in the sequence of modernist and avantgardist movements which began in Paris in the 1850s and
1860s and which maintained an ethos of cultural progress and vanguardism through the 1960s. On this level, postmodernism cannot be
regarded simply as a sequel to modernism, as the latest step in the never-
ending revolt of modernism against itself. The postmodern sensibility of
our time is different from both modernism *and* avantgardism precisely in
that it raises the question of cultural tradition and conservation in the
most fundamental way as an aesthetic and a political issue. It doesn't
always do it successfully, and often does it exploitatively. And yet, my
main point about contemporary postmodernism is that it operates in a
field of tension between tradition and innovation, conservation and renewal, mass culture and high art, in which the second terms are no longer
automatically privileged over the first; a field of tension which can no
longer be grasped in categories such as progress vs. reaction, left vs. right,
present vs. past, modernism vs. realism, abstraction vs. representation,
avantgarde vs. *Kitsch*. The fact that such dichotomies, which after all are
central to the classical accounts of modernism, have broken down is part
of the shift I have been trying to describe. I could also state the shift in the
following terms: Modernism and the avantgarde were always closely
related to social and industrial modernization. They were related to it as
an adversary culture, yes, but they drew their energies, not unlike Poe's
Man of the Crowd, from their proximity to the crises brought about by
modernization and progress. Modernization – such was the widely held
belief, even when the word was not around – had to be traversed. There
was a vision of emerging on the other side. The modern was a world-scale
drama played out on the European and American stage, with mythic

modern man as its hero and with modern art as a driving force, just as Saint-Simon had envisioned it already in 1925. Such heroic visions of modernity and of art as a force of social change (or, for that matter, resistance to undesired change) are a thing of the past, admirable for sure, but no longer in tune with current sensibilities, except perhaps with an emerging apocalyptic sensibility as the flip side of modernist heroism.

Seen in this light, postmodernism at its deepest level represents not just another crisis within the perpetual cycle of boom and bust, exhaustion and renewal, which has characterized the trajectory of modernist culture. It rather represents a new type of crisis *of* that modernist culture itself. Of course, this claim has been made before, and fascism indeed was a formidable crisis *of* modernist culture. But fascism was never the alternative to modernity it pretended to be, and our situation today is very different from that of the Weimar Republic in its agony. It was only in the 1970s that the historical limits of modernism, modernity, and modernization came into sharp focus. The growing sense that we are not bound to *complete* the "project of modernity" (Habermas' phrase) and still do not necessarily have to lapse into irrationality or into apocalyptic frenzy, the sense that art is not exclusively pursuing some telos of abstraction, non-representation, and sublimity – all of this has opened up a host of possibilities for creative endeavors today. And in certain ways it has altered our views of modernism itself. Rather than being bound to a one-way history of modernism which interprets it as a logical unfolding toward some imaginary goal, and which thus is based on a whole series of exclusions, we are beginning to explore its contradictions and contingencies, its tensions and internal resistances to its own "forward" movement. Postmodernism is far from making modernism obsolete. On the contrary, it casts a new light on it and appropriates many of its aesthetic strategies and techniques, inserting them and making them work in new constellations. What has become obsolete, however, are those codifications of modernism in critical discourse which, however subliminally, are based on a teleological view of progress and modernization. Ironically, these normative and often reductive codifications have actually prepared the ground for that repudiation of modernism which goes by the name of the postmodern. Confronted with the critic who argues that this or that novel is not up to the latest in narrative technique, that it is regressive, behind the times, and thus uninteresting, the postmodernist is right in rejecting modernism. But rejection affects only that trend within modernism which has been codified into a narrow dogma, not modernism as such. In some ways, the story of modernism and postmodernism is like the story of the hedgehog and the hare: The hare could not win because there always was more than just one hedgehog. But the hare was still the better runner. . . .

The crisis of modernism is more than just a crisis of those trends within it which tie it to the ideology of modernization. In the age of late capitalism, it is also a new crisis of art's relationship to society. At their most emphatic, modernism and avantgardism attributed to art a privileged status in the processes of social change. Even the aestheticist withdrawal from the concern of social change is still bound to it by virtue of its denial of that status quo and the construction of an artificial paradise of exquisite beauty. When social change seemed beyond grasp or took an undesired turn, art was still privileged as the only authentic voice of critique and protest, even when it seemed to withdraw into itself. The classical accounts of high modernism attest to that fact. To admit that these were heroic illusions – perhaps even necessary illusions in art's struggle to survive in dignity in a capitalist society – is not to deny the importance of art in social life.

But modernism's running feud with mass society and mass cultures as well as the avantgarde's attack on high art as a support system of cultural hegemony always took place on the pedestal of high art itself. And certainly that is where the avantgarde has been installed after its failure, in the 1920s, to create a more encompassing space for art in social life. To continue to demand today that high art leave the pedestal and relocate elsewhere (wherever that might be) is to pose the problem in obsolete terms. The pedestal of high art and high culture no longer occupies the privileged space it used to, just as the cohesion of the class which erected its monuments on that pedestal is a thing of the past; recent conservative attempts in a number of Western countries to restore the dignity of the classics of Western Civilization, from Plato via Adam Smith to the high modernists, and to send students back to the basics, prove the point. I am not saying here that the pedestal of high art does not exist anymore. Of course it does, but it is not what it used to be. Since the 1960s, artistic activities have become much more diffuse and harder to contain in safe categories or stable institutions such as the academy, the museum, or even the established gallery network. To some, this dispersal of cultural and artistic practices and activities will involve a sense of loss and disorientation; others will experience it as a new freedom, a cultural liberation. Neither may be entirely wrong, but we should recognize that it was not only recent theory or criticism that deprived the univalent, exclusive, and totalizing accounts of modernism of their hegemonic role. It was the activities of artists, writers, film makers, architects, and performers that have propelled us beyond a narrow vision of modernism and given us a new lease on modernism itself.

In political terms, the erosion of the triple dogma modernism/modernity/avantgardism can be contextually related to the emergence of the problematic of "otherness," which has asserted itself in the sociopolitical sphere as much as in the cultural sphere. I cannot discuss here the various and multiple forms of otherness as they emerge from differences in subjectivity, gender and sexuality, race and class, temporal *Ungleichzeitigkeiten* and spatial geographic locations and dislocations. But I want to mention at least four recent phenomena which, in my mind, are and will remain constitutive of postmodern culture for some time to come.

Despite all its noble aspirations and achievements, we have come to recognize that the culture of enlightened modernity has also always (though by no means exclusively) been a culture of inner and outer imperialism, a reading already offered by Adorno and Horkheimer in the 1940s and an insight not unfamiliar to those of our ancestors involved in the multitude of struggles against rampant modernization. Such imperialism, which works inside and outside, on the micro and macro levels, no longer goes unchallenged either politically, economically, or culturally. Whether these challenges will usher in a more habitable, less violent, and more democratic world remains to be seen, and it is easy to be skeptical. But enlightened cynicism is as insufficient an answer as blue-eyed enthusiasm for peace and nature.

The women's movement has led to some significant changes in social structure and cultural attitudes which must be sustained even in the face of the recent grotesque revival of American machismo. Directly and indirectly, the women's movement has nourished the emergence of women as a self-confident and creative force in the arts, in literature, film, and criticism. The ways in which we now raise questions of gender and sexuality, reading and writing, subjectivity and enunciation, voice and performance are unthinkable without the impact of feminism, even though many of these activities may take place on the margin or even outside the movement proper. Feminist critics have also contributed substantially to revisions of the history of modernism, not just by unearthing forgotten artists, but also by approaching the male modernists in novel ways. This is true also of the "new French feminists" and their theorization of the feminine in modernist writing, even though they often insist on maintaining a polemical distance from an American-type feminism.

During the 1970s, questions of ecology and environment have deepened from single-issue politics to a broad critique of modernity and modernization, a trend which is politically and culturally much stronger in West Germany than in the United States. A new ecological sensibility manifests itself not only in political and regional subcultures, in alternative life styles and the new social movements in Europe, but it also affects art and literature in a variety of ways: the work of Joseph Beuys, certain land art projects, Christo's California running fence, the new nature poetry, the return to local traditions, dialects, and so on. It was especially due to the growing ecological sensibility that the link between certain forms of modernism and technological modernization has come under critical scrutiny.

There is a growing awareness that other cultures, non-European, non-Western cultures, must be met by means other than conquest or domination, as Paul Ricoeur put it more than twenty years ago, and that the erotic and aesthetic fascination with "the Orient" and "the primitive" – so prominent in Western culture, including modernism – is deeply problematic. This awareness will have to translate into a type of intellectual work different from that of the modernist intellectual who typically spoke with the confidence of standing at the cutting edge of time and of being able to speak for others. Foucault's notion of the local and specific intellectual as opposed to the "universal" intellectual of modernity may provide a way out of the dilemma of being locked into our own culture and traditions while simultaneously recognizing their limitations.

In conclusion, it is easy to see that a postmodernist culture emerging from these political, social, and cultural constellations will have to be a postmodernism of resistance, including resistance to that easy postmodernism of the "anything goes" variety. Resistance will always have to be specific and contingent upon the cultural field within which it operates. It cannot be defined simply in terms of negativity or nonidentity a la Adorno, nor will the litanies of a totalizing, collective project suffice. At the same time, the very notion of resistance may itself be problematic in its simple opposition to affirmation. After all, there are affirmative forms of resistance and resisting forms of affirmation. But this may be more a semantic problem than a problem of practice. And it should not keep us from making judgments. How such resistance can be articulated in art works in ways that would satisfy the needs of the political *and* those of the aesthetic, of the producers and of the recipients, cannot be prescribed, and it will remain open to trial, error, and debate. But it is time to abandon that dead-end dichotomy of politics and aesthetics which for too long has dominated accounts of modernism, including the aestheticist trend within poststructuralism. The point is not to eliminate the productive tension between the political and the aesthetic, between history and the text, between engagement and the mission of art. The point is to heighten that tension, even to rediscover it and to bring it back into focus in the arts as well as in criticism. No matter how troubling it may be, the landscape of the postmodern surrounds us. It simultaneously delimits and opens our horizons. It's our problem and our hope.

Printed in the United Kingdom
by Lightning Source UK Ltd.
121489UK00002B/27/A